DRUG-FACILITATED SEXUAL ASSAULT

All royalties from this book will be donated to the
following non-profit charities:

Rape, Abuse and Incest National Network (RAINN), Washington, DC, USA
Santa Monica Rape Treatment Center, Santa Monica, CA, USA
The Drug Rape Trust, Essex, England

These organizations have proved instrumental in the investigation of drug-
facilitated sexual assault and the care and treatment of rape survivors.

DRUG-FACILITATED SEXUAL ASSAULT

A FORENSIC HANDBOOK

Edited by Marc A. LeBeau and Ashraf Mozayani

ACADEMIC PRESS

A Harcourt Science and Technology Company

San Diego   San Francisco   New York   Boston
London   Sydney   Tokyo

ACADEMIC PRESS
A Harcourt Science and Technology Company
Harcourt Place, 32 Jamestown Road, London NW1 7BY, UK
http://www.academicpress.com

ACADEMIC PRESS
A Harcourt Science and Technology Company
525 B Street, Suite 1900, San Diego, California 92101-4495, USA
http://www.academicpress.com

ISBN 0-12-440261-5

Library of Congress Control Number 2001090231
A catalogue record for this book is available from the British Library

Typeset by Kenneth Burnley, Wirral, Cheshire, England
Printed in Spain by Grafos SA Arte Sobre Papel, Barcelona
01 02 03 04 05 06 GF 9 8 7 6 5 4 3 2 1

CONTENTS

CONTRIBUTORS

Gail Abarbanel, LCSW
Director, Rape Treatment Center, Santa Monica-UCLA Medical Center, Santa Monica, CA 90404, USA.

Sergeant Joanne Archambault
San Diego Police Department, Sex Crimes Unit, San Diego, CA 92101, USA.

Santo Davide Ferrara, PhD
Full Professor, Centre of Behavioural and Forensic Toxicology, Università di Padova, Padova, Italy.

Giampietro Frison, PhD
Assistant Professor, Centre of Behavioural and Forensic Toxicology, Università di Padova, Padova, Italy.

James C. Garriott, PhD, D-ABFT
16031 Oak Grove, San Antonio, TX 78255, USA.

Amanda J. Jenkins, PhD
Chief Toxicologist, The Office of the Cuyahoga County Coroner, Cleveland, OH 44106, USA.

Graham Jones, PhD, D-ABFT
Chief Toxicologist, Alberta Medical Examiner's Office, Edmonton, Alberta, Canada.

Rebecca A. Jufer, PhD
Federal Bureau of Investigation, Washington, DC 20535, USA.

Karla Kerlin, JD
Deputy District Attorney, Los Angeles County District Attorney's Office, Los Angeles, CA 90012, USA.

Marc A. LeBeau, MS
Chemistry Unit Chief, Federal Bureau of Investigation, Washington, DC 20535, USA.

Linda Ledray, RN, PhD, FAAN
Director, Sexual Assault Resource Service, Minneapolis, MN, USA.

Ashraf Mozayani, PharmD, PhD, D-ABFT
Laboratory Director/Chief Toxicologist, Harris County Medical Examiner's Office, Houston, TX 77054, USA.

Carla M. Noziglia, MS
Laboratory Director (Retired), Tulsa Police Department, Tulsa, OK 74103, USA.

Stephen J. Paterson
President, Vinson & Dimitrius, LLC, Rolling Hills Estates, CA 90274, USA.

Trinka D. Porrata
Drug Consultant, Retired California Narcotics Detective, Pasadena, CA 91105, USA.

Lionel Raymon, PharmD, PhD
University of Miami, Department of Pathology, Miami, FL 33177, USA.

Diana M. Riveira, JD
Senior Attorney, The American Prosecutors Research Institute, Alexandria, VA 22314, USA.

Michael Robertson, PhD
Toxicologist, San Diego, CA 92122, USA.

Peter Singer, PhD
Deputy Chief Toxicologist, Alberta Medical Examiner's Office, Edmonton, Alberta, Canada.

Peter Sturman, BA, Cert Ed
Detective Chief Inspector, Metropolitan Police, London, England.

Luciano Tedeschi, PhD
Assistant Professor, Centre of Behavioural and Forensic Toxicology, Università di Padova, Padova, Italy.

Michael Welner, MD
Chairman, The Forensic Panel, Clinical Associate Professor of Psychiatry, New York University School of Medicine, New York, NY 10001, USA.

The opinions or points of view expressed in this book are a consensus of the authors of the individual chapters. These views are not necessarily the views of the organizations with whom the authors are employed (or otherwise associated), nor the views of the authors of other chapters.

PREFACE

Marc LeBeau
Ashraf Mazayani

Over the past decade, there has been a dramatic increase in media reports about sexual assault victims who describe being "knocked out" or "incapacitated" by their assailant through the use of drugs. The classic example involves a male secretly slipping the drug into a woman's beverage. After consumption of the beverage, the woman becomes severely incapacitated or unconscious. The male, taking advantage of the female's state of mind, sexually assaults the woman.

This book was written to aid the "investigators" of drug-facilitated sexual assault (DFSA). This includes law enforcement, medical professionals, rape crisis personnel, attorneys, and forensic scientists who are put into the difficult situation of dealing with this crime. It was also written to help dispel a number of myths that exist surrounding the crime of DFSA in order to better educate these investigators.

It is important that the reader understand that DFSA exists in a variety of formats. While the above example is what most often is deemed as DFSA, there are other scenarios that must also be considered and treated as DFSA. The first involves the voluntary ingestion of one or more of the recreational drugs (including ethanol) mentioned in this book. As the individual drug chapters explain, the effects of these drugs may incapacitate the victims, rendering them unconscious and unable to consent to sexual acts. The second scenario involves the co-ingestion of prescription or over-the-counter medications with ethanol and/or recreational drugs. Again, the combined effect of these drugs may sedate the victim to a point that is analogous to being under anesthesia. Investigators and prosecutors, in particular, must understand this point and treat each of these scenarios with the same degree of urgency.

This book addresses the many challenges that face the "investigators" of DFSA. These challenges include:

1. being aware of the many drugs used to commit DFSA, their effects upon the human body, and their pharmacokinetic properties;
2. understanding and acknowledging the complexities of reporting this type of crime; and
3. properly collecting and analyzing the physical evidence.

Furthermore, this book proposes ways to overcome such challenges in order to improve our capabilities in DFSA investigations.

One key element that makes DFSA difficult to investigate is the drugs used. By far, most of the problems faced in this type of investigation are directly related to the effects that these drugs have on the victim and the complications in detecting their presence after ingestion.

The term "drug-facilitated sexual assault" is used throughout this book. It should be understood that this term is used interchangeably with all drug-facilitated crimes. This includes drug-facilitated rape, drug-facilitated sexual abuse, and, at times, drug-facilitated robbery. Finally, the reader should recognize that the term "date rape" is not routinely used in this book. While this is a term the media has adopted when describing DFSA, it is an inappropriate term for the vast majority of sex crimes that rely on incapacitating drugs to facilitate a sexual assault.

CHAPTER 1

THE VICTIM

Gail Abarbanel

Sexual assault victims provide the most telling descriptions of the crimes committed against them:

> My boyfriend was gone for the weekend. I went to an off-campus party with my friends. One of my boyfriend's teammates, Mike, asked me to go with him to a nearby liquor store to get more beer for the party. The clerk asked him for identification. He didn't have it with him. He said he had some six-packs at his house. We went there to get them. When we got to the apartment, his roommate was there. The two guys went into another room to talk. All of a sudden, the roommate reappeared with no clothes on. He pinned me down on the couch and raped me while Mike watched. When he was done, I screamed at him, "How could you do this to me?" He raped me again.[1]

> I went to the gas station in the morning on my way to work. Just as I got back into my car, a man came up to the window. He had a knife. He shoved me over on the front seat towards the passenger side. He tied my wrists behind my back. He drove me to his house. He kept me there for six hours. He raped me three times and forced me to orally copulate him. He burned my legs with a blowtorch.

> John and I have been good friends for over 25 years. Sometimes, I spend holidays with his family. He invited me to his apartment for dinner. He offered me a glass of wine. After a few sips, I felt dizzy and nauseous. The next thing I remember is waking up in the morning handcuffed to his bed. There were black lace stockings on my legs. I was really sore and I had this burning sensation in my vagina. There were dildos on the floor.

[1] The cases described in this chapter involve victims who were seen at the Rape Treatment Center at Santa Monica-UCLA Medical Center. Their stories are told with their permission.

Rape has been described as "a form of torture" (Benedict, 1992) and as a psychological annihilation (Rose, 1986). Most sexual assault victims feel that the rapist "kills" a part of them. Afterwards, many victims say that a part of them is "dead." The sexual assault takes something away that victims can never wholly regain. One victim described it as "a moment that cannot be undone and changes life for ever" (Raine, 1998).

In addition to the severe emotional trauma sexual assault victims sustain, they may suffer genital and/or other physical injuries. They are at risk for sexually transmitted diseases (Reynolds *et al.*, 2000) and unwanted pregnancy (Holmes *et al.*, 1996). If they seek legal redress, they may confront discriminatory treatment in the criminal justice system. If they reach out to friends, family members or other agencies and institutions for help, they may be re-victimized by blaming and judgmental attitudes. For some victims, the experience of being raped carries with it a perceived or real stigma. They may be seen as "damaged goods" in their own cultures and communities. As a result of these and other factors, the physical, emotional, and social consequences of sexual assault are often long lasting. For some victims, the repercussions are lifelong.

Victims of drug-facilitated sexual assault (DFSA) describe their trauma as a "double crime." They suffer the horror, loss of control, physical violation, and health risks that are inherent in other forms of sexual assault. They are also subjected to what they call "mind rape." In addition to physically disabling them, the sedating effects of the drugs they ingest rob them of cognition and conscious awareness during the assault. The anterograde amnesia produced by the drugs robs them of the ability to retrieve memories of the trauma afterwards. These drug-induced conditions reduce victims to an extreme – and prolonged – state of helplessness.

DFSAs present unique challenges for victims and for professionals who provide victim assistance services. Victims of these crimes describe experiences during the assault and in the aftermath that differ significantly in many respects from those reported by other sexual assault victims. This chapter highlights some of the defining features of DFSAs from the victim's perspective by comparing them to the common characteristics of other types of sexual assault.

The remainder of this chapter has three sections. Section I contains an overview of rape and sexual assault, including definitions and commonly used terminology, prevalence and incidence of these crimes, risk factors for victimization, and similarities and differences between sexual assaults committed by strangers versus acquaintances. Section II describes typical victim experiences during and following a sexual assault, including the methods used by offenders, victim responses to the threat of rape, reporting patterns and help-seeking behaviors, and the immediate and longer-term psychosocial impacts of victimization. Section III discusses some of the unique aspects of DFSAs, including the distinguishing features of this crime pattern, ways in which these crimes and their aftermath may differ from other types of sexual assaults, and effective techniques for interviewing these victims.

The information presented in this chapter applies to both female and male victims. Although males are sexually assaulted, the vast majority of victims are females. Occasionally, the terms "she" and "her" are used to refer to victims, rather than references to both genders, for ease of writing. Similarly, since almost all rapists are male, the pronoun "he" is used to refer to offenders.

SECTION I: RAPE AND SEXUAL ASSAULT – AN OVERVIEW

DEFINITIONS AND TERMINOLOGY

Legal definitions of rape vary from state to state. These definitions also change over time as a result of rape reform legislation. Rape is generally defined in state laws as forced or nonconsensual sexual intercourse. In some states, rape statutes refer only to penile–vaginal penetration. Other states have broadened their legal definitions to include penetration of the victim's vagina, mouth, or rectum by a penis, fingers, or objects (Crowell and Burgess, 1996; Spohn and Horney, 1992).

Rape may be accomplished by the use of fear, threats of harm, and/or actual physical force. Rape also includes nonconsensual sexual intercourse accomplished without using force or threats, such as when victims are unable to give consent, prevented from resisting, or unaware of the nature of the act due to a mental or physical disability, or due to being intoxicated, drugged, unconscious, or asleep.

The term "sexual assault" is generally used to describe a broader range of sexual offenses that involve touching or penetration of an intimate part of a person's body without consent. Sexual assault includes rape, forced sodomy, forced oral copulation, and sexual battery (the unwanted touching of an intimate part of another person for the purpose of sexual arousal or sexual gratification).

"Drug-facilitated sexual assault" is a relatively new term. It is being used to define offenses in which victims are subjected to nonconsensual sexual acts while they are incapacitated or unconscious due to the effects of alcohol and/or drugs, and are therefore prevented from resisting and/or are unable to consent. The defining element in drug-facilitated sexual assaults is the victim's state of incapacitation resulting from the ingestion of alcohol and/or drugs. The other critical variable, from the victim's perspective, is whether the disabling drugs were given to the victim surreptitiously (i.e. without the victim's knowledge or consent) or under fraudulent conditions (i.e. the nature and effects of the drugs were misrepresented to the victim).

In common usage, the terms "rape" and "sexual assault" are often used interchangeably as they are in this chapter.

SCOPE OF THE PROBLEM: PREVALENCE AND INCIDENCE

One measure of the incidence of rape is the number of victimizations reported to the police. According to the annual Uniform Crime Report (UCR) published by the US Department of Justice (2000), over 90,000 "forcible rapes" were reported to law enforcement agencies throughout the United States in 1999. However, these statistics are very limited because they are based upon a narrow definition of "forcible rape" that excludes forcible oral copulation and sodomy, statutory rapes, and rapes accomplished without force when victims are incapacitated (Russell and Bolen, 2000). Moreover, because of the large number of unreported rapes, the crimes known to the police represent a very small percentage of the number of rapes and other sexual assaults that are actually committed.

Many victimization surveys have been conducted to obtain a more accurate estimate of the prevalence of rape, i.e. the number of rapes actually committed versus the number that have been reported. In a landmark study (Russell, 1984) that utilized face-to-face interviews with a randomly selected sample of women 18 years of age and older, 44% reported being victims of rape or attempted rape. Only 9.5% of these crimes were reported to the police. In the National Women's Study (Rape In America, 1992), one in eight women reported being raped. The researchers concluded that this number equated to 683,000 incidents of rape in a one-year period, nearly seven times the number reflected in the Uniform Crime Report for the same time period. The most recent national victimization survey sponsored by the National Institute of Justice (NIJ) and Centers for Disease Control and Prevention (CDC) indicates that one in six women in the United States is a victim of rape or attempted rape (Tjaden and Thoennes, 1998). This study used a definition of rape that includes forced oral, vaginal, and anal intercourse.

The differences in findings across various victimization surveys are related to how rape and sexual assault are defined, characteristics of the sample selected for study, screening questions, interviewer training and techniques, and other methodological and procedural issues. However, in virtually every victimization survey conducted, the number of unreported rapes far exceeds those that are reported to authorities.

VULNERABILITY TO SEXUAL ASSAULT

The most significant risk factor for rape and sexual assault is being a woman. Every woman is vulnerable to rape regardless of her age, race, ethnicity, marital status, socio-economic circumstances, neighborhood, education, physical characteristics, or lifestyle. However, some women are at higher risk. Rape is often called a "tragedy of youth" because younger women (children and adolescents) are more likely to be victimized. In the NIJ/CDC survey noted above (1998), 50% of the women who had been raped were victimized before they reached 18 years of age. In another study conducted to examine the incidence of childhood rape in a national sample of adult women, one out of eight women reported suffering at least one completed rape prior to their eighteenth birthday (Saunders *et al.*, 1999). Another significant risk factor for rape is childhood sexual abuse (Browne and Finkelhor, 1986; Messman-Moore and Long, 2000; Wyatt *et al.*, 1992).

Various studies indicate that male victims represent about 5 to 10% of reported rapes (Hodge and Canter, 1998). The NIJ/CDC study found that 1 in 33 men had been sexually assaulted. Like acts of sexual violence against women, these crimes are highly under-reported to the police (Scarce, 1997).

STRANGER VS. ACQUAINTANCE ASSAILANTS

Most rapes are committed by someone the victim knows (Bachman and Saltzman, 1995; Saunders *et al.*, 1999). In the National Women's Study (Rape in America, 1992), approximately 80% of the rapes disclosed to researchers were acquaintance rapes. Stranger rapes, the most feared form of sexual violence, account for about 20% of the victimizations. There are important differences, as well as similarities, in these two types of sexual assaults.

In stranger rapes, the victim has no prior relationship with the offender. The offender uses force, verbal threats, and/or the element of surprise to establish contact with the victim. From the victim's perspective, the attack is sudden. In many cases, as soon as the victim is aware of the offender's presence, he has control of the situation.

> Shana was walking back to work from the coffee store near her office. A man came up behind her on the street and grabbed her. He stuck his hand under her dress and digitally penetrated her.

In acquaintance rapes, the victim and the assailant have a prior relationship. The relationship is initiated in a socially acceptable way, rather than by force or threats. When the sexual assault occurs, the relationship may be new or casual, or well established. The offender may be a friend, neighbor, teacher, employer, medical care provider, fellow student at school, work colleague, business associate, social companion, new acquaintance, date, boyfriend, or spouse/partner. He may also be someone the victim met and became acquainted with on the Internet.

The situations in which acquaintance rapes occur usually begin as a voluntary, consensual encounter. For example, a woman agrees to a date with a man she met through a mutual friend, a college student goes to a male student's dorm room to study or allows him into her apartment for non-sexual purposes, or a woman agrees to stay late at work to finish a project with her boss. Then, something goes wrong. The assailant demands sex and uses physical force or other forms of intimidation to obtain it. He violates the boundaries of the victim's consent.

> Teresa, a seventy-five-year-old grandmother, returned home alone after attending a family party. As she got ready for bed, she heard a knock at the door. The visitor was an old family friend who had been at the party earlier in the evening. He seemed distressed and said that he needed to talk with her, so she opened the door. After they talked for a while, he began making sexual advances. When she resisted, he became angry, pushed her down on the couch, and raped her.

Victims of acquaintance rape feel a profound sense of betrayal. The offender is usually someone whom the victim has had no reason to fear prior to the rape. In fact, there is usually reason to trust him. Most of us make certain assumptions about people we know from work, school, our neighborhood, or through mutual friends, family, or business and professional relationships. We assume that these people are "safe." We usually make the same assumptions about people with whom we have built a relationship over time. We assume mutual trust and expect personal boundaries to be respected in the context of these relationships. Thus, acquaintance rapes often happen in situations in which the victim is understandably not on guard.

The unique characteristics of acquaintance rape may produce intense feelings of self-blame (Katz, 1991). The experience of being raped by people whom they initially consented to be with and trusted often causes these victims to feel that there is something wrong with their own judgment. They blame themselves for failing to foresee the dangerousness and the malevolent intent of the person who raped them. Many victims of acquaintance rape fear that they will be similarly judged and blamed by others.

Acquaintance rape is one of the most misunderstood forms of criminal violence. It is commonly, and mistakenly, viewed as less serious, less criminal, and less traumatic for the victim than stranger rape. In fact, many people believe that acquaintance rape is not "real rape" (Estrich, 1987). The prevalence of these misconceptions often results in discriminatory treatment. Victims who are raped by someone they know are frequently blamed or disbelieved, whereas victims of stranger rape are more likely to receive empathy and support. However, several studies that have compared the impact on victims of stranger versus acquaintance rapes find that the severity of the trauma that victims sustain is the same, regardless of their relationship to the rapist (Katz, 1991; Koss *et al.*, 1988). In addition, because victims of acquaintance rape often receive less support and validation from significant others and from "the system," they may be at greater risk for longer-term psychosocial problems. Acquaintance rape victims may also receive differential treatment in the criminal justice system. They are far less likely to have their assailants prosecuted (Frazier and Haney, 1996).

WITNESSES AND BYSTANDERS

With the exception of group and gang rapes, most rapists attack their victims in a situation or location where there are no witnesses. Typically, there are differences in how stranger and acquaintance rapists isolate their victims.

The stranger rapist often approaches victims in locations that provide privacy for the commission of the crime, such as a deserted parking lot, a dark street, or the victim's home when she is alone or asleep in the middle of the night. In contrast, the acquaintance rapist may conduct some of his relationship with the victim in a social environment or public place where there are other people around. However, he usually eventually lures or maneuvers the victim into a location where there is more privacy before he issues threats or applies the force required to carry out the crime. For example, a guy spends time with a girl at a fraternity party, but then he invites her up to his room on another floor of the fraternity house; a photographer invites a woman to his studio so he can take pictures of her that she can use to pursue her dream of a modeling career; or a man takes a co-worker to a restaurant for dinner and then, while ostensibly driving her home, stops the car on a deserted street.

SECTION II: THE VICTIM'S EXPERIENCE DURING AND FOLLOWING A SEXUAL ASSAULT

HOW RAPISTS GAIN ACCESS TO THEIR VICTIMS AND OVERPOWER THEM

Rapists use many methods to overpower their victims and maintain control of them. These methods include using the element of surprise to catch a victim off guard (e.g. approaching from behind, awakening a person from a sound sleep), brandishing or using weapons (e.g. guns, knives), inflicting physical injury (e.g. grabbing, hitting, choking), applying restraints (e.g. handcuffs, telephone cord, gags, blindfolds), and/or making verbal threats to harm the victim and/or significant others (e.g. children). Rapists also use other forms of intimidation. For example, undocumented immigrants may be threatened by someone posing as an immigration officer who says, "If you don't do what I tell you, I'll have you deported," or "I'll have your children taken away." This is called a "badge of authority rape." Some offenders exploit people who are especially vulnerable and unlikely to be able to defend themselves, e.g. a person who is developmentally disabled, under the influence of alcohol, or hospitalized for a physical or mental illness.

The particular style of attack to which a victim is subjected depends upon the type of rapist committing the crime (Groth, 1979). In "blitz" style rapes, offenders initiate contact with their victims by using threats or force (Burgess and Holmstrom, 1974; Silverman *et al.*, 1988). The victim senses danger immediately. This is often the *modus operandi* (MO) of the stranger rapist.

> Susan returned home from an evening class. When she turned on the light in her
> bedroom, she saw a man standing by the bed. He said, "Shut up or I'll kill you."

In "confidence" rapes, offenders establish non-threatening relationships with their victims, gain their trust, and then lure, manipulate, or maneuver them into situations where they are more vulnerable, i.e. less likely to be able to resist, summon help, or escape. In these cases, the offender establishes rapport, "grooms" the victim, gains the victim's trust, and then betrays it. Although the initial approach to the victim is accomplished in a socially acceptable manner, at some point in the encounter, the victim senses danger and becomes afraid because the assailant demonstrates through physical force or threats that he will resort to harming the victim to get what he wants.

> Rosa met a young man at her high school graduation party. He asked her out but she
> declined. She felt that she did not know him well enough to accept a date. Over the
> next few weeks, he called her frequently. She finally agreed to have dinner with him.
> He picked her up at her home, met her parents, and took her to an expensive restau-
> rant for dinner. On the way home, he turned the car in a direction away from where
> Rosa lived. She told him she wanted to go home. He told her he wanted to take a short
> ride first. He drove Rosa to a deserted mountain road, parked the car next to the edge
> of a cliff, put on black leather gloves, and raped her.

Despite differences in their MO, almost all sex offenders trigger fear in their victims. Research has demonstrated that the majority of rape victims fear they will be injured or killed by the rapist (Rape in America, 1992; Saunders *et al.*, 1999). Victims report these fears in stranger and acquaintance rapes, in "blitz" and "confidence" style assaults, and in cases where there are no weapons present and no explicit threats of bodily harm are verbalized by the offender. Many victims also report that, during their encounter with the rapist, they experience the physiological correlates of fear, including trembling or shaking, racing heart, muscle tension, and/or rapid breathing. These physiological reactions may become conditioned responses to stimuli that trigger fear in the future (Resnick *et al.*, 1997). In the aftermath of sexual assault, fear often remains as a constant companion to the victim.

RESPONDING TO THE THREAT OF RAPE: THE ISSUE OF RESISTANCE

The ability to sense danger and identify threats to one's safety enables a person to mobilize self-protective strategies. When faced with the threat of being raped, many victims attempt to defend themselves. They try to avert the attack or dissuade the assailant.

Victims typically use a variety of cognitive and behavioral strategies for self-defense. Many victims describe scanning the environment and making a mental assessment of the situation. They may recall advice they have been given about how to respond in a dangerous situation. They evaluate the offender and assess available options. Some victims try to bargain or negotiate with the offender. Verbal tactics are common responses because, in many situations involving interpersonal conflict, reasoning with the other person is an effective strategy. Some victims scream, hoping that this will scare off the attacker or attract the attention of potential rescuers. Some try to escape or stall for time. Other victims physically resist and attempt to fight off the assailant.

In certain situations, the victim finds that one or a combination of these resistance strategies is successful. The victim averts the assault and the crime is an attempted rape. In other circumstances, the same strategies escalate the dangerousness of the situation. The victim's resistance – talking, screaming, stalling, and/or fighting – is countered by more force and/or increased threats. In these circumstances, many victims fear that they will be killed or seriously injured if they continue to resist. Therefore, they may decide to submit to the sexual assault in order to get out of the situation alive and/or without suffering more serious harm. In effect, victims make a conscious choice to adopt a strategy of nonresistance to protect themselves. At this point, the victim's goal changes from preventing rape to ensuring survival. The victim's behavior also changes dramatically. The victim complies with the rapist's demands.

Some victims who adopt an outward stance of non-resistance continue to "fight back" in other ways. They may use their sensory and cognitive abilities to identify and memorize details about the offender's physical characteristics, the location of the crime, and other details that can later be used to aid authorities in apprehending and prosecuting the offender. This is an active coping strategy.

Another psychological response to the threat of rape is "frozen fright." Frozen fright is a state of panic. The victim is essentially immobilized by fear.

This combination of shock and terror may be engendered in victims in situations where their attempts to resist seem futile, they fear annihilation, they feel trapped, and they see no avenue of redress or escape. The wrenching feeling of terror overwhelms the victim, producing a kind of psychological paralysis. The victim is reduced to a state of helplessness or "psychological infantilism" (Symonds, 1976). This condition has also been described as a "state of surrender" that ensues when a victim finds that any effort to resist or escape is futile (Herman, 1992, p. 42). Moreover, in these circumstances, the victim often believes that survival is dependent on the whims of the rapist because he has control of the situation. Fear overrides other responses, such as fight or flight. The victim becomes passive, obedient, and compliant with the rapist's demands, avoiding any actions that might anger, startle, or provoke him. The victim's behaviors may even appear friendly and solicitous. The victim perceives the rapist as being unpredictable and capable of the worst imaginable acts. The victim has one goal: self-preservation. The victim attempts to stay in the rapist's "good graces."

Dissociation is yet another response to the extreme horror and terror victims experience during a sexual assault. This reaction is commonly described by victims as "spacing out" or "zoning out." It is a self-protective coping strategy. In the face of rape, and when resistance is likely to result in dire consequences for the victim, the victim is reduced to a state of powerlessness. The victim finds a way to survive by disengaging. A 30-year-old victim of a stranger rape said, "I decided he could take my body, but not my soul. I protected my self." Another victim said, "I kept a part of myself away from what was happening. It was like I left my body. I was an observer, watching what was happening from a far away place as if it were happening to someone else." Because of its behavioral manifestations, dissociation during a sexual assault may be viewed by others as a passive response. For the victim, however, it can be seen as an active coping strategy. Dissociation has many repercussions in the aftermath of the crime. It may affect the victim's ability to give a detailed, sequential, complete narrative account of what transpired immediately following the assault. This is because dissociation affects how information about the trauma is organized and stored in the victim's memory. The information is compartmentalized (van der Kolk *et al.*, 1996).

In most sexual assault cases, the victim's resistance or non-resistance becomes a very significant issue. It is often an area of focus during the police investigation, a consideration in case filing decisions made by prosecutors, a subject of examination in the courtroom, a cause for misunderstanding between victims and significant others, and a source of strong feelings of guilt and self-blame experienced by victims. In our culture, there has always been a strong expectation of rape victim resistance. This standard is reflected in our laws, as well as in public attitudes and institutional practices. Historically, most states incorporated victim resistance provisions from English common law in their rape statutes. Proof of resistance was often required as evidence of non-consent. In some states, the legal standard was "resistance to the utmost." The societal standard was communicated in the common adage, "death before dishonor." As a result of rape reform legislation enacted during the past few decades, state laws have been changed and most resistance standards have been eliminated. But legal reforms have not significantly changed public attitudes or institutional practices, such as prosecutor criteria for case filing decisions (Spohn and Horney, 1992). Victim resistance is still an expectation, albeit unwritten. Many people continue to believe that if they faced the threat of rape, they would resist. These beliefs are particularly likely to be imposed in cases of acquaintance rape and cases where victims are not threatened with lethal weapons or subjected to actual physical violence.

REPORTING THE CRIME AND OTHER HELP-SEEKING BEHAVIORS

Although one way to "fight back" against rape is to report the crime, relatively few victims exercise this option (Kilpatrick *et al.*, 1987). In fact, rape is called the most under-reported violent crime in America (Rape in America, 1992; Chaiken, 2000). The majority of victims do not officially notify authorities. In the National Women's Study, only about one in six of the victims reported their rapes to the police. In a study of childhood rapes among women, only about one in eight of the victimizations were reported (Saunders *et al.*, 1999).

Certain crime characteristics are related to victim reporting decisions, including the relationship between the victim and the offender and victim injuries (Bachman, 1998; Bachman and Saltzman, 1995; Frazier and Haney, 1996; Russell and Bolen, 2000). Victims who are raped by strangers are more apt to notify authorities. Victims who sustain physical injuries are also more likely to contact law enforcement. They often feel that they have visible "proof" of the force that was used against them. In contrast, victims of acquaintance rape are much more likely to remain silent or to make delayed reports (Koss *et al.*, 1988; Renner and Wackett, 1987).

The reasons victims give for not filing police reports include actual threats and/or fear of retaliation by the assailant(s); feelings of shame, guilt, and self-blame; concerns about being blamed or disbelieved by others; believing there is a stigma associated with being raped; viewing the assault as a private matter; not labeling the experience as "rape;" and reluctance to participate in the criminal justice process because of concerns about revictimization by "the system" (Bachman, 1998; Wyatt, 1992; Wyatt *et al.*, 1990).

In addition to making a police report, victims have the option of turning to other community agencies for assistance. And yet, despite the pervasive and disruptive effects of rape on physical and emotional health and/or psychosocial functioning, the number of victims who seek help from mental health providers, rape crisis centers, and victim assistance programs is extremely low (Kimerling and Calhoun, 1994).

When sexual assault victims turn to others for help, they are far more likely to visit medical care providers than mental health and specialized victim assistance providers. Several studies have documented a pattern of increased physician visits and higher utilization of medical care services by victims in the first few years following a sexual assault (Koss *et al.*, 1991; Waigandt *et al.*, 1990). In one study, over 70% of the victims sought medical services whereas only 19% sought mental health treatment of any kind in the first year after being sexually assaulted (Kimerling and Calhoun, 1994). Nevertheless, even though these victims obtain medical attention, they still "remain silent," in that they typically do not disclose their sexual assault histories to their health care providers. Instead, they seek treatment for various physical and somatic concerns and far too often, the etiology of their trauma-related symptoms is never identified.

The cost of silence is high, for the victim and for society. Telling and taking action are important steps in the healing process. As Judith Herman so poignantly stated in her book *Trauma and Recovery*, when secrecy prevails, "the story of the traumatic event surfaces not as a verbal narrative but as a symptom" (Herman, 1992, p. 1). The symptoms and long-term effects of unresolved rape trauma have been well documented in the professional literature, and are discussed in the next section of this chapter. In addition to the personal consequences of remaining silent, a victim's decision not to make a police report may also have an impact on public safety. Rapists are high recidivist offenders. When a rape is not reported, the offender is not apprehended or incarcerated. He remains free to victimize others.

THE MEANING OF RAPE TO THE VICTIM

For many victims, rape is a life-shattering event. The magnitude of the trauma is reflected in their descriptions of what the rapist did to them:

"My life is divided into two parts: before the rape and after the rape."

"He broke my soul."

"I constantly feel weak and dirty. It left a stain inside of me that I can't wash away."

"I am not the same person that I was before this happened to me."

One victim who was treated at our Center talked about the person who survived:

> "For weeks after the rape, I would look at myself in the mirror expecting to see someone else. I no longer knew the person I saw. I lost my connection to myself, my belief in myself, my ability to function in life. There was no innocence, no joy, no trust, no competence, no control and no belief in the possibility of tomorrow . . . I had experienced death without dying."

Because of the meaning of sexual assault to the victim, and the range and intensity of the resulting trauma symptoms, every aspect of a victim's life may be affected – activities of daily living (e.g. eating, sleeping), relationships (friends, family), other aspects of social adjustment (work, school), physical and psychological health, basic attitudes and beliefs, values, self-confidence, self-esteem, and hopes and dreams for the future (Abarbanel and Richman, 1990). One victim described the pervasiveness of the trauma: "It's not just your body that's raped, it's your whole life."

Research conducted over the past 25 years has documented both the immediate and long-term effects of sexual assault on victims. Although there are individual variations in the occurrence, timing, intensity, and duration of various symptoms, many victims experience similar reactions. These after-effects are described below.

Victim impact: physical/somatic symptoms

Regardless of whether victims sustain any physical injuries during the assault, they often develop physical symptoms that represent physiological and somatic responses to extreme stress, anxiety, and/or depression. The most common post-assault physical symptoms reported by rape victims are headaches, nausea, back pain, allergies, skin disorders, gastrointestinal distress, menstrual symptoms and other gynecological problems, sudden weight changes, and chronic pain syndromes (Golding, 1994; Kimerling and Calhoun, 1994; Koss and Heslet, 1992; Waigandt *et al.*, 1990). Sexual assault victims also tend to have poorer health perceptions than non-victims (Golding *et al.*, 1997; Koss *et al.*, 1991). This is consistent with the feeling victims commonly express that their bodies are "broken and defiled" (Resnick *et al.*, 1997).

Victim impact: acute stress disorder and post-traumatic stress disorder symptoms

One of the significant developments in clinical understanding about the nature and characteristics of sexual assault trauma has been the growth of a body of knowledge about human responses to certain types of traumatic events.

The *Diagnostic and Statistical Manual of Mental Disorders* (DSM-IV) published by the American Psychiatric Association (1994) defines characteristic symptom patterns that may follow exposure to an extremely traumatic event that involves a perceived threat to a person's survival or physical integrity and a response of intense helplessness, fear, or horror. The characteristics of the traumatic event, the person's response, and the resulting symptoms are the diagnostic criteria for Post-traumatic Stress Disorder (PTSD). The DSM-IV includes sexual assault as a traumatic event that may cause this anxiety disorder in victims.

Researchers have demonstrated that most rape victims suffer from symptoms of post-traumatic stress disorder in the immediate aftermath of the assault (Foa and Rothbaum, 1998; Kramer and Green, 1991; Rothbaum *et al.*, 1992). For some victims, these symptoms abate over time. For other victims, the symptoms are longer lasting and may become chronic (Foa and Rothbaum, 1998; Kilpatrick *et al.*, 1987; Rape in America, 1992). Regardless of their timing or duration, PTSD symptoms are extremely distressing and can be disabling for many victims.

In 1994, the American Psychiatric Association (DSM-IV) introduced the new diagnosis of Acute Stress Disorder (ASD) to describe similar symptoms that may be evident in the immediate aftermath of the trauma. Many sexual assault victims experience the symptoms of ASD, as well as PTSD. The ASD symptoms include the following:

- Dissociative symptoms during or following the traumatic event, such as a subjective sense of numbing, detachment, or absence of emotional responsiveness, depersonalization, derealization, reduced awareness of surroundings (e.g. the victim appears to be "in a daze"), or dissociative amnesia (e.g. the victim is unable to recall an important aspect of the trauma).
- Persistent re-experiencing of the trauma, such as flashbacks, recurrent images, thoughts, or dreams, a sense of reliving the experience, or distress on exposure to reminders of the trauma.
- Marked avoidance of stimuli that arouse recollections of the trauma, including thoughts, feelings, conversations, activities, places, people.
- Marked symptoms of anxiety or increased arousal, such as difficulty sleeping, irritability, problems with concentration, hypervigilance, exaggerated startle response.

The diagnosis of ASD may be made if certain combinations of these symptoms develop within one month of the sexual assault, last for at least two days, and are not due to the effects of a substance. During this time, the victim may experience significant distress and disruption in social, occupational, and other areas of functioning, including family relationships. Many victims find it difficult to perform their usual activities. In addition, the symptoms may delay disclosure and reporting, and make it difficult for victims to mobilize support systems or pursue needed assistance.

The diagnosis of PTSD is made if certain combinations of the symptoms below persist for at least one month. The symptoms of PTSD include the following:

- Persistent re-experiencing of the trauma in the following ways: recurrent and intrusive recollections of the event, distressing dreams, acting or feeling as if the sexual assault is recurring, intense distress or physiological reactivity when exposed to stimuli that resemble or are symbolic of the event.
- Persistent avoidance of people, activities, or situations associated with the trauma; and numbing of general responsiveness, including efforts to avoid thoughts and feelings related to the trauma, diminished interest or participation in significant activities, inability to recall an important aspect of the trauma, feeling detached or estranged from others, restricted range of affect, and/or sense of a foreshortened future.
- Persistent symptoms of increased arousal, such as sleep disturbances, irritability, mood swings, difficulty concentrating, hypervigilance, and exaggerated startle response.

There is considerable overlap in the symptoms of ASD and PTSD. The major difference between these diagnoses is the timing and duration of symptoms. In addition, there is an emphasis on numbing and dissociative symptoms in ASD. Several studies have demonstrated that dissociation during a traumatic event predicts the development of chronic PTSD afterwards (van der Kolk *et al.*, 1996).

Victim impact: other sequelae to sexual assault

In addition to the debilitating symptoms of PTSD, rape victims are at risk for many other psychosocial sequelae. When compared to women who are nonvictims of crime, rape victims have significantly higher rates of depression during the first few months post-assault (Atkeson *et al.*, 1982; Foa and Rothbaum, 1998) and over their lifetimes (Rape in America, 1992; Wyatt, 1992). Depressive symptoms may be related to other trauma sequelae, such as PTSD, social withdrawal, discontinuing previously enjoyed activities, loss of self-confidence and self-worth, shame, and blaming or negative reactions from significant others.

Rape victims have higher rates of suicidal thoughts and suicide attempts than nonvictims (Davidson *et al.*, 1996; Koss, 1988; Rape in America, 1992). Rape victims are also more likely to engage in increased use of alcohol or drugs and to develop substance abuse problems, even if they have no prior history of substance use or abuse (Kilpatrick *et al.*, 1997). Sexual assault victims may use substances to self-medicate, in an effort to dull or escape their emotional pain.

Rape victims may also experience immediate and/or long-term changes in their sexual functioning, including fears and avoidance and/or diminished sexual satisfaction (Burgess and Holmstrom, 1979; Gilbert and Cunningham, 1986; Holmes *et al.*, 1998; Wyatt, 1992; Wyatt *et al.*, 1990). Sexual contact may trigger flashbacks to the sexual assault.

A victim's social adjustment may also be significantly affected by sexual assault victimization (Calhoun and Atkeson, 1991; Resick *et al.*, 1981). Social adjustment includes work or school, relationships with significant others, and leisure time activities. Many victims withdraw from previously enjoyed relationships and activities as they struggle to cope with the after-effects of victimization. They constrict their lifestyle in order to contain their anxiety about personal safety. Some victims change jobs or find it necessary to take a leave of absence from school or work. Some move their residence because of safety concerns or to avoid other reminders of the assault. These lifestyle changes may have a significant economic impact if they involve increased expenses (e.g. relocation) or loss of wages. These actions may also disrupt relationships and deprive victims of needed social support. This, in turn, compounds their feelings of aloneness and isolation.

Feelings of guilt and self-blame are common. Many victims have exaggerated feelings of personal responsibility for the assault, regardless of the actual circumstances. These feelings, in part, represent a search to find a reason to explain the traumatic event. Victims struggle with the question, "Why me?" This is part of a normal process of working through a traumatic event. Victims replay and review what happened. They struggle with feelings that perhaps they could have, or should have, avoided, escaped, or successfully resisted the attack. Self-blame may represent an attempt to undo what happened and regain control. It is a defense against being vulnerable. If the rape happened because of something victims did or did not do, then they may feel that they could have prevented it from happening again. This type of self-blame may be easier for some victims to tolerate emotionally than the reality that rape is a random event. If it is random, it could happen again.

Many rape victims suffer deep feelings of shame. Their shame may be evident in lowered or averted eyes, avoidance of social contact with other people, and, all too often, in their secrecy about the rape. Shame is different from self-blame. Whereas self-blame reflects a sense of responsibility for acts of commission or omission, shame involves a diminished, devalued self. Because of what happened during the rape, the victim is ashamed of herself. Nathanson (1987) discusses shame as a "family of emotions," including humiliation, degradation, embarrassment, disgrace, dishonor, and mortification. Shame has several origins in the rape victim. In part, it stems from the humiliation and degradation to which the victim is subjected by the rapist during the assault. It is also related to the ways in which the rapist forces the victim to participate in the crime. One victim who was ordered by the rapist during the assault to act as if she enjoyed what he was doing to her said, "I became an unwilling participant." Afterwards, she was filled with a persistent sense of humiliation and disgust (Craven, 1978). Betrayal, a central element in rape, also produces shame. The victim believes her judgment and competence are inadequate because she failed to detect the dangerousness of the situation or the person who sexually assaulted her. Another source of shame is the special meaning our society attaches to rape victimization. Some victims feel they are "damaged goods." In some cultures, there is a stigma associated with being a rape victim. The victim is treated as a ruined woman. She not only suffers dishonor herself; she also visits disgrace upon her family. She may no longer be marriageable.

Self-blame, guilt, and shame are also related to other unique burdens placed upon sexual assault victims. Our culture is permeated by misconceptions about rape, such as "Rape only happens to women who ask for it or women who let it happen" and "Rape only happens to certain kinds of (bad) women." Many women who become victims carry these beliefs, consciously or unconsciously, within themselves. When they are raped, they impose these judgments on themselves. The victim's own reactions may be compounded when these attitudes are expressed and reinforced by significant others or people with whom the victim interacts in medical settings, law enforcement agencies, and the courts. Victims of acquaintance rape and victims who are under the influence of alcohol and/or drugs when they are sexually assaulted are much more likely to experience blame and censure.

HOW VICTIMS PRESENT IN EMERGENCY MEDICAL SETTINGS AND LAW ENFORCEMENT INTERVIEWS

There are two characteristics of rape victim reactions, observed by others, that are frequently misunderstood, misinterpreted, and mistakenly used to discredit victims. First, in the initial aftermath of rape, the way victims typically present is the opposite of what people expect. Second, over time, as victims cope with the impact of rape on their lives, they typically shift back and forth between two seemingly opposite states. Sometimes, the dramatic changes in their mood and affect are misinterpreted as an indicator of "inconsistencies in their story," rather than as the normal course of rape trauma symptomatology. These two features of rape victim reactions may impact the interactions victims have with law enforcement personnel and prosecutors, as well as the demeanor of victims in the courtroom. It is important to understand the reasons for these behaviors.

Immediately following a sexual assault, most victims experience shock. They are stunned. They feel numb. Outwardly, they may appear calm, subdued, or dazed. They have flat affect. They are often in a state of disbelief. Many victims say, "I can't believe this happened to me." Victims often find it difficult to focus and concentrate. Therefore, they may appear confused or disoriented, inattentive or distracted. Sometimes they seem distant.

This behavioral presentation is contrary to common expectations. It is often called "counterintuitive." Most people expect to see a visibly upset victim following a sexual assault, i.e. a victim who is crying, angry, and/or agitated. The more likely, seemingly calm presentation has many consequences. It belies the horror of the crime the victim has experienced. It hides the severity of the trauma the victim has sustained. It also masks the victim's need to have the traumatic nature of the assault and its impact acknowledged by others. When flat affect is coupled with a lack of visible physical injuries that is common in many rape cases, it may result in misdiagnosis, mistreatment, and misunderstanding about victim needs and appropriate interventions. Often, the victim's shock reaction is followed by a period of denial and numbing. The victim may want to try to "forget" what happened. Denial may be evident in behaviors such as late reporting, attempts to resume normal/usual activities, and avoidance of stimuli that remind the victim of the assault (e.g. interviews with police and prosecutors). It is too painful to think about. For all of these reasons, rape trauma is often called an "invisible wound," especially in its initial manifestations. The invisibility of the psychological injury rape victims sustain is also related to their characteristic silence and secrecy about the victimization.

The second common characteristic of rape victim behavior in the aftermath of the crime is what is called "oscillation" between two opposite states. The victim shifts back and forth between being "immersed in the trauma" and "psychic numbing" (Horowitz, 1986). When victims are immersed in the trauma, they have symptoms such as nightmares, flashbacks (recurrent, intrusive images of the rape), preoccupation with the trauma, and a sense that they are re-living it. The symptoms re-create the loss of control and sense of powerlessness they had during the assault. They become hypervigilant; they are on guard to protect themselves from being vulnerable again. They reckon with the losses that they have sustained, e.g. safety, control, autonomy, self-confidence, self-esteem, and the ability to trust other people. They experience intense emotions and acute distress. In striking contrast, when they shift to a state of "psychic numbing," they may appear outwardly disinterested and unaffected. They attempt to ward off feelings and avoid or deny the significance and meaning of the trauma. They withdraw from activities and relationships. They feel disconnected. They narrow their focus and constrict their lifestyle.

The diverse feelings and behaviors associated with these seemingly polar opposite states of mind are expressed in the victim's interactions with "the system." For example, the victim may make an immediate police report, indicating her interest in the prosecution of the offender. In her first interview with the prosecutor, the victim may be very emotional and expressive, giving specific details as she describes the rape. The prosecutor feels confident that the victim's testimony in court will be powerful and moving for the jury. When the prosecutor contacts the victim a few weeks later, the victim may be distant and unwilling to engage in the tasks at hand. In the first court hearing, the victim may be very "bland." She may also give much less detail about the rape. This variability reflects the "oscillation" (and the underlying distress) that is so common in rape victims during the aftermath of the crime. These issues have practical applications for law enforcement and criminal justice personnel. For example, victims who miss appointments should not always be viewed as "unco-operative witnesses." There are usually other reasons for their avoidance and reluctance. If the professionals involved in these cases understand the reasons for the variability in victim reactions, they can respond appropriately, and they will have more "cooperative witnesses."

SECTION III: DRUG-FACILITATED SEXUAL ASSAULTS

The first two sections of this chapter provide information about the scope of rape and sexual assault victimization in the United States, common patterns of occurrence, strategies used by offenders to overpower and control victims, typical victim responses during and following their encounters with rapists, and the immediate and long-term physical and psychosocial impacts of rape. This section discusses how these general characteristics of rape relate to the unique aspects of DFSA, including the emergence of the phenomenon as a distinct crime pattern, the prevalence of these crimes, victim–offender relationships, methods used to overpower victims, victim reactions during and following the assault, and special considerations and guidelines for victim interviews in the aftermath of DFSA.

Victims give poignant descriptions of this type of victimization:

> It was my 45th birthday. I was at a club with my girlfriends. It was about 9 o'clock at night. I ordered a drink. I remember taking a few sips. The next thing I remember is waking up in a bed in an apartment with a stranger. I was naked. It was morning. There was semen on my stomach. I felt sore inside. I knew someone had had sex with me. But I couldn't remember the last ten hours. I felt like I was waking up from being dead . . . Being drugged and raped is like being shot in the head, only you never see the gun. Afterwards, your brain doesn't work. No matter how hard you try to remember what happened, it's a black hole, total darkness . . . Whatever I was given, it knocked me out. I just keep wondering why anyone would want to have sex with a corpse.

> I am 18 years old. I went to a club with a friend. We left at about midnight. When we crossed the street to go to the parking lot, two men came up behind us. They had

guns. They grabbed me and dragged me to a car. They left my friend behind. I remember being shoved into the car. They drove me to a hotel. I asked for a drink of water. I woke up 12 hours later in the hotel room. My vagina and rectum hurt. There was one guy asleep in the room. I went to the bathroom. There was a window that led to a balcony. I climbed out and went for help. The police came and took me to the hospital. They found semen on my legs. I had bruises on my forehead. I was so sore. I couldn't sit down. I had a large laceration inside my rectum.

I am 15 years old. After school, I went to visit my boyfriend at the food store where he works. He gave me some fruit juice with guava in it. He said it was a health drink. I must have passed out. My memory is fuzzy about what happened next. I remember being put in a car. I woke up in my own bed, but I don't remember going home. My boyfriend's name was tattooed on my shoulder. There was blood in my underpants. I told him before this happened that I didn't want to have sex with him. I wasn't ready.

I went to college on an athletic scholarship. Our team was ranked one of the top three in the country. At my school, the male athletes and the female athletes spent a lot of time together. We were close friends. One night, after studying, one of the star male athletes on campus invited me to a party at his apartment. When I arrived, no one else was there yet. He offered me a glass of wine. The next thing I remember is waking up eight hours later on the floor of this guy's living room. I was on my back, completely naked. Next to me was a used condom. My clothes were rolled up in a ball across the room. I had been raped. Guys were asleep in the other room. They would have had to walk over me to get into their bedroom. They either saw what happened, or maybe they participated.

All rape victims experience a loss of control and are reduced to a state of powerlessness at the hands of another person. But most victims still have some of their "faculties" during the assault. In contrast, victims of DFSA experience an extreme degree of powerlessness. In addition to other common characteristics of sexual assault victimization, the offender takes away their cognition and consciousness and then sexually assaults them. One victim said, "It's like you're dead."

The unique features of these crimes that differentiate them from the experiences victims have in most other sexual assaults are related to the meaning to victims of being surreptitiously drugged and severely incapacitated by another person, how these victims experience the encounter with the rapist, and the effects of the drugs these victims unknowingly ingest: sedation, impaired motor skills, altered levels of consciousness and anterograde amnesia. The drug effects alter a victim's experience during the assault, as well as in the aftermath of victimization.

VICTIMS HELP DEFINE A NEW CRIME PATTERN

It was not until the mid-1990s that the phenomenon of DFSA began to be viewed as a distinct crime pattern. Victims of a specific type of DFSA played a key role in bringing this issue to the public's attention (Abarbanel, 2000).

Clearly, the sexual victimization of women who are under the influence of alcohol and/or drugs is not a new crime pattern. Sexual assaults committed against victims who voluntarily consume substances that impair their physical ability to defend themselves are relatively common. DFSA crimes have also been reported in other circumstances, such as when victims are under anesthesia during medical procedures. However, in these cases, the rapist exploits an already incapacitated or vulnerable person. This is quite different from crimes in which an offender arranges for, or acts to cause (surreptitiously or otherwise), a victim's substance-induced incapacitation or vulnerability.

It also is not an entirely new phenomenon for offenders to slip drugs into victims' drinks to incapacitate them. The most well-known version of this cruelty is "slipping someone a Mickey," a crime often committed in conjunction with the intent to rob the victim.

What changed dramatically in the mid-1990s was an increase in surreptitious druggings of victims for the purpose of sexually assaulting them, and the use of substances with certain characteristics, such as drugs that produce anterograde amnesia (LeBeau, 1999). Rape crisis centers, hospitals, police departments, and hotlines began seeing a significant number of victims who reported that someone had drugged them, without their knowledge or consent, in order to rape them. These victim reports had several common elements:

> The victim was in a social or business situation that seemed non-threatening – at a party, in a restaurant or a club, at a business lunch, in a friend's home, or on a date. The victim consumed a drink. Within a very short time, "a curtain seemed to come down" on the victim's awareness of what was happening. Most victims reported that they lost consciousness for a period of time. When they regained consciousness, hours had passed. They had little or no memory of the intervening time period. In many cases, they had been moved to another location. Some were unsure about whether they had been sexually assaulted. Others identified signs that they had been, such as semen stains on their bodies or clothing, vaginal and/or anal soreness, or physical bruises and lacerations.

These victims were describing substance-induced states in which they became physically and mentally impaired, often experiencing altered levels of consciousness. The onset of the drug-related symptoms was rapid. The victims' loss of control was profound. Many of the victims who had been drinking prior to their loss of consciousness reported that the amount of alcohol they consumed voluntarily was not sufficient to cause the level of sedation and loss of control they experienced. Some victims had no recall of events that took place after the drugs took effect. Other victims had very fragmented and/or vague memories.

Initially, many of the victims who reported these crimes were dismissed. For example, one victim was told, "He has his memory, you don't have yours. There is no evidence. The case is closed." Often, the victim's trauma was discounted. A victim was asked, "If you can't remember what happened, how bad can it be?" In addition to indifferent attitudes, the options available to victims for redress were very limited. Because of a lack of knowledge and training on the part of law enforcement and medical personnel, in many of the cases, crucial evidence was never collected from victims or crime scenes. There was very little information available in the professional literature to guide the responses of victim service providers. No research had been conducted. There were no established protocols for hospitals or law enforcement agencies that specifically addressed the unique issues presented in these cases. As a result of these conditions, many victims felt revictimized by the agencies that were supposed to help them (Abarbanel, 2000).

As more victims of these crimes came forward, their voices were eventually heard. The issues they identified led to the implementation of new policies and protocols in communities across the country. It is important to recognize victims for their crucial role in furthering our understanding of these crimes. Through their reports, we have been able to identify some of the unique characteristics of this form of victimization.

DEFINING THE PROBLEM

Currently, the term "drug-facilitated sexual assault" is used to refer to sex offenses committed under three different conditions:

- *Condition #1* (Involuntary ingestion of incapacitating substances). Victims are sexually assaulted after involuntarily or unknowingly consuming incapacitating drugs given to them surreptitiously by another person or persons. For example, the victim consumes food or a beverage that has been surreptitiously "dosed" or "spiked" with a drug. The victim does not voluntarily consume any alcohol or drugs.
- *Condition #2* (Voluntary and involuntary ingestion of incapacitating substances). Victims are sexually assaulted after voluntarily consuming alcohol and/or drugs *and* involuntarily ingesting other drugs given to them surreptitiously by another person or persons. For example, the victim has two drinks and then consumes a third drink that unbeknownst to her has been spiked with an incapacitating substance.
- *Condition # 3* (Voluntary ingestion of incapacitating substances). Victims are sexually

assaulted after voluntarily consuming alcohol and/or drugs. No substances are surreptitiously administered to the victim.

From the perspective of victims, although there may be some similarities among these three conditions, there are important differences between situations in which a person is sexually assaulted after being surreptitiously drugged, and thereby incapacitated, by another person (Conditions #1 and # 2) and situations in which someone is sexually assaulted after voluntarily consuming incapacitating substances (Condition # 3). As stated earlier, the victim experiences the first two conditions as "double crimes." These "double crimes" are the focus of the remainder of this chapter.

SCOPE OF THE PROBLEM

The prevalence and incidence of DFSAs are unknown and there are currently no systematic efforts under way to measure this form of victimization. Although there are anecdotal reports from victim services agencies across the country, as well as documented cases in which these crimes have been prosecuted, there are many methodological challenges confronting researchers and criminal justice agencies in their efforts to accurately assess the prevalence of these offenses. Some of the difficulties associated with identifying these cases are discussed in other chapters of this book. However, it should also be noted that, historically, in most survey research designed to measure the scope of sexual violence in this country, these types of crimes (i.e. rapes and other sexual assaults in which incapacitated women are victims) have generally not been included within the definitions used by researchers to identify sexual assault victims or incidents (Russell and Bolen, 2000).

The omission of these crimes in previous research may be a reflection of public attitudes about the nature and significance of these types of offenses. Incapacitated victims who have voluntarily ingested alcohol or drugs are often viewed as "asking for it." Our laws reflect public attitudes. In some states, even though these crimes involve nonconsensual sex, they are treated differently under the law, or special requirements are imposed for them to qualify as sex crimes. It is noteworthy that, as discussed earlier, these offenses are generally not included in the Uniform Crime Report (US Department of Justice, 2000) which uses a definition of "forcible rape" that requires the use of "force or threat of force" (Russell and Bolen, 2000).

VICTIM–OFFENDER RELATIONSHIPS

In drug-facilitated crimes, the relationships between victims and offenders may be similar to the stranger and acquaintance relationships that characterize other types of sexual assaults. However, victims of drug-facilitated crimes also describe two additional and unique types of relationships with their assailants.

In some cases, the victim does not know the identity of the rapist until she awakens from a drug-induced unconscious state.

> Maria went to a local restaurant-bar where she frequently had dinner. She ordered a beer while she looked at the menu. The last thing she remembers is her meal being served. She woke up five hours later on the beach. A stranger was raping her.

In other DFSAs, the offender remains anonymous. The victim may never learn his identity. The "anonymous rapist" may have no direct interaction with his victims until they are in an unconscious state. He can "knock out" his victims from a remote location by slipping a drug in their drink or food. Once the victim is incapacitated, he can transport the victim to another location, sexually assault the victim's body, and flee the scene before the victim regains consciousness. Consequently, his victims may never see him, hear him, or feel his body. One victim who was drugged at a party and woke up naked, in the back seat of her car, said, "The person who did this to me doesn't have a face." The mother of a college student who was drugged and raped by an unknown assailant said, "It's the perfect crime. A guy can walk into a bar and say I want a vodka tonic and I'll have that blonde over there . . ." (ABC News, 1996).

Because DFSAs are "double crimes," the person who drugs the victim may not be the same person who commits the sexual assault. Accomplices can help rapists drug their victims. One victim commented on the cloak of anonymity that protects offenders in these cases: "It could have been anyone in the room – the waiter, the bartender, my date. I will never know who put the drugs in my drink."

HOW OFFENDERS GAIN ACCESS TO VICTIMS

In drug-facilitated crimes, it is typically very easy for rapists to overpower their victims. The cases in which victims are taken by force and restrained while they are being drugged are relatively rare. In these instances, the drugs are administered with the victim's knowledge, but without her consent.

> I was living in a high-security building. I was sound asleep. I felt someone sit on the bed. I opened my eyes and saw a man with a bandana over his face. He said, "Shut up

or I'll kill you." Before I could move, he held a dirty, wet rag over my nose and mouth. He was pushing my head against the pillow. I felt him pulling my nightgown up over my stomach. Then I lost consciousness. When I woke up, he was gone. I had been raped. There were bruises on my thighs.

Victims have a different experience in the majority of DFSAs. The offender avoids any confrontation with the victim. He does not have to use threats or physical force get compliance. He does not have to overcome any form of resistance. He does not have to worry about a victim's screams attracting attention. He does not have to foil a victim's attempts to escape. The drugs that are administered surreptitiously quickly incapacitate, immobilize, and silence the victim.

THE VICTIM'S PERCEPTION OF DANGER AND SELF-PROTECTIVE STRATEGIES

Unlike other victims, most victims of drug-facilitated crimes do not perceive a threat to their safety at the time they are being rendered powerless by an offender. This is because the offender behaviors (e.g. force, threats, and intimidation) that commonly trigger fear in other victims are absent.

A 42-year-old woman was drugged in a restaurant and then raped, sodomized, and photographed while she was unconscious. Afterwards she said, "I never saw it coming, not even for a second."

This characteristic of drug-facilitated rape (i.e. the absence of anticipatory fear and dread) significantly alters the victim's experience during the encounter with the rapist. It may also account for differences in the victims' symptomatology in the aftermath of the crime, particularly in the appearance of traumatic stress symptoms that are fear-related.

As discussed earlier in this chapter, fear is a signal to victims to mobilize defensive behaviors. Because victims of DFSAs are usually deprived of any "warning" of the harmful intent of the offender, they are unable to implement self-protection strategies. They are denied the opportunity to offer resistance.

Afterwards, in striking contrast to other sexual assaults, in these crimes, the victim's nonresistance is usually not an issue, either in the court of public opinion or the criminal justice system. The incapacitating effects of the drugs provide an "acceptable" explanation for the victim's state of powerlessness and inability to fend off the attacker(s). Nevertheless, many victims of these assaults feel "robbed" of the opportunity, and of their ability, to utilize any coping and self-protective strategies during their encounter with the assailant. This is yet another example of the meaning of victims' categorization of drug-facilitated rape as a "double crime." One victim said, "Rape is never a fair fight, but I didn't even have a chance to try to defend myself."

WITNESSES AND BYSTANDERS

The secrecy and anonymity that are possible when drugs are used to overpower victims, and the ability to administer them from a remote location, offer considerable advantages for offenders. This characteristic of drug-facilitated crimes may also affect how victims are perceived – or misperceived – by other people.

In other types of sexual assaults, offenders usually overpower their victims in situations and locations that provide privacy. By using drugs as a weapon, an offender can render the victim helpless in a public place and bystanders may not recognize that a crime is being committed or pay attention to the identity of the offender. Moreover, in some cases, to bystanders and witnesses, the rapist may appear to be a rescuer. The behavioral effects of the drugs administered surreptitiously to the victim are very similar to the effects of voluntary alcohol consumption. To onlookers, the victim may appear to be drunk. When the rapist provides assistance, such as by offering to lead or carry the victim to another location (where he plans to sexually assault her), he may be mistakenly viewed by others as "helping" a vulnerable person get to a safe place. In addition, the victim may appear cooperative. Onlookers may not know that the victim is under the influence of drugs ingested involuntarily and unknowingly. These misperceptions may influence subsequent assessments of the victim's credibility.

THE MEANING OF DRUG-INDUCED INCAPACITATION TO THE VICTIM

The type and degree of incapacitation that a victim experiences during a DFSA is dramatically different from the powerlessness that victims experience in other types of sexual assaults.

One of the most striking features of the victim's incapacitation is an unexpected, and usually sudden, altered level of consciousness. Victims describe two different types of experiences. Some victims report that they completely lose consciousness when the drugs take effect, e.g. "I passed out. I was gone. He could have sawed my body in half and I would never have known." Other victims describe losing and then regaining consciousness for brief, intermittent periods of time. These victims have "flashbulb" or fragmented memories. However, even when they regain consciousness for short time intervals, they are severely incapacitated. They often say they feel "paralyzed." One victim gave a vivid description of her state of helplessness: "I came to for thirty seconds. This guy was on top of me raping me, but I couldn't move my arms or legs. I couldn't speak. Then I passed out again."

In some instances, observations and reports by witnesses indicate that the victim may not actually be unconscious for the entire time period that she cannot recall. Rather, the victim may have no memory of her behavior during a certain time period. This may be similar to an "alcohol blackout."

Another substance-induced impairment that these victims suffer is anterograde amnesia (i.e. absence of memory for events that occur after the drugs take effect). This has far-reaching consequences. In the aftermath of the crime, while other victims struggle to cope with trauma memories that recur repeatedly in the form of flashbacks and nightmares, victims of DFSAs live with the agony of not being able to recall some or all of the details of what was done to them. Some of these victims may never find answers to the questions that plague them: "Who sexually assaulted me?", "What sexual acts and other forms of abuse did they inflict on me?", "What objects did they insert inside of my body?", "How many people participated?", "How many people watched?" Others may have very fragmented memories. Not having the memories – not knowing – compounds their feelings of powerlessness. Many of these victims say, "I would rather have the nightmare."

Anterograde amnesia also haunts victims of DFSAs if they seek legal action. It may severely limit their access to redress through the criminal justice system. In most rape cases, the victim is a key witness and, in many cases, the only witness. In drug-facilitated rapes, the victim may be robbed of the ability to provide significant details about the identity of the offender, the criminal acts committed by him and any accomplices, and the location(s) where the crime was committed. Their memory deficit serves as a continuing reminder to victims that they have suffered a "double crime."

Over and over, victims may feel revictimized by the amnestic effects of the drugs (e.g. in police interviews, court testimony, and in the therapy office). Their inability to recall pertinent information perpetuates their sense of powerlessness. It also recreates – and prolongs – the helplessness they experienced during the sexual assault. This is one of the reasons that the anterograde amnesia is often experienced by victims as a permanent disability, a disability caused by the offender.

REPORTING AND OTHER HELP-SEEKING BEHAVIORS

Many victims of DFSAs are reluctant to make police reports. They have the same fears and concerns about reporting that inhibit other victims from contacting the police. However, they have additional and unique reasons for making late reports, as well as for not notifying the police. Specifically, their ability to immediately contact the police and/or seek other types of assistance can be severely limited by the initial and residual effects of the substances they ingest. Typically, the drugs cause impaired motor skills and altered levels of consciousness for extended periods of time. Some victims report being "out" for 8 to 12 hours. Even those victims who experience intermittent periods of awakening often report that they feel "paralyzed" and "unable to move," and quickly pass out again. When drugged victims do regain consciousness, many suffer "hangover effects," such as confusion and disorientation. These cognitive and physical impairments significantly delay decisions regarding reporting.

Victims of DFSAs often feel that they cannot provide sufficient information to law enforcement for action to be taken. They may also be reluctant to make an accusation of sexual assault without personal knowledge or memory of the assault circumstances. In some cases, they may feel certain that they were drugged, but uncertain about whether they were sexually assaulted. In these circumstances, they may prefer to seek drug testing before they consider a police report or a sexual assault examination. This decision delays what may eventually become a police report.

> Lara returned to school for her sophomore year after spending the summer vacation at home. Some of her friends invited her to go with them to a fraternity party. She knew a lot of the people at the party. She felt safe. She also knew her own alcohol tolerance. She had a few drinks. A guy offered her a shot. She remembers getting half way through the drink. She woke up eight hours later on a couch in the living room of the fraternity house. She had bruises on her head. Her pants were unzipped. There was urine on her clothes. She couldn't remember anything after taking a few sips of the drink. She went to the Student Health Center for a drug test.

Victims who voluntarily consume alcohol in the same incident in which they are drugged may have strong feelings of guilt and self-blame. Victims who voluntarily ingested illicit drugs may fear that legal action will be taken against them if they report the sexual assault. Victims who are drugged in situations where they were socializing with peers (e.g. a high school graduation party) may not want to "get friends in trouble." Victims may also have concerns about the confidentiality of drug-test results and the implications of positive findings if these results become part of their permanent health records.

UNIQUE SEQUELAE IN DFSAS

The unique characteristics of DFSAs, and their implications for victim impact, have not been examined scientifically. For example, no research has been conducted to determine whether victims of DFSAs evidence ASD and/or PTSD symptom patterns to a greater or lesser extent than other rape victims. Anecdotal evidence indicates that specific sexual assault sequelae that appear to be related to characteristics of a traumatic event (e.g. the victim experiences a threat to life or physical integrity) and a victim's responses during the traumatic event (e.g. the victim experiences intense fear or horror; the victim dissociates) may vary somewhat for some victims of drug-facilitated crimes because their assault experience is usually qualitatively different from that of other victims. The sequelae that are related to other characteristics of rape victimization (e.g. the meaning of rape in our culture, feelings of personal responsibility, and stigmatization) may be more similar across all victims. As cases of DFSA continue to be reported in alarming numbers, this is a critical area for research.

Another factor that may account for differences in victim reactions is the nature of the victim's amnesia. Victims who have fragmented memories may have different symptom constellations than victims who have no recall of any aspect of the sexual assault or other acts of abuse and degradation inflicted on them by the offender. Victims who experienced fear during their encounter with the assailant may also have a different course in the aftermath because fear is such a significant factor in the etiology and persistence of trauma symptoms in other victims. However, it appears that many victims of DFSAs have fear-related after-effects even though they did not experience fear during the assault itself. The fact of being reduced to a state of helplessness engenders within them subsequent fears about personal safety, as well as anxiety about personal vulnerability to harm in the future.

Victims of DFSAs may encounter unique forms of discrimination. It is not uncommon for other people to misjudge the nature and severity of their trauma. Because these victims often have no memory, or only vague or spotty memories, of the sexual assault, their trauma may be minimized. Victims may encounter these attitudes among professional service providers and within their social support networks of family and friends. One victim was told, "You're lucky you can't remember, you won't suffer as much as other victims." Another victim was told, "It's a blessing." Victims who encounter these attitudes may develop a sense of "illegitimacy" about their victimization experience. They may feel that they do not have the same rights as other victims – the right to seek justice, the right to support, the right to trauma symptoms. They also feel misunderstood. For these victims, not being able to remember is one of the most distressing symptoms of their trauma. One victim who was drugged and raped in a fraternity house over a year ago described the significance of this issue for her:

> I feel humiliated all of the time. Other people out there know what happened to me.
> They watched. I will never know what they saw. For me, not knowing is worse than
> knowing. It's like the rapist gets to take something more from me and keep it for ever.

HOW VICTIMS PRESENT IN EMERGENCY MEDICAL SETTINGS AND LAW ENFORCEMENT INTERVIEWS

In many ways, the initial presentation of victims of DFSAs is similar to the behaviors seen in other victims, although some of the contributing factors may be different. It is important to understand the unique trauma experiences that underlie the responses of victims who have been drugged in order to develop effective approaches for victim interviews.

In the aftermath of DFSAs, the shock and dismay expressed by victims may be compounded by the fact that they never perceived a "threat" to their safety before they lost control of their faculties. It is often very difficult for these victims to reckon with the fact that they "never saw it coming." They feel that their internal "alarm system" failed them. In addition, what may be trauma-related initial shock, confusion, and disorientation in other sexual assault victims, may be intensified for victims of drug-facilitated crimes by the residual or hangover effects of the drugs.

For drugged victims, the sense that the traumatic event is "surreal" may be magnified by their inability to recall details or piece together what happened to them, as well as by the effects of the drugs they ingested. They may be distanced or tenuous in their interactions with other people because of their self-consciousness about their memory impairment. While other sexual assault victims may appear preoccupied or unresponsive during a police interview because they are having flashbacks or dissociating, these victims are often literally "stumped" by the questions they are asked. They can't find the answers in their "memory bank." Their inability to provide answers compounds their sense of powerlessness and inadequacy.

Whereas other victims may experience some relief when they are able to talk about what happened to them with professionals who are supportive and understanding (e.g. after giving an assault history to police, advocates, and medical or mental health professionals), victims who have been drugged may become more anxious when they are questioned during investigative interviews because of their growing realization of the extent and the persistence of their memory impairment.

EFFECTIVE STRATEGIES FOR VICTIM INTERVIEWS

Knowledge about the unique characteristics of DFSA should be used to develop effective victim interviewing techniques for these cases. The strategies that are effective with other sexual assault victims are appropriate for use with victims of DFSA, but with certain modifications. Special interventions should be implemented to address the differences in victim experiences in these cases.

The following general principles for victim interviewing should be followed.

- The setting should provide privacy and safety. It should be a location where interruptions and distractions are minimized.
- Victims should always have the option of having support persons of their choice present.
- The interviewer's verbal and non-verbal language should communicate support and respect. For example, the interviewer should sit at eye level with the victim, rather than stand over the victim in a "command position."
- The interviewer should acknowledge the trauma the victim has experienced. This helps establish rapport by communicating acceptance and understanding. It also gives the victim permission to express feelings and concerns.
- The interviewer should always explain what they wish to do, and why, before they do it. The victim's consent should be obtained for various steps in the process. These procedures give victims a sense of control and safety. They make the situation predictable. Information also reduces anxiety. If victims understand the reasons for the questions they are being asked, e.g. how the information requested will be used to aid the investigation, they will be more able and willing to cooperate.
- The victim should be permitted to participate in making decisions about various issues. Making choices and exercising autonomy helps re-establish feelings of control, self-confidence, and self-esteem. The victim can be given choices about how, when, and where the interview is conducted, and who is present. Victims can also be given some control of the situation by being offered the option of stopping the interview whenever they feel uncomfortable or wish to take a break.
- Victims should always be encouraged to tell the investigator as much as they can remember. They should be advised to share details even if they think they are unimportant or out of sequence. Victims should be asked about sensory and peripheral details.

Special consideration should be given to ways that the unique needs and concerns of victims of drug-facilitated crimes can be addressed:

- The interviewer should communicate to the victim the seriousness of drug-facilitated offenses and the commitment of the agency to investigate and prosecute these crimes to the fullest. This helps overcome the "hopelessness" that many victims of these crimes feel about their chances of being believed and supported by the police.
- In appropriate cases, the interviewer may give the victim some general information about this form of victimization. This helps validate the victim's experience. It can be reassuring to victims to know that, if they have been drugged, some of the reactions they are experiencing are "normal" and "usual" effects of certain types of substances. Otherwise, victims may interpret certain drug-induced or trauma-related memory impairments as a personal defect or failing.

- The interviewer can focus initially on areas of inquiry and timeframes that the victim can remember, such as the time period prior to ingestion of the drugs and the period after the drug-effects wore off. This helps build the victim's confidence and encourages participation in the process. The interviewer should also acknowledge and reinforce the importance of the information that the victim can recall, versus the problems presented by the gaps in the victim's memory.

- Questions that focus on the time periods when victims experienced altered levels of consciousness should be introduced with an acknowledgement of the fact that the victim may not be able to remember certain facts and details.

- The interviewer should be aware of the hangover effects associated with DFSAs. Victims may be extremely fatigued in the immediate aftermath of the assault. The interviewer and the victim should determine together the best timing for various interviews.

- The victim should be informed about other avenues that will be pursued in the investigation, such as interviews with suspects and witnesses, preservation and examination of the crime scene(s), and the medical/evidentiary examination. It is important for victims to understand that the entire case does not rest on their ability to recall details that they may not be able to remember.

- Victims should be advised about the types of medical evidence that will be collected during the sexual assault examination. Victims should be informed about the realities of drug testing. In many cases, there are no findings in the forensic toxicology laboratory. The victim should be given information about the meaning of negative test results.

These approaches will assist investigators in forming a working alliance with the victim and enhance the victim's ability to contribute to the process.

CONCLUSIONS

Victims of DFSA have broken souls, like other rape victims. The unique aspects of the trauma they suffer should be recognized and respected – in specialized protocols to guide the delivery of services that are responsive to their needs and concerns, in the laws that guide criminal prosecutions and charging decisions in these cases, and in research dedicated to developing more knowledge abut this form of victimization. Encouraging these reforms and innovations is one of the goals of this book.

REFERENCES

Abarbanel, G. (2000) "Assessing Drug-Facilitated Rape: Learning From Victims", *Nat. Inst. Just. J.*, April, pp. 11–12, US Department of Justice.

Abarbanel, G. and Richman, G. (1990) "The Rape Victim". In Parad, H.J. and Parad, L.G. (eds) *Crisis Intervention Book 2: A Practitioner's Sourcebook for Brief Therapy*, pp. 93–118. Milwaukee, WI: Family Service America.

ABC News (1996) *20/20* (video recording).

American Psychiatric Association (APA) (1994) *Diagnostic and Statistical Manual of Mental Disorders* (4th edn). Washington, DC: American Psychiatric Association.

Atkeson, Beverly M., Calhoun, Karen S., Resick, Patricia A. and Ellis, Elizabeth M. (1982) "Victims of Rape: Repeated Assessment of Depressive Symptoms", *J. Consult. Clin. Psychol.,* 50 (1), pp. 96–102.

Bachman, R. (1998) "The Factors Related to Rape Reporting Behavior and Arrest: New Evidence from the National Crime Victimization Survey", *Crim. Just. Behav.*, 25 (1), pp. 8–29.

Bachman, R. and Saltzman, L.E. (1995) "Violence Against Women: Estimates from the Redesigned Survey", *Bureau Just. Stat. Spec. Rep.,* Washington, DC: US Department of Justice.

Benedict, H. (1992) *Virgin or Vamp: How the Press Covers Sex Crimes.* New York, NY: Oxford University Press.

Browne, Angela and Finkelhor, David (1986) "Impact of Child Sexual Abuse: A Review of the Research", *Psychol. Bulletin,* 99 (1), pp. 66–77.

Burgess, A.W. and Holstrom, L.L. (1974) *Rape: Victims of Crisis.* Bowie, MD: The Robert J. Brady Co.

Burgess, A.W. and Holmstrom, L.L. (1979) "Rape: Sexual Disruption and Recovery", *Am. J. Orthopsych.*, 49 (4), pp. 648–657.

Calhoun, K.S. and Atkeson, B.M. (1991) *Treatment of Rape Victims.* Elmsford, NY: Pergamon Press.

Chaiken, J.M. (2000) "Crunching Numbers: Crime and Incarceration at the End of the Millennium", *Nat. Inst. Just. J.*, January, pp. 10–17.

Craven, Carolyn (1978) NBC interview with Tom Snyder (video recording).

Crowell, N.A. and Burgess, A.W. (eds) (1996) *Understanding Violence Against Women.* Washington, DC: National Academy Press.

Davidson, J.R.T., Hughes, Dana C., George, Linda K. and Blazer, Dan G. (1996) "The Association of Sexual Assault and Attempted Suicide Within the Community", *Arch. Gen. Psych.*,
53, pp. 550–555.

Estrich, S. (1987) *Real Rape.* Cambridge, MA: Harvard University Press.

Foa, E.B. and Rothbaum, B.O. (1998) *Treating the Trauma of Rape.* New York, NY: The
Guilford Press.

Frazier, P.A. and Haney, B. (1996) "Sexual Assault Cases in the Legal System: Police, Prosecutor, and Victim Perspectives", *Law Hum. Behav.*, 20 (6), pp. 607–627.

Gilbert, B. and Cunningham, J. (1986) "Women's Postrape Sexual Functioning: Review and
Implications for Counseling", *J. Couns. Devel.*, 65, pp. 71–73.

Golding, J.M. (1994) "Sexual Assault History and Physical Health in Randomly Selected Los
Angeles Women", *Health Psychol.*, 13 (2), pp. 130–138.

Golding, J.M., Cooper, M. Lynne and George, Linda K. (1997) "Sexual Assault History and
Health Perceptions: Seven General Population Studies", *Health Psychol.*, 16 (5), pp.
417–425.

Groth, A.N. (1979) *Men Who Rape: The Psychology of the Offender.* New York: Plenum
Press.

Herman, J.L. (1992) *Trauma and Recovery: The Aftermath of Violence.* Boulder: BasicBooks.

Hodge, S. and Canter, D. (1998) "Victims and Perpetrators of Male Sexual Assault", *J. Interpersonal Viol.*, 13 (2), pp. 222–239.

Holmes, M.M., Resnick, Heidi S., Kilpatrick, Dean G. and Best, Connie L. (1996) "Rape-related
Pregnancy: Estimates and Descriptive Characteristics from a National Sample of
Women", *Am. J. Obstet. Gynecol.*, 175 (2), pp. 320–325.

Holmes, M.M., Resnick, Heidi S. and Frampton, Dale (1998) "Follow-up of Sexual Assault
Victims", *Am. J. Obstet. Gynecol.*, 179 (2), pp. 336–342.

Horowitz, M.J. (1986) *Stress Response Syndromes.* Northvale, NY: Jason Aronson Inc.

Katz, B.L. (1991) "The Psychological Impact of Stranger Versus Nonstranger Rape on Victims'
Recovery". In Parrot, A. and Bechhofer, L. (eds) *Acquaintance Rape: The Hidden Crime,*
pp. 251–269. New York: John Wiley and Sons, Inc.

Kilpatrick, D.G., Acierno, Ron, Resnick, Heidi S., Saunders, Benjamin E. and Best, Connie L.
(1997) "A 2-Year Longitudinal Analysis of the Relationships Between Violent Assault and
Substance Use in Women", *J. Consult. Clin. Psychol.*, 65 (5), pp. 834–847.

Kilpatrick, D.G., Saunders, Benjamin E., Veronen, Lois J., Best, Connie L. and Von, Judith M.

(1987) "Criminal Victimization: Lifetime Prevalence, Reporting to Police, and Psychological Impact", *Crime Delinq.*, 33 (4), pp. 479–489.

Kimerling R. and Calhoun K.S. (1994) "Somatic Symptoms, Social Support, and Treatment Seeking Among Sexual Assault Victims", *J. Consult. Clin. Psychol.*, 62 (2), pp. 333–340.

Koss, M.P. and Heslet, L. (1992) "Somatic Consequences of Violence Against Women", *Arch. Fam. Med.*, 1, pp. 53–59.

Koss, M.P., Dinero, Thomas E., Seibel, C.A. and Cox, Susan L. (1988) "Stranger and Acquaintance Rape: Are There Differences In the Victim's Experience?", *Psychol. Women Quart.*, 12, pp. 1–24.

Koss, M.P., Koss, P.G. and Woodruff, W.J. (1991) "Deleterious Effects of Criminal Victimization on Women's Health and Medical Utilization", *Arch. Int. Med.*, 151, pp. 342–347.

Kramer, T.L. and Green, B.L. (1991) "Posttraumatic Stress Disorder as an Early Response to Sexual Assault", *J. Interpersonal Viol.*, 6 (2), pp. 160–173.

LeBeau, M. (1999) 'Toxicological Investigations of Drug-Facilitated Sexual Assaults", *For. Sci. Comm.*, 1 (1).

Messman-Moore, T.L. and Long, P.J. (2000) "Child Sexual Abuse and Revictimization in the Form of Adult Sexual Abuse, Adult Physical Abuse, and Adult Psychological Maltreatment", *J. Interpersonal Viol.*, 15 (5), pp. 489–502.

Nathanson, D.L. (1987) "A Timetable for Shame". In Nathanson, D.L. (ed.) *The Many Faces of Shame*, pp. 1–63. New York, NY: The Guilford Press.

Raine, N.V. (1998) *After Silence: Rape and My Journey Back*. New York: Three Rivers Press.

Rape in America: A Report to the Nation (1992) Arlington, Virginia: National Victim Center and Crime Victims Research and Treatment Center.

Renner K.E. and Wackett, C. (1987) "Sexual Assault: Social and Stranger Rape", *Can. J. Comm. Mental Health*, 6 (1), pp. 49–55.

Resick, P.A., Calhoun, Karen S., Atkeson, Beverly M. and Ellis, Elizabeth M. (1981) "Social Adjustment in Victims of Sexual Assault", *J. Consult. Clin. Psychol.*, 49 (5), pp. 705–712.

Resnick, H.S., Acierno, Ron and Kilpatrick, Dean G. (1997) "Health Impact of Interpersonal Violence 2: Medical and Mental Health Outcomes", *Behav. Med.*, 23, pp. 65–78.

Reynolds, M.W., Peipert, J.F. and Collins, B. (2000) "Epidemiologic Issues of Sexually Transmitted Diseases in Sexual Assault Victims", *Obstet. Gynecol. Survey*, 55 (1), pp. 51–57.

Rose, D.S. (1986) "'Worse Than Death': Psychodynamics of Rape Victims and the Need for Psychotherapy", *Am. J. Psych.*, 143 (7), pp. 817–824.

Rothbaum, B.O., Foa, Edna B., Riggs, David S., Murdock, Tamera and Walsh, William (1992) "A Prospective Examination of Post-Traumatic Stress Disorder in Rape Victims", *J. Traum. Stress*, 5 (3), pp. 455–475.

Russell, D.E.H. (1984) *Sexual Exploitation: Rape, Child Sexual Abuse, and Workplace Harassment.* Beverly Hills, CA: Sage Publications.

Russell, D.E.H. and Bolen, R.M. (2000) *The Epidemic of Rape and Child Sexual Abuse in the United States.* Thousand Oaks, CA: Sage Publications.

Saunders, B.E., Kilpatrick, Dean G., Hanson, Rochelle F., Resnick, Heidi S. and Walker, Michael E. (1999) "Prevalence, Case Characteristics, and Long-Term Psychological Correlates of Child Rape Among Women: A National Survey", *Child Maltreat.*, 4 (3), pp. 187–200.

Scarce, M. (1997) *Male on Male Rape: The Hidden Tale of Stigma and Shame.* New York, NY: Insight Books.

Silverman, D.C, Kalick, S. Michael, Bowie, Sally I. and Edbril, Susan D. (1988) "Blitz Rape and Confidence Rape: A Typology Applied to 1,000 Consecutive Cases", *Am. J. Psych.*, 145 (11), pp. 1438–1441.

Spohn, C. and Horney, J. (1992) *Rape Law Reform: A Grassroots Revolution and Its Impact.* New York: Plenum Press.

Symonds, M. (1976) "The Rape Victim: Psychological Patterns of Response", *Am. J. Psychoanal.*, 36, pp. 27–34.

Tjaden, P. and Thoennes, N. (1998) *Prevalence, Incidence, and Consequences of Violence Against Women: Findings From the National Violence Against Women Survey.* Washington, DC: US Department of Justice, Office of Justice Programs.

U.S. Department of Justice (2000) *Crime in the United States: Uniform Crime Report 1999.* Washington, DC.

van der Kolk, B.A., McFarlane A.C. and Weisaeth L. (eds) (1996) *Traumatic Stress: The Effects of Overwhelming Experience on Mind, Body, and Society.* New York, NY: The Guilford Press.

Waigandt, A., Wallace, David L., Phelps, LeAdelle and Miller, Deborah A. (1990) "The Impact of Sexual Assault on Physical Health Status", *J. Traum. Stress*, 3 (1), pp. 93–102.

Wyatt, G.E. (1992) "The Sociocultural Context of African American and White American Women's Rape", *J. Soc. Iss.*, 48 (1), pp. 77–91.

Wyatt, G.E., Guthrie, Donald and Notgrass, Cindy M. (1992) 'Differential Effects of Woman's Child Sexual Abuse and Subsequent Sexual Revictimization", *J. Consult. Clin. Psychol.*, 60 (2), pp. 167–173.

Wyatt, G.E., Notgrass, Cindy M. and Newcomb, Michael (1990) "Internal and External
Mediators of Women's Rape Experiences", *Psychol. Women Quart.*, 14, pp. 153–176.

CHAPTER 2

THE PERPETRATORS AND THEIR MODUS OPERANDI

Michael Welner[1]

Any effort to obtain an understanding about the perpetrators of drug-facilitated sexual assault (DFSA) and what drives their offending confronts major obstacles. First of all, many DFSAs go unreported. Even when these assaults are reported to authorities, many are never prosecuted and there is no public record of what occurred. To prepare this chapter, we considered primarily, but not exclusively, 34 cases where there was a successful prosecution. The data we considered consisted primarily of public records, as well as detailed interviews with prosecutors about offenders' background, function, psychiatric history, and psychosocial history. In some instances, media reports, particularly from Canada and England, were reviewed and factored into our analysis if we had strong reason to believe them reliable. Naturally, there was more information available about some cases than others. Therefore, careful consideration was taken to draw conclusions based only upon confirmed factual history about the *modus operandi* and backgrounds of the DFSA offenders in our sampling.

We are mindful that the cases we considered represent a random sample of all DFSAs committed in North America, so we avoid sweeping conclusions. However, we found some common themes among the cases – themes that will be useful to investigators, prosecutors, mental health professionals, and others. We were able to categorize the perpetrators of DFSA by the settings in which they staged their crimes; we also shed light on what psychological factors may motivate some perpetrators to commit the crime – in other words, to the extent possible, we answer the question "Why?" As far as we know, we are the first to do so in DFSA cases; we hope to inspire other investigators to build upon our efforts.

Beyond *modus operandi* – we recognized the need to understand more psychologically about the perpetrators. This, too, proved challenging. Although many sex offenders admit their crimes and submit to mental health examinations for classification, risk assessment, and even mitigation, defendants in DFSA cases often deny that any crime occurred and, at trial, argue that the evidence is too weak to justify a guilty verdict. Because such a defense does not require psychiatric testimony, the defendants do not necessarily submit to probing forensic psychiatric examination.

Our analysis of the details we obtained about various DFSA cases and the

[1] The author would like to acknowledge the important input of Robert Lipman, an attorney and former prosecutor who shared his expertise and effort; and the assistance of Radha Gholkar and Callia Piperides in the editing of this manuscript.

perpetrators has led us to what we consider to be an important conclusion about both the crime and the perpetrators: expect the unexpected.

OVERVIEW

It was only several years ago that the news media raised public awareness about DFSA. The information available to the public suggested that the typical scenario involved a social setting, such as a singles bar or a party, at which a male would target a woman, surreptitiously spike her drink with a sedative, and then, when the woman was incapacitated, sexually assault her. In this scenario, the perpetrator often had no previous contact with the victim. The perpetrator was, in effect, a stranger. Because the drug often affected the victim's memory, the perpetrator, at least in some instances, remained a stranger. This frightening prospect – that a rapist could so furtively offend and remain at large because victims could not remember the rape – focused early attention on the bar and club scene.

However, a review of cases demonstrates that the world of DFSA is not that simple. The victim might be on a date, obtaining medical treatment, applying for a job, looking for an apartment, hitchhiking, getting her house cleaned, or just eating a meal at home. And everyone is potentially vulnerable – some perpetrators have targeted and victimized females; other perpetrators have targeted and victimized males.

Prosecutor Linda Fairstein, in her book *Sexual Violence* (1993), accurately describes the challenge often faced by police and prosecutors, as well as victims seeking justice, in such cases:

> "But he doesn't look like a rapist." . . . I have had women repeat to me this response they have received from family and friends when they have described a sexual assault by a mutual acquaintance. [O]ne of the most persistent myths about rapists is that they are physically unattractive, uneducated, and from the lower socioeconomic class. Since so many intelligent people make their preliminary judgments about guilt based on a man's appearance and station in life, imagine the response women get when they report assaults by professional men they have consulted for treatment or business purposes. They are universally disbelieved. Doctors, dentists, lawyers, accountants, religious leaders, teachers – educated, articulate, charming, sometimes married professional men – are often the toughest target of law enforcement . . . precisely because they do not fit the public's stereotypical portrait of a rapist."

Significantly, almost all the perpetrators we studied were repeat offenders. Some victimized many people. In the far less common scenario, where the perpetrator assaulted the same victim more than once, the perpetrator had some relationship with the victim that provided the perpetrator continued access to the victim. For example, in one instance the perpetrator shared living quarters in a remote location with a co-worker, whom he repeatedly victimized.

Perpetrators range from teenagers to seniors. And the ages of victims range at least as widely.

We propose that a perpetrator's *modus operandi* generally has four components:

1. *Means:* access to sedating drugs and knowledge about their effects on a victim's alertness and memory.
2. *Setting:* an occupation, a residence, or other circumstance in which the perpetrator controls the environment or answers to no one, such that he can execute a plan in that environment without interruption or unexpected discovery.
3. *Opportunity:* the capacity to orchestrate circumstances leading to a setting where the intended victim is alone and the crime will not be interrupted. This generally requires establishing a degree of trust by the victim. The perpetrator may exploit his dominant or supervisory position (for example, over a woman seeking a job or an apartment – where the woman would expect a professional, non-sexual interaction), or by deploying his social and communications skills.
4. *A plan to avoid arrest and prosecution:* this ranges from misinforming the victim that consensual sex – or even no sexual contact – took place, to dissuading the victim from reporting the crime.

Variations within *modus operandi* reflect the perpetrator's occupation, social circle and skills. One perpetrator, for example, was a celebrated chef-restaurateur who spiked a food dish he prepared for a waitress and her friend. This perpetrator, like others, exploited the established relationship he had with the victims to gain their trust, and access to them, as they visited him at his home to bid adieu before his trip abroad.

The sedating effects of some of the central nervous system (CNS) depressants, particularly GHB and certain benzodiazepines, can be abrupt and powerful (Greenblatt *et al.*, 1990; Welner, 1997). Once the victim has ingested the spiked drink, she may soon be too sedated to walk. For this reason, many perpetrators try to drug their victims in settings within their complete control – settings where they can immediately carry out their attack. This avoids the risks involved in moving a victim who is unable to walk. Indeed, in one case the perpetrator was spotted carrying a drugged woman to his residence where, undoubtedly, he intended to sexually assault her.

Occasionally, however, the drugging occurs at a restaurant, nightclub, bar, or party. According to Gail Abarbanel, Director of the Rape Treatment Center at Santa Monica-UCLA Medical Center (2000), "when victims are drugged in such places where other people are present, the rapist may appear to bystanders and witnesses to be a rescuer." A sedative slipped into a drink can cause effects similar to voluntary alcohol consumption – indeed, both sedatives and alcohol are CNS depressants. According to Abarbanel, "to onlookers, the victim may seem drunk; when the rapist carries or leads the victim to another location where the sexual assault will be committed, he may be viewed as 'helping' or transporting a vulnerable person to a safe place."

The perpetrator may be sophisticated and charming. He often has highly developed verbal and social skills, and uses those abilities to gain the trust of the victim so that he can isolate her and commit the crime. After the crime, the perpetrator may again rely upon his verbal advantage to persuade the victim – if she confronts him – that nothing happened or that she was a willing sexual partner or even an intoxicated aggressor. Indeed, another possibility – that she was raped while she was unconscious – may be so disturbing, that the victim, through protective denial, may accept the perpetrator's explanation.

The perpetrator's effort to convince the victim may progress to an attempt to persuade her not to report a crime, using approaches dictated by the circumstances of their encounter. If the victim was drinking alcoholic beverages or voluntarily using illicit drugs, the perpetrator may say: "You got drunk (or were using marijuana, cocaine, etc.) – no one will believe you."

In some cases the perpetrator's *modus operandi* may include efforts to both enhance the vulnerability of the victim and destroy her later credibility as a potential prosecution witness. For example, the perpetrator may offer the intended victim an illicit drug (cocaine, Ecstasy, etc.) and also surreptitiously spike the victim's drink with a CNS depressant (such as a sedative). If the victim voluntarily uses the illicit drug and then is sexually assaulted after becoming incapacitated by the sedative, the victim may be particularly reluctant to report the crime to police because the fact that she willingly engaged in illicit drug use might be revealed publicly at a trial. And, even if the victim reports the crime, prosecutors may be reluctant to bring charges because a jury may be hesitant to believe a victim who, at the time of the incident, may have been under the influence of an illicit drug she took voluntarily.

Also, a perpetrator may surreptitiously spike the victim's drink with both a sedative and some illicit drug (or otherwise cause the victim to unknowingly ingest an illicit drug, such as cocaine). In the event the victim reports the DFSA and urine testing is performed, both drugs might well be detected. This would create the false impression that the victim is a drug abuser. The perpetrator's goal may be to destroy the credibility of the prosecution's most important witness – the victim.

The perpetrator may be emboldened to incapacitate and sexually assault a victim even when others are nearby, based on circumstances that still reflect the isolation of the victim. In one such case, a woman and the two men who accompanied her to a party were all given "spiked drinks" and incapacitated. She was also raped.

In a number of cases, the perpetrators have either photographed or video-taped their victims. In such photographs and videotapes, the victim is often undressed. For example, in one such videotape the perpetrator can be seen sexually assaulting an unconscious victim – yet the drug used was so powerful that the victim had no recollection of the assault. In another instance the victim appeared to be fully conscious, yet, as a result of the effect of the drug, she had no recollection of being photographed.

Remnants from the scene of the crime are not limited to videotaping and photographing. One perpetrator not only photographed the victims, but he also stole valueless property from them, such as locks of hair, nylon stockings, and tampons. The taking of photographs and theft of valueless property, sometimes referred to as "trophies," has been described in other sexual assaults as well.

Various settings, including business offices, medical facilities, and social encounters, have all been used by perpetrators to approach victims. We discuss these settings separately because each has its unique features.

DFSAS IN BUSINESS SETTINGS

The businessman was charged under a statute that defined rape as including sexual intercourse where the defendant administered an intoxicating narcotic or anesthetic substance to prevent the victim from resisting. At trial, evidence was presented that the businessman had contacted a woman and offered her employment. She accepted and, on her first day of work, the businessman took her to a restaurant for wine and dinner. It was the prosecution's theory that the businessman drugged the woman during the meal and later, at a hotel, raped her. At trial, the victim testified that, after leaving the restaurant, she felt "weak and dizzy." She also provided other details about the crime.

The victim's mother testified that, on the day after the incident, her daughter was nervous, her eyes were dull, her memory was impaired, she seemed dazed, and, at times, spoke but did not make sense. Additionally, the prosecution offered testimony from a physician who came into contact with the victim approximately a day after the incident. According to the physician, the victim appeared to be nervous, somewhat dazed, and had a rapid and irregular pulse. The physician further testified that he was not certain what caused this condition, but that, in his opinion, the woman (the victim) was suffering from the effects of a drug – a narcotic or something similar. The jury convicted the businessman of rape. On appeal, the court reversed the conviction because of errors at trial, but held that the evidence, though weak, was sufficient to justify the verdict of guilt on the rape charge. The year was 1911.

No doubt both before 1911 and after, some business owners and executives, exploiting their power over job applicants and employees, have engaged in DFSA. The perpetrator may manipulate the situation to isolate the intended victim. The businessman or executive exploits the fact that the victim accords him the presumption of trustworthiness normally accorded someone in a position of responsibility. Consider, for example, this factual statement recently submitted by a prosecutor before a trial:

> Defendant is a dangerous sexual offender who employs a common plan or scheme to carry out his rape. Defendant lures his victim to his apartment or office, providing financial incentive to meet him such as a job offer or other opportunity to make money. He then offers his victim a drink. The drink is usually champagne or some other alcoholic beverage containing an intoxicating substance that defendant has mixed into the drink. Once the effects of the "drink" takes place, i.e. the victim was unconscious or unable to resist, defendant undresses the victim and rapes her. His victim has no memory of what happened after sipping on the drink given to her.
>
> In the instant case, one of the victims refused to drink the alcohol offered to her by the defendant. Instead, she drank water. Defendant later raped this victim by force. The other three victims accepted the champagne or other alcohol offered to them. All three of these victims have no memory of what happened other than waking up the next morning without all their clothes on, with the defendant either on top of them or next to them engaged in sexual activity.

The prosecutor, in her submission to the court, went on to summarize the evidence underlying the charges:

> On February 2, 1997, [Victim 1] went to a celebration at defendant's office. She was planning to make a business presentation to defendant at his request. While she was there, [she] drank some champagne offered to her by defendant. [Victim 1] has no more memory other than waking up naked with defendant on top of her, inserting his penis into her vagina.
>
> On March 19, 1998, [Victim 2] went to a job interview at defendant's office. She met with defendant at his request. At the interview, [she] drank some champagne offered her by defendant. Defendant then wanted to continue their discussion over dinner. On the way to dinner, defendant stopped by his apartment, claiming that he left his cellular phone inside. Defendant invited her into his apartment, and offered more champagne. When [Victim 2] refused, defendant gave her a glass of an alleged non-alcoholic drink. Within minutes of consuming this alleged non-alcoholic drink, [she] had no more memory of what happened aside from waking up naked the following morning in defendant's bed.

On September 25, 1998, [Victim 4] went to a job interview at defendant's office. This was her second interview with defendant. While there, defendant offered her champagne in celebration of a new business contract he acquired. She drank some champagne at his office. At his request, [Victim 4] went to defendant's apartment with the understanding that they were going to meet mutual friends for dinner. Defendant again offered her more drinks once they were inside his apartment. Within minutes of taking a sip, [Victim 4] has no more memory of what happened other than waking up the next morning naked in defendant's bed with him on top of her, inserting his penis in her vagina.

On June 26, 1995, [Victim 6], who was looking for a place to live, went to view defendant's apartment. Once there, defendant offered her some alcohol (beer). She drank it. During their discussion about the apartment, defendant asked if she had a boyfriend. While they were sitting on his couch, defendant kissed her on the lips. [Victim 6] jumped up and told him, "No!" Defendant tried to kiss her again, but she managed to leave his apartment, by promising that she will phone him. A police report was filed on June 27, 1995.

This case demonstrates that law enforcement officers, during efforts to seize evidence and to identify additional victims, need to consider that the perpetrator may use more than one location to encounter, drug, and sexually assault victims. Here, for example, the perpetrator used both his office and residence during his criminal activity. When there are others working at the business, the business may be used simply as a staging area to encounter the victim and another location used to drug the victim and carry out the attack. It is entirely possible that the perpetrator may work in one county, live in another county, and regularly travel to other locations while on business. Investigators will need to check the records of those jurisdictions to determine whether other victims have identified the same individual as the perpetrator of a drug-facilitated crime.

When the perpetrator runs a business from his home, the home office may be the ideal setting for the crime. Drugs can be readily stored in accessible and unremarkable refrigerators and medicine cabinets. Beverages, which can be spiked, are handy. And the perpetrator may be alone with the intended victim. In such situations, even a perpetrator without significant social skills can isolate, drug, and sexually assault an intended victim. In a case where a home office was the scene of the crime, the prosecution's appellate brief summarized the evidence:

[Victim 1] began a secretarial job at the home of the defendant . . . The defendant brought [her] a cup of coffee. The defendant made a sexual comment to her as she watched an instructional video regarding his company. As [she] worked, the defendant brought her another cup of coffee. [She] began to become very dizzy. She stumbled up the steps and laid down on the upstairs couch. When she woke, her bra was pushed above her breast. The defendant was beside her kissing, touching and fondling her breast and the defendant's erect penis was on her leg. Still woozy, she struggled to the bathroom knowing that she had been drugged. A urine sample found a drug called [lorazepam] in her system.

[Victim 3] was an exotic dancer, and she and a friend were paid to go to the defendant's house and dance naked while the defendant masturbated. Six to eight months later, she was unemployed and began working for the defendant as a secretary. [She] was asked to stay late one day so a computer expert could show her how to work the computer. At nine o'clock in the evening, the defendant offered her a beer. For about 45 minutes, she didn't remember anything. The next thing she remembered is waking up the next morning in her home. One month later, her boyfriend got pictures of her in the mail. [She] was posing, eyes wide open, smiling in the nude. [She] has no idea when or how those pictures were taken.

[Victim 4] cleaned house for the defendant in February of 1997. The last time she cleaned, he offered her a beer. She left the defendant's house and got into an automobile accident. The urine test found the drug [a benzodiazepine] in her system.

[Victim 8] did clerical work for the defendant and her stepfather, who were business partners. The defendant asked [Victim 8] to come to his house to help him do paperwork. The defendant offered her a [soft drink]. After drinking the [soft drink], [she] got very sleepy. When [she] woke up, the defendant was sucking on her breasts. She immediately left.

Perpetrators have used classified ads to lure victims. Ads offering money for unskilled work or an inexpensive place to live may attract victims who are vulnerable either because they lack sophistication or because they have financial problems.

In one instance, the perpetrator placed a newspaper ad offering a room for rent. When a female applicant arrived to see the room, the perpetrator informed her that she could earn $90 if, as part of a medical "survey," she took some pills. After taking the pills, the victim fell asleep. When she awoke, she realized that her underwear had been removed. According to a police report: "When she woke up that morning she realized that she did not remember anything after she fell asleep at [the perpetrator's] house. She began to suspect that she may have been raped." A sexual assault examination confirmed her suspicions.

She was not the only victim. To lure other victims, the perpetrator placed a variety of classified ads in newspapers, some offering a position for a house-sitter, others listing an opening for a sales assistant.

Another case illustrates the need to expect the unexpected, as the perpetrator committed drug-facilitated crimes in the homes of his victims. While operating his house-cleaning business, he spiked the non-alcoholic drinks (tea, coffee, etc.) of his elderly clients. Once they were incapacitated, he would take sexually graphic photos of them and steal locks of their hair, nylon stockings, or tampons. This evidence was seized by investigators. The perpetrator was about 48 years old and married; his victims were aged 47 to 89. Though this case has unusual aspects, its core features are often present in DFSA cases: the perpetrator targeted victims who knew him and trusted him; and he was a repeat offender.

DFSAS IN HEALTHCARE SETTINGS

Physicians, dentists, paramedics, and nurses have all been implicated in drug-facilitated sexual crimes. These crimes have characteristically taken place in private offices where the perpetrator/healthcare provider was in charge of the premises. In at least one case, a physician drugged and raped a woman while treating her at her home. In another, a male nurse reportedly sexually assaulted a drugged, sedated patient in a hospital.

In some cases, doctors, while treating female patients, sedated and sexually assaulted them. Such offenders may act professionally with most of their patients and carefully select a few others to victimize. In one case, for example, the victim was a new patient and the doctor arranged to be alone with her for an extended period in his office. When such a victim comes forward, police and prosecutors may be unwilling to bring charges because the healthcare provider may appear sufficiently credible to create a reasonable doubt in the minds of jurors.

A healthcare provider who commits drug-facilitated sexual crimes may have considerable respect in his professional and personal community and appear to be a member of a solid nuclear family. Many members of the community may be willing to attest to his professional skills and good deeds. Thus, the healthcare provider's stature may insulate him from prosecution for a considerable period of time. However, in some cases law enforcement authorities have been able to identify several victims and successfully prosecute the healthcare provider.

In one case a respected dentist sedated patients with Valium® and Seconal®, which he administered during a consented procedure; three patients reported to police that he sexually abused them while they were sedated. The police became convinced of his *modus operandi* and obtained a court order authorizing them to place a hidden video camera in his treatment room. Then, they recruited an undercover officer to pose as a patient. Like the three patients who had reported incidents to police, the undercover officer was young and female. Conveniently, she also had an abscessed tooth. She made an appointment with the dentist. During the appointment, the dentist sedated the undercover officer and removed the abscessed tooth. He then lifted her blouse and again examined her bare chest with his stethoscope. The court decision described what then happened:

> As [the undercover officer] began to regain consciousness, [the dentist] asked her to stand and put her arms around him. Since she had no control over her body at this time, [the undercover officer] told the [dentist] that she was unable to stand. [The dentist] then lifted her out of the dental chair and pulled her toward him. While sitting on a stool in front of the dental chair with [the undercover officer] between his legs, [the dentist] lifted her blouse and began moving his hands across the upper part of her back and around toward her breasts. He then slid both hands down across her back and grabbed her buttocks. While massaging her buttocks in a circular motion he drew her body toward his. All of these actions were recorded on the video tape which was later admitted into evidence.
>
> At this point the officers who were monitoring the video tape in the basement signaled other officers to arrest [the dentist]. [A detective] and [an investigator] were the first to enter the treatment room. [The investigator] testified at trial that when he first opened the door he observed that defendant's hands were on [the undercover officer's] sides, and that his thumbs were massaging the nipples of her breasts.

After the police officers entered the room, the dentist placed the "patient" back in the chair and asserted, "She's in respiratory distress – I was just trying to help her breathe and ventilate."

Depending on the circumstances, the defense may argue that the defendant, acting in the regular course of his practice, sedated the victim. The defense may further argue that while the victim was sedated she probably had a dream and, perhaps as a result of the victim's reaction to the drug, the victim now innocently mistakes the dream for reality. Indeed, a drug-facilitated rape victim's memory of the incident may resemble the fragmented recollection of a dream.

DFSAS IN SOCIAL SETTINGS

Some perpetrators use social encounters to ensnare intended victims. Singles bars, parties, and dates have all been used as staging areas to encounter and drug the victim. An appellate court, in affirming the conviction in one such case, described the facts. Here is an excerpt:

The victim . . . testified that she met appellant in August 1996. She testified that on the night of August 31, 1996, she went to [a restaurant] with friends . . . As she was leaving the [restaurant] around 11:30 p.m., [the defendant] invited her to go to a nightclub with him. She testified that appellant actually took her to the [restaurant] where he was the manager. When they arrived, [the defendant] gave her the keys to the restaurant and told her to make herself a drink. [The defendant] then left in his truck and did not tell her where he was going. She subsequently went into the restaurant and got a beer. She testified that [the defendant] returned approximately 30 minutes later and made drinks for them in the restaurant. The victim testified that she told him that she did not like mixed drinks, but he told her to drink it anyway. She took two sips of the drink and then poured it out.

The victim testified that they then went to [defendant's] home. She testified that they sat on a couch inside the house and began kissing. The victim testified that the next thing she remembered was waking up on the floor to find [the defendant] raping her. She stated that [the defendant] was on top of her, having intercourse with her. She testified that she was lightheaded and unable to focus. She further stated that she did not remember taking off her clothes, and that while she was on the floor she . . . could not move, and was unable to tell [the defendant] to stop.

After passing out again, the victim awoke to find herself naked and curled up on the floor. She testified that she then passed out again and the next thing she recalled was waking up in [the defendant's] bed. She testified that [the defendant] told her that he would not take her home. She stated that she was very tired and confused, and it was difficult for her to find her clothes because she could not focus on what she was doing. The victim eventually began walking home. She testified that she did not make it home until approximately five hours later because she kept getting lost and had a hard time focusing.

After arriving home, the victim noticed that her back was hurting. She discovered that she had bruises on her back and other parts of her body, and bumps on her head. She was unable to recall how she received the injuries. The victim then drove . . . to an emergency room where a medical exam was performed.

In another case, a married man drugged, sexually assaulted, and videotaped a number of women, including two he had "wined and dined" and with whom he had consensual sexual relations. The sedative administered was so powerful, the victims did not know they had been sexually assaulted and videotaped. Here is an excerpt of the court decision affirming the conviction:

[Defendant's wife] testified that until mid-1996, she believed she and [the defendant] had a strong marriage, and she became pregnant with the couple's second child in July, 1996. She testified that [the defendant] was "thrilled" with the news. But, by early 1997 she suspected [the defendant] was having an affair . . . According to [the defendant's wife], she found the videotape sometime in mid-June 1997 after she and [the defendant] had separated . . . [She] explained that she had gone to their house (she was living in an apartment at the time) to get the video camera . . . to record an upcoming family event. [She] still had a key and thus access to the home. After returning to her apartment, she [viewed] the videotape in the camera and saw the videotaped incidents of [the defendant] with three women, including her own younger sister . . . [The defendant's wife] called her divorce attorney who told her to give the tape to [the private investigator] who in turn gave it to the police after having copies made.

The . . . police department reviewed the tape. They contacted [Victim 1] who came down and viewed the tape. After witnessing it, she became physically sick according to the testimony of [a police officer]. The Texas authorities contacted their Arkansas counterparts when they suspected an Arkansas resident might be included on the tape. They were correct. [Victim 2] was eventually identified as one of the women appearing on the tape. She, too, expressed disgust and shock upon being informed of her appearance on the videotape.

A perpetrator operating in a social setting may urge the intended victim to drink a liquid – claiming it is an exotic mixed drink or other alcoholic beverage – but concealing the fact that the liquid also contains an additional drug. That drug may be an illegal drug obtained on the street (for example, GHB) or a sedative secured by prescription.

In those instances, the victim generally knows she is ingesting one central nervous system (CNS) depressant – alcohol – but does not realize that she, in fact, is ingesting a second CNS depressant – for example, Rohypnol®. The victim accounts for her expected response to alcohol, but nothing more. In other cases, the perpetrator may offer the intended victim a pill or capsule and encourage the victim to ingest it. ("It will make you relax," "It will make you feel better," or "It will get you high".) The victim may voluntarily ingest the tablet – but will not fully appreciate the identity or effect of the tablet, specifically, its capability to render her unconscious (and vulnerable to sexual assault).

OLDER PERPETRATORS

At least two perpetrators were over age 60 – and one of these was a grandfather. By using drugs, such perpetrators are able to control the victims without the need to use coercion. Indeed, in at least one instance, the perpetrator incapacitated a victim considerably younger than himself. In that case, the prosecutor submitted to the court a summary of what she intended to prove at trial:

The defendant was indicted for offenses committed against four different victims over a one year seven month period . . . All the offenses took place at the defendant's apartment . . .

On June 8, 1995, the defendant drove 42-year-old [Victim 1] and 70-year-old [Victim 2] to his apartment . . . Both [Victim 1] and [Victim 2] were acquainted with the defendant, having met him at a nightclub . . . three years earlier. A friend of the defendant's . . . stopped in. All four danced and talked, and the women put on clothing the defendant gave them, a negligee and a minidress. The defendant prepared alcoholic mixed drinks. He put temazepam . . . into the women's drinks. The defendant told [his friend] that he added something to the women's drinks "to make them relax." Once they finished their drinks, [Victims 1 and 2] remembered nothing else until they woke up the next day in the defendant's bed. They felt sick. Both women recalled having their underpants on the night before, but in the morning, their underpants were off. Suspecting that they had been drugged and raped, [Victims 1 and 2] went by ambulance to the . . . Hospital, where blood tests showed the presence of [a] benzodiazepine in their systems.

[Victim 3], a 29-year-old woman, was acquainted with the defendant. On June 14, 1996, the defendant drove [Victim 3] to his apartment, where she expected to meet one of his friends to discuss buying a car. When she got there, she asked the defendant for a glass of water. Instead, he prepared fruit punch and chowder, into which he put temazepam. After she consumed the drink and soup, [Victim 3] lost consciousness. She felt the defendant hitting her in the vagina, but was unable to move to stop him. [Victim 3] awoke the next morning in her own apartment, suffering pain in her vagina and rectum. She was certain she had been raped. [The defendant told Victim 3 that] he tried to, but did not rape her. She asked him what did he do to her. He said he had put something in her drink. [Victim 3] went to the hospital for medical care. An examination confirmed abrasions, lacerations, and trauma in [her] genital area. The . . . Crime Laboratory tested [her] blood, which was positive at a level of 4.4 micrograms per deciliter, for temazepam, a benzodiazepine.

On December 27, 1996, the defendant drove 58-year-old [Victim 4] from her home . . . to his apartment . . . [Victim 4] had previously spoken to the defendant over the phone, after being introduced to him by her neighbor . . . This was the first time [Victim 4] met the defendant in person. After they arrived at the defendant's apartment, the defendant prepared alcoholic mixed drinks. He put temazepam into [Victim 4's] drink. Early the next morning, the . . . Fire Department was called to [defendant's apartment]. When paramedics arrived, they found [Victim 4] dead. [Victim 4] had temazepam present in her blood at a level of 98 micrograms per deciliter, and ethanol (alcohol) at a level of .22. The medical examiner determined the cause of [Victim 4's] death to be a combination of alcohol and temazepam.

The defendant had legally obtained temazepam by prescription for an extended period. Temazepam, a sleeping medication, depresses the central nervous system (Kaplan and Sadock, 1993), as does alcohol (Kaplan *et al.*, 1994). Taken together, the sedating effect of one is added to the other. In some cases, respiratory suppression and even death may result (Physicians' Desk Reference, 2000).

The prosecutor's account of what she expected to prove at trial reflects two factors present in some DFSA cases:

1. there was some previous relationship between the perpetrator and each of the victims – in other words, the perpetrator knew (or communicated with) each of the victims before the day of the crime; and
2. the perpetrator was a repeat offender.

In this case there was another noteworthy aspect: the age of the victims varied widely – one victim was age 29, another was age 70.

USE OF FORCE BY DFSA PERPETRATORS

Drug-facilitated sexual crimes are carried out by an offender who defers to the drug to subdue the victim. In at least two of the cases we considered, the perpetrators were also willing to use physical force. In one case, a businessman, who drugged and sexually assaulted a number of women, used force after he offered a drink to an intended victim and she refused. Here is an excerpt from the prosecutor's submission to the court describing what she expected to prove at trial.

> On June 10, 1998, [Victim 3] went for job training at defendant's office. Defendant offered her more money if she would clean his apartment. At his request, they went to his apartment to see if she would accept the job of cleaning it. Once there, defendant offered her champagne, which she refused several times. Instead, [Victim 3] drank only water. Consequently defendant raped her by force.

The prosecutor's submission to the court reflected that she also expected to prove that the defendant engaged in additional conduct that was similar to the charged crimes:

> On January 25, 1993, [Victim 5] responded to defendant's advertisement in the local newspaper for a room-mate to share a two-bedroom apartment. She made arrangements to see the apartment and to be interviewed by defendant at 8 p.m. on this date. [Victim 5] went to the meeting dressed in a blue business suit. Upon arrival, she noticed that the apartment was not a two-bedroom, but rather it was a studio.

Defendant offered her an alcoholic drink. She refused. Instead, she asked for a soft drink. After viewing the balcony, [Victim 5] was grabbed from behind by defendant as she was walking back inside. Defendant threw her on his bed and started kissing her on the lips and neck. [Victim 5] struggled and continued to resist, saying "No!" Defendant forced her legs open and raped her. A police report was filed on January 27, 1993.

Perhaps surprisingly, a perpetrator over age 60 was one of those willing to use physical force. The court's opinion included a description of critical events. Here is an excerpt:

In July 1996, [Victim 1] answered a personal ad in [a] newspaper. After speaking on the phone with the man, [she] met him for dinner. The man was [the] 67-year-old [defendant]. [Victim 1] immediately decided she was not romantically interested in [defendant] as he was far too old for her. However, she felt they could be friends. When [defendant] telephoned her a week later and suggested he accompany her in her real estate search, she accepted. After viewing several properties, they had an early dinner together at which [Victim 1] abstained from drinking any alcohol.

After dinner, the two walked around the harbor for an hour, and then [defendant] drove [Victim 1] home, stopping *en route* once to allow [her] to get a few groceries. At [defendant's] request, she purchased juice for him. Arriving at her home, [she] poured the juice into glasses for the two of them, and they sat in her den to talk. During this conversation, [defendant] expressed the opinion that if two people liked each other, they should go to bed right away. [Victim 1] was completely disinterested in him, and told him that she did not engage in sex with men she hardly knew. At one point in the conversation, she excused herself to go upstairs to retrieve some checks. Upon her return, she finished off her glass of juice and immediately felt very strange. She could barely walk and her legs felt as if they were made of lead. Trying to light some logs in the fireplace, she fell backwards and collapsed on the floor. [The defendant] was immediately on top of her, kissing and fondling her. She did not want to engage in such activity with him, but was unable to push him off. She told him she was not feeling well and agreed with him when he suggested she go to bed.

[The defendant] followed [Victim 1] upstairs as she half-consciously disrobed and got into bed. Suddenly, she noticed that [the defendant] was also in bed with her, undressed. She felt him groping her; then suddenly she could feel his fingers in her vagina. [The defendant] pushed something metallic in her vagina and "grabbed" her hands, forcing them out of the way. She tried with all her might to push him "out of [her]." She told him to stop because he was hurting her. She passed out and was unable to recall anything else until her daughter called the next morning.

[Victim 1's] daughter . . . was shocked when she heard her mother's voice on the phone. It was slow and slurred, unlike anything she had heard before. Moreover, her mother was always quite alert and awake by that hour of the morning, whereas that morning her mother failed to make any sense.

Later in the day, [Victim 1] phoned the poison control center, fearing she had eaten bad shellfish. She then phoned [defendant] to inquire whether he was sick, too. She was finally able to get out of bed around 3 p.m., although she still felt numb. At this point, she noticed her sheets were stained, and slowly came to remember that [defendant] had raped her.

In February 1995, [Victim 2] answered a personal ad in [a] newspaper, which had been placed by [defendant]. They dated for a while and developed a sexual relationship. Eventually, [Victim 2] decided to end the relationship because [defendant] was far too possessive. [Defendant] responded most uncivilly to [her] decision, leaving vulgar epithets on her telephone answering machine. After confirming that she truly wanted to end their relationship, [defendant] arrived at her home late one evening, letting himself in with a key he had made from one [she] had lent him during their relationship. [Defendant] was visibly and uncontrollably angry, and [Victim 2] realized she was in serious trouble. Trying to divert him, she picked up her cat and tried to maneuver past [him]. He barred her way, however, and told [her] he was going to rape her for having "humiliated" him. She attempted to calm him down and de-escalate the situation, offering him a drink and suggesting that they talk about it. He refused, telling her "I want you sober when I hurt you." He then picked her up and carried her into the bedroom, while she cried and begged him to stop.

[Victim 2] has very little memory of what occurred next, but she knew she never consented to any sexual activity with [defendant] that night. The next morning she awakened to find [defendant] next to her. She immediately ordered him to leave. She was extremely sore through the genital area and believed [defendant] had raped her. By the time her girlfriend . . . phoned her at 8 a.m., she was hysterical and crying.

[Victim 2] reported the incident to police, who took her to a hospital where she was examined. The examination found bruising and abrasions on her cervix and the genital area between vagina and rectum. No sperm was present. A blood sample drawn from her was found to contain diazepam, commonly known as Valium®.

MALE-ON-MALE OFFENSES

There have been a number of cases in which a male perpetrator used drugs to surreptitiously incapacitate another male for sexual purposes. In one case the perpetrator, a divorced father employed as a pastry-maker, would drive down a highway and pick up young male hitchhikers. He would incapacitate them by providing them pastries laced with a prescription sedative and would then sexually assault them. After the sexual assault, he would abandon them near a road. One such victim, abandoned by a road while still under the influence of the drug, was struck by a car and killed.

In another case also involving young male victims, the perpetrator was both a high school principal and a foster parent. The prosecutor submitted to the court a memorandum of what she expected to prove at trial. Here is an excerpt:

> Generally, it is alleged that the defendant . . . who has been employed as a principal with the . . . High School, took advantage of his status as an authority figure with the . . . High School, as well as his status as a foster parent to sexually molest [Victim 1] and [Victim 2].
>
> First, with respect to the allegations involving [Victim 1], it is alleged that defendant took him shopping . . . for clothes in October of 1995. According to [Victim 1], he and defendant . . . returned to defendant's house after shopping . . . The defendant asked [Victim 1] to try on one of the new shirts. . . . Then, the defendant got [Victim 1] a drink of juice. [Victim 1] then went to bed. As [Victim 1] was climbing the stairs to go to his bedroom, his legs became weak and he became dizzy. Eventually, [Victim 1] found himself in bed. [Victim 1] . . . believed the defendant began touching [Victim 1's] [sexual organs] . . . [Victim 1] was not sure what was happening and thought it may have been a dream. [Victim 1] awoke to find his underwear wet . . . [Victim 1] also realized that when he awoke he had different clothes on from those he had on when he went to bed. [Victim 1] also relates that he felt dizzy and had a "hung-over feeling" when he woke up.
>
> With respect to [Victim 2], it is alleged that in September 1995, [Victim 2] was placed in the foster care of the defendant. At the time, the defendant was [Victim 2's] principal at school . . . In October of 1995, [Victim 2] claims to have used the defendant's bed because he [(Victim 2)] was having trouble sleeping. However, [Victim 2] moved to a different bed because he was "having dreams" about the defendant touching his [Victim 2's] butt and genital organs . . . [Victim 2] said that when he would wake up, he would be in a groggy state, as if he had a hangover. [Victim 2] could not understand or explain why he felt this way. [Victim 2] had also told investigators that the defendant was always trying to get [Victim 2] to drink bottled juice before going to bed. [Victim 2] preferred to drink water, but sometimes accepted the juice.

ASSAULTS ON FAMILY MEMBERS AND CO-HABITANTS

Assaults by a perpetrator living in the same residence as the victim have occurred. For example, in one case the perpetrator and the victim were co-workers, living in the same residence while they worked in a remote location.

It is hardly surprising that many intra-familial DFSAs may go unreported. Since the perpetrator may be the head of the house, each of the constraints confronting incest victims (threatened loss of family integrity, confusion over an act of aggression, vulnerability to psychological manipulation, self-blame, fear of eviction, lack of support of other family members) must be considered as affecting the reporting rate for intra-familial drug-facilitated assaults. On the data available to us, no meaningful appraisal was possible on the nature and frequency of drug-facilitated sexual crimes in the home. However, we did learn about two cases: one in which a stepfather victimized his stepdaughter, and, as noted above, one in which a foster parent victimized young men he was supposed to protect.

ACCOMPLICES AND CONSPIRACIES

More than one perpetrator may collaborate and conspire to commit DFSAs. Friends have conspired with each other, a male and female in a relationship have conspired with each other, and even brothers have conspired with each other. In one case, a man and his common-law wife drugged and sexually assaulted children and teenagers – and videotaped the assaults.

A perpetrator may use an accomplice who does not actually participate in the assault. For example, a female accomplice may be deployed to gain the trust of an intended female victim and engender in her a false sense of security and safety.

In almost all the cases we considered where there was an accomplice or a co-conspirator, there were high numbers of victims. During our consideration of cases involving co-conspirators and accomplices, a few interesting cases in Southern California came to our attention. Most of these perpetrators had histories notable for the use of recreational drugs (cocaine or Ecstasy (MDMA)) and direct or indirect links to the pornography industry.

WHO IS THE PERPETRATOR?

The perpetrator of DFSA generally carries out his crimes in secret, is aware of societal rules, and is able to conform to them. He may, in a variety of contexts, exploit trust and people, and, basically, do what he wants to do if he thinks he can get away with it, even if such conduct is outside societal norms. Such behavior has been described in malignant narcissists (Kernberg, 1989), who also abuse positions of domination and physical, financial or occupational control to exploit situations (Price, 1994). Malignant narcissists may be quite overtly law-abiding, but are so self-absorbed and motivated by entitlement as to trample over the boundaries of others (DSM-IV, 1994). These qualities are characteristic of high functioning, sometimes even famous (Horowitz, 1989), individuals who rape as they tell themselves that "No" means "Yes", are implicated in *quid pro quo* sexual harassment, various frauds, and tax evasion, for example (Stone, 1993).

The grandiosity, entitlement, and self-absorption of many of the DFSA perpetrators reviewed evokes consideration of pathological narcissism. Psychopathy is also characterized by some of the same personality qualities presented in this DFSA sample, such as lying, manipulation, and poor empathy. However, the great majority of the randomly selected sample of DFSA offenders did not have a criminal history, criminal versatility, juvenile deliquency, parasitic lifestyles, poor behavior controls, irresponsibility, or short-term marital relationships (Hare, 1991). Psychopathy, therefore, is not as prevalent among DFSA offenders as might be suggested by their manner and behavior.

Any notion that the perpetrators of DFSA are generally enslaved by lusts and fantasies and unable to control themselves is not supported by the cases we considered. Drug-facilitated rape is far more frequently the handiwork of composed, selective offenders, careful to strike when access, setting, and concealment are reasonably ensured.

Antisocial personality disordered individuals, with long histories for a variety of criminal conduct (DSM-IV, 1994), often exhibit the same impulsivity in their sexual offenses (Hazelwood and Warren, 2000), as evidenced by their use of force. Perpetrators of DFSA in our sample, on the other hand, showed impulsive and improvizational qualities only when the orchestrated plan hits a snag. Rather than using force, perpetrators consistently allowed elusive victims to escape, even to the end of driving them home on the victim's request. The majority of case histories reflects more passive offenders who struck only when a victim was unfortunate enough to be secluded and receptive to being drugged after some orchestration.

All but a few of the perpetrators lived alone. Only ten of a sample that ranged in ages from 18 to 60 had been in a committed relationship before. Four of these ten had been married. Twenty-five of the perpetrators were age 30 or older. For those with undeveloped intimate relations, the opportunity to have sex with something (rather than someone) impersonal, compliant, and ephemeral, may have been all they were emotionally capable of.

The combination of isolation, poorly developed intimacy, and lack of empathy explains how a person who seemingly functions well could commit such an egregious crime. Those who are emotionally disconnected from others, as well as the emotional qualities of themselves, more readily relate to acquaintances, colleagues, neighbors, and others as if they are objects, remote from their conscience and consideration (Paris, 1997). People, to such individuals, are mere vehicles for getting needs met. As for those perpetrators who have been married, there is no indication of the quality of intimacy in their relationships. The data available to us does not explain what prompts individuals with well-developed emotional and interpersonal relations to engage in drug-facilitated sexual offenses.

Given that the men who commit drug-facilitated rape are often charming or attractive, it is not surprising that some victims indicated that they would have willingly consented to have intercourse with the men. In these instances, notably one case where the conspirators endeavored to have sex with as many women as possible, the perpetrators chose to act immediately, rather than to cultivate a personal relationship.

Several of those drug-facilitated perpetrators studied who were socially unsuccessful exhibited a clingy relatedness to prospective victims. This quality suggests a sexualized idea of intimacy in someone unable, if desperate, to form personal attachment. Perpetrators who utilize personal ads more consistently evidence this quality; their poor interpersonal skills and otherwise unappealing nature make it more difficult for them to lure victims. Nevertheless, even with those who were quite solicitous in seeking relationships, it is unclear whether their objective was anything other than sexual intercourse. Only a closer forensic examination would discern whether other personality forces are at work, or whether the history described merely reflected the best efforts of a socially awkward person to entrap a prospective victim.

The preference for drug-facilitated sexual activities with a heavily sedated or essentially inanimate victim may, for some homosexual perpetrators, reflect continued conflicted feelings about relating to same sex in a manner that reflects human, or object relations (Stone, 1989).

Notable in the case of the school principal who victimized male high school students under his guardianship was the history that no one had any awareness of him as a homosexual, and he had represented himself as a heterosexual. More cases need to be considered to draw substantive conclusions; still, the dynamics of male-on-male drug-facilitated sexual offenses may be different in important respects.

In our data, the male was the dominant figure in the accomplice cases with male and female offenders. Cases in Southern California consistently involved objectifying, hedonistic and highly sexualized sub-populations indigenous to Hollywood and those who choose to emulate its lifestyle.

In a few cases that we considered there were co-conspirators involved in the DFSAs; these characteristically involve large numbers of victims. In male perpetrators, the existence of an internal drive to sexually conquest as much as possible demonstrates a narcissistic quest for omnipotence, rather than the satisfaction of a compulsive sex addiction. Dominant perpetrators in several cases were glib, highly manipulative, disarming, self-involved, and without meaningful personal relationships.

In one case where male twins collaborated in numerous drug-facilitated rapes, the brothers would mug for the videotapes they took. To the other brother who would later watch, one would brag, "We have fucked more women than anybody."

Despite the fact that some of the brothers' unsuspecting victims found the brothers to be attractive, the brothers appeared to have had a greater interest in hunting new targets than in re-victimizing women they had already violated.

In most of the over 30 cases we considered, the perpetrators assaulted or abused multiple victims. Thus, our data suggest that drug-facilitated sexual offenses such as rape, are crimes of very high likelihood of repetition before capture. Of course, our sample comes primarily from successful prosecutions and may have selected for repeat offenders; indeed, because of the proof problems in DFSA cases, such prosecutions are often only initiated when law enforcement has been able to identify multiple victims.

No information is available to determine whether the likelihood of recidivism persists after imprisonment, prosecution, or even arrest. However, at least two perpetrators committed DFSAs after they had been convicted for committing sexual assaults by coercion. (This elegantly illustrates how a sexual offender might resort to a more sophisticated *modus operandi* – such as the use of drugs to incapacitate intended victims – to lessen the chance for arrest and conviction.)

Does imprisonment deter re-offense by the drug-facilitated rapist? Or does the drug-facilitated rapist merely refine his *modus operandi* after release? There is no available information to answer these questions; and given the high risk for re-offense designation often assigned to such convicted offenders, we will wait for years before enough numbers emerge from prison to draw meaningful conclusions about their prospective risk.

DOES THE PERPETRATOR HAVE A PSYCHIATRIC ILLNESS?

Those perpetrators who offended in a social setting maintained adequate interpersonal skills, communication and appearance. In many instances, occupational function underscores how they were not suffering from psychotic illness at the time of the rape; bizarre behavior would have frightened potential victims away (except for those interested in helping him obtain medical treatment). Rather, perpetrators of DFSA generally plan their crimes and use the resources at their disposal – such as their charm (social skills) or their ability to offer employment – to ensnare targeted victims. This distinguishes drug-facilitated rape from certain other forms of rape, which may be occasionally committed by someone especially irrational or responding to hallucinations (Smith and Taylor, 1999).

While psychosis is highly unlikely, it remains at least a theoretical possibility. One example from the author's forensic case experience involves a 55-year-old clergyman-writer who placed ads for assistance at his home office. He attempted to commit DFSAs on women who responded to the ads. Later, when experiencing a manic episode of his bipolar illness, he became sexually preoccupied, and he was referred to me after he again attempted to sexually assault a woman he had sedated with a spiked drink. He could never have qualified for an insanity defense, as he appreciated the wrong of his actions, but he was driven by the heightened sexual preoccupation of his mania. The clergyman, indeed, committed a DFSA by relying upon the *modus operandi* he had already devised well before his manic episode came on. He also, nevertheless, offended when his mania resolved. Expect the unexpected.

Forcible rape in the context of psychotic illness or severe psychiatric distress is more likely to be impulsive (Phillips *et al.*, 1999). Again a distinction from drug-facilitated rape, which is carried out through a *modus operandi* that involves planning the setting where the victim is to be drugged and assaulted. Drug-facilitated sexual assaulters must maintain a certain measure of control.

Socially inept perpetrators may well be suffering from undiagnosed depressive or anxiety spectrum conditions that contribute to otherwise withdrawn personalities. However, this determination cannot be made without carefully interviewing perpetrators and screening for latent conditions. Highest suspicion for undiagnosed depression should be held when drug-facilitated rape follows a significant loss (such as death or separation), or represents a substantial change from previous behavior and personality. That alleged personality change may not be an actual change, but rather a revelation of a person's hidden proclivities.

A history of drug abuse should also be explored; the substance abuse may, in certain instances, be medicating an anxiety disorder or depression (Kushner *et al.*, 2000; Williams and Adams-Campbell, 2000). Sexual preoccupation has been described in individuals with depressive and substance abuse disorders (Black *et al.*, 1997).

Despite surprisingly well-integrated functioning in many drug-facilitated perpetrators, one must remember that some offenders obtain prescriptions legally – from doctors who treat them with sedatives characteristically prescribed for symptoms of anxiety or insomnia.

DOES THE PERPETRATOR HAVE A COMPULSIVE SEXUAL DEVIANCE?

Psychiatrists and other examiners should not presume that all perpetrators of DFSA are cool and collected, based on their veneer and *modus operandi*. Pedophiles, for example, are notorious for how smooth and engaging they can be (Blum, 2000). Yet some of these same pedophiles, who maintain a veneer of control, are locked into a cycle of re-offense where triggers initiate their hunting, targeting, and offending (Pithers *et al.*, 1988). For this reason, this subgroup of pedophiles exhibits alarmingly high rates of recidivism (Doren, 1998; Hanson and Thornton, 2000).

Many offenders in our sample did not present this sort of history of a flip into an uncontrollable urge. Nonetheless, some perpetrators of DFSA repeat the offense with astonishing frequency; therefore, any psychiatric interview should explore the possibility of compulsive behavior relating to deviant sexual fantasy (paraphilia), contributing to the offending behavior.

Paraphilias and antisocial (criminal) personality are not mutually exclusive; an offender may have both (Kafka, 1995). Therefore, the motivating force of the DFSA must be determined from a careful appraisal of history, circumstances, and the offender's inner sexual fantasy life. Such examinations are now commonly performed with risk classification of all sex offenders (Janus and Meehl, 1997; Witt *et al.*, 1996).

In our data, histories of DFSA perpetrators engaging in pedophilia or molestation were relatively rare. However, this may only reflect the offenders being identified by law enforcement. Already we understand how difficult it is for the adult victim to piece together that she has been violated. Certainly children are even more vulnerable, more likely to be at the mercy of a custodial adult, or more likely to place themselves in riskier situations, particularly in late adolescence (Raj *et al.*, 1997), less willing to report attack (Colings and Payne, 1991), and more likely to respond to the suggestive historical revisionism of the adult offender (Back and Lips, 1998).

In some cases, once the drug has rendered the victim unconscious, the perpetrator may exploit his control over the victim by acting out sexual fantasies. For example, he may violate the victim anally, shave her genital areas, or ejaculate on her face.

Some perpetrators of DFSA reflect a persistent fantasy in their *modus operandi*. For example, in three cases where the perpetrator sought out victims who were either hitchhiking or in public places, or repeatedly telephoned prospective targets, the drive to offend appeared to be relentless in comparison to the other 31 cases. Further study is needed to determine the basis of exceptional drive to locate victims.

However, psychiatry draws the line for addictive disorders – from substance abuse, to gambling, to the Internet – at a level of activity that consumes enough time and attention as to interfere with social or occupational activities (DSM-IV, 1994). Obsessive thoughts and associated compulsive actions involve the same over-involvement to the end of impairment. These standard models, applied to drug-facilitated rapists, can therefore illustrate how much a specific offender is responding to a compulsive drive, as opposed to merely exploitative opportunism.

Photographs and videotapes taken and collected have been more closely studied among serial killers and pedophiles (Burgess *et al.*, 1984; Warren *et al.*, 1996). In those cases, the preservation of material from the assault was later used to fuel masturbatory fantasy. This behavior is also a function of more ritualized, more carefully imagined sexual fantasy (Douglas *et al.*, 1992). More planning must be devoted to an assault that fulfills a sexual fantasy. If videotapes are taken to perpetuate the experience, the offender not only must orchestrate the luring of a victim to an isolated setting, but also to one where the video production can be carried out to conform to the dimensions of the perpetrator's fantasy. This includes proper positioning of the camera to capture the elements of the assault most stimulating, and at the optimum imagined angle.

Videotaping in DFSA cases suggests the presence of a paraphilia, as the materials are kept but not distributed. It may be carried out by a perpetrator who wants to create and preserve a masturbatory scenario – a scenario that his spouse or other consenting partners would not participate in (Hucker *et al.*, 2001). In other words, such perpetrators live double lives. Such paraphilia may relate to power and control, even necrophilia and sadism. Without specific probing of the offender's fantasy life, no generalizations are possible, only an accounting for the range of possibilities.

Based, however, on available data, one might also conclude that the video-taping of drugged partners may reflect narcissistic expression, especially likely when the perpetrator casts himself in the starring role of his own porn film. Consistent with this, one videotaping rapist had a history of cosmetic surgeries, including liposuction.

Sex offenders whose assaults or murders have followed highly ritualized plans often retain "trophies" (property of the victim, etc.) in order to more vividly recreate the events as part of masturbatory fantasy. Trophy taking is also closely associated with deviant sexual interest, or with re-enactment through sexual fantasy (Douglas *et al.*, 1992). One may experience any number of fetishes, or arousal from sexual contact with an inanimate object (DSM-IV, 1994). Therefore, a person who collects underwear from a scene may be maintaining a trophy to remind him of the specific scenario he orchestrated, or merely satisfy his arousal by a certain feeling of undergarments, or even arousal from his dressing in those undergarments. Each perpetrator needs to be examined on a case-by-case basis.

Given the privacy of sexual fantasy and preference, it is yet to be determined whether these and other paraphilias are found with similar coincidental frequency in DFSA perpetrators to that noted in coercive rapists.

The drug-facilitated rapist is not known to show empathy for his victims. Again, this also distinguishes the drug-facilitated perpetrators from those sex offenders who respond to compulsive and sometimes unwanted urges (Pithers, 1993). A lack of empathy is an antisocial or narcissistic personality feature (Kernberg, 1989). Investigators and examiners should probe for the sincerity of empathy; a lack or absence of such feeling is a basis to consider the sexual assault as a crime of entitlement or exploitation, not a compulsive condition.

WHAT DISTINGUISHES THE DRUG-FACILITATED RAPIST FROM THE COERCIVE RAPIST?

Violent histories are very uncommonly found in DFSA perpetrators. Only two perpetrators of 27 with confined data had a history of arrest. Only four perpetrators of 32 with available social histories were known to have been violent in the past. The drugs are not administered by force. The victims are not brought to the scene of the assault by force. Clothes are not commonly torn off. The victim is seldom mutilated in the assaults studied, and injuries described are more frequently part of the act of intercourse. The perpetrator's non-coercive, non-menacing, polite, even sometimes friendly persuasion and manipulation after the fact additionally characterize his nature. This differs markedly from the histories of coercive rapists (Douglas *et al.*, 1992). While some perpetrators may resort to coercion if the attempt to control the victim by chemical means is unsuccessful, most do not.

Forcible rape is alternatively viewed as a crime of varying degrees of anger, violence, or self-indulgent gratification, depending on the psychological make-up of the offender (Hall *et al.*, 1993). DFSA perpetrators, in their pattern of opportunistic offending, seductive *modus operandi*, objectification of the victim, detachment from the victim, unremarkable psychiatric histories, and unremarkable violent histories display more prominent self-gratification elements. While many violent sex offenders employ social skills and other seductive ruses, they characteristically employ violence when needed or overindulgently – rather than allow a prospective victim to readily slip away.

In a number of cases, there is evidence that the perpetrator sodomized victims. However, gratuitous mutilation is not generally seen in victims after attacks. Injuries suffered occur during the act of intercourse. This represents an important contrast to sexual sadists, who draw sexual gratification not only from the control of the victim, but the degree of her overt suffering as well (Raine, 1993). An effort to injure or to mutilate would make it more difficult for the drug-facilitated rapist to conceal the crime.

Stranger child molesters, pedophiles, and rapists typically confront victims with threats to their safety if they report the crime (Douglas *et al.*, 1992). Drug-facilitated rapists more commonly attempt to convince the victim that the act was consensual, nothing happened, or that she will not be believed, and may even attempt to meet the victim again. This distinction, however, may not be so absolute; coercive rapists of dates and other acquaintances also commonly attempt to convince the victim that they did not knowingly force someone to have intercourse against her will (Bownes *et al.*, 1991).

While violence and criminality have been reported in the past histories of a small number of convicted drug-facilitated rapists, violence is less a dominant force in their lives. Specifically, histories of convictions for previous violent offenses are very uncommon. Moreover, while drug-facilitated rapists have access to the unconscious victim's valuables, robbery is unusual to this crime.

Some rapists are suffering from paraphilias (deviant sexual interest) of control or sadism, or are acting out antisocial personalities (Berger *et al.*, 1999). However, given the nature of our data, we cannot draw any conclusions about the frequency of paraphilias among DFSA perpetrators.

Drug-facilitated rapists very uncommonly meet criteria for antisocial personality disorder. Only one person in our sample showed a history of antisocial behavior on a variety of psychosocial levels of function. This condition is very frequently diagnosed, however, among coercive rapists (Henn *et al.*, 1976).

Drug-facilitated rape has generally not been described in heterosexual serial killers. However, Jeffrey Dahmer and John Wayne Gacy, the notorious serial killers, also verbally manipulated and then immobilized male victims by sedating them before sexual assaults.

While Dahmer's and Gacy's assaults were murderous, they, like the high school principal mentioned above, harbored strongly conflicted feelings about their own homosexuality (Stone, 1989). Gacy was married, a local businessman, and politically and socially active in a conservative community (Bell, 2001). His reputation in the community was further softened by his dressing up as a clown for events. He had been imprisoned for sexual assault before becoming a serial killer. Like a number of the perpetrators described above, he lured victims with the promise of a job; he attacked victims in his home after he persuasively drew them there under false pretenses (Bell, 2001). Gacy was a sadist, but not a necrophiliac; murder enabled him to continue to offend, since his victims would have otherwise identified him. Murder may also, for Dahmer and Gacy, have resolved conflict and self-loathing relating to homosexuality.

Impulsive rapists – specifically those who attack, while they, themselves, are under the influence of a drug, or while committing some other crime against a vulnerable victim, or who do so during a period of anger – should be less likely to opt for a *modus operandi* of drug-facilitation than those rapists who carefully target and deliberately stalk their victims. Again, this question warrants further study; rapists who act impulsively earlier in life may have better impulse control, yet the same antisocial or rape proclivities, at a more mature age.

DFSA perpetrators are distinguished from coercive rapists as a group by the prevalence of well-developed communications and social skills (Scott *et al.*, 1984). This glibness assists the perpetrator to gain access to the victim and engender a sense of comfort. By contrast, many coercive rapists have numerous neuropsychological abnormalities and more poorly developed communications skills. Those poor communications skills are linked to problems in anger management and interpersonal isolation that often contribute to violence as expressed through coercive rape (Hall *et al.*, 1993).

It is important to distinguish communications skills from social skills. Communications skills, such as verbal agility and vocabulary, help the perpetrator explain and obfuscate. A perpetrator armed with only communications skills could not effectively inspire potential victims to trust him. Social skills, on the other hand, arm the perpetrator with an ability to persuade – to lure a potential victim to an isolated setting, to trick an even cautious person to accept a drink, to convince a woman who has been drugged and raped that, in fact, no rape occurred.

Many DFSA perpetrators have excellent social skills and are charming and personable, even very attractive. Those DFSA perpetrators who lack such charm and physical attractiveness may attract victims through classified ads and other schemes that passively bring victims to them. Some socially inept perpetrators of DFSA resemble those coercive rapists who are interpersonally isolated (though the latter are violent and more impulsive). Ironically, communications and social skills are part of the effective treatment of those coercive rapists who reveal these limitations in testing and evaluation (Alexander, 1999).

WHAT LAW ENFORCEMENT NEEDS TO KNOW

THE PERPETRATORS

The perpetrators of DFSA occupy all rungs of the socioeconomic ladder. They often have well-developed social skills. The DFSA perpetrator may use charm and looks, or the appearance of wealth or authority, to gain the trust of his intended victim, to isolate her, and then incapacitate her for his sexual exploitation. Superior social skills may also explain how a perpetrator could persuade another person to become an accomplice or co-conspirator in this egregious crime.

The perpetrator – despite overwhelming evidence of guilt – seldom displays remorse and far more commonly denies that he did anything wrong, even in the face of clear evidence of guilt. For example, during an interview with a television journalist, one perpetrator denied he had done anything wrong. He maintained this denial despite the fact that he had videotaped himself sexually assaulting at least one unconscious woman – and law enforcement had obtained a copy of the tape.

While the offenders studied were a subset of DFSA perpetrators, there is every indication that DFSA perpetrators, as a population, have a very high likelihood of being repeat offenders – re-offense if not apprehended. No information is available to appraise whether a risk for recidivism exists after incarceration.

THE DRUGS AND THEIR EFFECTS

Perpetrators use drugs that are available and familiar to them. Physicians and other healthcare professionals utilize the drugs they prescribe or administer in clinical practice. Within the nightclub scene, rapists may use GHB or other drugs of abuse that are readily distributed in the "club" environment. Some perpetrators may use sedatives, muscle relaxants or pain relievers for which they have a prescription (or which they have purchased illicitly from either drug dealers or via the Internet from overseas distributors).

The drugs often chosen by perpetrators not only sedate the victims, they also render them unable to defend themselves when sedation is incomplete; they may also impair the victims' ability to recall events that occur while they are under the influence of the drug. Memory and alertness are headquartered in different areas of the brain. Sedatives' effects on memory are independent of their effects on alertness. Therefore, a victim may be unable to recall an attack even if she never lost consciousness.

In some instances, the amnesic effect of the drug is so powerful that the victim is unaware that she has been raped. In one such case, the victim continued to trust the perpetrator – and he drugged and raped her a second time. Because of the effects of the drug, the victim may have little or no recollection of the events and many victims do not report the crime.

At least two intended victims died after drinking spiked drinks. Toxicology testing is often a component of an autopsy. In non-traumatic death cases of unclear cause, law enforcement and medical examiners should consider the possibility that the decedent died from drinking the contents of a spiked beverage, especially when traces of a drug are present in the deceased's biological fluids. In such cases, law enforcement officers should determine whether anyone who was near the victim in the hours before her death has ever been suspected of committing a DFSA or some other crime involving sedatives or other drugs.

MODUS OPERANDI

The perpetrator will typically try to commit the crime in a setting where he has complete control. The setting may be the perpetrator's home or office, or even the home of the victim if she can be isolated.

A perpetrator may take some action beforehand to decrease the likelihood that the victim will report the crime. For example, the perpetrator may offer marijuana (or some other illicit drug) to the intended victim – and then offer the intended victim a drink surreptitiously spiked with a sedative. The sedative renders the victim unconscious and impairs her memory of what occurred, and the victim, knowing that she voluntarily used an illicit drug, may be very reluctant to report the incident to police.

Also, a perpetrator may surreptitiously spike the victim's drink with both a sedative and some illicit drug (or otherwise cause the victim to unknowingly ingest an illicit drug, such as cocaine). In the event the victim reports the DFSA and urine testing is performed, both drugs might well be detected. This would create the false impression that the victim is a drug abuser. The perpetrator's goal may be to destroy the credibility of the prosecution's most important witness – the victim.

In an effort to cover his tracks, the perpetrator may, after the rape, dress the victim while she is still under the influence of the drug. Reportedly, some victims first become suspicious that they were raped when, after gaining consciousness, they realize that their underwear is on backwards or their clothes feel out of place.

Victims are targeted by their vulnerability in the eyes of the perpetrator. For example, the perpetrator may consider the intended victim to be vulnerable simply because the intended victim is alone with the perpetrator in a business, healthcare, or social context; however, in some cases other factors may also be involved, such as the intended victim's youth or old age, willingness to use illicit drugs, financial dependence, lack of sophistication, or occupation (e.g. exotic dancer). Virtually anyone, male or female, no matter how intelligent or street-wise, can find himself or herself in a vulnerable enough circumstance to be victimized.

Some perpetrators may target a woman with whom they have had consensual sexual relations, such as a current girlfriend. There may be a considerable age difference between the perpetrator and the victim.

In a number of cases, there has been more than one perpetrator. At least a few perpetrators have used accomplices, including female accomplices. In these cases there have often been many victims over a period of time. Indeed, the use of an accomplice may significantly enhance the success of the trap and, to an extent, this may account for the especially high number of victims in cases involving conspiracies.

WHATEVER THE FACT PATTERN, THE RESPONSE BY LAW ENFORCEMENT SHOULD BE THE SAME

Every complaint of a DFSA must be taken seriously, even if the victim can remember little or nothing, even if the victim voluntarily used illicit drugs during the incident, and even if the suspect is wealthy, well respected, handsome, and charming.

Some perpetrators photograph their unconscious victims or steal some property from their victims – a deviant behavior sometimes referred to as taking a "trophy." Other perpetrators have also videotaped their victims, and, in at least one instance, the perpetrator videotaped himself sexually assaulting an unconscious victim. Such property and videotapes, as well as the drugs used, represent crucial evidence, and police, armed with a warrant, may be able to find such evidence in the perpetrator's residence or vehicle.

Perpetrators of DFSA are most frequently repeat offenders. Therefore, the investigator's search for other victims should at least include a search of police reports in jurisdictions at or near where the suspect now resides, works, or travels – and at or near where he previously resided, worked, or regularly traveled on business or for other purposes. There is a high probability that identifying the perpetrator's other victims will significantly enhance both the outcome of the prosecution and the sentence imposed.

The perpetrators of DFSA – and their *modus operandi* – are often much more sophisticated than those observed in some other forms of rape. Be prepared – expect the unexpected.

REFERENCES

Abarbanel, G. (2000) "Assessing Drug-Facilitated Rape: Learning From Victims", *Nat. Inst. Just. J.*, 243, pp. 11–12.

Alexander, M.A. (1999) "Sexual Offender Treatment Efficacy Revisited", *Sex. Abuse J. Res. Treat.*, 11 (2), pp. 101–116.

American Psychiatric Association (APA) (1994) *Diagnostic and Statistical Manual of Mental Disorders* (4th edn). Washington, DC: American Psychiatric Association.

Back, S. and Lips, H.M. (1998) "Child Sexual Abuse: Victim Age, Victim Gender, and Observer Gender as Factors Contributing to Attributions of Responsibility", *Child Abuse Negl.*, 22 (12), pp. 1239–1252.

Bell, Rachel (2001) John Wayne Gacy from the Crime Library. Available Internet: URL: *www.crimelibrary.com/serial/gacy/gacybegin.html* *www.crimelibrary.com/serial/gacy/gacytrial.html*

Berger, P., Berner, W., Bolterauer, J., Gutierrez, K. and Berger, K. (1999) "Sadistic Personality Disorder in Sexual Offenders: Relationship to Antisocial Personality Disorder and Sexual Sadism", *J. Personality Dis.*, 13 (2), pp. 175–186.

Black, D.W., Kehrberg, L.L., Flumerfelt, D.L. and Schlosser, S.S. (1997) "Characteristics of 36 Subjects Reporting Compulsive Sexual Behavior", *Am. J. Psych.*, 154 (2), pp. 243–249.

Blum, A. (2000) "Seduction Typology OK at Sentencing: Testimony Relevant on Moral Culpability of Sex Offender", *For. Pan. Lett.*, 4 (12), 13 November 2000, *www.forensicpanel.com*

Bownes, I.T., O'Gorman, E.C. and Sayers, A. (1991) "Rape – A Comparison of Stranger and Acquaintance Assaults", *Med. Sci. Law*, 31 (2), pp. 102–109.

Burgess, A.W., Hartman, C.R., McCausland, M.P. and Powers, P. (1984) "Response Patterns in Children and Adolescents Exploited Through Sex Rings and Pornography", *Am. J. Psych.*, 141 (5), pp. 656–662.

Collings, S.J. and Payne, M.F. (1991) "Attribution of Causal and Moral Responsibility to Victims of Father–Daughter Incest: An Exploratory Examination of Five Factors", *Child Abuse Negl.,* 15 (4), pp. 513–521.

Doren, D.M. (1998) "Recidivism Base Rates, Predictions of Sex Offender Recidivism, and the 'Sexual Predator' Commitment Laws", *Behav. Sci. Law,* 16, pp. 97–114.

Douglas, J.E., Burgess, A.N., Burgess, A.G. and Ressler, R.K. (eds) (1992) "Rape and Sexual Assault". In *Crime Classification Manual: A Standard System for Investigating and Classifying Violent Crimes.* New York: Lexington Books.

Douglas, J.E., Burgess, A.N., Burgess, A.G. and Ressler, R.K. (eds) (1992) "Homicide". In *Crime Classification Manual: A Standard System for Investigating and Classifying Violent Crimes.* New York: Lexington Books.

Fairstein, L.A. (1993) *Sexual Violence: Our War Against Rape.* New York, NY: William Morrow & Co.

Greenblatt, D.J., Miller, L.G. and Shader, R.I. (1990) "Neurochemical and Pharmacokinetic Correlates of the Clinical Action of Benzodiazepines Hypnotic Drugs", *Am. J. Med.,* 88 (3A), 18S–24S

Groth, A.N., Burgess W. and Holmstrom L.L. (1977) "Rape: Power, Anger, and Sexuality", *Am. J. Psych.,* 134 (11), pp. 1239–1243.

Hall, G., Hirschman, R., Graham J. and Zaragoza M. (eds) (1993) *Sexual Aggression: Issues in Etiology, Assessment, and Treatment.* Kent, OH: Taylor & Francis.

Hanson, R.K. and Thornton, D. (2000) "Improving Risk Assessments for Sex Offenders: A Comparison of Three Actuarial Scales", *Law Hum. Behav.,* 24, pp. 119–136.

Hare, R. (1991) *The Hare Psychopathy Checklist – Revised Manual.* Toronto, Ontario: MHS, Inc.

Hazelwood, R.R. and Warren, J.I. (2000) "The Sexually Violent Offender: Impulsive or Ritualistic?", *Aggress. Viol. Behav.,* 5, 267–279.

Henn, F.A., Herjanic, M. and Vanderpearl, R.H. (1976) "Forensic Psychiatry: Profiles of Two Types of Sex Offenders", *Am. J. Psych.,* 133 (6), pp. 694–696.

Horowitz, M.J. (1989) "Clinical Phenomenology of Narcissistic Pathology", *Psych. Clin. N. Am.,* 12, pp. 531–540.

Hucker, S., Bartlik, B., Moser, C., Berlin, F. and Quinsley, V. (Commentators) (2001) "Cases in Headlines: Sado-masochism. Harmless, or Ominous?", *For. Pan. Lett.,* 4 (12), *www.forensicpanel.com*

Janus, E.S. and Meehl, P.E. (1997) "Assessing the Legal Standard for Predictions of Dangerousness in Sex Offender Commitment Proceedings", *Psychol. Pub. Pol. Law,* 3, pp. 33–64.

Kafka, M.P. (1995) "Sexual Impulsivity". In Hollander, E. and Stein, D. (eds) *Impulsivity and Aggression,* pp. 201–228. Chichester: Wiley & Sons.

Kaplan, H.I. and Sadock, B.J. (1993) *Pocket Handbook of Psychiatric Drug Treatment.* Baltimore: Williams & Wilkins.

Kaplan, H.I., Sadock, B.J. and Grebb, J. A. (1994) *Kaplan and Sadock's Synopsis of Psychiatry: Behavioral Sciences, Clinical Psychiatry* (7th edn). Baltimore: Williams & Wilkins.

Kernberg, O.F. (1989) "The Narcissistic Personality Disorder and the Differential Diagnosis of Antisocial Behavior", *Psych. Clin. N. Am.,* 12, 553–570.

Kushner, M.G., Abrams, K., Thuras, P., Thuras, P. and Hanson, K.L. (2000) "Individual Differences Predictive of Drinking to Manage Anxiety Among Non-problem Drinkers with Panic Disorder", *Alcohol Clin. Exp. Res.,* 24 (4), pp. 448–458.

Paris, J. (1997) "Antisocial and Borderline Personality Disorders: Two Separate Diagnoses or Two Aspects of the Same Psychopathology?", *Comp. Psych.,* 38, pp. 237–242.

Phillips, S.L., Heads, T.C., Taylor, P.J. and Hill, G.M. (1999) "Sexual Offending and Antisocial Sexual Behavior Among Patients with Schizophrenia", *J. Clin. Psych.,* 60 (*3*), pp. 170–175.

Physicians' Desk Reference (54th edn). Montvale: Medical Economics Company, Inc.

Pithers, W.D. (1993) "Treatment of Rapists: Reinterpretation of Early Outcome Data and Exploratory Constructs to Enhance Therapeutic Efficacy". In Nagayama Hall, G.C., Hirschman, R., Graham, J.R. and Zaragoza, M.S. (eds) *Sexual Aggression: Issues in Etiology, Assessment, and Treatment.* Kent: Taylor & Francis.

Pithers, W.D., Kashima, K., Cumming, G.F., Beal, L.S. and Buell, M. (1988) "Relapse Prevention of Sexual Aggression". In Prentky, R. and Quinsey, V. (eds) *Human Sexual Aggression: Current Perspectives,* pp. 244–260. New York: New York Academy of Sciences.

Price, D.R. (1994) "Personality Disorders and Traits". In McDonald Jr, J.J. and Kulick, F.B. (eds) *Mental and Emotional Injuries in Employment Litigation,* pp. 93–140. Washington, DC: The Bureau of National Affairs.

Raine, A. (1993) *The Psychopathology of Crime: Criminal Behavior as a Clinical Disorder.* San Diego, CA: Academic Press, Inc.

Raj, A., Silverman, J.G. and Amaro, H. (1997) "The Relationship Between Sexual Abuse and Sexual Risk Among High School Students: Findings From the 1997 Massachusetts Youth Risk Behavior Survey", *Matern. Child Health J.,* 4 (2), pp. 125–134.

Scott, M.L., Cole, J.K., McKay, S.E., Golden, C.J. and Liggett, K.R. (1984) "Neuropsychological Performance of Sexual Assaulters and Pedophiles", *J. Forensic Sci.,* 29 (4), pp. 1114–1118.

Smith, A.D. and Taylor, P.J. (1999) "Serious Sex Offending Against Women by Men with

Schizophrenia. Relationship of Illness and Psychotic Symptoms to Offending", *Brit. J. Psych.,* 174, pp. 233–237.

Stone, M.H. (1989) "Murder", *Psych. Clin. N. Am.,* 12, pp. 643–652.

Stone, M.H. (1993) *Abnormalities of Personality: Within and Beyond the Realm of Treatment.* New York: Norton.

Warren, J.I., Hazelwood, R.R. and Dietz, P.E. (1996) "The Sexually Sadistic Serial Killer", *J. Forensic Sci.,* 41 (6), pp. 970–974.

Welner, M. (1997) "Rapist in a Glass: The Big Picture of the Rohypnol Wars", *Forensic Echo,* 1, pp. 4–10.

Williams, C.D. and Adams-Campbell, L.L. (2000) "Addictive Behaviors and Depression Among African Americans Residing in a Public Housing Community", *Addictive Behavior,* 25 (1), pp. 45–46.

Witt, P.H., DelRusso, J., Oppenheim, J. and Ferguson, G. (1996) "Sex Offender Risk Assessment and the Law", *J. Psych. Law,* Fall, pp. 343–376.

CHAPTER 3

ETHANOL

James C. Garriott
Ashraf Mozayani

Alcohol in the Biblical Days
The daughters of Lot, sensing the end of the world, endeavored to get Lot
drunk in order to seduce him and continue the human race. (Book of Genesis)

Ethanol (ethyl alcohol), also commonly known as alcohol, is the most prevalent
drug in Western society, with *per capita* consumption exceeding 2.54 gallons of
ethanol per year for each person in the United States over 14 years of age. This
equates to 5.8 billion gallons of beer (53% of the total consumption), 585.3
million gallons of wine, and 394.7 million gallons of spirits sold in the United
States (CDC, 1989). Considering such extensive use of alcohol in our society, it
is not surprising that its use also results in many ills for modern society. For
example, there are over 100,000 deaths due to excessive alcohol consumption
each year in the United States, including alcohol-induced illnesses such as
cirrhosis, overdoses of alcoholic beverages, and accidental deaths (McGinnis
and Foege, 1993). In 1998, there were approximately 15,000 alcohol-related
traffic deaths in the United States (NHTSA, 1998). Alcohol is the most common
drug used to facilitate sexual assault, with estimates of its involvement in up to
75% of cases.

PHARMACOKINETICS OF ETHANOL

To understand the pharmacokinetics of alcohol, it is necessary to know the
manner in which it is absorbed from the site of administration, distributed into
body tissues, and eliminated from the body. Since alcohol is soluble and
miscible with water in all proportions, its disposition in the body is relatively
simple compared with more fat-soluble (or water-insoluble) drugs.

ABSORPTION

Alcohol is absorbed from all the mucosal surfaces of the gastrointestinal tract at
a rate that is best described by simple diffusion. This rate is proportional to the
concentration gradient of alcohol across the membrane and to a diffusion

coefficient that is a constant for ethyl alcohol and the specific membrane being studied. Fasting individuals absorb 20% to 25% of a dose from the stomach and 75% to 80% from the small intestine proximal to the pyloric sphincter. Negligible amounts are absorbed from the mouth and colon (Baselt, 1995). When alcohol is consumed with food it results in a lower, delayed peak blood alcohol concentration. This reduction in area under the blood alcohol concentration–time curve due to food intake has been shown to be the result of two factors: first, the reduction in efficiency of absorption of alcohol due to prolonged gastric emptying time, and second, the Michaelis-Menton kinetic behavior of alcohol elimination, such that lower amounts of alcohol in the body are metabolized at a proportionately higher rate (Baselt, 1995).

Various authors, employing several hundred experimental subjects, have shown that fasting subjects exhibit peak blood alcohol concentrations within 0.5 to 2.0 hr (average 0.75–1.35 hr, depending on dose and time of last meal), while non-fasting subjects exhibit peak levels within 1.0 to 6.0 hr (average 1.06–2.12 hr). The type of food (e.g. carbohydrate, fat, protein) apparently has relatively little influence, but the extent of the effect is directly proportional to the size of the meal and inversely proportional to the elapsed time between food and alcohol consumption. The reduction of peak blood alcohol concentration by food in these studies ranged, on average, from 9% to 23% (Abele and Kropp, 1958; Herbich and Prokop, 1963; Krauland et al., 1967).

Alcohol is absorbed most rapidly when the concentration of the ingested solution is between 10% and 30% (20- to 60-proof). More dilute solutions result in a lower concentration gradient across the absorbing membrane and, because of the larger volume involved, may also delay gastric emptying. More concentrated solutions are irritating to the gastric mucosa and to the pyloric sphincter, causing increased secretion of mucus and delayed gastric emptying (Kalant, 1971; Schwar, 1979). The type of alcoholic beverage ingested probably has little effect except in the first 30 minutes after consumption (Schwar, 1979).

DISTRIBUTION

Alcohol is very hydrophilic and is therefore distributed to body tissues and fluids as a function of the water content of that tissue or fluid. The blood concentration that is produced at time zero (C_p) after instantaneous equilibration of a dose of alcohol (D) within an individual of body weight W may be estimated using the standard pharmacokinetic equation:

$$C_p \ (g/L) = \frac{D}{V_d \times W}$$

where:

V_d = the volume of distribution for ethanol in that individual (in L/kg),
D = the alcohol dose (in grams)
W = the body weight of the individual in kilograms.

Since alcohol is distributed throughout the body's water, then the V_d for alcohol in an individual is also an expression of total body water (Widmark, 1981). The V_d of alcohol for adult males has been found to average 0.62 to 0.79 (range 0.59–0.90) and for adult females 0.55 to 0.66 (range 0.46–0.86). Schwar (1979) determined average values of 0.70 and 0.60 for males and females, respectively, in calculations of amount of alcohol consumed from known blood alcohol concentrations (for comparison, Widmark's average values, obtained some 40 years earlier, were 0.68 and 0.55, respectively). For individuals of the same sex and similar body weight, differences in V_d (which may be considerable) are largely due to differences in body fat ratios. This is because alcohol is, to a great degree, excluded from adipose tissue. Age is another important factor as total body water, and therefore the V_d of alcohol, decreases with increasing age. Total body water decreases from an average of 61% of body weight in males aged 18 to 40 years to 52% in those over 60 years, and from 51% in females aged 18 to 40 years to 46% in those over 60 years (Schwar, 1979).

A general rule of thumb is that 1.0 g of alcohol per kg of body weight produces a blood alcohol concentration (BAC) of 0.15 g/dL (based on an average V_d value of 0.66). Using the English system, one ounce of alcohol, or the equivalent of two regular beers (5% alcohol content) or two mixed drinks containing 1.5 ounces of 80-proof alcohol each will produce a peak blood alcohol content of about 0.05 g/dL in an average 150-pound male. This rule must be adjusted for lower or higher body weights and lower or higher fat distribution ratios, and does not account for metabolism. For accurate evaluations of BAC to alcohol consumption levels, it is necessary to apply Widmark's formula.

ELIMINATION

The elimination of alcohol is the sum of all processes that remove alcohol from the systemic circulation, including biotransformation and excretion.

The major portion of ingested alcohol undergoes biotransformation to oxidation products in the liver. Biotransformation occurs in three steps:

1. ethanol $\longrightarrow$ acetaldehyde
2. acetaldehyde $\longrightarrow$ acetic acid
3. acetic acid $\longrightarrow$ $CO_2 + H_2O$

The transformation of ethanol to acetaldehyde is accomplished by three systems:

1. alcohol dehydrogenase;
2. catalase; and
3. the microsomal ethanol-oxidizing system.

Of these mechanisms, alcohol dehydrogenase (and its several isozymes) is by far the most important (Goldstein, 1983). The basic mechanism is outlined in the reaction below:

$$CH_3CH_2OH + NAD^+ \longrightarrow CH_3CHO + NADH + H^+$$

The rate-limiting factor in this reaction is the regeneration of nicotine adenine dinucleotide (NAD).

An ethanol load imposed on the liver causes practically all metabolic dynamics to be directed toward the metabolic handling of alcohol, causing a marked diminution and "shortchanging" of other hepatic metabolic functions to the extent that fatty acids coming to the liver are stored and unmetabolized, producing fatty infiltration (Goldstein, 1983; Tottmar *et al.*, 1973). This "fatty liver" occurs acutely after alcohol ingestion, and is not limited to chronic heavy alcohol consumption.

The vast majority (95%) of ingested alcohol is metabolized in the liver. This metabolic removal begins as soon as the alcohol in the blood reaches the liver. The decline in blood alcohol concentrations resulting from metabolism and excretion is generally considered to be a zero-order (linear) process, at least at midrange concentrations. Dubowski (1976) has shown this rate of decline to average 0.015 g/dL/hr (range 0.011–0.022) for 25 males and 0.018 g/dL/hr (range 0.011–0.022) for 15 females. Shajani and Dinn (1985) reported an average of 0.018 g/dL/hr (range 0.013–0.023) for eight females. Thus normal healthy adult females appear to eliminate alcohol at a slightly higher rate than normal healthy adult males. Chronic drinkers develop metabolic tolerance to alcohol, resulting in increased metabolic rates. Researchers comparing rates of blood alcohol elimination in nondrinkers, social drinkers, and alcoholics found marked differences in the three groups. The mean rates were: 0.012 ± 0.004 g/dL/hr in nondrinkers, 0.015 ± 0.004 g/dL/hr in social drinkers, and 0.030 ± 0.009 g/dL/hr in alcoholics (Winek and Murphy, 1984). A group of 15 patients admitted to a treatment facility for alcohol dependency had serial blood alcohol measurements performed on admission. The average initial blood alcohol concentration (BAC) was 0.24 g/dL. The average rate of decline was 0.0266 ± 0.007 g/dL/hr (range 0.0159–0.043 g/dL/hr) (Clothier *et al.*,

1985). These rates are considerably greater than the rates of 0.015 to 0.018 g/dL/hr often considered as representing the "average" rate of alcohol metabolism.

Wagner *et al.* (1976) showed that first-order kinetics (nonlinear) predominate at very low blood alcohol concentrations (0.02 g/dL or less). At very high blood alcohol concentrations (over 0.30 g/dL) first-order kinetics may also apply, and a more rapid rate of decline than normally expected occurs, at least until blood concentrations fall into the range where zero-order kinetics would again be observed (Bogusz *et al.*, 1977; Hammond *et al.*, 1973).

PHARMACODYNAMICS

Alcohol acts as a central nervous system (CNS) depressant, and generally depresses all body functions. The desirable effect of alcohol to a sexual offender is its similarity to therapeutic and abused drugs such as tranquilizers, narcotics, sedatives, and hypnotics. Alcohol and narcotic drugs (e.g. morphine and heroin) are CNS and respiratory depressants and can induce euphoria, tolerance, and physical dependence. The major distinctions between these drugs are the strong analgesic effects of narcotics versus the very weak pain-killing action of alcohol. Generally, alcohol has a weaker potency, requiring tens of grams for effectiveness rather than a few milligrams. Due to this low potency, ethyl alcohol must be present in the body at high concentrations to be effective, and consequently, it affects the functioning of virtually all physiological and biochemical systems (Garriott, 1995).

Forensic scientists are primarily concerned with alcohol's effects as a drug and its impact on the CNS. Its effect as a depressant leads to impairment and alteration of a variety of behavioral actions. Alcohol's effects on vision, auditory discrimination, decision-making, response and reaction time, and driving skills have been described in numerous studies. The CNS is the bodily system most severely affected by alcohol, causing a multitude of behavioral aberrations. Therefore, the effects of alcohol on the CNS are the most important element to consider for medicolegal interpretation of alcohol-related situations.

The intensity of the CNS effects of alcohol is proportional to the concentration of alcohol in the blood. These general effects are outlined in relation to alcohol concentrations in Table 3.1 (Dubowski, 1997). It is important to emphasize that these effects are considerably more pronounced when the blood alcohol level is rising rather than falling. This is believed to be a result of so-called "acute," or functional, tolerance to alcohol, so that a greater tolerance to its effects exist as the blood level is declining versus when it is rising (Mellanby, 1919; Moskowitz *et al.*, 1977). The magnitude of alcohol's effects could also be a function of the rate that the alcohol is consumed. It was observed that the more rapid the rate of drinking, the greater the degree of

Table 3.1

Stages of acute alcoholic influence/intoxication. Copyright © by K.M. Dubowski, University of Oklahoma College of Medicine, Oklahoma City, OK, 1997.

Blood alcohol concentration (g/dL)	Stages of alcoholic influence	Clinical signs/symptoms
0.01–0.05	Subclinical	Influence/effects not apparent or obvious Behavior nearly normal by ordinary observation Impairment detectable by special tests
0.03–0.12	Euphoria	Mild euphoria, sociability, talkativeness Increased self-confidence; decreased inhibitions Diminution of attention, judgment, and control Some sensory motor impairment Slowed information processing Loss of efficiency in critical performance tests
0.09–0.25	Excitement	Emotional instability Loss of critical judgment Impairment of perception, memory, and comprehension Decreased sensitory response; increased reaction time Reduced visual acuity, peripheral vision, and glare recovery Sensory motor incoordination; impaired balance Drowsiness
0.18–0.30	Confusion	Disorientation; mental confusion Dizziness Exaggerated emotional states (fear, sorrow, rage, etc.) Disturbances of vision and perception of color, form, motion, dimensions Increased pain threshold Increased muscular incoordination; staggering gait Slurred speech Apathy Lethargy
0.25–0.40	Stupor	General inertia Approaching loss of motor functions Markedly decreased response to stimuli Marked muscular incoordination Inability to stand or walk Vomiting Incontinence of urine and feces Impaired consciousness Sleep or stupor
0.35–0.50	Coma	Complete unconsciousness; coma Anesthesia; depressed or abolished reflexes Subnormal temperature Incontinence of urine and feces Impairment of circulation and respiration Possible death
0.45 +	Death	Death from respiratory arrest

performance decrements at the same blood alcohol concentration (BAC) (Moskowitz *et al.*, 1977).

The effects of alcohol on the CNS are related to its impact on various locations of the brain. The frontal lobes are sensitive to low concentrations of alcohol, resulting in alteration of thought and mood. At low and moderate blood levels the effects are often considered stimulant actions, mediated by depression of the reticular activating system and release of the cortex from selective control and inhibition. Increased confidence, a more expansive and vivacious personality, mood swings, garrulousness, and increased social interactions are all characteristic behaviors. These effects are actually due to depression of the inhibitory central mechanisms. Thus, the behavior and actions of an intoxicated individual may be altered and uncharacteristic by nature.

In terms of DFSA, alcohol has other effects that may be desirable to a sexual offender. As the blood alcohol level rises (usually 0.10 g/dL and above), memory, fine discrimination, and concentration functions are dulled, with vision (occipital lobe) and coordination (cerebellum) also becoming impaired. All bodily functions and abilities governed by the brain are impaired progressively. With acute intoxication (blood levels in excess of 0.40 g/dL), autonomic (automatic) functions governed by the medulla and the brain stem are affected, resulting in loss of control of bodily functions and possibly causing death from depression of the respiratory centers (Dubowski, 1985).

The negative impact of alcohol on driving-related skills exemplifies the general impairment induced by alcohol. The same weakened responsiveness, reduction of decision-making abilities, loss of judgment and control, reduced perception and awareness, and other impaired abilities increase the vulnerability of an individual to a potential predator, and increase the likelihood of sexual assault, robbery, or violence. Alcohol use is highly associated with violent death. A study of drugs and alcohol incidence in homicides found an average 57% of all cases were alcohol-related (Garriott, 1993).

INTERPRETATION OF BLOOD ALCOHOL CONTENT

The usual forensic specimen for determination of alcohol content is whole blood; however, it is more likely in clinical practice that a serum or plasma specimen will be obtained by allowing blood to clot upon exposure to air or by centrifuging anticoagulated blood, respectively.

Plasma–whole blood alcohol concentration ratios ranged from 1.10 to 1.35 and averaged 1.18 in a study of heparinized blood samples (Payne *et al.*, 1968). These ratios are similar for the serum–whole blood ratio (Schwar, 1979). These differences can be accounted for by the relative water content of these fluids. Normal variations in the percentage of whole blood volume occupied by the red cells (hematocrit) make it difficult to apply a uniform correction factor when attempting to convert a serum or plasma alcohol concentration to a whole blood concentration.

EFFECTS OF ALCOHOL IN COMBINATION WITH OTHER DRUGS

To intensify the effect of alcohol, it is a common practice in DFSA cases to administer it in combination with other drugs. Alcohol exerts a potentiating or synergistic effect when ingested in the presence of other drugs having CNS depressant effects such as sedatives, hypnotics, anticonvulsants, some antidepressants, tranquilizers, some analgesics, and opiates.

The enhanced intoxication effect of drugs can occur with low levels of alcohol. This effect can be profound, therefore, it is not surprising that numerous sexual assaults have occurred while the victim was under the influence of both alcohol and drugs. Alcohol may also interact with drugs to produce reduced (antagonistic) or severe toxic effects. Below are some specific drug groups often combined with alcohol in sexual assault cases.

BARBITURATES

Historically, barbiturates were prescribed as sedatives. Their use has declined due to their high occurrence in suicide and accidental overdose cases. Barbiturates are CNS depressants that lessen polysynaptic pathways and enhance the effect of γ–aminobutyric acid (GABA), an inhibitory neurotransmitter.

Barbiturates are divided into different categories depending on their duration of action: 2–4 hr for ultra short acting, 4–6 hr for short acting, 6–10 hr for intermediate and 12–24 hr for long acting. The shorter the duration of action, the more lipid soluble the barbiturate, thereby achieving high CNS concentration and more toxicity. Ethanol potentiates the effects of barbiturates as do other CNS depressants. Typical symptoms of barbiturate overdose are low blood pressure, reduced and shallow respirations, acidosis, and dilated fixed pupils with no reflex.

BENZODIAZEPINES

Benzodiazepines are well known by many forensic toxicologists to facilitate sexual assaults. Diazepam, lorazepam, alprazolam and more recently flunitrazepam (Rohypnol®) have all been used in "doping" circumstances, often being placed in an unsuspecting victim's alcoholic drink. Extreme sedation, helplessness, and prolonged sleep may result, during which a sexual assault, robbery or other crime can occur. In general, the benzodiazepines interact with GABA neuroreceptors causing increased chloride ion conductance in response to GABA. The result is sedative and hypnotic effects. Another desirable effect for the sexual offender is the capacity of benzodiazepines to abate the victim's memory. Therapeutic doses of lorazepam (1 mg) have been studied in combination with and without 0.6 g/kg alcohol (Kerr *et al.*, 1992). Lorazepam alone produced sedation and disrupted performance, an effect potentiated when mixed with alcohol. Lorazepam mixed with alcohol has historically been used as an incapacitating drug. At moderate, therapeutic doses, benzodiazepines have been shown to not significantly add to the effect of low or moderate alcohol concentrations (Forney and Hughes, 1968). However, as the dosage of either drug increases, the combined effect is more marked. The interactions of benzodiazepines with alcohol has led to drug-induced deaths, clinical drug overdoses, traffic accidents, etc. The effects of alprazolam, currently a very popular benzodiazepine tranquilizer, were studied in 48 human volunteers given 1 mg alone and in combination with 0.5 g/kg of alcohol and then challenged with psychological testing. Alprazolam caused subjective sedation, unsteadiness, dizziness, fatigue, and impaired performance on all tasks studied. Although the effects of the combination were greater than those using either alprazolam or alcohol alone, they were generally additive, and no more than would be predicted (Bond *et al.*, 1991; Bond *et al.*, 1992).

ANTIHISTAMINES

Classical antihistamines such as chlorpheniramine, diphenhydramine and brompheniramine are competitive antagonists of histamine. Antihistamines appear to potentiate the abuse potential of other drugs, and all members of this group enhance the depressant and sedative effects of alcohol.

TRICYCLIC ANTIDEPRESSANTS

Some tricyclic antidepressants (TCAs) potentiate sedation with alcohol, causing enhanced CNS depression and hypothermic coma in high doses. In addition, inhibition of intestinal movement and fatty changes in the liver may result from this interaction (Griffin and D'Arcy, 1975). TCAs are a leading cause of death from drug overdoses, and often these deaths involve alcohol.

The newer antidepressants (non-TCAs) may have fewer effects with alcohol. Therapeutic doses of paroxetine (20 mg) and 1 mg of lorazepam were studied in combination with and without 0.6 g/kg alcohol (Kerr *et al.*, 1992). Paroxetine had little to no effect on most of the tests, while lorazepam produced sedation and disrupted performance. However, paroxetine did have a slight antagonistic effect on alcohol-induced sedation.

MARIJUANA

Marijuana is the most widely used illicit drug in our society, so it is not surprising to see the combination of this drug with alcohol in many cases of sexual assault. Tetrahydrocannabinol (THC), the active psychoactive component of marijuana, may affect complex performance skills for up to 24 hr after drug ingestion. Marijuana alone induces impairment of some skills in road-driving simulation experiments, especially divided attention tasks, while alcohol impairs psychomotor performance on virtually all driving related skills (Heishman *et al.*, 1989). Since the effects of the two drugs are different, the effect of marijuana in combination with alcohol appears to be primarily additive. In one study, marijuana alone did not impair driving performance, but when alcohol was given in combination, the interaction resulted in greater impairment in driving performance than with alcohol alone (Sutton, 1983).

GHB

Gamma-hydroxybutyric acid (GHB), a natural component of human cells, is a CNS depressant that has anesthetic properties. GHB has been used as an adjunct for anesthesia in Europe. In the United States, GHB is a controlled substance and is often illicitly manufactured. It causes CNS depression, amnesia and hypotension. GHB is an ideal DFSA drug due to its ability to induce drowsiness, amnesia, and muscle relaxation. It acts synergistically with ethanol to intensify CNS and respiratory depression.

NARCOTICS

Opiates are a class of compounds that, while depressing the CNS and relieving pain, also produce euphoria. Hydrocodone, meperidine, codeine and morphine are the most common drugs in this class to be detected in DFSAs. Combining alcohol and opiates intensifies the depression of the CNS, especially respiratory depression, which can lead to coma and respiratory arrest.

WHY IS ETHANOL SUCH A COMMON FINDING IN SEXUAL ASSAULT CASES?

Recent studies indicate that ethanol is commonly found in both the victim and the assailant in sexual assault cases. In a study of offenders convicted of rape/sexual assault, approximately one-third reported drinking at the time of the assault (Bureau of Justice Statistics, 1998).

According to David Anderson of George Mason University in his "College Alcohol Survey", a poll of college and university administrators showed that alcohol is believed to be involved in 75% of acquaintance rapes that occur on campuses (George Mason University, 1997). In a study of female students who were victims of sexual aggression while in college, 68% of these women reported that their assailants had been drinking at the time of the attack. The acts of sexual aggression ranged from intimidation to illegal restraint with intent to rape (Frinter and Rubinson, 1993).

Dr Mahmoud ElSohly recently published the results of a three-year study conducted by his laboratory on urine samples from rape victims who believed they were drugged (ElSohly *et al.*, 1999). The specimens were collected by law enforcement agencies in all 50 states during investigations of reported sexual assaults. The specimens were subjected to a general drug screening protocol which included all of the reported DFSA drugs, as well as an extensive screen for other drugs, both prescription and illegal. A total of 2,366 urine specimens were tested from June 1996 to July 1999. More than 20 different substances were identified, with alcohol being found in 954 of the specimens (40%). The other most prevalent drugs identified were marijuana (434 cases, 18%), cocaine (194 cases, 8%), gamma-hydroxybutyrate (GHB, 71 cases, 3%) and fluni-trazepam (9 cases, 0.3%). In 873 of the cases (37%), no drugs or alcohol were identified.

From these studies it appears that alcohol plays a significant role in sexual assaults. The self-reporting of offenders is probably low, while the "belief" of college administrators may be high. Even with those caveats, the data suggest that at least 40%, and maybe as many as 60%, of all sexual assaults involve alcohol.

There are a number of factors contributing to the prevalence of alcohol in sexual assault cases. Alcohol has been used throughout history in situations that require the loosening of inhibitions. Most people hear stories and jokes at an early age suggesting that alcohol can be used in this manner. Everyone has probably heard the old joke "Candy is dandy, but liquor is quicker." Thus, most young adults become familiar with the concept of using liquor to assist in advancing their sexual desires.

Of course, one of the reasons that alcohol has achieved this reputation is that it works. A small amount of alcohol eases tension, a large amount removes inhibitions, and a still larger amount prevents the potential victim from resisting the aggressor.

This effectiveness, coupled with the fact that drinking alcohol is socially acceptable, facilitates the process of administration. Unlike many other potential DFSA drugs, alcohol is legal and readily available. There are no illegal drugs to buy, no surreptitious mixing of drugs in drinks, no convincing the victim to "try this." Drinking alcohol, even in excess, is legal and socially acceptable.

ANALYTICAL METHODS THAT ALLOW FOR DETECTION OF ETHANOL

During sexual crime investigations, a number of different sample types may be collected from the victim. The samples are usually collected from the victim during an examination at a medical facility such as a hospital. In order for any results obtained from the analysis of these specimens to be used in subsequent legal actions, a chain of custody must be established and maintained, from the collection of the specimens through the analytical procedures. After collection, the sample containers must be sealed with tamper-evident tape or retained in a tamper-evident container. Any transfer of custody from one individual to another must be documented, and the specimen containers must be sealed until the forensic laboratory personnel open them to begin the analysis for drugs and alcohol.

In many cases, clinical blood alcohol tests are performed in the hospital during the post-rape examination. Clinical testing generally does not comply with the strict chain of custody standards required for forensic testing, so clinical results are much more likely to be challenged during court proceedings. In addition to chain of custody issues, clinical alcohol testing may be performed using a number of different methodologies that may give conflicting results. In general, urine alcohol is 10 to 15% higher than blood alcohol, and serum alcohol is approximately 10 to 20% higher than those results obtained from whole blood.

The analytical methods used for the determination of alcohol are essentially identical for blood, serum, and urine. The presence of alcohol may be determined by a number of screening tests, the most common of which involves the use of alcohol dehydrogenase (ADH). This enzyme reacts with ethanol in the presence of NAD to form a product that may be detected by an UV spectrophotometer. Many clinical methods used in hospitals are based on this reaction, although it is subject to interferences by some of the other alcohols.

Forensic detection and quantitation of alcohol in blood or urine is predominantly done by gas chromatography. By selecting an appropriate gas chromatograph (GC) column, ethanol can be cleanly separated from other drugs and endogenous components of body fluids and can be accurately quantitated.

There are two commonly used methods for the introduction of the sample into the GC. The first is headspace sampling, where a sample of the body fluid is placed in a sealed container. After a period of equilibrium, a sample of the vapor generated above the body fluid is extracted and injected into the GC.

The second method of sample introduction is direct injection. In this method, a sample of the body fluid is injected into a specially prepared injection port that separates the non-volatile substances from the sample prior to their introduction into the GC column. Both methods are widely used in forensic applications.

Most forensic laboratories employ flame ionization detectors (FID) for the detection and quantitation of alcohol. These detectors respond to any substance, such as alcohol, that burns in a hydrogen/oxygen flame. A small number of laboratories have begun to use mass spectral detectors in alcohol analysis. These detectors are highly sensitive and much more specific than FIDs.

CONCLUSION

Alcohol is the drug most commonly associated with sexual assault cases due to its easy availability. It is rapidly absorbed into the bloodstream after ingestion and distributes to the entire body, including the CNS. After distribution alcohol is rapidly metabolized and eliminated from the body. The amount of time that alcohol can be detected after it is consumed will depend upon a number of factors including the amount of alcohol consumed, the individual's weight and gender, and tolerance to alcohol. In DFSA cases, the victims most often consume the alcohol voluntarily. Alcohol decreases inhibitions, impairs perception, and may cause amnesia and/or loss of consciousness, especially if used in conjunction with other drugs.

REFERENCES

Abele, G. and Kropp, R. (1958) *Dtsch. Z. Ges. Gerichtl. Med.*, 48, pp. 68–72.

Baselt, R.C. (1995) In Garriott, J.C. (ed.) *Medicolegal Aspects of Alcohol* (3rd edn), pp. 65–83. Tuscon: Lawyers & Judges Publishing Co.

Bogusz, M., Pach, J. and Stasko, W. (1977) "Comparative Studies on the Rate of Ethanol Elimination in Acute Poisoning and In Controlled Conditions", *J. Forensic Sci.*, 22, pp. 446–451.

Bond, A., Silveira, J.C. and Lader, M. (1991) *Hum. Psychopharm.*, 6, pp. 219–228.

Bond, A., Silveira, J.C. and Lader, M. (1992) *Clin. Pharmacol.*, 42, pp. 495–498.

Bureau of Justice Statistics, Alcohol and Crime (1998).

Centers for Disease Control (1989) *Morb. Mortal. Wkly Rep.*, 38, pp. 800–803.

Clothier, J., Kelly, J.T. and Reed, K., *et al.* (1985) *Alcohol*, 2, pp. 443–445.

Dubowski, K.M. (1976) *Alcohol Tech. Rep.*, 5, pp. 55–63.

Dubowski, K.M. (1985) "Absorption, Distribution and Elimination of Alcohol: Highway Safety Aspects", *J. Stud. Alc. Supp.*, 10, pp. 98–108.

Dubowski, K.M. (1997) *Stages of Acute Alcoholic Influence/Intoxication.* Oklahoma City: The University of Oklahoma College of Medicine.

ElSohly, S.J. Salamonei (1999) *J. Anal. Toxicol.*, 23, pp. 141–146.

Forney, R.B., and Hughes, F.W. (1968) In *Combined Effects of Alcohol and Other Drugs,* pp. 82–83. Springfield: Charles C. Thomas.

Frinter, M.P. and Rubinson, L. (1993) *J. Sex Ed. Ther.*, 19, pp. 373–384.

Garriott, J.C. (1993) *Am. J. Forens. Med. Pathol.*, 14, pp. 234–237.

Garriott J.C. (1995) In Garriott, J.C. (ed.) *Medicolegal Aspects of Alcohol* (3rd edn), pp. 35–63. Tucson: Lawyers and Judges Publishing Company.

Garriott, J.C., DiMaio, V.J.M and Rodriguez, R. (1986) *J. For. Sci.*, 31, pp. 1274–1282.

George Mason University (1997) *College Alcohol Survey* George Mason University, Fairfax, VA.

Goldstein, D.B. (1983) In *Pharmacology of Alcohol,* p. 80. New York: Oxford University Press.

Griffin, J.P. and D'Arcy, P.F. (1975) In *A Manual of Adverse Drug Interactions,* p. 57. Bristol, England: John Wright & Sons.

Hammond, K.B., Rumack, B.H. and Rodgerson, D.O. (1973) *JAMA,* 226, pp. 63–64.

Hansten, P.D. (1976) In *Drug Interactions* (3rd edn), pp. 156–161. Philadelphia: Lea & Febiger.

Heishman, S.J., Stitzer, M.L. and Bigelow, G.E. (1989) *Pharm. Biochem. Behavior*, 31, pp. 649–655.

Herbich, J. and Prokop, L. (1963) *Wien. Klin. Wchnschr.*, 75, pp. 421–427.

Kalant, H. (1971) In Kissin, B. and Begleiter, H. (eds) *The Biology of Alcoholism* 1, pp. 1–62. New York: Plenum Press.

Kerr, J.S. Fairweather, D.B., Mahendran, R. and Hindmarch, I. (1992) *Int. Clin. Psychopharmacol.*, 7, pp. 101–108.

Krauland, W., Wojahn, H. and Glass, F. (1967) In Schleyer, F. (ed.) *Forschungsergebnisse der gerichtlichen Medizin,* pp. 162–182. Lubeck, West Germany: Verlag Max Schmidt-Romhild.

McGinnis, J.M. and Foege, W.H. (1993) *JAMA*, 270 (18), pp. 2207–2212.

Mellanby, E. (1919) Medical Research Committee. Special Report Series, 31.

Morb. Mortal. Wkly Rep. (1989) 38 (46), pp. 800–803.

Moskowitz, H., Daily, J. and Henderson, R. (1977) *Proc. Seventh Int. Conf. on Alc. Drugs and Traffic Safety*, Melbourne.

NHTSA (1998) Annual Report File, *http://www.ars.nhtsa.dot.gov/www/cfm/wizard/frame.cfm?qryID=DRI2*

Payne, J.P., Hill, D.W. and Wood, D.G.L. (1968) *Nature*, 217, pp. 963–964

Schwar, T.G. (1979) In Cooper, W.E., Schwar, T.G. and Smith, L.S. (eds) *Alcohol Drugs and Road Traffic*. Capetown, South Africa: Juta & Co.

Shajani, N.K. and Dinn, H.M. (1985) *Can. Soc. Forensic Sci. J.*, 18, pp. 38–48.

Sutton, L.R. (1983) *J. Stud. Alc.*, 44, pp. 438–445.

Tottmar, S.O.C., Pettersson, H. and Kiessling, K.H. (1973) *Biochem. J.*, 135, pp. 557–586.

Wagner, J.G., Wilkinson, P.K. and Sedman, A.J., *et al.* (1976) *J. Pharm. Sci.*, 65, pp. 152–154.

Widmark, E.M.P. (1981) In Baselt, R.C. (ed.) *Principles and Applications of Medicolegal Alcohol Determination.* Davis, Calif.: Biomedical Publications.

Winek, C.L. and Murphy, K.L. (1984) *Forensic Sci. Int.*, 25, pp. 159–166.

CHAPTER 4

ROHYPNOL® AND OTHER BENZODIAZEPINES

Michael Robertson
Lionel Raymon

HISTORY AND DISCOVERY OF BENZODIAZEPINES

Ever since the discovery of chlordiazepoxide (Librium®) in the early 1950s, benzodiazepines have been of utmost medical importance. Their high therapeutic index results in the safe management of insomnia and anxiety in ambulatory patients. Their use also includes more specialized indications appropriate for hospital setting, such as inducers of anesthesia, amnestic agents to help the patient forget about frightful pre-operative procedures, and the management of severe seizure disorders, such as life-threatening status epilepticus. Benzodiazepines have largely supplanted barbiturates in these indications. However, as has already been described with barbiturates, the potential for abuse of benzodiazepines casts a shadow on this class of therapeutic agents. Flunitrazepam is one of more than 30 marketed benzodiazepine medications worldwide. Introduced as an hypnotic in Europe, South America and Asia in the mid-1970s, flunitrazepam gained medical popularity due to its potency (ten times that of diazepam, on average (Stovner *et al.*, 1973)) and rapidly became a "drug of choice" prior to induction of anesthesia to decrease patient anxiety, and produce a dose-dependent amnesia while keeping an awake, compliant patient. Flunitrazepam has never been approved by FDA for the United States benzodiazepine market.

Generic name	Trade name
Alprazolam	Xanax®
Chlordiazepoxide	Librium®
Clonazepam	Klonopin®
Clorazepate	Tranxene®
Diazepam	Valium®
Estazolam	Prosom®
Flurazepam	Dalmane®
Lorazepam	Ativan®
Oxazepam	Serax®
Prazepam	Centrax®
Quazepam	Doral®
Temazepam	Restoril®
Triazolam	Halcion®

Table 4.1

Generic and trade names of commonly prescribed benzodiazepines.

RELEVANCE

The abuse potential of benzodiazepines in general, and flunitrazepam in particular, has been assessed and studied since their first appearance on drug markets. The abuse liability of a drug is characterized by its capacity to produce psychological or physiological dependence. Dependence to a drug is defined by the presence of a withdrawal syndrome upon abrupt cessation of drug intake. When a drug is associated with psychological dependence, withdrawal results in intense craving for the drug, a desire to seek and resume the treatment. When a drug is associated with physical dependence, withdrawal results in physical symptoms that can be clinically measured; these symptoms may represent a rebound of the initial disease, or are opposite to the pharmacological actions of the drug abused. Therapeutic doses of benzodiazepines do not have a high potential for abuse, compared with more classically abused drugs, such as cocaine, opiates, ethanol, or barbiturates (Woods and Winger, 1997). Nevertheless, pharmacological doses of these agents can show reinforcing properties in individuals with history of long-term sedative use, or in individuals who suffer from polydrug addiction. The report that opiate addicts in particular abuse benzodiazepines has led to the erroneous belief that benzodiazepines are addictive substances. The recent popularization of flunitrazepam by the media as a "date-rape drug", referred to as DFSA subsequently in the text (drug-facilitated sexual assault), added to the seizures of this benzodiazepine at United States borders, has confounded the problem.

The abuse liability of flunitrazepam and other benzodiazepines has been studied and has yielded conflicting results. Woods and Winger (1997) have reviewed the abuse liability of flunitrazepam and concluded that it offered no tangible difference compared with other benzodiazepines and that only supratherapeutic doses of the drug could show potential reinforcing effects. More importantly, their review of the literature failed to demonstrate any greater abuse liability for flunitrazepam when compared to other benzodiazepines such as diazepam, lorazepam, alprazolam or triazolam. The current belief that benzodiazepines differ from one another on kinetic parameters only and not on their way of interacting with the $GABA_A$ receptor can easily lead to those generalizations. Nevertheless, it is established that selected populations do abuse benzodiazepines in general and flunitrazepam in particular. Proposed reasons for this are to produce sedation and "slow down" the rush of stimulants; to sleep; to enhance the depressant effects of ethanol or cannabis and be more detached from the reality of everyday life; to ameliorate symptoms of withdrawal, particularly the stressful opiate withdrawal; or to possibly reduce stress, anxiety and depression associated with crash that follows a binge of psychostimulant like cocaine or amphetamines.

CLINICAL INDICATORS OF IMPAIRMENT

CNS DEPRESSANT

Individuals under the influence of a benzodiazepine may look like people under the influence of alcohol. Psychophysicals show divided attention impairment and poor coordination and balance. One's internal clock is generally slowed down. Eye indicators of a CNS depressant are that a horizontal nystagmus is generally present, even vertical at high doses. But pupil size is normal. The eyelids may be droopy, and the eyes watery. The individual may seem sluggish, drowsy, with thick slurred speech and flaccid muscle tone.

DIFFERENTIAL DIAGNOSIS

Other conditions may result in similar symptoms: extreme fatigue, head injury, hypotension, severe depression, diabetic hypoglycemia are some of the common clinical situations with similar presentation that have to be ruled out.

PHARMACOKINETICS OF FLUNITRAZEPAM

CLASSIFICATION OF BENZODIAZEPINES

Benzodiazepines can be classified as diazepam-like, oxazepam-like (3-OH-benzodiazepines), flunitrazepam-like (7-nitrobenzodiazepines) and alprazolam-like (triazolobenzodiazepines).

Flunitrazepam is a member of the 7-nitrobenzodiazepine class (Figure 4.1). In addition to a nitro group on position 7, it also has a fluorine on the 2´ position of the phenol ring. These chemical characteristics have generally resulted in an increase in the pharmacological potency of the drug, particularly of its hypnotic properties.

CHEMISTRY

Flunitrazepam has a molecular weight of 313.3, a pKa of 1.82 and its solubility in water is 6.0 µg/mL at pH 7.4 and 37°C (Boxenbaum et al., 1978).

PHYSICOCHEMICAL DETERMINANTS OF FLUNITRAZEPAM KINETICS

Absorption of a drug is defined as the processes allowing the drug to reach systemic administration, thereby having relevance in extravascular administration only. A major determinant of absorption is the lipid/water solubility of the

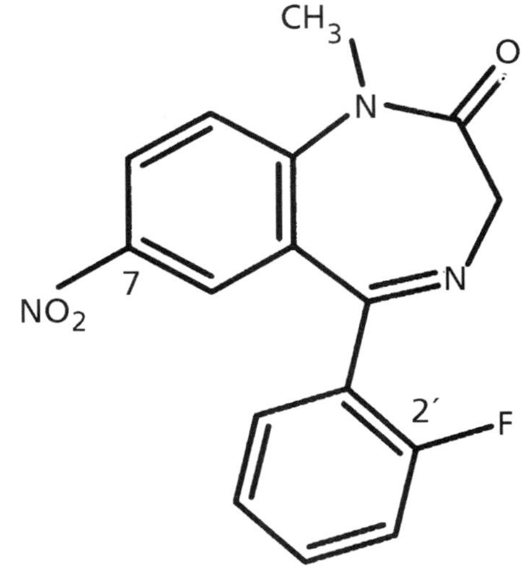

Figure 4.1
Structure of flunitrazepam.

drug. Whereas lipid solubility is required for flunitrazepam to leave the blood-stream, distribute and cross the blood–brain barrier, water solubility is needed for transport of the molecules across the various body compartments, hence either extremes are not good for absorption and reaching the central nervous system. Flunitrazepam has the required intermediate solubility to have a fast absorption after oral administration: the peak plasma concentration occurs within 30 min, and the half-life for absorption (the time required for 50% of the drug to reach systemic circulation) is classically between 10 and 30 min. Certainly, co-ingested drugs may dramatically enhance or delay this absorption process. For example, it would be expected that alcohol may enhance fluni-trazepam absorption by enhancing gastric emptying, whereas an opiate would delay such an absorption by delaying gastric emptying and slowing transit of the drug to the small intestine where most of its absorption occurs. It is important to mention that drugs with high abuse liability are generally associated with a rapid plasma rise, and a fast onset of activity. Flunitrazepam does not appear to have extremely favorable kinetics of absorption and distribution after oral adminis-tration to be associated with a significant "rush" from a sudden presence of the drug at key receptor sites. Other determinants of absorption involve the surface area and vascularization of the membrane which the drug crosses to reach the systemic circulation. Orally administered drugs are generally best absorbed from the small intestine, and flunitrazepam is no exception.

Heroin addicts have abused flunitrazepam using unconventional routes: they have ground the tablets so that they can inject the drug (thereby by-passing the absorption phase, allowing the drug to rapidly reach the brain). They have also snorted or smoked the drug. These are all routes of administration that have extremely fast absorption, much faster than ingestion, owing to the large surface area and rich vascularization of the alveolar surface of the lungs, or the large vascularization and thin mucosal membrane of the nose. Flunitrazepam may well show more addictive liability using these routes than after oral administration. There are no studies comparing the subjective feelings induced by flunitrazepam after smoking or intranasal administration and after oral intake of the drug.

DISTRIBUTION

Distribution is a function of lipid solubility. Chronic administration of drugs can result in accumulation of the parent compound and/or metabolites. There is generally a discrepancy between the clinical half-life (the duration of action) and the elimination half-life of the parent benzodiazepine. The elimination half-life of flunitrazepam is approximately one day (Boxenbaum *et al.*, 1978). Yet the clinical effects are much shorter, in the order of a few hours at the most. If a steady efficacy of the drug is required over time, chronic dosing will have to be implemented and will result in accumulation of the compound. This phenomenon is generally due to redistribution of the lipid soluble flunitrazepam to adipose tissue. The drug has no efficacy while in adipose tissue, but has not yet left the body by the time a second dose of flunitrazepam is given. Plasma levels are therefore expected to rise, and they will do so for four to five half-lives (therefore four to five days), after which a steady state will be reached. At this time, the adipose tissue will be saturated and elimination will be matched by administration.

Flunitrazepam distributes well as its volume of distribution of 3 L/kg (210 L in a healthy 150 lbs male) indicates. This distribution is classically bi-phasic, with a first half-life of 2–4 hrs and a second terminal half-life of 20 hrs (Boxenbaum *et al.*, 1978). The volume of distribution remains small for a central nervous system drug, and this is explained by a plasma protein binding of 95%, which keeps a large concentration of the drug in the bloodstream. When drugs have high plasma protein binding, any displacement from binding site can dramatically increase free concentrations of flunitrazepam and could cause toxicity. Any situation where plasma proteins are low, such as hypoalbuminemia due to liver dysfunctions, could also result in higher plasma concentrations of the drug and an exaggerated pharmacodynamic effect. Flunitrazepam shows a blood-to-plasma ratio of 0.65–0.80.

METABOLISM

Metabolism of flunitrazepam (Figure 4.2) yields one active metabolite, N-desmethylflunitrazepam, and several inactive metabolites: 7-amino- and 3-hydroxy-flunitrazepam. The 7-amino-metabolite can be further acetylated to 7-acetamido or hydroxylated to 3-hydroxy-7-aminoflunitrazepam. Additionally the 7-acetamido-metabolite can also be hydroxylated at position 3. These hydroxylated metabolites can be further conjugated by O-glucuronidation prior to renal excretion (Baselt and Cravey, 1995). The 7-amino-metabolite has been the main target of flunitrazepam forensic analysis due to its high concentrations in urine and its good gas chromatography properties. The presence of CYP450s in the gut and in the liver results in 10–15% first pass metabolism of the parent drug and a bioavailability of 85–90%.

Figure 4.2

Flunitrazepam metabolism.

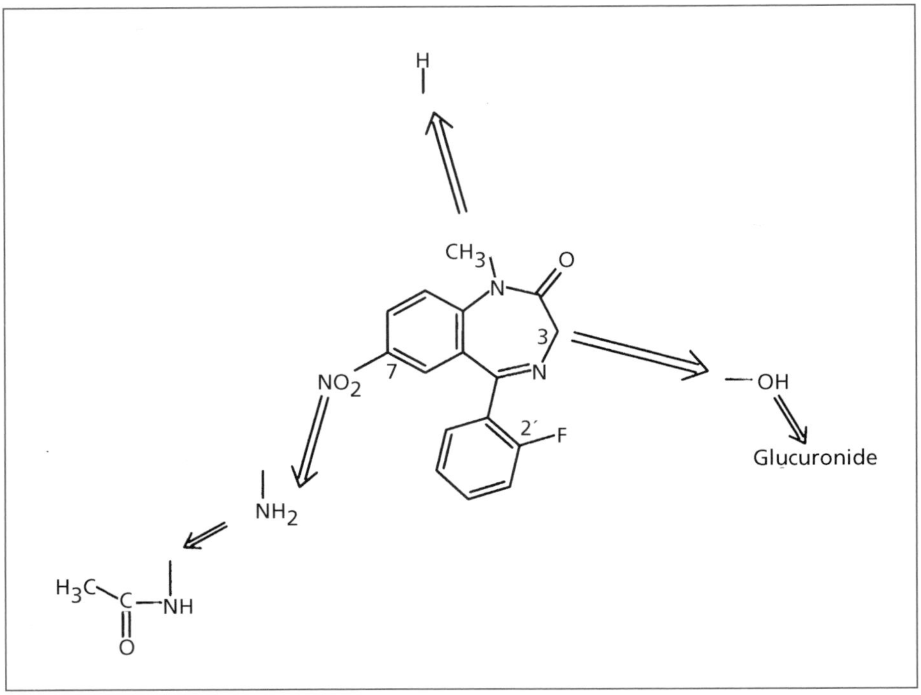

EXCRETION

Kinetic data are readily available from the *Drugs Compendium of Switzerland 1998* (1997). Flunitrazepam has an elimination half-life of 20–35 hrs. Its active metabolite N-desmethylflunitrazepam has a longer half-life of 23–33 hrs, whereas the inactive 7-amino-metabolite is cleared rapidly, with a half-life of 10–16 hrs. The plasma clearance of flunitrazepam in a normal, healthy male is of 1.7–2.4 mL/min/kg. Glucuronides can be secreted through the bile and enterohepatically recirculated, leading to a "double surge" phenomenon: the plasma concentration of a metabolite that is conjugated can show oscillations as the glucuronide is reabsorbed and recirculated.

PHARMACOKINETIC INTERACTIONS

Benzodiazepines are metabolized extensively by CYP450 isozymes. Whereas the 3-OH metabolites are likely the result of CYP2D6, the reduction of the nitro position at carbon 7 can be attributed to CYP3A4. The use of these enzymes can create a competitive inhibition for the metabolism of other co-administered drugs. Benzodiazepines have been shown to inhibit the metabolism of antipsychotics for example (Otani, 1992) and flunitrazepam in particular inhibited the metabolism of bromperidol (Suzuki *et al.*, 1998). Although the risk of pharmacological interactions is minor, it is a possibility that should not be omitted in the case of higher than therapeutic doses (abuse) or presence of multiple drugs competing for the same enzymatic pathway. Further, there is large interindividual variation in CYP3A4 activity. The metabolite pattern may also be affected by genotypic variations in CYP2D6, possibly shifting the metabolism in the direction of the reductive pathways and the N-dealkylation, potentially resulting in more active metabolite in poor metabolizers of the 3 position. This would also lead to less glucuronide formation, and possibly more 7-amino and acetamido metabolites. Such a scenario remains to be proven but could clearly explain the discrepancies in 7-amino metabolite concentrations in individuals and would complicate, if not prevent, any interpretation of metabolite concentrations with dose ingested or possible impairment from the parent or the active metabolite. Oxidative metabolism of flunitrazepam may also be significantly inhibited by cimetidine or fluvoxamine while smoking, and rifampin could increase metabolism. More relevant drug interactions are pharmacodynamic, with an additive CNS depressant effect to alcohol, anticholinergics (antipsychotics, antidepressants, antihistamines), other sedative/hypnotics, or β-blockers.

PHARMACODYNAMICS OF FLUNITRAZEPAM AND OTHER BENZODIAZEPINES

SITES OF ACTION: CNS AND PERIPHERY

GABA (γ-aminobutyric acid) is the most widely distributed inhibitory neurotransmitter in the brain of human and other vertebrates (Sivilotti and Nistri, 1991).

GABA owes its pharmacology to at least three receptor subtypes: $GABA_{A-C}$. $GABA_A$ is coupled to a chloride channel (Figure 4.3) and has the modulatory

Figure 4.3

*General structure of a
GABA$_A$ receptor.*

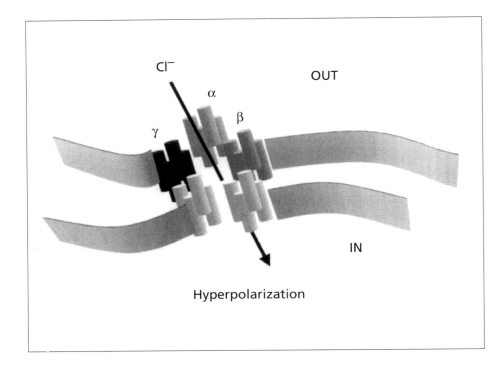

Hyperpolarization

sites for benzodiazepines. GABA$_B$ receptor is coupled to cationic channels (K$^+$, Ca^{2+}) via G-proteins and second messenger systems (it responds to baclofen), and GABA$_C$ are chloride channels with totally different pharmacology than GABA$_A$. A chloride channel allows negatively charged Cl$^-$ ions to enter the neurons and lower the resting membrane potential (hyperpolarization), resulting in a less excitable tissue and decreased neuronal function. The three GABA receptors have distinct structure, distinct function, different cellular localization and pharmacology. GABA$_A$ receptors are made of five sub-units and each sub-unit spans the neuronal membranes four times. These sub-units are chosen in mammals from a family of 6 α, 4 β, 3 γ, 1 δ, 1 ε, 1 π, 3 ρ and 1 θ (Alexander and Peters, 2000). There are even more isoforms if one considers the possible splice variants of some of the gene products. This complex stoichiometry can clearly give rise to several sub-types of GABA$_A$ receptors: the most abundant human CNS receptor type is the α1β2γ2 isoform. Classically, GABA$_A$ receptors have modulatory (allosteric) sites for the binding of benzodiazepines, barbiturates and neurosteroids.

The functional response of the channel to both GABA and to its modulators is dependent on the sub-unit composition of the receptor complex. α and β sub-units contribute to the GABA binding site whereas α and γ sub-units are necessary for benzodiazepine binding to the GABA$_A$ receptor. Whereas certain amino acid residues of the α and γ sub-units are critical for the binding of ben-

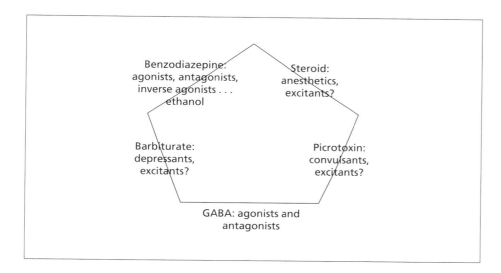

Figure 4.4
Modulatory sites associated with the GABA$_A$ receptor.

zodiazepines, the γ sub-unit type can also influence the efficacy (EC50) of the benzodiazepines (Hadingham *et al.*, 1995). Molecular studies have revealed interesting differences in the binding selectivity of benzodiazepines to subtypes of the GABA$_A$ receptor. These are the first insights in a possible different pharmacodynamic of benzodiazepines and will contradict the common notion that all benzodiazepines act in a similar manner and are only different through their respective pharmacokinetics. Pharmacological analysis has underlined the importance of phenylalanine and methionine at positions 77 and 130 on γ2 sub-units: high affinity binding of flunitrazepam and other benzodiazepines such as clonazepam and triazolam requires Met130, whereas high affinity binding of other ligands, such as flumazenil, depends more on Phe77 (Wingrove *et al.*, 1997). Certain aminoacid residues of the α subunits are just as critical for flunitrazepam binding, such as the histidine residue at position 102 (Duncalfe *et al.*, 1996). Allosteric regulation of flunitrazepam binding by other GABA ligands, such as barbiturates, can depend on the sub-unit composition of the receptor: for example α1γ2 receptor binding of flunitrazepam is inhibited by pentobarbital and etomidate, whereas α1β3γ3 binding is actually stimulated by the same compounds (Slany *et al.*, 1995). Even more disturbing is the report that flunitrazepam can behave as an inverse agonist (thereby no longer causing sedation but insomnia, not causing anxiolysis but anxiety) on α6β2γ2 receptors (Hauser *et al.*, 1997). This inverse agonist pharmacology could well explain the paradoxical effects of hyperactivity, insomnia, aggression, hallucinations and anxiety sometimes seen with flunitrazepam. Some GABA$_A$ receptors are actually insensitive to benzodiazepines: αβδ and αβε isoforms are not recognized by benzodiazepines but are still inhibited by bicuculline, a ligand of the chloride channel; and more recently, ρ-containing GABA receptors are found to be insensitive to both (Bormann, 2000). It is these subtle differences that could explain why certain benzodiazepines, such as flunitrazepam, may be more likely to be abused, or may cause a more powerful amnestic effect, a more potent anxiolysis, or a marked sedative effect. A better understanding of the sub-unit composition and brain region localization of the various $GABA_A$ subtypes will undoubtedly shed some light on pharmacodynamic differences between benzodiazepines.

ACUTE EFFECT

All benzodiazepines share to a certain extent the properties of potentiating GABA binding to its receptor and result in a certain degree of CNS depression. This is clinically exhibited as a sedative, anxiolytic and amnesic effect. High potency benzodiazepines, such as flunitrazepam, can be used as hypnotic, to induce anesthesia and have a more pronounced anterograde amnesia effect. It is this action that is sought in the potential use of flunitrazepam as a drug for DFSA. An anterograde amnesia refers to a lack of memorization by the individual from the time of administration of the drug (parenteral) or after adequate absorption of the drug (oral). There is no change in previously memorized events (i.e. no retrograde amnesia). Small therapeutic doses of flunitrazepam given intravenously or orally can clearly result in impaired memory: however, this effect is short lived and seems to decline rapidly within 30 min after the drug administration (Mattila and Larni, 1980). The relatively short time window of the effect may be a reason for the small number of drug-facilitated rapes associated with flunitrazepam. Enhancement of $GABA_A$ receptor function has been shown to disrupt the formation of memories in the hippocampal formation. The excitatory aminoacid transmitter glutamate and aspartate are involved in plastic changes in neurons of the cerebral structures known as long-term potentiations (LTPs) involving the NMDA receptor. Flunitrazepam suppressed LTP induction and this effect was prevented by pre-administration of the benzodiazepine receptor antagonist flumazenil (Seabrook et al., 1997).

Flunitrazepam also has significant vasodilatory properties and the relaxation of vascular smooth muscle with ensuing drop in blood pressure and barorecep-tor-mediated reflex increase in heart rate are quite specific to this drug. Diazepam is devoid of such effect (Mattila and Larni, 1980). Drugs are sometimes abused due to their vasodilatory properties: the draining of brain blood due to the pooling in dilated peripheral vessels is commonly understood as the reason for the abuse of nitrates ("poppers") and certain inhalants. It is possible that the cardiosuppressant effects of flunitrazepam may add to the feeling of euphoria that addicts report after the use of this drug. In a survey, liking scores for flunitrazepam by heroin addicts was higher than for other benzodiazepines, and a clinical study has suggested that 2 mg flunitrazepam produces pleasurable feelings in healthy patients, a property not shared with another benzodiazepine, triazolam (Farre *et al.*, 1996).

CHRONIC ADMINISTRATION

Benzodiazepines have a number of effects on various neurotransmitters when taken chronically. The role of GABA may actually only be a small part of the efficacy of these drugs. Like meprobamate and barbiturates, benzodiazepines have been shown to reduce the turnover of dopamine in the limbic system and in the cortex and of norepinephrine in the locus ceruleus, probably through GABA-mediated inhibition of catecholamine neuron cell bodies. The decrease in dopamine/norepinephrine may be related to the lack of serious abuse potential and to the decreased arousal of the CNS. Further, benzodiazepines also decrease the turnover of serotonin, likely cause of the anxiolytic effects of these drugs (Feldman *et al.*, 1997). The abuse liability of long-term treatment of benzodiazepines has been a concern. The risk of developing dependence using chronic therapeutic doses of these anxiolytics/sedatives occurs beyond three to six months of treatment and an abstinence syndrome is more likely the shorter the half-life of the drug administered (lorazepam more than diazepam or clorazepate, for example). Katz *et al.* (1991) have shown that drug-naïve subjects, in contrast to sedative abusers, did not experience significant reinforcing effects and may even have found drugs such as flurazepam and lorazepam aversive at moderate doses. Drug-naïve subjects could not discriminate between placebo and therapeutic doses of these benzodiazepines. Research has therefore shown that the recreational use of benzodiazepines is generally associated with subjects having histories of alcohol, methadone or drug abuse. And even under these conditions, these abusers chose barbiturates over benzodiazepines (Woods *et al.*, 1992).

Withdrawal to benzodiazepines is characterized by rebound anxiety or insomnia, sometimes associated with headaches, nausea, vomiting and muscle tremors. The symptoms are proportional to the duration of treatment and the abruptness of the cessation of use. Despite the lack of obvious dependence, benzodiazepines represent a potential of abuse: they are illegally traded as street drug, are low cost, and can give symptoms reminiscent of opiates or alcohol to abusers of those drugs.

ROHYPNOL® – THE DEBATE

Awareness of the use of drugs as "chemical tools" to facilitate sexual assault has been highly publicized in the recent years. Particular media attention has focused on the use of Rohypnol® as a DFSA drug. In virtue of its sedative and anterograde amnestic effects, flunitrazepam has been portrayed as a "drug of choice" in such criminal acts. Several studies have failed to confirm the widespread use of this benzodiazepine in drug-facilitated rape. Hindmarch and Brinkmann (1999) showed that only six urine specimens out of 1033 samples collected from alleged rape victims were positive for flunitrazepam. More importantly, alcohol and cannabinoids were present in close to 40% and 20% of these samples, respectively. Other benzodiazepines were present in more than 12% of the specimens analyzed. A similar study conducted by ElSohly and Salamone (1999) essentially yielded the same data, with again six samples positive for flunitrazepam out of 1179 specimens tested. Alcohol, followed by cannabinoids and other benzodiazepines, were found much more often. Flunitrazepam may not be commonly used in DFSA; however, significant abuse of the drug exists. Flunitrazepam has been reported as the most prevalent benzodiazepine confirmed in urine samples from DUI drivers in South Florida for several years and has been found in more than 10% of all DUI urine analyzed in Miami-Dade County in 1996 (Raymon et al., 1999). Rohypnol® is therefore more likely to be abused for its alcohol-like intoxicating effects by selected segments of the population, rather than used as a tool to commit DFSA. Further, the recent addition of blue dye in the manufacturing of flunitrazepam tablets should act as a deterrent against its surreptitious addition to beverages.

ANALYTICAL METHODS

ANALYTICAL METHODS IN CASES OF DFSA

The analysis of compounds of toxicological interest, particularly with forensic implications, requires the collection of well-preserved, appropriate specimens whose integrity can be well established. Although benzodiazepines are generally stable in whole blood and urine for many weeks, it is recommended to preserve the blood using a tube containing preservative (e.g. gray-top tube containing sodium fluoride and potassium oxalate) and store refrigerated until analysis. Note: preservatives will not compromise the testing for benzodiazepines. In cases where greater than 48 hours has passed, the collection of hair may also be considered; however hair should not be collected for at least seven days post-incident, to allow drug-incorporated hair to grow out of the scalp. This is discussed later in this chapter.

It is imperative to keep in mind that all DFSA cases have the potential of ending up in court. All specimens should therefore be handled with appropriate documentation and chain of custody, which may include such things as the date and time of collection, the donor, the collector, any persons handling the specimen up to and including the analyses, and how the specimen was stored prior to analysis.

The analysis of benzodiazepines and interpretation of analytical results are particularly problematic in DFSA cases due to the large number of potential drugs used within the family of the benzodiazepines. Worldwide there are in excess of 24 benzodiazepines available, many of which are not prescribed in any individual country.

A few of the most frequently encountered problems with the analysis and interpretation of benzodiazepines associated with DFSA are:

1. specimens collected too many hours after the incident;
2. the analysis of all the possible benzodiazepines which may have been ingested;
3. correct interpretation of the results, particularly negative results.

Benzodiazepines (in particular flunitrazepam and alprazolam) may only be present at low ng/mL concentrations in blood and urine. When specimens are not collected for many hours or even days following the alleged incident, which is common, the concentrations present in biological specimens may be so small that routine analyses of the specimens are inappropriate. Therefore a laboratory may not be able to detect these low concentrations and may report a "Not detected" result, which may be misleading if not interpreted correctly.

The analysis of benzodiazepines can be performed using many different analytical techniques. These include a presumptive screen using one or other form of commercial immunoassay (IA) analysis, with or without confirmation by high-performance liquid chromatography (HPLC) or gas-chromatography with mass selective detection (GC-MS).

IMMUNOASSAY PROCEDURES AND THEIR LIMITATIONS IN DFSA

Immunoassays are probably the most widely used screening technique used for the detection of benzodiazepines. Variations of this technology exist and include:

- Radioimmunoassay (RIA);
- Enzyme-multiplied immunoassay technique (EMIT);
- Fluorescence polarization immunoassay (FPIA);
- Cloned enzyme donor immunoassay (CEDIA);
- Kinetic interaction of microparticles in solution (KIMS);
- Enzyme-linked immunosorbent assay (ELISA); and
- Micro-Plate enzyme immunoassay.

All of these immunoassay technologies have similar capabilities in a practical sense, with the possible exception of Micro-Plate enzyme immunoassay which has recently been used to correctly detect very low ng/mL concentrations of flu-nitrazepam, a capability no other IA is currently able to do.

Although immunoassays are both rapid and inexpensive, they are often inappropriate in cases of drug-facilitated sexual assault. The reasons are as follows. The immunoassay technology in general uses a competitive binding process between an antibody and a drug-antigen. The antibody is generally most specific and sensitive to the drug used to generate the antibodies. In the case of benzodiazepines, this drug is typically oxazepam. As a result, immunoassays are primarily designed to detect oxazepam; however, they will detect most of the other benzodiazepines with various degrees of success. Given the wide range of benzodiazepines available, many of which do not produce oxazepam during metabolism, the range of successful detection is vast and includes some which may not be able to be detected even if present in psychoactive concentrations (e.g. lorazepam, alprazolam, triazolam). In addition there are many benzodiazepines, even oxazepam which, if present at low concentrations (which is often the case in DFSA) may not be detected by immunoassay in blood or urine. Although it has been demonstrated that pre-treatment of the specimens and de-conjugation may increase the concentration of unconjugated benzodiazepines and therefore improve the usability of immunoassays, the major limitations associated with sensitivity to some benzodiazepines remains and precludes this form of screen to be used as an exclusionary screen, i.e. a negative result does not mean no benzodiazepine is present. This is particularly noteworthy when hospitals may have excluded the presence of benzodiazepines during some routine toxicology, due to their typical access to only IA technology.

CHROMATOGRAPHIC PROCEDURES USED IN DFSA

There are many peer reviewed publications describing the procedures for the extraction and chromatographic analysis of benzodiazepines; therefore this section will not describe in detail the methods of analysis. Benzodiazepines are typically recovered from blood and urine by a buffered alkaline liquid/liquid extraction that may or may not be associated with an acid clean-up step. Extraction solvents vary from ether to chloroform to butylchloride. Solid phase extraction (SPE) has also been employed for benzodiazepines; however, this is a less frequently described form of extraction. The removal of the glucuronide conjugate from the benzodiazepine molecule may facilitate detection when present at low concentrations by increasing the concentration of free-unconjugated benzodiazepines. In general an enzymatic hydrolysis is preferable over acid hydrolysis as acid conditions may produce benzophenones. This hydrolysis step may be particularly warranted in cases of DFSA, when concentrations of benzodiazepines may only be small. Separation, detection, identification, and quantification may be made by gas chromatography with nitrogen-phosphorus detection (GC-NPD), electron capture detection (GC-ECD) or, by far the most generally accepted and widely used, gas chromatography mass-spectroscopy (GC-MS). The drawbacks of GC such as poor elution of the more polar benzodiazepines or thermal instability of some compounds may be overcome by the use of HPLC in combination with UV, photodiode array detector or mass spectrometer. HPLC-MS, although still relatively expensive, is highly specific, sensitive and avoids the above described GC-related drawbacks; however, any of these techniques, when used appropriately, are adequate for the identification and quantitation of benzodiazepines.

INTERPRETATION OF RESULTS IN DFSA

Immunoassay

A negative result does not imply the absence of "any" benzodiazepines and should never be relied upon to exclude the presence of benzodiazepines in either blood or urine. A positive result suggests the presumptive presence of a benzodiazepine and requires chromatographic confirmation by one or more of the confirmation techniques or equivalents described above.

Chromatography

A positive result identifies the presence of a benzodiazepine; however, in the absence of any other evidence or analytical result, also requires confirmation, preferably by a different technique from the one originally used. A negative result indicates none of the benzodiazepines looked for were present, i.e. a benzodiazepine not looked for may be present, or that the concentration of benzodiazepine present is below the limit of detection for that analysis.

Analysis of alternate specimens

In the absence of suitable blood or urine specimens, often due to a report not being made for many days or weeks following the alleged incident, alternate specimens or samples may still be available. These specimens are primarily hair. Benzodiazepines have been detected in hair following a single ingestion; however, this requires the aid of laboratories experienced at handling these samples and with the analytical equipment capable of detecting the small concentrations expected. Hair typically grows at a rate of approximately 1 cm per month and a few hundred milligrams of hair is typically all that is required for the analysis of benzodiazepines. In addition, blood-, urine- or vomit-stained clothing may also be of value in the investigation of DFSA.

In summary, it can be generally assumed that the analysis for benzodiazepines following DFSA will be an attempt to find low concentrations of one or more of a vast family of compounds. As a consequence, immunoassay results must be interpreted cautiously and by an experienced toxicologist. When interpreting results it is imperative that toxicologists understand the limitations of the technologies being used. The toxicologists must be aware of the range of benzodiazepines the analyses rule out and, based on the specimen type and time of collection, make some assessment of the likelihood of benzodiazepine ingestion. In addition, the investigator must be aware that a report which states "Benzodiazepines – not detected" must not be interpreted as no benzodiazepines were present. Clarification must be gained for the toxicologists with regard to which benzodiazepines were not detected, and which ones were not able to be analyzed for. In these cases, it is always wise to exclude the presence of any benzodiazepines by techniques more sensitive and selective than immunoassays such as HPLC or GC.

REFERENCES

Alexander, S.P.H. and Peters, J.A. (2000) In 2000 Receptor and Ion Channel Nomenclature Supplement (11th edn). *Trends Pharmacol. Sci.*, pp. 40–42.

Baselt, R.C. and Cravey, R.H. (eds) (1995) (4th edn). Chemical Toxicology Institute, Foster City, CA.

Bormann, J. (2000) *Trends Pharmacol. Sci.*, 21, pp. 16–18.

Boxenbaum, H.G., Posmanter, H.N., Macasieb, T., Geitner, K.A., Weinfeld, R.E., Moore, J.D., Darragh, A., O'Kelly, D.A., Weissman, L. and Kaplan, S.A. (1978) *J. Pharmacokin. Biopharm.*, 6, pp. 283–293.

Drugs Compendium of Switzerland 1998 (1997) (19th edn). Documed AG, Basel.

Duncalfe, L.L., Carpenter, M.R., Smillie, L.B., Martin, I.L. and Dunn, S.M. (1996) *J. Biolog. Chemistry*, 271 (16), pp. 9209–9214.

ElSohly, M.A. and Salamone, S.J. (1999) *J. Anal. Toxicol.*, 23, pp. 141–146.

Farre, M., Teran, M.T. and Cami, J. (1996) *Psychopharmacol.*, 125 (1), pp. 1–12.

Feldman, R.S., Meyer, J.S and Quenzer, L.F. (1997) *Principles of Neuropsychopharmacology*, pp. 698–700. Sunderland, Massachusetts: Sinauer Associates, Inc., Publishers.

Hadingham, K.L., Wafford, K.A., Thompson, S.A., Palmer, K.J. and Whiting, P.J. (1995) *Eur. J. Pharmacol.*, 291 (3), pp. 301–309.

Hauser, C.A., Wetzel, C.H., Berning, B., Gerner, F.M. and Rupprecht, R. (1997) *J. Biolog. Chemistry*, 272 (18), pp. 11723–11727.

Hindmarch, I. and Brinkmann, R. (1999) *Hum. Psychopharmacol. Clin. Exp.*, 14, pp. 225–231.

Katz, J.L., Winger, G.D. and Woods, J.H. (1991) In Rogers, R.J. and Cooper, S.J. (eds), pp. 317–341. New York: Wiley.

Mattila, M.A.K. and Larni, H.M. (1980) *Drugs*, 20, pp. 353–374.

Otani, K. (1992) *Hum. Psychopharm.*, 7, pp. 331–336.

Raymon, L.P., Steele, B.W. and Walls, H.C. (1999) *J. Anal. Toxicol.*, 23 (6), pp. 490–499.

Seabrook, G.R., Easter, A., Dawson, G.R. and Bowery, B.J. (1997) *Neuropharmacol.*, 36 (6), pp. 823–830.

Sivilotti, L. and Nistri, A. (1991) *Prog. Neurobiol.*, 36, pp. 35–92.

Slany, A., Zezula, J., Fuchs, K. and Sieghart, W. (1995) *Eur. J. Pharmacol.*, 291 (3), pp. 99–105.

Stovner, J., Endresen, R. and Osterud, A. (1973) *Acta Anaesth. Scand.*, 17 (3), pp. 163–169.

Suzuki, A., Otani, K., Mihara, K., Yasui, N., Kondo, T., Tokinaga, N., Furukori, H., Kaneko, S., Inoue, Y. and Hayashi, K. (1998) *Psychopharmacol.*, 135 (4), pp. 333–337.

Wingrove, P.B., Thompson, S.A., Wafford, K.A. and Whiting, P.J. (1997) *Molec. Pharmacol.*, 52 (5), pp. 874–881.

Woods, J.H. and Winger, G. (1997) *J. Clin. Psychopharmacol.*, 17 (3 Suppl 2), pp. 1S–57S.

Woods, J.H., Katz, J.L. and Winger, G.D. (1992) *Pharmacol. Rev.*, 44, pp. 151–347.

CHAPTER 5

GAMMA-HYDROXYBUTYRATE (GHB) AND RELATED PRODUCTS

Santo Davide Ferrara
Giampietro Frison
Luciano Tedeschi
Marc LeBeau

Although still considered a "new" drug of abuse, gamma-hydroxybutyrate (GHB) has been used clinically as an anesthetic and hypnotic agent since the early 1960s. It is a naturally occurring, endogenous compound found in most mammalian tissues, including the brain, where it is synthesized from the inhibitory neurotransmitter gamma-aminobutyric acid (GABA) (Roth and Giarman, 1969; Snead and Morley, 1981). GHB also appears to function itself as a neurotransmitter or neuromodulator (Vayer *et al.*, 1987).

Over the past decade, GHB and related products (i.e. gamma-butyrolactone (GBL), 1,4-butanediol (1,4-BD)) have been used repeatedly to commit drug-facilitated sexual assault (DFSA). Of all the drugs used to commit this crime, these chemicals are probably the most difficult to deal with in terms of analysis and interpretation because of the speed with which they leave the body.

This chapter will introduce the reader to GHB, and those chemicals that are converted into GHB after ingestion (GBL and 1,4-BD). It will address their structural relationships; synthesis; abuse; pharmacology; therapeutic applications; use in DFSA; and analytical methods to detect, identify, and interpret their presence in seized materials or biological specimens.

CHEMISTRY OF GHB AND RELATED PRODUCTS

GHB is a simple molecule composed of just four carbon, eight hydrogen, and three oxygen atoms. It has a straight chain structure with a hydroxyl group on one end and a carboxylic acid group on the other (Figure 5.1). As a chemical, GHB is usually supplied in the sodium salt form with a molecular weight of 126.1. The pure salt form is a white or off-white powder that is readily soluble in water. Table 5.1 lists chemical synonyms and street names for GHB.

GBL is an industrial solvent that may be purchased from chemical distributors or found in paint removers or engine degreasers. In contrast to GHB, GBL contains four carbon, six hydrogen, and two oxygen atoms. The difference between GHB and GBL is the loss of one molecule of water (H_2O) allowing for GBL to form a closed ring as indicated in Figure 5.1. With a molecular weight of 86.1, pure GBL is a colorless liquid with a mild caramel odor, a density of 1.12,

Compound	Chemical synonyms	Street names and trade names
γ-hydroxybutyrate (GHB)	γ-hydroxybutyric acid 4-hydroxybutyrate Sodium 4-hydroxybutyrate Sodium oxybate Sodium oxybutyrate	Easy Lay Fantasy G GBH G-Riffick Gamma 10 Gamma Hydrate Gamma OH Georgia Home Boy Gook Grievous Bodily Harm Liquid Ecstasy Liquid E Liquid G Liquid X Nature's Quaalude Organic Quaalude Salty Water Scoop Soap Somsanit Somatomac Somatomax PM Zonked
γ-butyrolactone (GBL)	Dihydro-2(3H)-furanone Butyrolactone 1,2-butanolide 1,4-butanolide γ-hydroxybutyric acid lactone 4-hydroxybutyric acid lactone 4-hydroxybutanoic acid lactone	Blue Nitro Firewater G3 Gamma G G.H. Revitalizer Insom-X Invigorate Longevity Remforce Renewtrient Revivarant Verve
1,4-butanediol (1,4-BD)	Butanediol Butane-1,4-diol Butylene glycol 1,4-butylene glycol 1,4-dihydroxybutane 1,4-tetramethylene glycol Tetramethylene 1,4-diol	Enliven Diol 14B Dormir FX GHRE Inner G NRG3 Revitalize Plus Serenity Soma SomatoPro Sucol B Thunder II Thunder Nectar Weight Belt Cleaner White Magic

Table 5.1

Chemical synonyms and street names for GHB, GBL and 1,4-BD.

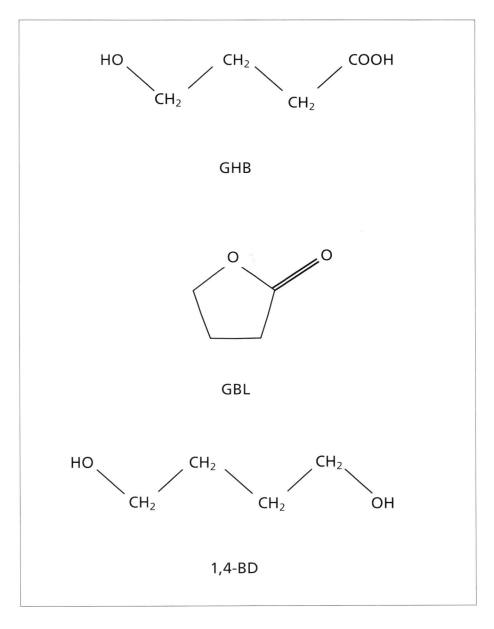

Figure 5.1
Structures of GHB, GBL, and 1,4-BD.

and a boiling point of 204°C. It is volatile with steam, miscible with water, and soluble in methanol, ethanol, acetone, and ether. GBL has a number of synonyms (Table 5.1), but the most common is dihydro-2(3H)-furanone.

1,4-BD is only slightly different in structure from GHB. It is composed of four carbon, ten hydrogen, and two oxygen atoms forming a straight chain structure with a hydroxyl group on each end. With a molecular weight of 90.1, a density of 1.02, and a boiling point of 228°C, 1,4-BD is a colorless, viscous liquid that is soluble in water, dimethyl sulfoxide, acetone, and ethanol. As indicated in Table 5.1, street names for 1,4-BD include FX and Thunder Nectar.

ABUSE OF GHB, GBL, AND 1,4-BD

Once the chemical structures are studied, it is easy to understand that GBL and 1,4-BD are rapidly converted into GHB after ingestion (Figure 5.2). Thus an individual who ingests these chemicals will experience pharmacological effects that mimic GHB ingestion (Irwin, 1996; Poldrugo and Snead, 1984; Rambourg-Schepens *et al.*, 1997; Roth and Giarman, 1966).

Figure 5.2

Metabolism of 1,4-butane-diol and γ-butyrolactone: A – alcohol dehydroge-nase; B – aldehyde dehy-drogenase; C – lactonase.

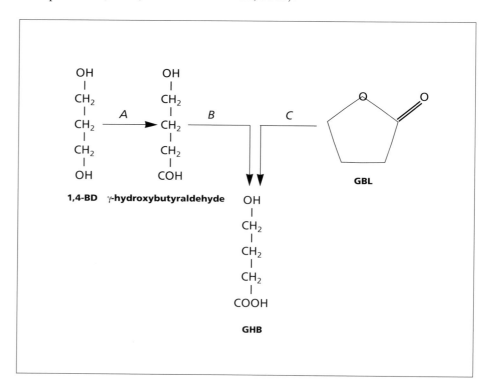

Abuse of GHB tends to occur in two groups. The first group includes body-builders who believe it to be a steroid alternative for building muscle mass. This belief is based on a 1977 report indicating that GHB causes an increased release in human growth hormone (Takahara *et al.*, 1977). It may also be used as a diet aid.

The other group of GHB-abusers are those who use it for the strong CNS (central nervous system) depressant effect that leads to euphoria, reduced inhi-bitions, and sedation. As with other CNS depressants (e.g. ethanol, benzodi-azepines, barbiturates, etc.), the effects are largely dependent upon the amount of chemical consumed. Thus an individual consuming GHB may experience any variety of effects ranging from wakefulness and euphoria to deep sleep or coma.

GHB, GBL, and 1,4-BD are nearly always abused orally. While they may be found as off-white or tan-colored powders in gelatin capsules, more often these chemicals are diluted in water where they can be disguised as "spring" water, sport drinks, or mouthwash. As law-enforcement agencies have caught on to these tricks, sellers and abusers of GHB have disguised it in other containers such as hair spray or eyedrop bottles.

These chemicals are usually consumed by the capful or teaspoon. A typical dose of one to five grams currently costs about $5 to $10 in the United States, but the street price may inflate with the increased state and federal penalties that have been attached to its sale and distribution.

There are a number of street names for GHB and its related products (Table 5.1). It is not surprising that many of these names are interchanged in reference to GHB or any of the GHB-like products.

GHB SYNTHESIS

To the abuser and seller, one of the attractive features of GHB is the ease with which it can be made from fairly common ingredients. The Internet is full of GHB recipes and even allows users to order these ingredients on-line. While some instructions are more elaborate than others, nearly all start with two main chemicals: GBL and sodium hydroxide. Simply mixing these two chemicals together will form GHB. Most recipes add additional purification steps; some even going as far as predicting a theoretical yield of GHB. Typically, the result is a fairly concentrated (50–80%) solution of GHB which is diluted to about 20% for use. Occasionally, the recipe will dry the GHB into a powdered, salt form for packing into gelatin capsules.

ENDOGENOUS GHB

One of the interesting yet challenging aspects of the use of GHB, GBL, or 1,4-BD in DFSA is that everyone has a small amount of natural GHB in their body. This is known as "endogenous GHB." It results, in part, from the normal metabolism of GABA in the brain (Figure 5.3) and from its production outside the brain. In the CNS, GABA is converted into succinic semialdehyde (SSA) via GABA aminotransferase. Most of the formed SSA is oxidized to succinic acid (SA) *via* a dehydrogenase where it enters the Krebs cycle and is converted to water and carbon dioxide. However, a small amount of the SSA is reduced to GHB via a reductase. The GHB is typically oxidized back to SSA via GHB ketoacid transhydrogenase where it too can be converted to SA and enter the Krebs cycle, but a small amount of GHB may instead undergo β-oxidation to 3,4-dihydroxybutyric acid and 3-keto-4-hydroxybutyric acid (Tunnicliff, 1997). Research has suggested that these metabolites of oxidized GHB may only occur at measurable levels when the ketoacid transhydrogenase pathway is blocked (Jakobs *et al.*, 1981).

Figure 5.3

GHB is naturally present in all mammalian tissues. It is a breakdown product of GABA and is removed from the body primarily by conversion to carbon dioxide and water.

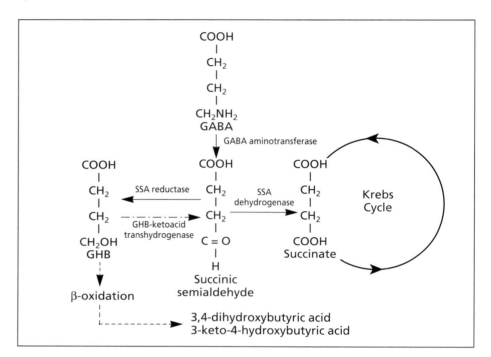

It is important to point out that there is evidence that suggests the presence of endogenous GHB precursors other than GABA. For example, GHB is present in extraneural sites (i.e. heart, lung, liver, skeletal muscle, kidney, and hair) that have either no or very little amounts of GABA present (Nelson *et al.*, 1981; Roth, 1970; Zachmann *et al.*, 1966; Ferrara *et al.*, 1995a). Research has shown that 1,4-BD, an endogenous product from fatty acids, may be a source of GHB in peripheral tissues (Barker *et al.*, 1985).

PHARMACOKINETICS

The first pharmacokinetic studies on GHB were carried out on animals in the 1970s. Following intravenous administration of high doses of GHB to dogs, evidence of nonlinear elimination kinetics was obtained, with apparent half-lives of 1–2 hr (Shumate and Snead, 1979; Van der Pol *et al.*, 1975). Both absorption and elimination were shown to be capacity-limited in rats (Arena and Fung,

1980; Lettieri and Fung, 1979). Of the same period is an anecdotal report of dose-dependent elimination kinetics with half-lives of 0.5–5 hr in man (Vree *et al.*, 1976).

Several clinical applications of GHB have been reported in the last two decades, especially in the treatment of sleep disorders (Mamelak *et al.*, 1986) and alcohol and opiate dependence (Gallimberti *et al.*, 1989, 1992, 1993). Due to the latter applications, the oral disposition kinetics of GHB have been studied in healthy volunteers (Palatini *et al.*, 1993) and in alcohol-dependent patients with either no or only mild hepatic dysfunction (Ferrara *et al.*, 1992). GHB pharmacokinetics have also been studied in patients with liver cirrhosis of increasing severity, as characterized by the absence or presence of ascites (Ferrara *et al.*, 1996).

In the study by Palatini *et al.* (1993), healthy male volunteers received single oral doses of GHB of 12.5, 25 and 50 mg/kg. Blood samples were collected at 0, 10, 15, 20, 30, 45 minutes and 1, 1.5, 2, 2.5, 3, 4 and 6 hours after dosing, and plasma GHB was determined as GBL by a GC-MS method (Ferrara *et al.*, 1993). Plasma protein binding of GHB and its possible dependence on concentration were also studied by equilibrium dialysis. In the study of Ferrara *et al.* (1992), alcohol-dependent subjects received single and repeated oral doses of GHB (25 mg/kg every 12 hours for 7 days) and some of them a single 50 mg/kg dose. Blood samples were collected as above, and urine samples before dosing and at 0 to 4, 4 to 8 and 8 to 12 hours after the 1st and 13th doses. GHB in both types of samples was determined by GC-MS (Ferrara *et al.*, 1993). The mean values of pharmacokinetic parameters proved to be very similar in both groups of patients and the results demonstrated that:

- GHB is rapidly absorbed and rapidly eliminated (peak plasma times, t_{max} = 20–45 minutes; terminal half-lives, $t_{1/2z}$ = 27 ± 5 sd minutes, after doses of 25 mg/kg);
- significant increases in t_{max} with little change in peak plasma concentration (C_{max}), decreases in oral clearance (CL_o) and increases in mean residence time (MRT) and $t_{1/2z}$ have all been found with increasing dosages;
- both oral absorption and elimination of GHB are capacity-limited processes;
- GHB does not bind to any significant extent to plasma proteins over the therapeutic concentration range;
- urinary recovery of unchanged GHB is negligible (<1% of dose);
- GBL, the lactonic form of GHB, cannot be detected in either plasma or urine, suggesting that lactonization does not occur *in vivo*;
- multiple-dose regimens of GHB result neither in accumulation nor in time-dependent modification of its pharmacokinetics.

Compared with healthy volunteers, cirrhotic patients showed double or even greater mean area under the curve (AUC) values. Accordingly, apparent oral clearance was markedly reduced in both non-ascitic and ascitic patients and the $t_{1/2}$ was significantly longer in non-ascitic patients than in control subjects (32 vs 22 min). A further significant prolongation of $t_{1/2}$, likely due to increased distribution volume, was observed in patients with ascites (56 min). Nonetheless, GHB plasma concentrations fell to either undetectable or negligible levels by the end of the usual dosing intervals (6–8 hr). Smaller changes were noted in absorption parameters. C_{max} increased only in non-ascitic patients, and t_{max} increased from 30 to 45 min in both cirrhotic groups. These data suggest that, although liver cirrhosis causes significant modifications of GHB disposition kinetics, the increase in $t_{1/2}$ is not such as to cause drug accumulation on repetitive dosing, and these modifications have no or little effect on GHB tolerability.

A recent study (Scharf *et al.*, 1998) evaluated the pharmacokinetics of GHB, given twice in one night to narcoleptic patients who had been taking GHB chronically. Results from this study confirm earlier reports showing the non-linear and, in some patients, capacity-limited pharmacokinetics of GHB.

GBL and 1,4-BD are rapidly metabolized to GHB following their ingestion (Figure 5.2). This occurs very rapidly and the conversion may be complete within ten minutes of ingestion of these chemicals. Once this has occurred, their existence in the body should be considered solely as GHB, thus their distribution and elimination will follow that of GHB (Irwin, 1996; Poldrugo and Snead, 1984; Rambourg-Schepens *et al.*, 1997; Roth and Giarman, 1966). Further, conversion of GBL and 1,4-BD occurs to such an extent (nearly 100%) that in most DFSA cases it is not expected to see them unchanged in a biological specimen except in extreme scenarios (i.e. rapid fatalities following ingestion of these drugs).

PHARMACODYNAMICS

Although the effects of GHB are not limited to the CNS but involve nearly every organ system, its primary effects are those of a CNS depressant and are the result of perturbations of several neurotransmitter systems. Administered GHB profoundly affects the cerebral dopaminergic system by mechanisms which still remain to be clarified. Some studies demonstrated increased dopamine concentrations in nerve terminals due to GHB inhibition of dopamine-releasing nerve cells (Bustos and Roth, 1972). GHB also seems to stimulate tyrosine hydroxylase, the enzyme catalyzing the first step in dopamine synthesis (Morgenroth *et al.*, 1976; Spano *et al.*, 1971). Other studies indicated that, although GHB initially inhibits dopamine release, a time-dependent stimulation of dopamine release ensues (Cheramy *et al.*, 1977). Another study indicated a dose-dependent effect of GHB, in which lower doses inhibit and higher doses stimulate the release of dopamine (Godbout *et al.*, 1995). GHB also has affinity for two receptor sites in the CNS, a GHB-specific receptor and the GABAB receptor. Experimental findings indicate that some of the GHB-induced alterations in dopaminergic activity are mediated by the GHB receptor (Godbout *et al.*, 1995). The cholinergic and serotoninergic systems also seem to be affected by GHB (Giarman and Schmidt, 1963; Waldmeier and Fehr, 1978). Lastly, within the CNS, GHB mediates sleep cycles, temperature regulation, cerebral glucose metabolism and blood flow, memory, and emotional control (Li *et al.*, 1998b).

Behavioural changes and neurologic effects are observed in subjects who have ingested GHB. Low doses of GHB (approximately 0.5–1.5 g) cause induction of a pleasant state of relaxation and tranquillity, placidity, sensuality, mild euphoria, a tendency to verbalize, emotional warmth, and pleasant drowsiness. Higher doses, like those probably involved in DFSA cases (1.5 g or more), can induce more obvious clinical manifestations and adverse effects ranging from relaxation and euphoria, confusion, dizziness and drowsiness, nausea and vomiting, agitation, nystagmus, loss of peripheral vision, hallucinations, short-term amnesia and somnolence, to uncontrollable shaking or seizures, combativeness, bradycardia, respiratory depression, apnea, and coma (Chin *et al.*, 1992; Chin *et al.*, 1998a; Dyer, 1991; Galloway *et al.*, 1997; Li *et al.*, 1998a; Li *et al.*, 1998b; Palatini *et al.*, 1993). Helrich *et al.* (1964) found that blood concentrations exceeding 260 µg/mL were associated with deep sleep, levels of 156–260 µg/mL with moderate sleep, 52–156 µg/mL with light sleep, and less than 52 µg/mL with wakefulness. In animal experiments, the median lethal dose is 5 to 15 times the coma-inducing dose (Vickers, 1969).

There have been some reported cases of possible physical dependence on GHB, with symptoms attributed to GHB withdrawal (Craig *et al.*, 2000; Galloway *et al.*, 1994). Additionally, there have been several fatalities resulting from GHB overdose, sometimes in combination with other drugs (CDC, 1997; Ferrara *et al.*, 1995b; FDA, 1997).

As mentioned earlier, since GBL and 1,4-BD are rapidly metabolized to GHB after oral ingestion, the effects of these drugs are analogous to the effects observed when GHB is ingested (Irwin, 1996; Poldrugo and Snead, 1984; Rambourg-Schepens *et al.*, 1997; Roth and Giarman, 1966).

THERAPEUTIC APPLICATIONS

GHB was first introduced into Europe in the 1960s as an intravenous general anesthetic agent that lacked analgesic properties. A short time later its use as such diminished due to reported side-effects of grand mal seizures and coma.

However, GHB is still employed as an anesthetic adjunct and hypnotic agent. It was also studied for its ability to suppress the symptoms of alcohol dependence (Addolorato *et al.*, 2000, Beghe and Carpanini, 2000; Poldrugo and Addolorato, 1999) and opiate-withdrawal syndrome (Gallimberti *et al.*, 1993; Gallimberti *et al.*, 2000). Finally, GHB has been used in the management of narcoleptic patients (Scharf *et al.*, 1998).

ADDITIVE EFFECTS WITH OTHER DRUGS

According to a large number of reported cases of GHB intoxication, DFSA, and driving under the influence, multisubstance abuse or administration in combination with GHB is a very common finding (Bismuth *et al.*, 1997; Chin *et al.*, 1992; Chin *et al.*, 1998; Couper and Logan, 2000; Elsohly and Salamone, 1999; Frommhold and Busby, 1998; Li *et al.*, 1998a; Li *et al.*, 1998b; Louagie *et al.*, 1997; Ross, 1995; Slaughter, 2000). Ethanol is the drug most commonly found in combination with GHB (Elsohly and Salamone, 1999) and is likely to be found in many DFSA cases. CNS depressants other than ethanol which can be mixed with GHB include benzodiazepines, opiates, barbiturates, and more specifically, in cases of sexual assault, short-acting benzodiazepines like triazolam, flunitrazepam, and lorazepam. GHB is almost tasteless in its pure form, but has a "salty" or "soapy" taste when it is not as pure. Further, it can easily be added in relatively large quantities to alcoholic beverages or mixed with other drugs. Co-administration of ethanol and other drugs of abuse may confound accurate assessment of symptoms produced by GHB administration alone. Since ethanol and many drugs act as CNS depressants they may synergistically increase the neurologic effects produced by GHB alone, resulting in a more severe adverse reaction and clinical picture. This should be carefully considered from both the laboratory and clinical points of view.

GHB AND DFSA

The strong CNS depressant effect of GHB has led to its use in a number of DFSA cases. Of all the drugs used to commit this crime, GHB and related products are probably one of the most favored by rapists, although statistics may never prove it.

Because of GHB's natural presence in the body, it complicates interpretation of its role in cases of suspected DFSA cases. As time passes after its ingestion, GHB's rapid elimination from the body results in only low levels remaining in the body. These levels often cannot readily be differentiated from those considered as natural or endogenous levels. As mentioned elsewhere, after ingestion, GHB may only be detected about eight hours in blood and about twelve hours in urine (Hoes *et al.*, 1980). Of course, as is often the case in DFSA, victims may not come forward until this time period has elapsed, thus preventing the detection of the drug if it was actually used.

Another factor that makes GHB, GBL, and 1,4-BD attractive to rapists is that they are readily available. Besides the fact that GHB is simple to make in one's kitchen, these drugs are easy to buy from the Internet, on the street, in numerous fitness facilities, and in dance clubs.

The strong sedative effect of GHB and its related products is unlike many other drugs that are used to commit DFSA. These drugs can cause the user to go from a completely alert state to unconsciousness in a matter of 10 to 15 minutes (Galloway *et al.*, 2000). Additionally, GHB may cause amnesia when the user is under its influence. Reportedly a GHB-assisted sleep lasts only 3–4 hr, after which the user awakes feeling unusually refreshed (Galloway *et al.*, 1997; Morgenthaler and Joy, 1995). This later effect is due to GHB's extremely short half-life and rapid clearance from the body.

A bystander who sees an individual under the influence of GHB is likely to assume the individual has consumed too much alcohol. This is another attractive characteristic of these drugs, as witnesses may claim the victim was intoxicated, which many juries may not be as sympathetic toward.

Yet another factor that favors rapists that use GHB is the fact that many forensic and clinical laboratories still do not have assays designed to detect its presence in blood or urine specimens. Thus this drug may often go undetected no matter how quickly the specimen is collected. While this appears to be improving with time, investigators must know the capabilities of the laboratory they are employing for the analytical testing in these cases.

Finally, due to the fact that GHB, GBL, and 1,4-BD have become such popular recreational drugs, the rapist may not need to slip the drug into the victim's drink in order to incapacitate her. Many victims voluntarily consume these products for the euphoric effect they provide at low doses.

DEATHS ATTRIBUTED TO GHB INGESTION

As of April 2000, the US Drug Enforcement Administration had documented 65 GHB-related deaths. Of these deaths, nearly 60% of the victims were in their 20s at the time of their deaths (*Microgram*, May 2000). These deaths may involve GHB alone or in combination with other drugs (CDC, 1997; Ferrara *et al.*, 1995b; FDA, 1997).

One of the most famous deaths attributed to GHB was that of 15-year-old Samantha Reid. While attending a suburban Detroit party in 1999, this high-school freshman lost consciousness and later died after drinking GHB-spiked soda. Three teenagers were convicted of involuntary manslaughter for slipping the fatal dose of GHB into Reid's soda. A fourth male was convicted of being an accessory to the crime for supplying the GHB to the young men. In her memory, the Hillary Farias and Samantha Reid Date-Rape Prohibition Act of 1999 was signed into law in early 2000 making GHB a federally controlled Schedule I substance in the United States.

ANALYTICAL METHODS

There are primarily two types of evidence that require testing for GHB in DFSA investigations. The first is biological specimens collected from the victim during the sexual assault examination. The other includes glasses, bottles, or other containers suspected of containing the drug in it. While some of the same types of analytical testing may be used on these different types of evidence, a different analytical approach will be required to adequately address these analyses.

SEIZED MATERIALS

Illicit samples may be analyzed by a variety of analytical techniques: color tests (Andera et al., 2000; Koppenhaver, 1997; Morris, 1999); GC-MS analysis with silylation (Johnson and Bussey); HPLC (Ciolino and Mesmer, 2000); or direct FTIR analysis (Backledge and Miller, 1991; Bommarito, 1993; Mesmer and Satzger, 1998; Walker, 1999).

With seized materials it is important to differentiate GHB, GBL, and 1,4-BD. In the United States, laws are currently written that have drastically different penalties for manufacturing, distributing, and possessing these different chemicals. Whatever the combination of analytical techniques used, the chemist should be certain that the combination is capable of identifying and distinguishing between GHB, GBL, and 1,4-BD.

BIOLOGICAL SAMPLES

Methods for GHB analysis in biological fluids have been proposed both to detect GHB as an endogenous substance and after its administration or intake. These applications have been suggested for serum, plasma, urine, cerebrospinal fluid (CSF), hair, and tissue analysis.

In many GHB methods, the procedure involves initial quantitative conversion of GHB to its lactonic form (GBL) at high temperatures and in acid conditions, and its subsequent liquid–liquid extraction and GC or GC/MS detection (Doherty et al., 1975; Ferrara et al., 1993; Ferrara et al., 1995a; Lettieri and Fung, 1978; Van der Pol et al., 1975). Alternatively, the species extracted from biological fluids is the original GHB, in conditions avoiding the incidental formation of GBL, which is then derivatized, usually to a bis-trimethyl-silylester, for efficient GC or GC-MS analysis, in the second case using electron impact or chemical ionization conditions (Couper and Logan, 2000; Ehrhardt *et al.*, 1988; Eli and Cattabeni, 1983; Elian, 2000; Gibson *et al.*, 1990; McCusker *et al.*, 1999).

A number of alternative analytical approaches have recently been reported. The first is applicable to serum (or plasma) analysis only, and includes acetonitrile deproteinization of serum, evaporation of the resulting supernatant to dryness, and GHB derivatization for GC/MS analysis (Louagie *et al.*, 1997). Another method is for detecting toxic, therapeutic and sub-therapeutic levels of GHB in plasma and urine samples by headspace solid-phase microextraction (SPME) and GC/MS positive ion chemical ionization (GC-PICI-MS) (Frison *et al.*, 2000). Still another reported method allows for headspace introduction of the analyte to a GC or GC/MS (LeBeau *et al.*, 2000d).

Most of these methods may be conveniently applied to quali-quantitative detection of GHB in cases associated with sexual assault. In addition, some overall analytical and pharmaco-toxicological aspects should be considered when dealing with such cases. First, whether GHB or pro-drugs GBL or 1,4-BD are presumed to be administered, GHB seems to be the analyte of choice to search for in biological fluids, due to *in vivo* conversion of the other two compounds to GHB (Doherty *et al.*, 1978; Fishbein and Bessman, 1966; Lettieri and Fung, 1978; Snead *et al.*, 1989). Second, due to the natural occurrence of GHB in fluids and tissues of mammals, working cut-offs should be considered when analyzing biological samples, in order to distinguish between endogenous levels and those coming from GHB ingestion (Frison *et al.*, 2000; McCusker *et al.*, 1999). Third, the well-known phenomenon of post-mortem GHB increase in blood and tissues due to its catabolism reduction as a result of the Krebs cycle decrease in anoxic tissues (Doherty *et al.*, 1978; Roth, 1970; Snead and Morley, 1981) should be recalled in cases of post-mortem specimen analysis (Fieler *et al.*, 1998; McCusker *et al.*, 1999). Lastly, although quite rare, the occurrence of the genetic disease 4-hydroxybutyric aciduria, in which an unusually large amount of succinic semialdehyde is diverted to GHB to the detriment of succinate, should be taken into consideration, particularly when urinary GHB analysis is to be carried out (Gibson *et al.*, 1990; Gibson *et al.*, 1998; Tunnicliff, 1997).

INTERPRETING GHB LEVELS IN BIOLOGICAL FLUIDS

There are a number of significant factors that need to be understood in order to properly interpret GHB levels in biological samples. For instance, it has been shown that endogenous levels of GHB in post-mortem blood can be influenced by the absence of sodium fluoride, as well as storage temperature of the specimen (Stevens and Coleman, 1999). These blood levels may be elevated to such a degree that apparent endogenous levels of GHB may overlap those reported to be lethal. This catabolism of GHB after death is a result of the Krebs cycle decrease in anoxic tissues (Doherty *et al.*, 1978; Roth, 1970; Snead and Morley, 1981). In a limited study, this effect was not observed in post-mortem urine specimens or in blood and urine specimens collected from living individuals (Stevens and Coleman, 1999).

Another study suggested that blood samples collected and stored in citrate buffer may artificially produce GHB (LeBeau *et al.*, 2000c). This study found that random blood specimens collected from sexual assault victims and stored in periods of 6 to 36 months contained an average endogenous GHB concentration of 8.7 µg/mL ± 3.1 µg/mL. The same authors report of a sexual assault case in which the measured differences between GHB in blood stored in a citrate buffered tube and a tube containing EDTA was 31 µg/mL and < 1 µg/mL, respectively.

It has been suggested here and by numerous other authors that there is a need to establish endogenous levels of GHB in biological fluids. This will allow toxicologists and investigators involved in DFSA cases to better evaluate the role that GHB may have played in the sexual assault.

Along these lines, most published data suggest that endogenous levels of GHB in urine exist at some concentration under 10 µg/mL (Fieler *et al.*, 1998; LeBeau, 1999; Robertson *et al.*, 1999; Stevens and Coleman, 1999). One report suggested urinary endogenous levels exist as high as 20 µg/mL (Eklund and Eriksson, 2000).

There have been a number of published reports on GHB concentrations in biological specimens following ingestion of GHB. In one study, a driver found asleep in his car had a urinary GHB concentration of 1975 µg/mL approximately two hours post-ingestion (Stevens and Baselt, 1994). Frommhold and Busby (1998) reported urine levels of 1085 µg/mL and 1041 µg/mL, respectively, in two impaired drivers. Still another case reported a comatose emergency room patient with levels of GHB of 141,000 µg/mL in urine and 101 µg/mL in serum hours after ingestion of alcohol and GHB (Dyer *et al.*, 1994). Couper and Logan (2000) described five cases of GHB intoxication with blood levels ranging between 3.2 and 221 µg/mL.

Another important factor to consider when interpreting GHB levels in biological fluids is whether the specimen came from an individual who has 4-hydroxybutyric aciduria, a rare genetic disease in which an unusually large amount of succinic semialdehyde is diverted to GHB. This usually leads to neurological abnormalities in the individual which include mild or moderate mental retardation, ataxia, convulsions, and speech disorders (Jakobs *et al.*, 1981). However, there have been reports of more severe neurologic symptoms (i.e. peripheral neuropathy, retinal damage, extrapyramidal signs) in patients suffering from 4-hydroxybutyric aciduria (Rahbeeni *et al.*, 1994).

A study by LeBeau *et al.* (2000d) found that intra-individual levels of endogenous GHB in urine may fluctuate rather dramatically over a one-week period. In their study, every urine void produced from four GHB-free subjects was collected and analyzed for the presence of endogenous GHB. The results found that the endogenous levels varied by a factor of about 10 within each subject, yet none of the specimens had levels that measured 7 μg/mL or higher.

Another issue surrounding endogenous GHB concentrations in urine specimens centers around the effect of long-term storage of specimens prior to analysis. It has been shown that while there were increases in endogenous GHB levels during extensive storage periods (up to six months) – even while stored at temperatures below freezing, the increases were rather mild and never reached a level that should be mistaken as "exogenous" (LeBeau *et al.*, 2000d).

GBL and 1,4-BD are rapidly metabolized into GHB, but are not excreted into the urine unchanged in appreciable amounts. However, there has been a report of the detection of GBL in a urine specimen (McCusker *et al.*, 1999). This observation is likely due to the pH of the urine in question. The pH of the matrix plays a significant role in the interconversion between GHB and GBL (Ciolino and Mesmer, 2000). At neutral and acidic pH levels, it should be expected that, with time, an equilibrium will be reached between GHB and GBL such that both may be present at measurable amounts. As the pH increases towards a more alkaline range, the equilibrium shifts in a dramatically rapid fashion to favor GHB. The pH range of biological specimens is normally in the range of 6.5–8.5 for urine and 7.2–7.6 for blood specimens. When interpreting findings of GBL in a biological specimen, one should remember that GBL's presence may only be a function of the pH-related interconversion from GHB and not necessarily an indication of GBL ingestion.

CONCLUSIONS

GHB and its related products are becoming increasingly popular recreational drugs. Their easy availability coupled with their strong sedative effects make them strong candidates for DFSA. Since both GBL and 1,4-BD are quickly metabolized to GHB, their pharmacological properties are, for all practical purposes, identical to GHB. All three drugs are rapidly eliminated from the body such that, on average, a laboratory will be able to discern between exogenous and endogenous levels of GHB only up to eight hours after ingestion in a blood specimen and up to 12 hours post-ingestion in a urine specimen.

REFERENCES

Addolorato, G., Caputo, F., Capristo, E., Stefanini, G.F. and Gasbarrini, G. (2000) *Alcohol*, 20, pp. 217–222.

Antera, K.M., Evans, H.K. and Wojcik, C.M. (2000) *J. Forensic Sci.*, 45, pp. 665–668.

Arena, C. and Fung, H.L. (1980). *J. Pharm. Sci.*, 69, pp. 356–358.

Backledge, R.D. and Miller, M.D. (1991) *Microgram*, 24, pp. 172–179.

Barker, S.A., Snead, O.C., Poldrugo, F., Liu, C.C., Fish, F.P. and Settine, R.L. (1985) *Biochem. Pharm.*, 34, pp. 1849–1852.

Beghe, F. and Carpanini, M.T. (2000) *Alcohol*, 20, pp. 223–225.

Bismuth, C., Dally, S. and Borron, S.W. (1997) *Clin. Toxicol.*, 35, pp. 595–598.

Bommarito, C. (1993) *JCLICA*, 3, pp. 10–12.

Bustos, G. and Roth, R.H. (1972) *Brit. J. Pharmacol.*, 44, pp. 817–820.

Center for Diseases Control (1997) *Morb. Mortal. Wkly Rep.*, 46, pp. 281–283

Cheramy, A., Nieoullon, A. and Glowinski, J. (1977) *J. Pharmacol. Exp. Ther.*, 203, pp. 283–293.

Chin, M.Y., Kreutzer, R.A. and Dyer, J.E. (1992) *West J. Med.*, 156, pp. 380–384.

Chin, R.L., Sporer, K.A., Cullison, B., Dyer, J.E. and Wu, T.D. (1998) *Ann. Emerg. Med.*, 31, pp. 716–722.

Ciolino, L. and Mesmer, M. (2000) Presented at the 52nd American Academy of Forensic Sciences Meeting, Reno, Nevada.

Couper, F.J. and Logan, B.K. (2000) *J. Anal. Toxicol.*, 24, pp. 1–7.

Craig, K., Gomez, H.F., McManus, J.L. and Bania, T.C. (2000) *J. Emerg. Med.*, 18, pp. 65–70.

Doherty, J.D., Snead, O.C. and Roth, R.H. (1975) *Anal. Biochem.*, 69, pp. 268–277.

Doherty, J.D., Hattox, S.E., Snead, O.C. and Roth, R.H. (1978) *J. Pharmacol. Exp. Ther.*, 207, pp. 130–139.

Dyer, J.E. (1991) *Am. J. Emerg. Med.*, 9, pp. 321–324.

Dyer, J.E., Isaacs, S.M., and Keller, K.H. (1994) *Vet. Hum. Tox.*, 36, p. 348.

Ehrhardt, J.D., Vayer, P. and Maitre, M. (1988) *Biomed. Environ. Mass Spectrom.*, 15, pp. 521–524.

Eklund, A. and Eriksson, M. (2000) Presented at the 38th Meeting of The International Association of Forensic Toxicologists, Helsinki, Finland.

Eli, M. and Cattabeni, F. (1983) *J. Neurochem.*, 41, pp. 524–530.

Elian, A.A. (2000) *Forensic Sci. Int.*, 109, pp. 183–187.

Elsohly, M.A. and Salamone, S.J. (1999) *J. Anal. Toxicol.*, 23, pp. 141–146.

Ferrara, S.D., Zotti, S., Tedeschi, L., Frison, G., Castagna, F., Gallimberti, L., Gessa, G.L. and Palatini, P. (1992) *Brit. J. Clin. Pharmacol.*, 34, pp. 231–235.

Ferrara, S.D., Tedeschi, L., Frison, G., Castagna, F., Gallimberti, L., Giorgetti, R., Gessa, G.L. and Palatini, P. (1993) *J. Pharm. Biomed. Anal.*, 11, pp. 483–487.

Ferrara, S.D., Tedeschi, L. and Frison, G. (1995a) In de Zeeuw, R.A., Al Hosani, I., Al Muntiri, S. and Maqbool, A. (eds) *Hair Analysis in Forensic Toxicology – Proceedings of the 1995 International Conference and Workshop for Hair Analysis in Forensic Toxicology,* pp. 225–260. Abu Dhabi, United Arab Emirates.

Ferrara, S.D., Tedeschi, L., Frison, G. and Rossi, A. (1995b) *J. Forensic Sci.*, 40, pp. 501–504.

Ferrara, S.D., Tedeschi, L., Frison, G., Orlando, R., Mazzo, M., Zordan, R., Padrini, R. and Palatini, P. (1996) *Eur. J. Clin. Pharmacol.*, 50, pp. 305–310.

Fieler, E.L., Coleman, D.E. and Baselt R.C. (1998) *Clin. Chem.*, 44, p. 692.

Fishbein, W. and Bessman, S.P. (1966) *J. Biol. Chem.*, 241, pp. 4842–4847.

Food and Drug Administration (1997) *FDA Consumer*, 31, p. 2.

Frison, G., Tedeschi, L., Maietti, S. and Ferrara, S.D. (2000) *Rapid Commun. Mass Spectrom.*, 14, pp. 2401–2407.

Frommhold, S. and Busby C. (1998) *DRE*, 10, pp. 2–4.

Gallimberti, L., Canton, G., Gentile, N., Ferri, M., Cibin, M., Ferrara, S.D., Fadda, F. and Gessa, G.L. (1989) *Lancet*, 2, pp. 787–789.

Gallimberti, L., Ferri, M., Ferrara, S.D., Fadda, F. and Gessa, G.L. (1992) *Alcohol. Clin. Exp. Res.*, 16, pp. 673–676.

Gallimberti, L., Cibin, M., Pagnin, P., Sabbion, R., Pani, P.P., Pirastu, R., Ferrara, S.D. and Gessa, G.L. (1993) *Neuropsychopharmacol.*, 9, pp. 77–81.

Gallimberti, L., Spella, M.R., Soncini, C.A. and Gessa, G.L. (2000) *Alcohol*, 20, pp. 257–262.

Galloway, G.P., Frederick, S.L. and Staggers, F.E. (1994) *Lancet*, 343, p. 57.

Galloway, G.P., Frederick, S.L., Staggers, F.E., Gonzales, M., Stalcup, S.A. and Smith, D.E. (1997) *Addiction*, 92, pp. 89–96.

Galloway, G.P., Frederick-Osborne, S.L., Seymour, R., Contini, S.E. and Smith, D.E. (2000) *Alcohol*, 20, pp. 263–269.

Giarman, N.J. and Schmidt, K.F. (1963) *Brit. J. Pharmacol.*, 20, pp. 563–568.

Gibson, K.M., Aramaki, S., Sweetman, L., Nyhan, W.L., De Vivo, D.C., Hodson, A.K. and Jakobs, C. (1990) *Biomed. Environ. Mass Spectrom.*, 19, pp. 89–93.

Gibson, K.M., Hoffmann, G.F., Hodson, A.K., Bottiglieri, T. and Jakobs, C. (1998) *Neuropediatrics*, 29, pp. 14–22.

Godbout, R., Jelenic, P., Labrie, C., Schmitt, M. and Bourguignon, J.J. (1995) *Brain Res.*, 673, pp. 157–160.

Helrich, M., McAslan, T.C., Skolnick, S. and Bessman, S.P. (1964) *Anesthesiology*, 25, pp. 771–775.

Hoes, M.J.A.J.M., Vree, T.B. and Guelen, P.J.M. (1980) *L'Encephale*, VI, pp. 93–99.

Irwin, R.D. (1996) *NIH Publication,* 96-3932.

Jakobs, C., Bajasch, M., Monch, E., Rating, D., Siemes, H. and Hanefeld, F. (1981) *Clinica Chimica Acta*, 111, pp. 169–178.

Johnson, R.E. and Bussey, J.L. *FDA Laboratory Information Bulletin*, 3532.

Koppenhaver, D.J. (1997) *Microgram*, 30, p. 130.

LeBeau, M.A. (1999) Presented at the 1999 Society of Forensic Toxicologists Meeting, Puerto Rico.

LeBeau, M.A., Huestis, M., and Darwin, D. (2000a) Presented at the 2000 Society of Forensic Toxicologists Meeting, Milwaukee, Wisconsin.

LeBeau, M.A., Miller, M., Levine, B. (2000b) Presented at the 2000 The International Association of Forensic Toxicologists Meeting, Helsinki, Finland.

LeBeau, M.A., Montgomery, M.A., Jufer, R.A. and Miller, M.L. (2000c) *J. Anal. Toxicol.*, 24, pp. 383–384.

LeBeau, M.A., Montgomery, M.A., Miller, M., and Burmeister, S.G. (2000d) *J. Anal. Toxicol.*, 24, pp. 421–428.

Lettieri, J.T. and Fung, H.L. (1978) *Biochem. Med.*, 20, pp. 70–80.

Lettieri, J.T. and Fung, H.L. (1979) *J. Pharmacol. Exp. Ther.*, 208, pp. 7–11.

Li, J., Stokes, S.A. and Woeckener, A. (1998a) *Ann. Emerg. Med.*, 31, pp. 723–728.

Li, J., Stokes, S.A. and Woeckener, A. (1998b) *Ann. Emerg. Med.*, 31, pp. 729–736.

Louagie, H.K., Verstraete, A.G., De Soete, C.J., Baetens, D.G. and Calle, P.A. (1997) *J. Toxicol. Clin. Toxicol.*, 35, pp. 591–594.

Mamelak, M., Scharf, M.B. and Woods, M. (1986) *Sleep*, 9, pp. 285–289.

McCusker, R.R., Paget-Wilkes, H., Chronister, C.W., Goldberger, B.A. and ElSohly, M.A. (1999) *J. Anal. Toxicol.*, 23, pp. 301–305.

Mesmer, M.Z. and Satzger, R.D. (1998) *J. Forensic Sci.*, 43, pp. 489–492.

Microgram (May 2000) 33, p. 83.

Morgenroth, V.H., Walters, J.R. and Roth, R.H. (1976) *Biochem. Pharmacol.*, 25, pp. 655–661.

Morgenthaler, J. and Joy, D. (1995) *Better Sex Through Chemistry.* Petaluma, CA: CERI and Smart Publications.

Morris, J.A. (1999) *Microgram*, 32, pp. 215–221.

Nelson, T., Kaufman, E., Kline, F. and Sokoloff, L. (1981) *J. Neurochem.*, 37, pp. 1345–1348.

Palatini, P., Tedeschi, L., Frison, G., Padrini, R., Zordan, R., Orlando, R., Gallimberti, L., Gessa, G.L. and Ferrara, S.D. (1993) *Eur. J. Clin. Pharmacol.*, 45, pp. 353–356.

Poldrugo, F. and Addolorato, G. (1999) *Alcohol Alcoholism*, 34 (1), pp. 15–24.

Poldrugo, F. and Snead, O.C. (1984) *Neuropharmacol.*, 23, pp. 109–113.

Rahbeeni, Z., Ozand, P.T. and Rashed, M. (1994) *Brain Dev.*, 7 (Suppl), pp. 90–92.

Rambourg-Schepens, M.O., Buffet, M., Durak, C. and Mathieu-Nolf, M. (1997) *Vet. Hum. Tox.*, 39, pp. 234–235.

Rigamonti, A.E. and Muller, E.E. (2000) *Alcohol*, 20, pp. 293–304.

Robertson, M., MacMillan, B., Watson, R.L. and Middleberg, R.A. (1999) Presented at the 1999 Society of Forensic Toxicologists Meeting, Puerto Rico.

Ross, T.M. (1995) *J. Em. Nursing*, 21, pp. 374–376.

Roth, R.H. (1970) *Biochem. Pharm.*, 19, pp. 3013–3019.

Roth, R.H. and Giarman, N.J. (1966) *Biochem. Pharm.*, 15, pp. 1333–1348.

Roth, R.H. and Giarman, N.J. (1969) *Biochem. Pharm.*, 18, pp. 247–250.

Scharf, M.B., Lai, A.A., Branigan, B., Stover, R. and Berkowitz, D.B. (1998) *Sleep*, 21, pp. 507–514.

Shumate, J.S. and Snead O.C. (1979) *Res. Comm. Chem. Path. Pharmac.*, 25, pp. 241–256.

Slaughter, L. (2000) *J. Reprod. Med.*, 45, pp. 425–430.

Snead, O.C. and Morley, B.J. (1981) *Dev. Brain Res.*, 227, pp. 579–589.

Snead, O.C., Furner, R. and Liu, C.C. (1989) *Biochem. Pharmacol.*, 38, pp. 4375–4380.

Spano, P.F., Tagliamonte, A., Tagliamonte, P. and Gessa, G.L. (1971) *J. Neurochem.*, 18, pp. 1831–1836.

Stevens, B. and Baselt, R. (1994) *J. Anal. Toxicol.*, 18, pp. 357–358.

Stevens, B.G. and Coleman, D.E. (1999) *J. Forensic Sci.*, 44, p. 231.

Takahara, J., Yunoki, S., Yakushiji, W., Yamauchi, J. and Yamane, Y. (1977) *J. Clin. Endocrinol. Metab.*, 44, pp. 1014–1017.

Tunnicliff, G. (1997) *Clin. Toxicol.*, 35, pp. 581–590.

Van der Pol, W., van der Kleijn, E. and Lauw, M. (1975) *J. Pharmacokin. Biopharm.*, 3, pp. 99–113.

Vayer, P., Mandel, P. and Maitre, M. (1987) *Life Sciences*, 41, pp. 1547–1557.

Vickers, M.D. (1969) *Int. Anesthesiol. Clin.*, 7, pp. 75–89.

Vree, T.B., van der Kleijn, E. and Knop, H.J. (1976) *J. Chromatogr.*, 121, pp. 150–152.

Waldmeier, P.C. and Fehr, B. (1978) *Eur. J. Pharmacol.*, 49, pp. 177–184.

Walker, L. (1999) *JCLICA*, 9, pp. 17–18.

Zachmann, M., Tocci, P. and Nyhan, W.C. (1966) *J. Biol. Chem.*, 241, p. 1355.

CHAPTER 6

HALLUCINOGENS

Lionel Raymon
Michael Robertson

Hallucinogens have lain in the cradle of some of Earth's oldest civilizations. Plant preparations causing perceptual distortions, illusions, hallucinations or other alterations of thinking have been fundamentals of religious beliefs throughout the world, and are now in the midst of heightened controversy in Western societies (Dobkin de Rios, 1984). First called by Lewin *phantastica*, then by Osmond *psychedelics*, the French pharmacologists Delay and Deniker placed drugs such as mescaline, tetrahydrocannabinol and psilocybin in the class of *psychodysleptics* (Stafford, 1992). Hallucinogens are a class of heterogeneous agents, of natural sources, such as plants (cannabis, ibogaine, harmala alkaloids, peyotl, kawakawa, khat), mushrooms (psilocybine from Psilocybe or Stropharia), or of synthetic sources, such as designer drugs (amphetamine derivatives). Other drugs are "abandoned" pharmaceuticals, such as phencyclidine, or even results of structure-activity relationships based on natural compounds, such as LSD.

There are two main chemical categories: the indoleamine derivatives, including LSD, N,N-dimethylamine (DMT), and psilocybin; the phenethylamines, including mescaline, dimethoxymethylamphetamine (DOM), methylenedioxyamphetamine (MDA) and methylenedioxymethamphetamine (MDMA) (Lister *et al.*, 1992; Nichols *et al.*, 1991).

PREVALENCE

While cannabis remains the most widely used drug worldwide, other hallucinogens have poorly defined prevalence. The use of hallucinogens was highly publicized in the 1960s and 1970s. After a short decade of waning, their popularity was again on the rise, and by the early 1990s, between 13 and 17 million individuals in the USA had used hallucinogens at least once (NIDA, 1991). The most recent data were released in August 2000 by the National Household Survey on Drug Abuse (NIDA, 1999). A total of 39.7% of persons aged 12 or older reported the use of an illicit drug in their lifetime (11.9% in the past year). Marijuana was used at least once by 34.6% of the individuals surveyed (11.9% in the past year). Of the individuals surveyed 11.3% have used hallucinogens in their lifetime (1.4% in the past year), and as expected, LSD is the most commonly reported hallucinogen (8.7% used it in their lifetime, 0.9% in the past year). Interestingly, the survey also reports that 24.1% (6.3% in the past year) have used any illicit drug other than marijuana, confirming polydrug use.

CLINICAL INDICATORS OF IMPAIRMENT

MARIJUANA

Marijuana causes complex behavioral changes. These include the classical lack of attention, divided attention impairment, and poor coordination and balance. Subjects under the influence also exhibit a slowed internal clock. An eye examination fails to reveal a nystagmus, and pupil size is generally normal or slightly dilated. The conjunctiva are red (bloodshot eyes), and classically eyelid and body tremors are prominent. The diminished inhibitions are a good reason for the use of cannabis as a tool in drug-facilitated sexual assault (DFSA).

HALLUCINOGENS

Hallucinogens cause . . . hallucinations! The user reports perceiving things differently from the way they are. Dysesthesias, the transposition of one sense for another, are common, such as seeing sounds or hearing colors. Mescaline from Peyote, psilocybin from mushrooms, LSD and MDMA cause an intoxicated subject to show lack of coordination, severe divided attention impairment, a poor perception of time and distance, and to have a poor balance. Pupils are generally dilated, but there should be no nystagmus. Body tremors and perspiration are possible.

PCP/KETAMINE

Although some effects are similar to that of CNS depressants, such as nystagmus, slurred speech, slowed responses, other effects are that of CNS stimulants: with elevated vital signs (blood pressure, heart rate) and agitated behavior; hallucinations are also typical. Intoxicated individuals exhibit divided attention impairment, "moon walking", and a slowed internal clock. An eye examination can reveal the presence of both horizontal and vertical nystagmus, but normal pupil size.

PHARMACOLOGY

MARIJUANA, ANANDAMIDE, AND CANNABINOID RECEPTORS

Cannabis: the plant, the alkaloids (THC)

The plant has been cultivated for thousands of years, for the production of hemp fiber and for its psychoactive properties. *Cannabis sativa* is the main species from which several varieties have arisen (*C. indica, C. sinensis, C. ruderalis,* etc.). The differences seem to be the result of plant adaptation to different climates, soils and modes of cultivation. A large herbaceous plant, it can reach up to 6 m in ideal conditions. The leaves are segmented and the segments are lanceolate and dentate. The resin, abundant in the bracts and leaflets of the female flowers (in the trichomes), is rich in psychoactive substances: delta-9-tetrahydrocannabinol (THC) is the main active constituent.

The receptors

Devane *et al.* (1988) first isolated a receptor for cannabinoids, and Matsuda *et al.* (1990) cloned it. The CB_1 receptor is a G-protein linked receptor, 473 amino acids long and with potential glycosylation sites. Although found in uterus, gonads, heart and spleen, it is mainly distributed in the central nervous system, particularly in the striatum, cerebellum and hippocampus (Herkenham, 1990). Whereas the striatum is involved with the initiation of movement and its fine control, the cerebellum allows the tuning of ongoing motor function. The inhibitory effect of CB_1 receptors in these structures can certainly offer basis to the impairing effects of marijuana in drivers, but also in victims of assault. The hippocampal formation is critical to the making and storing of short-term and recent memories, further underlying the potential for the use of this drug as a tool to commit DFSA. The notable absence of this receptor sub-type from medullary and pontine formations, where cardiovascular and respiratory centers are located, may underlay the absence of severe toxicity of cannabinoids (Glass *et al.*, 1997; Herkenham *et al.*, 1990).

The CB_2 receptor is also a G-protein linked receptor, which shares 44% homology with the aminoacid sequence of the CB_1 receptor. It is absent in the CNS. Peripherally, it is abundant on blood cells, notably B- and T-lymphocytes, monocytes and natural killer cells. Cannabinoids have been suspected of possessing immunosuppressant effects: the location of CB_2 receptors certainly offers a putative role for cannabinoids in the modulation of immune function (Pertwee, 1997). The binding of cannabinoids to their receptors results in the inhibition of the enzyme adenylate cyclase through an inhibitory G_i protein. The resulting decrease in cAMP may result in a decrease in phosphorylation by protein kinase A of ligand-gated ion channels. Cannabinoids have been shown to modulate potassium channels in the hippocampal formation and N-type calcium channels in the superior cervical ganglion. Devane *et al.* (1992) isolated an endogenous ligand, anandamide, a derivative of arachidonic acid. Anandamide has a high affinity for CB_1 receptors and a much lower affinity for the CB_2 receptors. The endogenous cannabinoid decreases neuronal activity. Anandamide is not classically packaged into vesicles as a neurotransmitter, but seems to exist as a phospholipid precursor in the cell membrane. A phosphodiesterase is involved in its release (Felder and Glass, 1998).

Medicinal use of marijuana

Several medicinal effects of cannabis have been described. Its use as an antiemetic during chemotherapy and its effect of increased hunger applied to wasting syndrome prevention in AIDS patients have been approved for many years. Other medical benefits include the ability to decrease intraocular pressure, therefore the potential therapeutic use in glaucoma, and some general muscle relaxant and anticonvulsant pharmacology (Nahas *et al.*, 1999). Unfortunately, these effects are undissociable from psychoactive properties of the preparation. The cloning of the receptor may allow the development of interesting molecules with possible medical applications in the near future.

Tolerance, dependence, and withdrawal

Tolerance develops, but also disappears rapidly to most of the effects of marijuana. Withdrawal symptoms are not generally seen in the addict population and may consist of restlessness, irritability, insomnia, and possible nausea and cramping. This syndrome is only seen in people who use marijuana on a daily basis and suddenly stop. There is no fear of withdrawal as an explanation for compulsive use (quite different from opiate abuse).

Pharmacokinetics

After inhalation of cannabis smoke, the bioavailability of THC approaches 18%. The absorption (process to reach systemic circulation) is extremely rapid, with a peak concentration C_{max} occurring at a t_{max} of 7 to 8 min. Concentrations around 10 ng/mL for an occasional user can reach 50 to 200 ng/mL for a daily abuser.

After oral administration, the bioavailability is significantly lower and the C_{max} occurs after 2–3 hr. After 20 mg THC, one can expect blood peak concentrations of 5 ng/mL (Cone and Huestis, 1993; Huestis *et al.*, 1992; Huestis *et al.*, 1995; Huestis *et al.*, 1996). Since THC is a lipid, its absorption can be greatly increased by the co-ingestion of fatty foods.

This high lipid solubility is also responsible for a rapid distribution to brain and redistribution to adipose tissues. The volume of distribution reflects this fact since it reaches values in excess of several hundreds of liters. The redistribution of the active constituents in and out of the adipose/brain tissues correlates with the long duration of action of cannabis and explains the long elimination half-life in excess of a week. Enterohepatic recirculation and reabsorption from the kidney tubule also participate in this slow pattern of excretion.

THC is rapidly metabolized to 8- and 11-hydroxy-THC. These are active metabolites. However, their short plasma half-lives and low concentrations suggest that they do not participate in the overall intoxication. The 8,11- and 8,9-dihydroxymetabolites are minor. Further oxidation to the carboxylic acid inactivates THC and yields the principal urinary metabolite, 11-nor-delta-9-tetrahydrocannabinoic acid (THCCOOH). THCCOOH appears within minutes of inhalation.

The slow elimination of cannabinoids is essentially biliary, with kidney, sweat, and breast milk being minor routes. Urine contains mainly acid metabolites and considerable amounts of conjugated hydroxy-metabolites. Urine THC can readily be detected in chronic users or in cases where a high dose was intaken.

Psychological effects

Acute effects of cannabis include disorders of thought processes, misperception of time, some disturbance of the senses, possible amnesia, and mood changes, which can range from euphoria to aggressiveness, with hallucinations and possible delirium (Perez-Reyes, 1981). These effects are variable and very much a function of the dose, the purity of the drug taken, the naïvety of the user, and the concomitant use of other drugs (alcohol, psychoactive substances).

Chronic users exhibit recent and short-term memory impairment, some anxiety, possibly to the extent of panic attacks with feelings of persecution. One of the most controversial effects produced by cannabis is an amotivational syndrome, where the abusers seem to have lost interest in normal sociological activities.

These behavioral toxicities are liable to impair drivers, and can of course be used against a potential victim to abuse.

Physiological effects

Cardiovascular effects consist of a marked tachycardia subsequent to hypotension, which can be postural. They may present a risk in patients suffering from pre-existing cardiovascular disease (Renault *et al.*, 1971).

The lung toxicity is similar to that of smoked tobacco, with inflammatory processes, chronic obstructive pulmonary disease, and tar deposits in the alveolar space, aggravating the consequences of the generally associated smoking. A notable carboxyhemoglobinemia is measured. The cancer potential for the buccopharyngeal mucosa and pulmonary tissue is probably linked to the high concentrations of carcinogens such as benzopyrenes in marijuana smoke, which are 70% more elevated than in tobacco smoke (Tashkin *et al.*, 1973).

Gastrointestinal disturbances are frequent at high doses, with vomiting, diarrhea and cramping. However, THC also slows down peristalsis (Senon, 1996). This effect can alter the absorption of other drugs.

Cannabis use has been associated with a significant decrease of sperm count and also with premature deliveries of smaller than normal babies (Nair *et al.*, 1994).

A number of studies have been published on the immunosuppressant effects of cannabis: the inhibition of interleukin-2 and interferon production inhibit the division and differentiation of immunocompetent cells when presented with antigens (Cabral and Vasquez, 1991; Nahas *et al.*, 1974). THC also inhibit macrophage function and may therefore interfere with tumor cell removal. Interestingly, an opposite effect is observed with respect to cytokines involved with inflammatory processes. THC administration to animals is associated with a greater incidence of bacterial and viral infections (Dewey, 1986).

Role of serotonin in hallucinations

Hallucinogens are commonly understood as $5HT_{2c}$, $5HT_{1a}$ and $5HT_{5-7}$ agonists. Indole hallucinogens share a similar structure with serotonin, and Wooley had already hypothesized of the role of serotonin in the mediation of the psychodysleptic effects of LSD in 1954. Hallucinogens have relatively high affinity for the serotonin $5HT_2$ receptor (Arnt and Hyttel, 1989; Glennon *et al.*, 1985). As early as 1971, scientists correlated the potency of psychodysleptics with their binding to this receptor: ritanserin, a $5HT_2$ receptor blocker could block the pharmacological effects of hallucinogens in animals. If a $5HT_2$ receptor is a common target for such a variety of drugs, their interaction with other subtypes of receptors defines the specific effects of all these drugs.

LSD

History reveals that ergot (*Claviceps purpurea*, a fungus that infects rye) and its alkaloids were used several thousands of years ago, particularly in China, but also in Central America by Precolombian civilizations, and in ancient Greece. A decoction of the infected grain was used to facilitate labor, thanks to the oxytocic actions of alkaloids such as ergonovine. Around the first millennium, in Europe, St Vitus' dance was associated with the intoxication following ingestion of bread made with flour from infected rye or barley. Epidemics were seen in times of famine. At the turn of the 20th century, Stoll isolated ergotamine, and in the mid-1930s Jacobs and Graig isolated lysergic acid as a

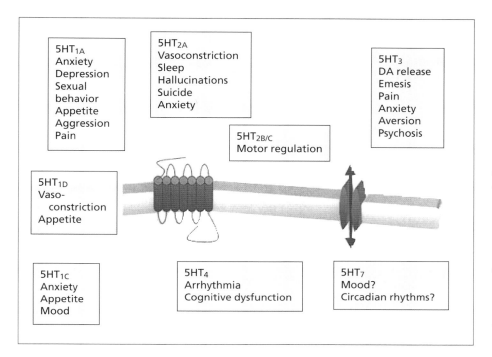

Figure 6.1

Serotonin receptors and their putative functions. $5HT_{1B}$ is a rat homologue of the human $5HT_{1D}$ receptor. There are two types of $5HT_{1D}$, α and β, depending on brain localization. $5HT_{1E}$ and $5HT_{1F}$ have no known functions yet; they are only found in brain, not in kidney, liver, spleen, heart, pancreas or testes where other sub-types may be found. $5HT_{5A}$ seems to be similar to $5HT_{1D}$ in function. $5HT_{5B}$ has no known function as of yet, but is found in adult neurons from CA_1 hippocampus and medial habenula, possibly involving it with memory and mood. Ergot alkaloid and LSD bind there. $5HT_6$ and $5HT_7$ have unknown function, but they are blocked by drugs like clozapine and amitriptyline. They increase cAMP in striatum, amygdala, cerebral cortex and olfactory tubercle for $5HT_6$ and in the hypothalamus, hippocampus, midbrain, cerebral cortex and olfactory bulb and tubercle for $5HT_7$.

precursor of all ergot alkaloids. The chemist Albert Hoffman, working for Sandoz, accidentally ingested the 25th of a series of analogs of LSD he had synthesized and suffered from hallucinations and delirium. He had just invented the most potent of all hallucinogens: LSD25. As little as 25 to 50 mg are efficacious. It is considered to be 3,000 times more potent than mescaline (Stoll, 1947).

After widespread use in the 1960s and 1970s, LSD was on the decline until the 1990s, where an interesting increase in seizures of the drug and use of it was seen not only in the USA but also in Europe. Commonly known as acid, it is sold as crystals or liquid. The liquid form is often deposited on a candy, a cube of sugar or a blotter ("fake tattoos").

Mostly orally ingested, LSD is rapidly absorbed from the gastrointestinal tract and is very highly liver metabolized. The first effects occur within 30–40 min post-ingestion. Most symptoms reflect an activation of the sympathomimetic system: mydriasis, tachycardia, sweating, tremors and hyperthermia, even hypertension are commonly seen. The "trip" starts with hallucinations and is accompanied by mood swings, rapidly cycling from ecstasy to anxiety, euphoria to apathy, "good" hallucinations to terrifying visions. Dysesthesias are common and body perception distortion allude to the depersonalizing effect of this drug. The powerful disturbance will last up to 12 hours and is generally followed by a prolonged fatigue of one to two days as the addict regains grasp of the outside world. Very little is known of its pharmacokinetics: ethics has prevented the

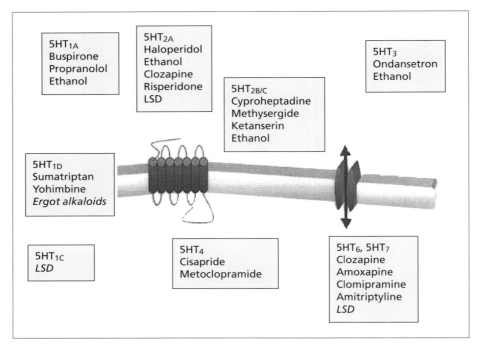

studying of this drug. Less than 1% of the LSD dose is found unchanged in the urine, about 1.2% in the demethylated form, and there are some hydroxy-metabolites that are excreted as glucuroconjugates (Lim *et al.*, 1988).

The detection of bufotenin and dimethyltryptamine in the urine of schizophrenia patients in the early 1960s suggested the possibility for humans to methylate serotonin and give rise to hallucinogenic chemicals (Karkkainen *et al.*, 1988). In 1969, indole amine N-methyl transferase was isolated from human brain and allowed scientists to speculate to the causes of schizophrenia and depression (Morgan and Mandell, 1969). In the mid-1980s, confirmation of the agonist activities of LSD to receptors 5HT$_{1A}$ and 5HT$_{2A}$ was finally provided (Glennon *et al.*, 1985; Spencer *et al.*, 1987). Interestingly, this came on the heels of discovering the potential relapse of flashbacks to LSD when a patient uses serotonin specific reuptake inhibitors such as fluoxetine (Strassman, 1992). Certainly, LSD also binds to other types of neurotransmitter receptors. For instance, LSD is a good agonist at dopamine receptors, in particular D$_1$ receptors, which agrees with the antipsychotic action of dopamine receptor blockers (Burt *et al.*, 1976).

There is no evidence of organ toxicity with LSD use. However, psychiatric complications are commonly reported. Particularly, users are prone to panic attacks, suicide attempts and can suffer homicidal tendencies (Strassman, 1995). The neurosis is often accompanied by psychotic behaviors which are reminiscent of schizophrenia. Flashbacks will occur, sometimes months after cessation of LSD intake. These symptoms are triggered by various situations, darkness, stress, alcohol or other CNS drugs (antidepressants, antihistamines). The perceptual changes and the intense arousal induced by LSD can be used against the victim's will as a tool to commit DFSA.

Dependence and withdrawal have not been readily observed for LSD. There is rapid cross-tolerance with mescaline and psilocybin, but none with ketamine, PCP or cannabis (Carroll, 1990).

MDMA AND MDA

Amphetamines are psychostimulants that are used therapeutically as anorexics, vasoconstrictors, in attention deficit hyperactivity disorders or narcolepsy. These are also street drugs abused by addicts and by athletes and students.

Amphetamine is an acronym for Alpha-Methyl PHenEThylAMINE, and the structure is the basis for many different derivatives, some of which are considered hallucinogens more than stimulants. A more appropriate terminology is that of *entactogens*, which means literally "generating contact within."

MDMA, 3,4-methylenedioxymethamphetamine, MDEA, 3,4-methylene-dioxyethylamphetamine, MDA, 3,4-methylenedioxyamphetamine, MBDB, methylbenzodioxazolylbutanamine, BDB, benzodioxazolylbutanamine, MMDA, 3-methoxy-4,5-methylenedioxyamphetamine, PMA, para-methoxyamphetamine, 2,5-DMA, dimethoxyamphetamine, TMA, 3,4,5-trimethoxyamphetamine, DOM, 2,5,-dimethoxy-4-methylamphetamine, DOB, 4-bromo-2,5-dimethoxyamphetamine, 2CB, 4-bromo-2,5-dimethoxyphenethylamine and DOET, 2,5-dimethoxy-4-ethylamphetamine are all derivatives of phenethylamines and are either considered entactogens, or hallucinogens. Chemically, trisubstitution at positions 3,4- and 5- or 2,4- and 5- results in potent hallucinogens, whereas 3,4- substitutions are more appropriately entactogen and only hallucinogens at high doses (Nichols, 1986).

MDMA is an oil, often referred to as Ecstasy, XTC, or Adam. MDMA is taken orally in doses of 50 to 150 mg and has a good absorption (20–60 min). C_{max} of 100 ng/mL occurs within 2 hr of a 50 mg intake in a normal adult male. Plasma peaks of a metabolite, MDA, are in the order of 20–30 ng/mL (Helmlin *et al.*, 1996; Verebey *et al.*, 1988). MDMA and MDA are also found in the urine, at high concentrations, peaking up to a day after ingestion and still measurable three days later. CYP2D6 is a major enzyme system that biotransforms MDMA type drugs (Tucker *et al.*, 1994). This is an enzyme which is associated with genotypic determination, and poor metabolizers represent close to 10% of Caucasians. Some of the hydroxylated metabolites produced by the action of this enzyme are neurotoxic (Verebey *et al.*, 1988).

MDMA has a strong affinity for $5HT_2$ (serotonin), M_1 (acetylcholine), $\alpha 1$

(norepinephrine) and H_1 (histamine) receptors. MDMA also blocks serotonin reuptake potently, and to a lesser extent, dopamine transport. MDMA also causes release of mobile pools of amine transmitters in the CNS, just like any amphetamine derivative (Battaglia *et al.*, 1988). One must remember that these are the acute effects of these drugs, and on a chronic basis, an actual *decrease* of serotonergic transmission is to be expected due to negative feedback from the high synaptic concentrations of serotonin, and possible plastic changes in the number of postsynaptic receptors and presynaptic transporters. In animals for instance, an 80% decrease in serotonin metabolites is measured only four hours after an injection of MDMA. The affinities for muscarinic M_1 and adrenergic α_1 receptors are the basis for autonomic disturbances, particularly for the cardiovascular effects of MDMA type of compounds. MDMA therefore causes some central effects of empathy, mood changes, euphoria, disinhibition (which can all be taken advantage of in the case of a potential MDMA-facilitated sexual assault), but also some significant unpleasant peripheral effects of tremors, diaphoresis, paresthesias, and tachycardias. At high doses and in overdoses, MDMA may cause a syndrome similar to a hypertensive crisis, with pronounced hyperthermia, arrhythmias, and possibly life-threatening convulsions. In cases of death associated with MDMA use, notable findings are disseminated intravascular coagulation and rhabdomyolysis (muscle breakdown with subsequent clogging of the renal glomerulus by myoglobin and acute renal failure). More typical findings of multiple drug overdoses are a pulmonary edema, and signs of liver dysfunction (Green *et al.*, 1995; Steele *et al.*, 1994 for reviews).

The neurotoxicity of MDMA compounds has been well established in animals, where a selective destruction of serotonergic nerve terminals has been observed within two weeks of chronic treatment. Upon cessation of the treatment, a complex adaptation to these effects was found, with some regeneration of serotonergic activity in some structures, sometimes an actual increased innervation, sometimes an actual decreased innervation, and in other areas, no regeneration at all. These findings have not been studied in human brains (although neurotoxicity has been described), but the deficits and changes in aminergic transmission in the human brain are likely causes to multiple neuropsychiatric disorders observed in chronic users (McCann *et al.*, 1994; McCann *et al.*, 1996; Ricaurte *et al.*, 1992).

MDEA, also known as Eve, and often combined with MDMA, has been much less studied: no data exist in humans, and certainly its pharmacokinetics are not established. However, due to the similarity in structure with MDMA, one would suspect MDEA to undergo the same metabolic pattern, with opening of the cycle by CYP2D6 and conjugation of the hydroxylated metabolites. In the urine, the principal metabolite is 4-hydroxy-3-methoxyethylamphetamine (HME), dihydroxyethylamphetamine (DHE) and MDA (Ensslin *et al.*, 1996). Similarly, the pharmacology of MDEA must be similar to that of MDMA, with rather alterations in emotions, empathy, more than a frank hallucinogenic effect (an "entactogen"). The arrhythmia potential is just as high for MDEA, and undesirable side-effects reported by subjects abusing the drug are those of drugs interfering with autonomic nervous system receptors: dry mouth, tachycardia, trismus, bruxism, etc. (Dowling *et al.*, 1987).

MDA is also known as the Love Pill. It is used as a drug, but is also an important metabolite of MDMA and MDEA. At high doses, MDA is more hallucinogenic than its two parent drugs. The pharmacology is similar to that of MDMA.

MBDB is the ethylated analog of MDMA. It is distributed as a pill. MBDB releases serotonin and has little effect on dopamine. According to Shulgin, 210 mg result in more relaxation than MDMA, but it would be less of a stimulant (Shulgin and Shulgin, 1992). MBDB has been shown neurotoxic to rat serotonin neurons, but to a lesser degree than MDMA.

BDB and MMDA have combined psychostimulant and hallucinogenic effects. Again, serotonin pharmacology seems to predominate in their effects.

PMA is much more hallucinogen than the other amphetamine derivatives: it is estimated that PMA is even five times more potent than mescaline. Used orally or intravenously, PMA is rapidly excreted in the urine as unchanged drug (15%) and hydroxylated metabolites (free and conjugated). It has the toxicity of amphetamines (stimulant and particularly cardiovascular toxicities), and appears more dangerous than MDA.

2,5-DMA appeared more recently in the late 1980s as gelcaps. It is a powerful hallucinogen, about eight times more so than mescaline. 2,5-DMA was shown to have high affinity for $5HT_2$ receptors.

Whereas TMA is a derivative of mescaline, DOM and DOB are powerful hallucinogens, 100- and 200-fold the potency of mescaline, respectively. DOB is sold as liquid impregnated paper, just like LSD. These phenethylamines have more psychoactivity than the MDMA counterparts. However, unlike LSD, these compounds retain some side-effects of cardiovascular toxicity and convulsions. More typical effects of psychodysleptics occur also, such as panic attacks, extreme anxiety, violent or aggressive behaviors. 2CB has often been found used together with MBDB. The intake of 10–20 mg seems to give effects similar to MDMA, but lasting up to eight hours. At high doses, addicts report similar effects to LSD. 2CB can also be inhaled for a faster absorption and stronger effects.

DOET is another hallucinogen with 100 times the potency of mescaline. Shulgin reports similar effects to LSD after ingestion of only 2–6 mg. (For a review of these substances, see Shulgin, 1981, and Shulgin and Shulgin, 1992.)

PCP, KETAMINE

Phencyclidine and its analog ketamine were developed as anesthetics. PCP was first synthesized in the 1950s but rapidly abandoned as an anesthetic since there were too many psychotic effects in patients. Known as "peace pills" in the 1960s, it was first used as a slightly stronger psychedelic than cannabis. However, in the 1980s, it was smoked and resulted in powerful toxicity. Ketamine is an analog of PCP and is still used medically and in veterinary medicine as an anesthetic. Its dissociative effects result in illegal use of the drug. PCP and ketamine are well known for their behavioral effects resembling schizophrenia and dissociative states. The impaired speech, attention, thought processes and memory make them ideal candidates for DFSA.

NMDA receptor blockers

Although part of the efficacy of PCP and ketamine resides in their interactions with opiate receptors (some μ agonist activity), most of the pharmacology of these two related compounds is the result of non-competitive blockade of the N-methyl-D-aspartate (NMDA) receptors. These are ion channels that are responsible for excitation of neuronal pathways throughout the brain. Endogenous ligands are excitatory amino-acids (glutamate, aspartate), and activation of the NMDA receptor results in depolarization of major neuronal pathways by calcium entry. Blockade of such a prevalent protein in the CNS is associated with the sensory perception blockade induced by ketamine and PCP. PCP and ketamine were initially thought to bind a novel sub-type of opiate receptor, the σ receptor. These are receptors that do not exactly share the distribution of NMDA binding site, and more importantly, these receptors are sensitive to antipsychotics whereas NMDA receptors are not. This would certainly suggest the participation of σ receptors in proprioceptive properties of ketamine and PCP. This fact also results in the contraindication to use neuroleptics in the treatment of PCP/ketamine addicts, since they would be expected to potentiate the action of the drugs.

Ketamine is still used owing to its ease of administration and its effects: a strong sedative, it is also associated with analgesia and amnesia. Certainly, these are characteristics that may make ketamine a "perfect" tool in DFSAs. Often, a patient under anesthesia with ketamine remains "awake" but is "dissociated" in the sense that although pain is occurring, the patient's brain does not integrate the feeling as being a noxious stimulus. Ketamine and PCP have the advantage to spare respiratory function and reflexes from the larynx/pharynx. However, ketamine use often results in vivid hallucinations, and nightmares in the patients, and it is these hallucinogenic effects that are sought by addicts. Serum concentrations of 0.15 μg/mL are sufficient to result in sedation/anesthesia and are the results of doses of 1–2 mg/kg given intravenously. Its half-life is short, generally a couple of hours, and it is metabolized to norketamine, then hydroxylated and conjugated, with 80% of the dose renally eliminated (Haas and Harper, 1992). It is important to know that for both ketamine and PCP, blood levels do not correlate with clinical findings and cannot guide clinical management.

The use of PCP is only seen illegally. The effects are subjective and depend on the individual's mood, the environment, etc. Interestingly, addicts have a 50% chance to experience a "good" effect. Whereas small doses of less than 10 mg can result in a state close to an alcohol intoxication, higher doses (up to 100 mg) cause agitation, extreme violence, including sexually oriented aggressiveness, which can result in aggressiveness and therefore augments the risk of DFSA. Psychotic symptoms, paranoid ideation with feelings of impending death are often reported by individuals abusing PCP. Convulsions and anesthesia with respiratory depression will lead to death in cases of overdose. Due to its over-stimulation of skeletal muscle contraction (catatonia), rhabdomyolysis is possible. The same effect is probably the basis for the "superhuman" strength reported by law enforcement officers attempting to apprehend an individual under the influence of PCP. Following an acute intoxication with PCP, a pronounced crash with depression and suicidal ideation is seen (Jerrard, 1990).

Other neurotransmitters involved

As is the case with many drugs, other receptor binding sites are known to participate in the pharmacology of ketamine and phencyclidine: acetylcholine (anti-cholinergic), dopamine (stimulates release and D_2 agonist), even possibly norepinephrine (especially in the periphery where hypertension and an increase in circulating levels of catecholamines are noted) (see Feldman *et al.*, 1997).

Tolerance, dependence and withdrawal

PCP/ketamine induce a weak psychological dependence in that the drugs do not particularly result in euphoria or pleasurable feelings. Tolerance seems to occur rapidly and disappears rapidly and no cross-tolerance with other hallucinogens is seen, due to the lack of serotonin effects (see Feldman *et al.*, 1997).

ANALYTICAL METHODS

The analysis for possible drugs used in DFSA and interpretation of analytical results are particularly problematic in DFSA cases. This is due to the large number of potential drugs used to drug victims, together with the typical delay between the alleged incident and the collection of specimens. Therefore the

Figure 6.3

Glutamate synapse. Excessive influx of calcium through NMDA receptors has been implicated in the neurotoxicity of a variety of insults to the CNS, including anoxia, hypoglycemia, seizures. Long-term changes in signaling in hippocampus and subiculum (hippocampal formation) are associated with memory consolidation. LTP (Long Term Potentiation) occurs in many pathways. NMDA receptors mediate LTP in hippocampus. Drugs can inhibit LTP, such as ethanol at low concentrations. More specifically, NMDA receptor is thought to mediate spatial learning and memory. PCP, ketamine, alcohol are examples of drugs that would potentially affect memory through such mechanisms.

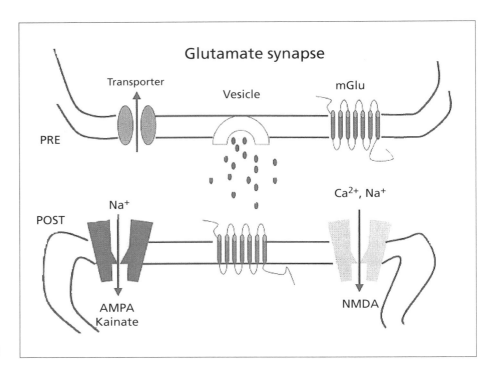

correct choice of specimens, the correct type of analyses and the careful interpretation of analytical findings are all imperative in DFSA cases. This section will investigate the analysis of the "hallucinogenic" compounds: tetrahydrocannabinol (THC); phencyclidine (PCP); ketamine; lysergic acid diethylamide (LSD); methylenedioxymethamphetamine (MDMA); methylenedioxyamphetamine (MDA); mescaline (Peyote); and psilocybin.

CHOICE OF SPECIMENS

Blood/serum-plasma/urine

Most "hallucinogenic" compounds are relatively stable in blood, serum-plasma and urine, with the exception of LSD which is sensitive to light and elevated temperatures. As a result, it is always wise, once collected, to store blood and serum-plasma specimens in a tube containing a preservative (e.g. gray-top tube containing sodium fluoride and potassium oxalate) and store refrigerated until analysis. Note: preservatives will generally not compromise the testing for "hallucinogenic" drugs. The collection of urine becomes more critical with compounds such as PCP and LSD which, due to their potency, are only present in very low concentration in blood/serum-plasma specimens. Urine specimens, however, generally contain higher concentrations of drug for a greater period of time than blood or serum-plasma. The timing of specimen collection is

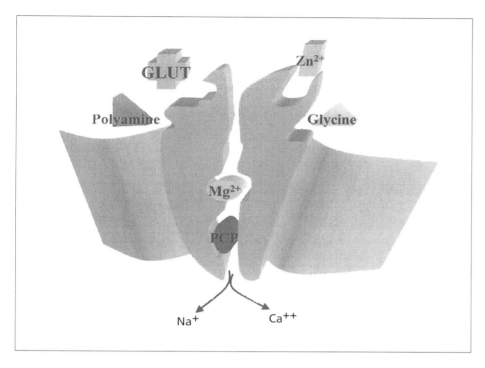

Figure 6.4
NMDA receptor. The NMDA receptor is a macromolecular complex analog to the $GABA_A$ receptor complex. The cation permeable channel is modulated by the binding of ligands at various sites. A glutamate and NMDA recognition site (where anticonvulsant drugs like felbamate work), a strychnine insensitive glycine site (where ethanol works for example), a site within the channel that is PCP sensitive, a voltage-dependent Mg^{2+} site and a modulatory site for Zn^{2+} all participate in the complex interactions of drugs and NMDA receptors.

therefore critical in DFSA cases. Every effort should be made to collect minimally blood and urine up to four days after the incident.

OTHER DRUGS POSSIBLY USED IN DATE-RAPE: CENTRALLY ACTING ANTICHOLINERGIC DRUGS

Centrally acting antimuscarinic drugs have mood-elevating effects that can be the cause for abuse. Trihexyphenidyl has been used for hallucinogenic properties sporadically, for example. The peripheral autonomic effects, mediated by blockade of the parasympathetic muscarinic receptors found on effector cells throughout the body, result in classical symptoms. The toxic psychosis can explain the potential role of these agents in drug-facilitated rapes.

SOURCE

A number of plants contain alkaloids that are of the atropine family: scopolamine, hyoscyamine for example. A complex herbal preparation from Colombia, Burundanga, is a soaring problem poised to invade Florida whereas the use of datura leaves or the ubiquitous jimson weed plants are classically associated with teenagers. Besides natural products, a number of drugs are antimuscarinic (benztropine, trihexyphenidyl) or have antimuscarinic side-effects (antihistamines, amantadine, antipsychotics, tricyclic antidepressants, quinidine, antimalarials, etc.).

PHARMACOLOGY

Blockade of acetylcholine muscarinic receptors results in an overactive sympathetic nervous system, with the following peripheral symptoms of mydriasis, tachycardia, dry mouth and blurred vision. Constipation and urinary retention are other, more chronic problems. Centrally, sedation and short-term memory blockade are obvious with all antimuscarinic drugs that cross the blood–brain barrier. At high doses, these alkaloids can cause hallucinations and result in a toxic psychosis, with paranoid ideation, disorientation, confusion, and excitement, and only occasionally, euphoria. Certainly, as alkaloids or herbal preparations, the bitter taste should be a deterrent, but with the advent of synthetic sources of pure drugs, the compounds could easily be part of larger, more "palatable" forms of administration. Patients who are therapeutically administered long-term treatments with antimuscarinic for Parkinson's disease or to treat the extrapyramidal symptoms associated with antipsychotic use show tolerance to the side-effects of benztropine-like medications. A physiological dependence may be present since withdrawal symptoms of muscle pain, gastrointestinal disturbances, anxiety, and rebound dyskinesias can be seen upon abrupt cessation of treatment.

ANALYTICAL TECHNIQUES

The analysis of hallucinogens can be performed using many different analytical techniques. The techniques used will be dictated by the drug in question and the availability of instrumentation. The most common types of analyses include a preliminary screen using thin layer chromatography (TLC) or a form of commercial immunoassay (IA) analysis. This may be followed by a confirmation analysis using high-performance liquid chromatography (HPLC) or gas-chromatography (GC) with or without mass selective detection.

Immunoassay procedures and their limitations in DFSA

Immunoassay technology is a frequently used screening technique for the detection of THC, PCP and LSD. The analysis of MDMA and MDA by IA is more difficult. Only a few commercial IA kits are capable of detecting MDMA/MDA with adequate sensitivity. Variations of commercial IA technology exist and include: radioimmunoassay (RIA), enzyme-multiplied immunoassay technique (EMIT), fluoresence polarization immunoassay (FPIA), cloned enzyme donor immunoassay (CEDIA), kinetic interaction of microparticles in solution

(KIMS) and enzyme-linked immunosorbent assay (ELISA). All of these immunoassay technologies have similar capabilities in a practical sense and all are typically designed to detect significant concentrations in urine, rather than any concentration in urine. As a result of the inadequate sensitivity of the immunoassays, they are often inappropriate in cases of DFSA.

It should be noted that ketamine, mescaline (Peyote) and psilocybin are unable to be detected by the common IA analyses.

Chromatographic procedures used in DFSA

There are many peer-reviewed publications describing the procedures for the extraction and chromatographic analysis of various hallucinogens in biological specimens; as a result this section will not describe in detail these methods of analysis, but rather summarize the more common types of analyses.

Most of the drugs described in this section are readily analyzable by gas chromatography (GC). For most hallucinogenic compounds, gas chromatography mass-spectrometry (GC-MS) remains the method of choice for detection, identification and quantitation. There are however a few exceptions. High-performance liquid chromatography (HPLC) is a more suitable method for the detection of psilocybin and psilocin. In addition, HPLC-MS or MS-MS appears more sensitive for the detection of LSD and the analysis of MDMA, and MDA may also be performed using LC-MS, with high sensitivity and specificity.

Interpretation of results in DFSA

Immunoassay

A negative result for THC, LSD, PCP and MDMA/MDA does not imply the absence of "any" of these drugs, but simply that not enough was present to produce a positive result, i.e. an immunoassay simply excludes the presence of a significant amount of that specific drug being present. As a result of the very low concentrations of drugs typically found in DFSA cases, IA screens should never be relied upon to exclude the presence of any of these drugs. A positive result suggests the presumptive presence of the specific drug or drug class analyzed, and requires some form of confirmation and identification, possibly by one or more of the GC/HPLC techniques described above.

Chromatography

A positive result identifies the presence of the specific hallucinogen analyzed for; however, in the absence of any other evidence or analytical result, it will also require confirmation. This may be done preferably by a different technique from the one originally used. A negative result indicates the absence of the compound of interest at the limit of detection for that technique. The "limit of detection" is simply that concentration of drug at which the instrument cannot detect below.

In summary, it can be generally assumed that the analysis for hallucinogens following DFSA will be an attempt to find low concentrations of one or more drugs. Due to these low concentrations, immunoassay results must be interpreted cautiously and by an experienced toxicologist. In these cases, it is always wise to exclude the presence of specific hallucinogens by techniques more sensitive and selective than immunoassays such as HPLC-MS or GC-MS.

During any interpretation it is imperative that the toxicologist understand the limitations of the technologies being used. The toxicologist must also be aware of the sensitivity of the analytical techniques being used. In addition, the investigator must be aware that a report which states "Drug X – not detected" does not imply nothing was present, but simply that the instrumentation used was not able to detect any drug. Clarification must be gained from the toxicologist with regard to the sensitivity of the instrumentation used in order to adequately rule out the presence of a drug.

REFERENCES

Arnt, J. and Hyttel, J. (1989) *Eur. J. Pharmacol.*, 161, pp. 45–51.

Battaglia, G., Brooks, B.P., Kulsakdinum, C. and De Souza, E.B. (1988) *Eur. J. Pharmacol.*, 149, pp. 159–163.

Burt, D.R., Creese, I. and Snyder, S.H. (1976) *Mol. Pharmacol.*, 12, pp. 800–812.

Cabral, G.A. and Vasquez, R. (1991) *Adv. Biosci.*, 80, pp. 93–105.

Carroll, M.E. (1990) In *PCP and Hallucinogens.* Minneapolis, Psychiatry Department, University of Minnesota: The Haworth Press.

Cone, E.J. and Huestis, M.A. (1993) *Therap. Drug Monitor.*, 15, pp. 527–532.

Devane, W.A., Dysarz, F.A., Johnson, M.R., Melvin, L.S. and Howlett, A.C. (1988) *Mol. Pharmacol.*, 34, pp. 605–613.

Devane, W.A., Hanus, L., Breuer, A., Pertwee, R.G., Stevenson, L.A., Griffin, G., Mandelbaum, A., Etinger, A. and Mechoulam, R. (1992) *Science*, 258, pp. 1946–1949.

Dewey, W.L. (1986) *Pharmacol. Rev.*, 38, pp. 151–178.

Dobkin de Rios, M. (1984) In *Hallucinogens: Cross-cultural Perspectives.* Albuquerque, NM: University of New Mexico Press.

Dowling, G.P., McDonnough, E.T. and Bost, R.O. (1987) *J. Am. Med. Assoc.*, 257, pp. 1615–1617.

Ensslin, H.K., Kovar, K.A. and Maurer, H.H. (1996) *J. Chromatog. B.*, 683, pp. 189–197.

Felder, C.C. and Glass, M. (1998) *Ann. Rev. Pharmacol. Toxicol.*, 38, pp. 179–200.

Feldman, R.S., Meyer, J.S and Quenzer, L.F. (1997) In *Principles of Neuropsychopharmacology,* pp. 750–765. Sunderland, Massachusetts: Sinauer Associates, Inc., Publishers.

Glass, M., Dragunow, M. and Faull, R.L.M. (1997) *Neurosci.*, 77, pp. 299–318.

Glennon, R.A., Titeler, M. and McKenney, J. (1985) *Life Sci.*, 35, pp. 2505–2511.

Green, A.R., Cross, A.J. and Goodwin, G.M. (1995) *Psychopharmacol.*, 119, pp. 247–260.

Haas, D.A. and Harper, D.G. (1992) *Anesth. Prog.*, 39, pp. 61–68.

Helmlin, H.J., Bracher, K., Bourquin, D., Vonlanthen, D., Brenneisen, R. and Styk, J. (1996) *J. Anal. Toxicol.*, 20, pp. 432–440.

Herkenham, M., Lynn, A.B., Little, M.D., Johnson, M.R., Melvin, L.S., de Costa, B.R. and Rice, K.C. (1990) *Proc. Nat. Acad. Sci. USA*, 87, pp. 1932–1936.

Huestis, M.A., Henningfield, J. and Cone, E.J. (1992) *J. Anal. Toxicol.*, 16, pp. 283–286.

Huestis, M.A., Mitchell, J.M. and Cone, E.J. (1995) *J. Anal. Toxicol.*, 19, pp. 443–449.

Huestis, M.A., Mitchell, J.M. and Cone, E.J. (1996) *J. Anal. Toxicol.*, 20, pp. 441–452.

Jerrard, D.A. (1990) *J. Emerg. Med.*, 8, pp. 733–741.

Karkkainen, J., Raisainen, M., Naukkarinen, H. Spoov, J. and Rimon, R. (1988) *Biol. Psych.*, 24, pp. 441–446.

Lim, H.K., Andrenyak, D., Francom, P., Jones, R.T. and Foltz, R.L. (1988) *Anal. Chem.*, 60, pp. 1420–1425.

Lister, M.B., Grob, C.S., Bravo, G.L. and Walsh, R.N. (1992) *J. Nerv. Ment. Dis.*, 180, pp. 345–356.

Matsuda, L.A., Lolait, S.J., Brownstein, M.J., Young, A.C. and Bonne, T.I. (1990) *Nature*, 346, pp. 561–564.

McCann, U.D., Ridenour, A., Shaham, Y. and Ricaurte, G.A. (1994) *Neuropsychopharmacol.*, 10, pp. 129–138.

McCann, U.D., Slate, S.O. and Ricaurte, G.A. (1996) *Drug Safety*, 15, pp. 107–115.

Morgan, M. and Mandell, A.J. (1969) *Science*, 165, pp. 492–493.

Nahas, G.G., Sucia-Foca, N., Armand, J.P. and Morishima, A. (1974) *Science*, 183, pp. 419–420.

Nahas, G.G., Sutin, K.M., Harvey, D.J. and Agurell, S. (eds) (1999) In *Marihuana and Medicine*. Totowa, New Jersey: Humana Press.

Nair, P., Rothblum, B.A. and Hebel, R. (1994) *Clin. Pediatr.*, 33, pp. 280–285.

National Institute on Drug Abuse (1991) *National Household Survey on Drug Abuse. Population Estimates 1990*. Rockville, Maryland: US Department of Health and Human Services.

National Institute on Drug Abuse (2000) *National Household Survey on Drug Abuse. Population Estimates 1999*. Rockville, Maryland: US Department of Health and Human Services.

Nichols, D.E. (1986) *J. Psychoactive Drugs*, 18, pp. 305–313.

Nichols, D.E., Oberlender, R.A. and McKenna, D.J. (1991) In Watson, R. (ed.) *Biochemistry and Physiology of Substance Abuse*. Boca Raton, FL: CRC Press.

Perez-Reyes, M., DiGuiseppi, S. and Owens, S.M. (1981) *J. Clin. Pharmacol.*, 21, pp. 201S–207S.

Pertwee, R.G. (1997) *Pharmacol. Therap.*, 74, pp. 129–180.

Renault, P.F., Schuster, C.R., Heinrich, R. and Freeman, D. (1971) *Science*, 174, pp. 589–591.

Ricaurte, G.A., Martello, A.L., Katz, J. and Martello, M.B. (1992) *J. Pharmacol. Exp. Therap.*, 261, pp. 616–622.

Senon, R. (1996) In *Le Cannabis* Paris: Presse Universitaires de France.

Shulgin, A.T. (1981) *J. Psychoactive Drugs*, 13, p. 99.

Shulgin, A.T. and Shulgin, A. (1992) In Pihkal (ed.) *A Chemical Love Story*. Berkely, CA: Transform Press.

Spencer, D., Glaser, T. and Traber, J. (1987) *Psychopharmacol.*, 93, pp. 158–166.

Stafford, P. (1992) *Psychedelics Encyclopedia* (3rd edn). Berkeley, CA: Ronin Press.

Steele, T.D., McCann, U.D. and Ricaurte, G.A. (1994) *Addiction*, 89, pp. 539–551.

Stoll, W.A. (1947) *Schweiz Arch. Neurol. Psychiat.*, 60, pp. 279–323.

Strassman, R.J. (1992) *Neuropsychopharmacol.*, 7 (3), pp. 241–243.

Strassman, R.J. (1995) *J. Nerv. Ment. Dis.*, 183 (3), pp. 127–138.

Tashkin, D.P., Shapiro, B.J. and Frank, I.M. (1973) *N. Engl. J. Med.*, 289, pp. 336–341.

Tucker, G.T., Lennard, M.S., Ellis, S.W., Woods, H.F., Cho, A.K. and Lin, L.Y. (1994) *Biochem. Pharmacol.*, 47, pp. 1151–1157.

Verebey, K., Albrazi, J. and Jaffe, J.H. (1988) *J. Am. Med. Assoc.*, 259, pp. 1649–1650.

CHAPTER 7

OPIOIDS

Rebecca A. Jufer
Amanda J. Jenkins

Opioids are a class of substances that include natural, semi-synthetic and synthetic alkaloidal agents derived from opium or substances which have a morphine-like activity. Naturally occurring opioids are typically referred to as opiates and include substances obtained by extraction from the opium poppy, *Papaver somniferum*. The opium poppy is an annual plant that grows in many climates, although it prefers warm, temperate regions with no frost. Opium is obtained from the milky exudate released from incisions of the unripe seed capsule. Mentions of opium poppies in the historical record date back to the ancient Greeks. The word for poppy in Greek was *opion*, and in Latin, *opium*. More recently, opium was used in the Middle Ages since its ability to induce sleep was recognized by the surgeons of the time. During the Renaissance, physicians prescribed opium to their patients as a cure for a variety of ailments. A well-known historical figure in toxicology circles, Philippus Aureolus Theophratus Bombast von Hohenheim (Paracelsus) prescribed opium in several different formulations. One formulation called "laudanum" comprised 1/4 opium (Karch, 1996).

Opium is a complex substance, containing numerous compounds including morphine, codeine, thebaine, papaverine, and noscapine (Kerrigan and Goldberger, 1999). The relative content of these alkaloids varies with geographic region but the principal constituents are typically morphine (10–17%), noscapine (6%), papaverine (1%), codeine (0.5%) and thebaine (0.2%). Although opium has been used historically for hundreds of years, morphine was not isolated until 1805. This principal alkaloid of opium was named after Morpheus, the god of dreams. Morphine is used as a building block for many of the semi-synthetic opioids. Semi-synthetic opioids derived from morphine include heroin, codeine, and hydromorphone. Opioids which may be synthesized from codeine include dihydrocodeine and hydrocodone. Although codeine occurs naturally in opium, often it is present in very low quantities such that it may be easier to synthesize the drug from morphine rather than use the natural source. Thebaine has little inherent pharmacological activity but is used as a building block for semi-synthetic opioids such as buprenorphine, oxycodone and oxymorphone.

The first synthetic opioid with a chemical structure dissimilar to morphine was meperidine, prepared in 1939, followed by methadone in 1946. Additional synthetic opioids include butorphanol, levorphanol, nalbuphine, pentazocine, propoxyphene, and tramadol. Table 7.1 summarizes additional information on these opioids.

PHARMACOKINETICS

Pharmacokinetics (PK) is the study of the relationship between administered doses of a drug and the observed blood concentrations. This relationship is often expressed quantitatively. Blood may be substituted for blood components such as serum or plasma or tissues. The PK model is a mathematical expression of this relationship. PK considers the processes of drug absorption, distribution, biotransformation, and elimination. These processes play a large role in determining how much of a given dose of drug reaches the effector site, and as a consequence, determine the intensity and duration of drug effect.

The concepts which apply to the transfer of chemical substances across biological membranes are involved in these PK processes. These concepts include membrane fluidity, the presence of membrane transport proteins and pores, physicochemical properties of the drug such as molecular size and shape, solubility, degree of ionization, and also plasma protein binding.

Opioids share many PK characteristics and therefore will be discussed in general here. Morphine, the classic naturally occurring opioid, may be administered orally, by subcutaneous, intramuscular, intravenous or epidural injection or by continuous intravenous infusion (Jenkins and Cone, 1998). After epidural administration of a dose of morphine, approximately 7% reaches the cerebrospinal fluid and spinal cord. A single epidural dose of 0.1 mg/kg of morphine produced a mean peak serum concentration of 80 ng/mL at 10 min in surgical patients (n = 9) (Drost, 1996). Intravenous administration bypasses the absorption PK step. A single IV dose of 0.125 mg/kg of morphine resulted in an average peak serum concentration of 440 ng/mL at 30 s, declining to 20 ng/mL at 2 hr (Aitkenhead, 1984). The peak serum concentration and the time to peak concentration were reduced when the same dose was administered intramuscularly (70 ng/mL at 10–20 min). Absorption processes also result in delayed peak concentrations after oral administration. Further, metabolism of the drug in the liver once it has been absorbed through the stomach and intestinal walls, reduces bioavailability to 15–64%. Doses of 20–30 mg of oral morphine were required to maintain serum concentrations above 20 ng/mL for 4–6 hr in terminally ill cancer patients (Sawe, 1981).

Once absorbed, morphine distributes slowly into tissues due to its relative hydrophilicity. Morphine does cross the blood–brain barrier but without the

Table 7.1 (opposite)
Natural, semi-synthetic and synthetic opioids.

Opioid	US trade names	Receptor binding characteristics	Primary metabolites
Natural			
Codeine	Nucofed	Has a very low affinity for opioid receptors; antitussive action likely due to the binding of codeine to distinct receptors	Morphine, norcodeine, C3G, M3G and other conjugates
Morphine	Duramorph MSContin	Mu and Kappa agonist	M3G, M6G and normorphine
Noscapine			
Papaverine	Cerebid, Pavabid	Smooth muscle relaxant	6-hydroxypapaverine, 4'-hydroxypa-paverine, 3'-hydroxypapaverine, 7-hydroxypapaverine and conjugates
Thebaine			
Semi-synthetic			
Buprenorphine	Buprenex	Partial Mu agonist and Kappa$_1$ antagonist	Norbuprenorphine, buprenorphine glucuronide and norbuprenorphine glucuronide
Dihydrocodeine	Synalgos-DC	Mu agonist	Nordihydrocodeine, dihydromorphine and conjugates
Heroin		Has a very low affinity for opioid receptors; thought to act as a prodrug	6-AM, morphine, M3G, M6G and normorphine
Hydrocodone	Lortab Vicodin	Mu agonist	Norhydrocodone, hydromorphone, hydrocodol, hydromorphol and conjugates
Hydromorphone	Dilaudid	Mu agonist	Hydromorphol, congugates
Oxycodone	Oxycontin Percocet Percodan	Mu agonist	Noroxycodone, oxymorphone, and conjugates
Oxymorphone	Numorphan	Mu agonist	6-oxymorphol and conjugates
Synthetic			
Butorphanol	Stadol NS	Weak Mu antagonist or partial Mu agonist and Kappa$_1$ agonist	Hydroxybutorphanol, norbutorphanol and conjugates
Fentanyl	Duragesic Actiq Sublimaze	Mu agonist	Norfentanyl, hydroxyfentanyl and hydroxynorfentanyl

Opioid	US trade names	Receptor binding characteristics	Primary metabolites
Levorphanol	Levo-Dromoran	Mu agonist and Kappa$_3$ agonist	Norlevorphanol and conjugates
Meperidine	Demerol	Mu agonist	Normeperidine, meperidinic acid, normeperidinic acid and conjugates
Methadone	Dolophine	Mu agonist	EDDP, EMDP, methadol and normethadol
Nalbuphpine	Nubain	Mu antagonist and Kappa$_{1+3}$ agonist	Nornalbuphine and glucuronide conjugates
Pentazocine	Talwin Talacen	Weak Mu antagonist or partial Mu agonist and Kappa$_{1+3}$ agonist	Cis- and trans-hydroxypentazocine, trans-carboxypentazocine and conjugates
Propoxyphene	Darvon Darvocet	Mu agonist	Norpropoxyphene
Tramadol	Ultram	Mu agonist	Nortramadol, O-desmethyltramadol and conjugates

Table 7.1 (continued)

rapidity of more lipophilic opioids such as heroin. The volume of distribution of morphine is 2–5 L/kg in humans. Plasma protein binding ranges from 12–35% and albumin is the major plasma protein to which morphine binds. The plasma elimination half-life of morphine ranges from 1.8–2.9 hr in healthy individuals and is not affected in individuals with renal failure but is increased in patients with significant liver disease.

Morphine is metabolized by Phase II biotransformation by conjugation with glucuronic acid to morphine 3- and morphine 6-glucuronide (M3G and M6G). The latter is pharmacologically active. Morphine is also N-demethylated to the active metabolite, normorphine. Morphine is primarily metabolized in the liver with 90% and 10% of a dose excreted in the urine and feces, respectively. Morphine is subject to enterohepatic recirculation of both the free and conjugated forms.

Heroin is an illicit opioid that is commonly abused in the US and other countries. Although heroin is used medically in some countries in Europe, it does not have an accepted medical use in the United States and is listed as a Schedule I substance of the federal Controlled Substances Act of 1970. It is mentioned here due to its wide availability as a street drug. It is typically purchased on the street in powder form for intravenous injection, nasal insufflation and, more recently, smoking. Peak blood heroin concentrations are achieved rapidly (within minutes) after intravenous or smoked administration. The time to peak concentrations after intramuscular and oral administrations is delayed and therefore these modes of self-administration are not commonly reported by heroin abusers since there is also a delay in feeling the "high." In addition, heroin is broken down in the stomach after oral administration and only its metabolite, morphine, may reach the blood.

Once absorbed, heroin is rapidly metabolized to 6-acetylmorphine (6-AM) by plasma and liver esterases. Clinical studies have reported a half-life in blood of 3–5 min after both intravenous and smoked administration. 6-Acetylmorphine is then converted to morphine, with a half-life of approximately 40 min. Morphine is produced from the hydrolysis of 6-AM by plasma and liver esterases. The morphine is then conjugated and excreted as previously described. A metabolic scheme for heroin, morphine and codeine is illustrated in Figure 7.1.

Of note, is the low affinity of heroin for the opioid receptors. It is generally thought that heroin acts as a prodrug. Since it is lipophilic, heroin gains entry to the brain rapidly, more rapidly than its more polar metabolites. Once in the brain it is rapidly converted to 6-acetylmorphine and morphine, which can then interact with the opioid receptors.

After heroin administration, very little of a dose is excreted as parent drug. Indeed, no heroin may be detected in blood or urine. 6-Acetylmorphine may also be present in low concentration and typically will not be detected after the first urine void unless the patient has overdosed. Therefore, the major metabolites excreted in urine after heroin administration are conjugated and free morphine.

Figure 7.1
Metabolic scheme for heroin, morphine and codeine.

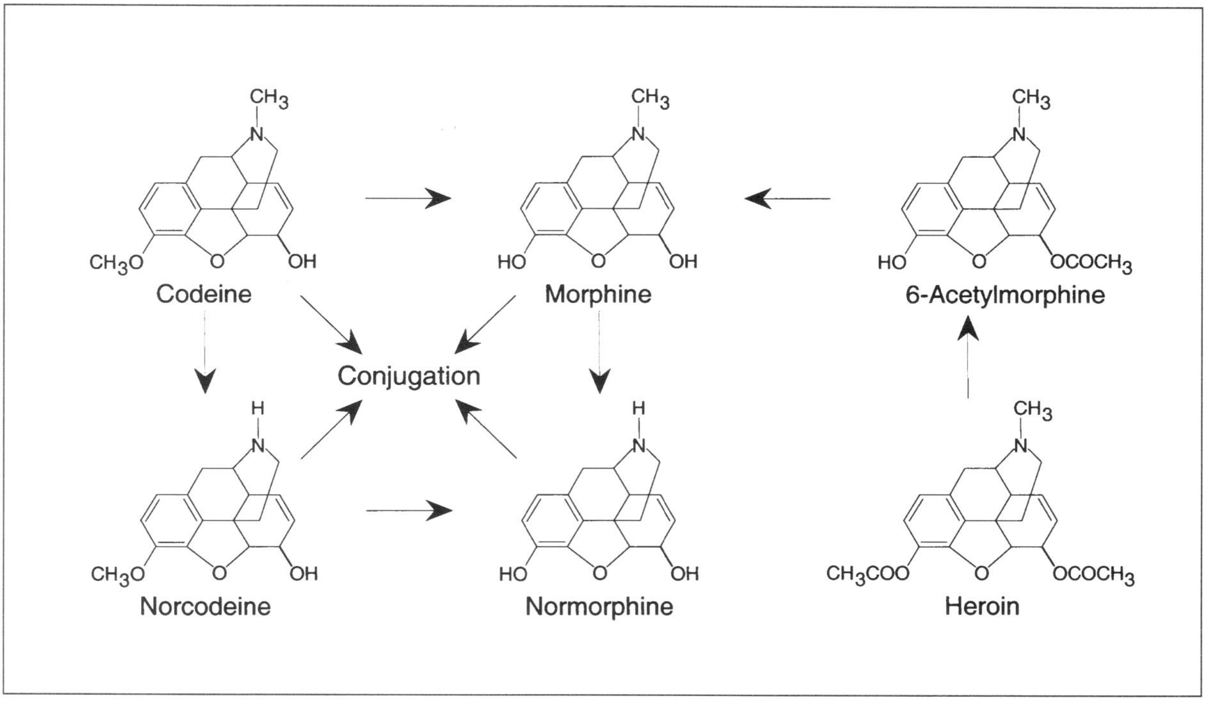

PHARMACODYNAMICS

Pharmacodynamics is the study of the relationship between administered drug and the observed effects in the body. The pharmacological effects of the opioids are due to their relative interaction with receptors in the central nervous system (CNS). Several "opioid" receptors have been identified in humans, namely the mu (μ), kappa (κ), delta (δ), and sigma (σ) receptors. Interactions at the mu receptor, of which at least two subtypes have been identified, result in central nervous depression, analgesia, respiratory depression, miosis, euphoria, bradycardia, decreased gastrointestinal motility, and hypothermia. Interactions at this receptor type are also responsible for the physical dependence and tolerance that may develop with opioid use. Kappa receptor interactions also produce analgesia of the spinal type, sedation, miosis, and some respiratory depression. Delta receptors are binding sites for endogenous peptides and binding results in spinal analgesia, dysphoria, and delusions. Sigma receptor binding may produce central excitation. This excitation results in increased heart rate and hypertension, tachypnea, mydriasis, and hallucinations. The effects of binding at opioid receptors are summarized in Table 7.2.

Table 7.2

Opioid receptor actions. Adapted from Karch (1996).

Opioid receptor type	Effect of binding
Mu	Central nervous system depression, spinal and supraspinal analgesia, respiratory depression, miosis, euphoria, bradycardia, decreased gastrointestinal motility and hypothermia
Delta	Spinal and supraspinal analgesia, dysphoria and delusions
Kappa	Spinal analgesia, sedation, miosis and some respiratory depression
Sigma	Central excitation resulting in increased heart rate and hypertension, tachypnea, mydriasis and hallucinations

The opioids bind to the receptors with differing affinity and this results in varying responses. The opioids are typically classified according to three modes of action: agonist, antagonist, and mixed agonist-antagonist. An agonist is a compound with affinity for a certain type of opioid receptor (e.g., morphine is a strong mu agonist). Drugs may be antagonists if they inhibit agonist binding. These compounds are typically utilized in the treatment of opioid intoxication (e.g. nalbuphine is a mu antagonist). Substances which act as agonists to one receptor but demonstrate antagonistic activity at another are called mixed agonist-antagonists (e.g. butorphanol is a kappa agonist and a mu antagonist). Antagonists can displace opioids from receptor binding sites due to affinity and potency differences. This property is used to treat cases of opioid intoxication. For example, naloxone can rapidly reverse the respiratory depression caused by morphine. One of the newer opioids, tramadol, has opioid properties, as it is a mu agonist. However, tramadol produces analgesia by a non-opioid pathway involving noradrenaline and serotonin inhibition.

A number of studies have been performed to assess the effects of opioids on human performance. A recently published chapter provides a useful review of these studies (Heishman, 1998). A limited number of studies have observed impaired cognitive abilities after opioid administration (Zacny, 1995). Veselis et al. (1994) observed impaired memory function after low doses of intravenous fentanyl. Schneider et al. (1999) also observed pronounced cognitive impairment (decrements in auditory reaction time, signal detection, sustained attention, and recognition) after fentanyl administration. In another study, subjects displayed a slowed reading time and impaired comprehension after receiving intravenous morphine (Kerr et al., 1991). A study in cancer patients demonstrated decreases in cognitive impairment tests including a visual memory test after an increase from their usual dose of various opioids (morphine, hydromorphone, oxycodone or codeine) (Bruera et al., 1989).

When considering drugs classes that may be associated with cases of drug-facilitated sexual assault (DFSA), one must consider the desired effects for such a use. These effects include sedation, muscle relaxation, anti-anxiety, and amnesia. As summarized above, opioids are capable of producing sedation and muscle relaxation. In addition, there are a limited number of studies that indicated that opioids impair cognitive function, including memory in some cases. Furthermore, many opioids produce a pleasant drowsy state and a decreased sensation of pain, both of which could conceivably decrease resistance from an intended victim of DFSA. However, the most important consideration may not be the effects of opioids alone, but their interaction(s) with other drugs, especially ethanol.

INTERACTIONS OF OPIOIDS WITH ETHANOL

In a recently published report, ElSohly and Salamone (1999) described the results of a study to estimate the prevalence of drug use in cases of sexual assault. They collected a total of 1,179 urine specimens over a period of 26 months from victims of sexual assault where drug use was suspected. The specimens were submitted to the laboratory by law enforcement agencies, emergency rooms and rape crisis centers across the US. Each specimen was screened by immunoassay for nine drugs and/or drug classes. Positive immunoassay results were confirmed by GC-MS. Opioids were detected in 25 (2.1%) of the 1,179 cases. This study also demonstrated a very high prevalence for ethanol among alleged sexual assault victims (451 of 1,179 were positive for ethanol). Due to the high prevalence of ethanol in sexual assault cases, it becomes essential to consider the potential interactions that ethanol may have with a co-administered substance.

When two or more drugs are taken in combination, one of several types of interactions may result. The simplest interaction is that of *addition*, where the response produced by the drug combination is equal to the combined responses of the individual drugs. Other possible interactions include *synergism*, *potentiation*, and *antagonism*. Synergism results when the response produced by the drug combination is greater than the combined responses of the individual drugs. Potentiation occurs when the effect of a toxic agent is enhanced by a nontoxic agent. When the response produced by a drug combination is less than the combined responses of the individual drugs, an antagonistic interaction occurs. As both alcohol and opioids are capable of producing sedative effects, a potentially significant interaction becomes apparent.

The effects of combining opioids and alcohol have been investigated in several animal studies. A study performed by Forney *et al.* (1962) investigated the effects of codeine, morphine and ethanol in mice. The effects of these drugs were evaluated when they were administered alone and in combinations of codeine–ethanol and morphine–ethanol. The drug effects were evaluated by the ability of the mice to move a specified distance following drug administration. Their results indicated that the co-administration of morphine significantly enhanced the depressant effects of ethanol. However, co-administration of codeine and ethanol did not result in an increase of the depressant effects of ethanol. Another study evaluated the acute co-administration of ethanol and morphine in mice (Venho *et al.*, 1955). The authors reported that the depression observed following administration of both drugs was greater than the sum of the effects of each drug. The same investigators also examined the sensitivity of "alcoholic" mice to toxic doses of morphine (Venho *et al.*, 1955). The "alcoholic" mice were administered ethanol for a six-week period prior to morphine administration. The authors found that the "alcoholic" mice displayed an increased sensitivity to the toxic effects of morphine compared with a control group that did not receive ethanol for the six-week period prior to morphine administration.

Aasmundstad *et al.* (1996) studied the effects of ethanol on morphine metabolism in isolated guinea pig hepatocytes. They found that all evaluated concentrations of ethanol (range tested = 0.023–0.46 g/dL) decreased the elimination of morphine compared to control conditions. In addition, they observed that the formation of morphine glucuronides was influenced by dose; at low ethanol concentrations, morphine glucuronide concentrations were increased, whereas at higher ethanol concentrations, morphine glucuronide concentrations were decreased. The authors suggested that a low ethanol concentration may have a more pronounced ethanol–morphine interaction because not only is morphine eliminated at a slower rate, but M6G, a metabolite with higher agonist potency than morphine, is produced at a faster rate.

Relatively few clinical studies of drug interactions between opioids and ethanol have been performed. An early report by White (1955) indicated that the amount of meperidine required to produce sedation and amnesia in women who had been administered ethanol and pitocin (both IV) for induction of labor was about 25–50% of what is typically needed. Kiplinger *et al.* (1974) evaluated the effects of combined ethanol and propoxyphene on human performance. They observed only an additive effect and found no evidence for a synergistic interaction between the two drugs. Cushman (1987) discussed potentially clinically important interactions between ethanol and opioids. These interactions included the possibility for slower elimination rates when opioids and ethanol are used in combination, which could lead to higher toxicity. Cushman also indicated that ethanol may modify some opioid receptors and possibly alter concentrations of endogenous opioid peptides in some brain areas. However, the clinical significance of these observations remains unclear.

CASE HISTORIES

Case examples of DFSA in which opioids were involved are limited. The two cases summarized below were submitted to the FBI Laboratory in Washington, DC.

CASE 1

A 20-year-old female was at a bar in a popular beach vacation area. When she complained of getting tired about 10 p.m., an unknown male offered her a green pill that he said was a "Vivarin". She ingested the pill and later woke up to find herself bruised and covered with sand. A blood specimen collected 20.5 hr following ingestion of the pill was submitted to the laboratory for analysis. Morphine was detected in the blood specimen at a concentration of 10 ng/mL and caffeine was detected at a concentration of 1500 ng/mL.

CASE 2

A 31-year-old female was at a bar where she was introduced to two men by an acquaintance. The two males accompanied her when she left the bar and, after much convincing, she agreed to return with them to one of their apartments for a drink. She was given some wine and noticed that it had a bitter taste and was orange in color. She does not remember how much of the wine she consumed. She awoke fully clothed at approximately 9 a.m. the next morning and went back to a friend's house where she slept for a few hours, then prepared for her trip home that she would be making that evening. When she arrived at home, she took a sleeping pill (temazepam) and slept for several hours. Upon awakening, she took a bath and noticed that there were multiple bruises on the inside of both of her thighs. The bruises appeared to be in the shape of hand and finger marks. She recalled nothing that had happened after she had consumed the wine. Later that day (approximately 40–48 hr following her visit to the apartment), she was examined by a physician and a urine specimen was collected and submitted to the laboratory for analysis. Codeine and temazepam were detected in her urine.

ANALYSIS

Typically, the forensic laboratory conducts two types of analyses on submitted specimens: screening and confirmation testing. Screening tests are designed to provide a rapid preliminary indication of whether a drug is present in the specimen. Screening techniques often involve minimal specimen preparation and have fast turnaround times. However, screening tests are not intended to positively identify the presence of a drug, but rather to indicate whether or not further testing is warranted. If a specimen has a positive screening test result, a confirmatory test must be performed. Confirmatory tests must be sensitive and specific for the analyte(s) of interest. Often, confirmatory tests require extensive sample preparation, have a longer analysis time and are fairly labor intensive.

SCREENING TECHNIQUES

Currently the most common screening technique for the detection of opioids are immunoassays. These techniques are typically instrument based and require little or no sample preparation, may be automated and analyze many samples in a short time-frame. Individual commercial assays are available for the opioid class of drugs, and also for specific drugs within the class such as methadone, buprenorphine, fentanyl, and propoxyphene. Since the technology is based on antibody–antigen complex formation, each assay will target a specific drug (e.g. morphine is typically the target substance for opioid assays). This means that the antibodies were raised to the morphine or morphine 3-glucuronide antigen and will give a positive result if there is morphine in the specimen above a specified concentration. However, the test may also produce a positive result if there are other opioids in the specimen (e.g. codeine). The degree to which an individual assay will cross-react with other substances varies between products but is noted on the package insert, which is provided by the manufacturer for each kit of reagents. It is obvious from the previous statements that if an immunoassay result is positive for a specimen tested for opioids, unless further testing is conducted, the precise opioid present is unknown. Therefore, immunoassay technology is considered a screening procedure and where the degree of proof may be sufficient for clinical diagnostic purposes, it lacks the degree of specificity to unequivocally state the presence of drug. Therefore, if the results of the testing are to be used for forensic purposes (i.e. any applicability to the law), confirmation testing must be performed.

Historically, immunoassay technology was marketed for the testing of urine specimens. More recently, assays have been produced for use with blood and other biological matrices. A variation on the instrument-based immunoassay technology is the use of on-site quick tests. These are self-contained tests that may detect a variety of drugs in urine. The advantage of these tests is that they are easy to use, require little technical training and provide preliminary results at the site of collection within 5–10 min. Devices are available with trade names such as Triage®, TesTcup®, TesTstik®, Syva Rapid Test®, Accusign®, Visualine®, Verdict®, and PharmScreen®. Presumptive positive results must be confirmed. One disadvantage of these tests is the limited number of assays available and the requirement for urine as a testing specimen. In the future, on-site testing devices may be available to test for drugs of abuse in saliva and other matrices that are minimally invasive.

An alternate screening procedure for opioids is thin layer chromatography (TLC). Commercial systems are available such as the ToxiLab® system by Ansys Diagnostics, Inc. (Lake Forest, CA). This is a self-contained system. The manufacturer provides the chromatographic material, development tanks, visualization reagents and sample extraction tubes. Alternatively, silica plates may be purchased by a laboratory, and reagents prepared in-house. Instead of dipping the chromatogram in a reagent, the visualization material may be sprayed on to the plate. Opioids may be assayed by TLC. An example of a procedure that may be used for opioid analysis follows.

Silica gel G plates of 250 μm thickness which should be pre-prepared by dipping or spraying with 0.1 M potassium hydroxide in methanol and dried. The mobile phase is methanol:ammonia solution (100:1.5). Visualization reagents include Marquis reagent which produces violet spots on the plate with alkaloids related to morphine (Moffat et al., 1986).

Typically, TLC procedures detect concentrations of opioids down to 500–1000 ng/mL when using 10 mL sample volume. TLC is a relatively rapid technique to perform and of low cost. Disadvantages include the relatively high limits of detection when compared to more sensitive techniques such as gas chromatography (GC) and high-performance liquid chromatography (HPLC).

SAMPLE PREPARATION FOR GC AND HPLC ANALYSIS

Biological specimens usually require pre-treatment prior to analysis by GC or HPLC. The pre-treatment consists of either liquid–liquid or solid phase extraction. In addition, preparation of specimens for gas chromatographic analysis often requires a hydrolysis step prior to extraction to convert the conjugated analytes to non-conjugated free drug. The most common hydrolysis methods are acidic and enzymatic hydrolysis. Acid hydrolysis is typically performed by acidifying the specimen and applying heat. Acid hydrolysis is often rapid (15–30 min) and complete. However, acid hydrolysis also converts heroin and 6-AM to morphine, which may make it difficult to distinguish between heroin and morphine exposure. To preserve any heroin and 6-AM present in the sample, an enzymatic hydrolysis can be performed. The enzyme of choice for this procedure is β-glucuronidase. Generally, enzymatic hydrolysis requires incubation at an optimal temperature and pH for a few hours up to an overnight period. The two hydrolysis methods have been demonstrated to be equally efficient for hydrolyzing M3G according to a study completed by Jennison *et al.* (1993).

Liquid–liquid extraction (LLE) methods for opioids employ a variety of different solvent mixtures, depending on the analyte(s) of interest. These solvents include *n*-butyl chloride, isobutanol:methylene chloride (1:9, v/v), ethyl acetate:chloroform:hexane (7:2:1, v/v), chloroform/2-propanol/*n*-heptane (60:14:26, v/v/v) and methylene chloride. LLE can be a very efficient and relatively low-cost extraction technique for a small number of chemically similar opioid analytes. However, it is often difficult to optimize an LLE scheme for multiple opioid analytes. Solid phase extraction (SPE) appears to be the preferred extraction method for the analysis of multiple opioids. Mixed-mode SPE columns, which use hydrophobic and cation exchange mechanisms, are frequently used and can provide good recovery of multiple opioid analytes. Also, C_{18} and C_2 SPE columns have been used to extract mixtures of morphine and its glucuronide metabolites.

GC SCREENING METHODS

A variety of GC methods have been reported for the detection of opioids in biological specimens. Capillary columns are utilized with detection performed by nitrogen phosphorus, electron capture or flame ionization detection. The particular drugs that are detected by a GC procedure depends upon several factors including extraction pH, the choice of extraction solvent, GC column specificity and the detector. In order to improve the chromatographic characteristics of an opioid, a derivatizing reagent may be added. These reagents include silylating and acylating agents such as heptafluorobutyric anhydride (HFBA), acetic anhydride, pentafluorobutyric anhydride (PFBA), trifluoroacetic anhydride (TFAA), and N,O-bis (trimethylsilyl) acetamide (BSTFA) (Lee and Lee, 1991). When the system is optimized, concentrations below 50 ng/mL may be routinely detected and quantitated.

HPLC SCREENING METHODS

HPLC procedures for the screening of opioids have been reported. The most common analytes measured by this technique are morphine and its glucuronide metabolites. One system used a 10-µ Waters C_8 Resolve cartridge installed in a Waters RCM 8 mm × 10 cm radial compression unit with an in line C_{18} u-Bondapak guard column. The mobile phase consisted of methanol:acetonitrile:phosphate buffer, 0.0125M pH 7.2 (12:12:76) in which 25 mg/L of acetyltrimethylammmonium bromide was dissolved. A Waters Model 460 electrochemical detector was utilized. Using sample preparation by solid phase extraction with C_{18}-SPE cartridges, extraction efficiencies were >90% (Wright and Smith, 1998). Morphine and morphine glucuronides may also be measured using UV and fluorescence detection (Aderjan et al., 1995). Limits of detection were typically <10 ng/mL.

The screening procedures outlined above are not useful for the detection of opioids in which the therapeutic concentration is low. These include fentanyl and buprenorphine. Detection methods for these drugs must be able to routinely measure concentrations as low as 1 ng/mL. Although several immunoassays are available to screen for these drugs (typically radioimmunoassay or enzyme linked immunosorbent assays), more sensitive and specific techniques are utilized as described below.

CONFIRMATORY TECHNIQUES

Given the substantial number of diverse drugs in the opioid class, it is necessary to have well-developed and highly sensitive confirmatory techniques that are capable of distinguishing between them. At the present time, the instrumental analyses that are best equipped to provide robust confirmatory techniques are gas chromatography with mass spectrometric detection (GC-MS) and liquid chromatography with mass spectrometric detection (LC-MS). A detailed summary of selected published confirmatory techniques is provided in Table 7.3. Prior to GC-MS or LC-MS analysis, specimen preparation is accomplished with liquid–liquid extraction or solid phase extraction and can vary according to the specimen type(s) that one is analyzing.

Table 7.3
(pages 162–165)

Methods for opioid confirmation.

Analytes detected	Specimen type(s)	Sample preparation	Instrumental details	Limit of detection	Comments	Ref.
GC-MS / GC-ECD Methods						
Codeine and morphine	Urine	Acid hydrolysis LLE: isobutanol:methylene chloride (1:9, v/v) with a back extraction derivatized with acetic anhydride and pyridine	GC-MS Column: DB-5 Hewlett Packard 5970A MSD	10 ng/mL (10 mL of urine analyzed)	The authors found derivatives formed with trifluoroacetic anhydride, pentaflouropropionic anhydride and hepta-fluorobutyric anhydride to be unstable	Paul et al. (1985)
Codeine, morphine and 6-AM	Urine	SPE: Bond Elut Certify™ (Varian) Derivatized with trifluoroacetic anhydride	GC-MS Column: HP Ultra-1 Hewlett Packard 5970 MSD	10 ng/mL (1 mL of urine analyzed)	The authors found derivatives formed with trifluoroacetic anhydride to be stable for 2–3 days	Fuller and Anderson (1992)
Heroin, 6-AM and morphine	Blood, urine and vitreous humor	LLE: ethyl acetate:chloroform:hexane (7:2:1, v/v) Derivatization with propionic anhydride and 4-dimethylaminopyridine	GC-MS Column: DB-1 Saturn II ion trap detector	0.75 ng/mL (1 mL of specimen analyzed)	This method was applied to postmortem samples	Guillot et al. (1997)
Heroin, 6-AM, morphine, codeine, normorphine, nor-codeine and cocaine analytes	Plasma, saliva, urine and hair	Hair samples were pre-treated with a methanol wash and extraction into methanol; both hair washes and extracts were analyzed SPE: Clean Screen® DAU derivatized with BSTFA	GC-MS Column: HP-1 Hewlett-Packard 5970B MSD	1–5 ng/mL (1 mL or 10 mg specimen analyzed)		Wang et al. (1994)
Heroin, 6-AM, morphine, acetylcodeine, codeine	Hair	Methanol wash incubation of hair with MSTFA derivatization mixture	GC-MS-MS Column: DB-5 Finnegan TSQ 700 triple quadrupole MS	25 pg/mg (10 mg of hair analyzed)	The authors found that this direct incubation of hair with derivatizing reagent produced comparable results to a prolonged methanolic extraction; however, they also found that frequent injector maintenance was required to minimize heroin degradation	Polettini et al. (1993)
Codeine, morphine, C6G, and M3G	Hair	Alkaline hydrolysis SPE: Bond Elut Certify Derivatized with TFAA	GC-MS Column: DB-5 MS Finnegan Magnum™ Ion Trap MS operated in positive ion chemical ionization mode	0.1 ng/mg (10 mg hair analyzed)	The authors used this method to detect codeine in hair following a single 120 mg dose of codeine phosphate	Wilkins et al. (1995)

Analytes detected	Specimen type(s)	Sample preparation	Instrumental details	Limit of detection	Comments	Ref.
Morphine, 6-AM, codeine, hydrocodone and cocaine analytes	Toenails	Toenail specimens were pretreated with a methanol wash and solubilized into buffer SPE: Clean Screen® DAU Derivatized with MSTFA	GC-MS Column: DB-5 Hewlett Packard 5970 MSD	0.025–0.050 ng/mg (100 mg toenail analyzed)	This method was used to analyze postmortem toenail specimens	Engelhart et al. (1998)
Morphine, codeine, 6-AM	Clothing	LLE: chloroform/2-propanol/n-heptane (60:14:26, v/v/v) with a back extraction Derivatized with BSTFA	GC-MS Column: HP5-MS HP 5972 MSD	N/A (1 g of textile sample analyzed)	The authors detected opioids in all pieces of garment analyzed; concentrations ranged from 0.02–9.27 µg/g	Tracqui et al. (1995)
Methadone, EDDP and EMDP	Plasma, urine and liver microsomes	SPE: Bond Elut Certify™ (Varian)	GC-PICI-MS Column: HP-1 Finnegan 4500 quadrupole MS (operated in positive ion detection mode)	5 ng/mL (1 mL of specimen analyzed)	The authors conducted stability studies indicating that the analytes are stable in plasma and urine at room temperature for at least 1 week	Alburges et al. (1996)
Norfentanyl and nor-3-methylfentanyl	Urine	LLE: methylene chloride Aqueous derivatization with pentafluoropropionic anhydride	GC-ECD Column: DB-1701 ^{63}Ni electron capture detector	2 ng/mL (1 mL of urine analyzed)	The authors found that the concentrations of the normetabolites were up to 10 times higher than the parent drug	Hammargren and Henderson (1988)
Fentanyl	Blood	LLE: n-chlorobutane with a back extraction	GC-MS Column: HP-5 Hewlett Packard 5988 MS	0.05 ng/mL (2 mL blood analyzed)	All glassware used in the extraction was silanized; this method is also suitable for the analysis of fentanyl analogs	Watts and Caplan (1988)
Buprenorphine and nor-buprenorphine	Plasma or serum	SPE: Clean Screen DAU (UCT) derivatization with heptafluorobutyric anhydride	GC-MS-MS Column: DB-5MS Finnegan MAT TSQ 700 operated in the negative chemical ionization mode	0.016–0.15 ng/mL (1 mL of plasma or serum analyzed)	The authors evaluated the assay for interferences from various drugs and found none	Kuhlman et al. (1996)

LC-MS Methods

Analytes detected	Specimen type(s)	Sample preparation	Instrumental details	Limit of detection	Comments	Ref.
Morphine, M3G and M6G	Plasma	SPE: Clean up C$_{18}$	LC-MS-MS Mobile phase: 0.1% formic acid in water: acetonitrile (95:5, v/v) Column: YMC-ODS-AQ Finnegan MAT TSQ 7000 with an ESI source	0.25–0.50 ng/mL (1 mL plasma analyzed)		Slawson et al. (1999)

Analytes detected	Specimen type(s)	Sample preparation	Instrumental details	Limit of detection	Comments	Ref.
Morphine, M3G, M6G and codeine	Serum	SPE: ethyl (C_2)	LC-MS Mobile phase: gradient from water: methanol (85:15, v/v) to (40:60, v/v) Column: Supelcosil ABZ TRIO 2 with electrospray interface	10–100 ng/mL (1 mL of serum analyzed)	The authors indicated that the use of C_2 SPE columns avoided the use of non-volatile buffers in the final eluate while producing acceptable recovery (70–95%) for all analytes	Pacifici et al. (1995)
Morphine, M3G and M6G	Serum	SPE: Sep pak light C_{18}	LC-MS Mobile phase: gradient from 3 mM formic acid in water:3 mM formic acid in acetonitrile (4:96, v/v) to (70:30, v/v) Column: ODS C_{18} Fisons Instruments VG platform electrospray	0.84–5.0 ng/mL (1 mL of serum analyzed)		Tyrefors et al. (1996)
Heroin, 6-AM, morphine, M3G, M6G	Serum	SPE: ethyl (C_2)	LC-MS (API) Mobile phase: methanol:water: acetonitrile:formic acid (59.8:5.2:34.65:0.35, v/v/v/v) Column: Supelco LC-Si Perkin-Elmer API MS	0.5–4.0 ng/mL (1 mL of serum analyzed)	The authors analyzed serum collected from mice; the authors found that the LC-Si with a silica stationary phase proved effective for separating these analytes without the addition of salts; this could not be accomplished with C_2,C_4,C_8 or C_{18} columns. The addition of salts could make the assay incompatible with mass spectrometry	Zuccaro et al. (1997)
Morphine, M3G, M6G, 6-AM and other illicit drugs	Urine	SPE: Sep pak C_{18}	LC-MS Mobile phase: gradient from 100 mM ammonium acetate to 100 mM ammonium acetate: acetonitrile (60:40, v/v) Column: L-column ODS Shimadzu QP-1100 EX thermospray LC-MS	2–40 ng/mL (5 mL of urine analyzed)	The authors did not use an internal standard in their assay	Tatsuno et al. (1996)

Analytes detected	Specimen type(s)	Sample preparation	Instrumental details	Limit of detection	Comments	Ref.
Morphine, M3G, M6G and 6-AM	Blood, cerebrospinal fluid, vitreous humor and urine	SPE: Bond Elut C$_{18}$, endcapped	LC-MS Mobile phase: 50 mM ammonium formate buffer (pH 3):acetonitrile (95:5, v/v); for 6-AM, (90:10, v/v) Column: Ecocart cartridge filled with supersphere select B SSQ 7000 operated in APCI positive ion mode	0.1–1.0 ng/mL (1 mL of specimen analyzed)	The authors reported that this technique displayed increased sensitivity over ECD and comparable sensitivity; also they concluded that this technique is acceptable for everyday use in routine casework	Bogusz et al. (1997)
Buprenorphine and nor-buprenorphine	Blood	Enzymatic hydrolysis SPE	LC-MS Mobile phase: 2 mM ammonium formate (pH 3): acetonitrile (55:45, v/v) Column: Nucleosil C$_{18}$ API-100 Perkin Elmer-Sciex API MS with electrospray type Ionspray	0.05 ng/mL (1 mL of blood analyzed)	This method was applied to clinical and postmortem samples	Hoja et al. (1997)
Heroin, 6-AM, morphine, codeine, buprenorphine and other drugs of abuse	Sweat	Sweat patches were extracted into methanol Derivatized with BSTFA (except for buprenorphine and amphetamines)	LC-MS (Buprenorphine) Mobile phase: acetonitrile: 2 mM ammonium acetate (pH 3) (80:20, v/v) Column: Nova Pak C$_{18}$ Perkin-Elmer Sciex API-100 mass analyzer GC-MS (all other analytes) Column: HP-5 MS Hewlett Packard 5989B engine	0.2–1.0 ng/patch	This method was used to analyze sweat patches from opioid users. The opioids detected included heroin, 6-AM, morphine and codeine. Buprenorphine was detected in sweat collected from individuals receiving buprenorphine therapy	Kintz et al. (1996)

GC-MS confirmation

The most common technique for the confirmation of opioid analytes is gas liquid chromatography with mass spectrometric detection (GC-MS). When GC-MS analysis is performed, derivatization is often necessary for a number of opioid compounds. The most widely used derivatizing reagents include acetic anhydride, trifluoroacetic anhydride (TFAA), pentafluoropropionic anhydride

(PFPA), propionic anhydride, heptafluorobutyric anhydride (HFBA), N-Methyl,N-trimethylsilyl trifluoroacetamide (MSTFA) and N,O-bis (trimethylsilyl) acetamide (BSTFA). Studies comparing the stability of various morphine and codeine derivatives have had varying results. Paul *et al.* (1985) compared the stability of TFAA, PFPA, HFBA and acetyl derivatives of morphine and codeine. They found the TFAA, PFPA and HFBA derivatives to be unstable, while the acetyl derivative was stable at room temperature for 72 hr. Chen *et al.* (1990) compared the stability of morphine and codeine derivatives prepared with PFPA, HFBA, MBTFA and BSTFA. They found that the PFPA and HFBA derivatives resulted in relatively poor spectra, due to the low abundance of secondary and tertiary ions. In addition, hydromorphone interfered with morphine when HFBA and PFPA derivatives were used. The authors concluded that acetyl derivatives were the most stable using their method. Grinstead (1991) examined the stability of the acetyl and pentafluoropropionyl derivatives of morphine and codeine. He reported that while the PFPA derivatives were stable and free from interferences, the codeine derivative displayed poor chromatography. The acetyl derivatives were stable and displayed good chromatography, but hydromorphone was found to interfere with the analysis of morphine. Although the conclusions on the stability of some derivatives were inconsistent across studies, each of these studies did find the acetyl derivatives of morphine and codeine to be stable. However, the use of an acetyl derivative makes it impossible to distinguish heroin and 6-AM from morphine. An alternative to acetyl derivatives of morphine and 6-AM is derivatization with deuterium labeled acetic anhydride, which creates essentially the same derivative, but the deuterium label results in a distinguishable derivative for each analyte (Bowie and Kirkpatrick, 1989).

The typical GC column phases for opioid analysis include 100% dimethylpolysiloxane (similar columns: HP-1, DB-1, Rtx-1, OV-1, SPB-1, SE-30, CP-Sil 5CB, RSL-150, MTX-1, BP-1, 007-1 and MDN-1) and 95% dimethylpolysiloxane with 5% diphenyl (similar columns: HP-5, DB-5, Rtx-5, PTE-5, CP-Sil 8CB, SE-54, Mtx-5, OV-5, SE-52, GC-5, 007-2, RSL-200, MDN-5 and BP-5). Full scan or selected ion monitoring in the electron impact ionization mode is the most widely used technique. A few methods employed positive or negative chemical ionization, ion trap MS and tandem MS. It should be noted that ion trap methods can provide increased sensitivity with MS-MS capabilities. Chemical ionization mass spectrometry may also produce analytical results with less background interference, providing lower limits of detection. The matrices analyzed by the reviewed GC-MS confirmation methods included blood, plasma, urine, hair, saliva, nails, and clothing. A unique application reported by Traqui *et al.* (1995) involved the analysis of clothing (T-shirts and underwear) from individuals who had died as a result of opioid overdose. The authors were able to detect opioid analytes in these clothing samples, presumably as a result of drug transfer to the clothing through sweat, sebaceous secretions and/or urine. Limits of detection for opioid analytes in biological fluids by GC-MS were usually less than 10 ng/mL, with a typical specimen analysis volume of 1 mL.

LC-MS confirmation of opioids

A limited number of methods for the confirmation of opioid analytes by LC-MS have been reported. A major advantage of LC-MS is that polar and thermally labile compounds, including glucuronide conjugates, may be analyzed without hydrolysis and/or derivatization. The elimination of these requirements results in a more complete analytical result (allowing direct quantitation of conjugated metabolites) in addition to a reduced analysis time. Similar to GC-MS techniques, the majority of LC-MS methods utilized mixed mode, C_{18}, or C_2 SPE columns for sample preparation. Pacifici *et al.* (1995) reported that the use of C_2 SPE columns provided acceptable recovery of morphine, M3G, M6G and codeine without the use of non-volatile buffers, which may not be compatible with LC-MS analysis.

The most common liquid chromatography technique for drug analysis is reverse phase chromatography, in which separation is dependent on the nonpolar properties of the substances. In the reviewed LC-MS confirmation methods, LC separation was most frequently performed on a C_{18} column. However, Zuccaro *et al.* (1997) reported that their use of an LC-Si column (Supelco, Bellafonte, PA) provided effective separation of heroin, 6-AM morphine, M3G and M6G without adding salts to the mobile phase. They were unable to achieve effective separation on C_2, C_4, C_8 or C_{18} columns without salt addition. Mobile phases for LC-MS confirmation of opioids are typically composed of a volatile buffer such as ammonium formate or ammonium acetate in water and acetonitrile and/or methanol. The following isocratic mobile phases have been used with a C_{18} phase column for the LC-MS analysis of opioids including morphine, M3G, M6G, buprenorphine and norbuprenorphine:

0.1% formic acid in water: acetonitrile (95:5)
2 mM ammonium formate (pH 3): acetonitrile (55:45)
acetonitrile: 2 mM ammonium acetate (pH 3) (80:20).

Examples of gradient mobile phases employed for the analysis of opioids (including morphine, M3G, M6G and 6-AM) on a C_{18} phase column include:

3 mM formic acid in water: 3 mM formic acid in acetonitrile (4:96) to (70:30)
100 mM ammonium acetate to 100 mM ammonium acetate: acetonitrile (60:40).

Mobile phases used for the analysis of opioids on column phases other than C$_{18}$ are summarized in Table 7.3. The specimens analyzed by LC-MS in the reviewed methods included blood, plasma, serum, urine, sweat, cerebrospinal fluid and vitreous humor. Detection limits better than 10 ng/mL (with 1 mL of sample analyzed) can generally be achieved with LC-MS opioid confirmatory methods.

SUMMARY

In cases of DFSA where opioid involvement is suspected, it is important to consider testing for opioids that require specialized analyses, in addition to the routinely analyzed opioids including morphine, codeine and 6-AM. If it is unclear which opioid(s) may be involved, immunoassay testing may assist in narrowing the target analytes without consuming a large amount of specimen. However, any immunoassay positive result must be confirmed by an accepted confirmatory procedure. A number of the confirmatory methods summarized were applied to the analysis of alternative specimens, including sweat and hair. These specimens may provide information that cannot be obtained from traditional specimens in cases of DFSA, where a significant time lapse may have occurred between the time of the alleged assault and the time of specimen collection. However, research on the applicability of these types of specimen analyses to DFSA cases is only in its early stages. In addition, there are many unresolved issues with the interpretation of analytical results from alternative specimens, so analytical results from these specimens are of most value when they are supported by an analytical result from a traditional specimen, such as blood or urine.

ACKNOWLEDGMENTS

The authors would like to thank W. David Darwin (IRP, NIDA, NIH Baltimore, MD) for his assistance with the construction of Figure 7.1.

REFERENCES

Aasmundstad, T.A., Lillekjendlie, B. and Morland, J. (1996) "Ethanol Interference with Morphine Metabolism in Isolated Guinea Pig Hepatocytes", *Pharm. Toxicol.*, 79, pp. 114–119.

Aderjan, R., Hofmann, S., Schmitt, G. and Skopp, G. (1995) "Morphine and Morphine Glucuronides in Serum of Heroin Consumers and in Heroin Related Deaths Determined by HPLC with Native Fluorescence Detection", *J. Anal. Toxicol.*, 19, pp. 163–168.

Aitkenhead, A.R., Vater, M. and Achola, K. (1984) "Pharmacokinetics of Single Dose i.v.

Morphine in Normal Volunteers and Patients with End Stage Renal Failure", *Brit. J. Anaesth.*, 56, pp. 813–818.

Alburges, M.E., Huang, W., Foltz, R.L. and Moody, D.E. (1996) "Determination of Methadone and Its N-demethylation Metabolites in Biological Specimens By GC-PICI-MS", *J. Anal. Toxicol.*, 20 (6), pp. 362–368.

Bogusz, M.J., Maier, R.D. and Driessen, S. (1997) "Morphine, Morphine-3-glucuronide, Morphine-6-glucuronide, and 6-monoacetylmorphine Determined By Means of Atmospheric Pressure Chemical Ionization-mass Spectrometry-liquid Chromatography in Body Fluids of Heroin Victims", *J. Anal. Toxicol.*, 21, pp. 346–355.

Bowie, L. and Kirkpatrick, P. (1989) "Simultaneous Determination of Monoacetylmorphine, Morphine, Codeine, and Other Opiates by GC/MS", *J. Anal. Toxicol.*, 13, pp. 326–329.

Bruera, E., Macmillan, K., Hanson, J. and MacDonald, R.N. (1989) "The Cognitive Effects of the Administration of Narcotic Analgesics in Patients with Cancer Pain", *Pain*, 39 (1), pp. 13–16.

Chen, B.H., Taylor, E.H. and Pappas, A.A. (1990) "Comparison of Derivatives for Determination of Codeine and Morphine by Gas Chromatography/Mass Spectrometry", *J. Anal. Toxicol.*, 14 (1), pp. 12–17.

Cushman, P., Jr. (1987) "Alcohol and Opioids: Possible Interactions of Clinical Importance", *Adv. Alcohol Subst. Abuse*, 6 (3), pp. 33–46.

Drost, R.H., Ionescu, T.I., van Rossum, J.M. and Maes, R.A. (1996) "Pharmacokinetics of Morphine After Epidural Administration in Man", *Arz. Forsch.*, 36, pp. 1096–1100.

ElSohly, M.A. and Salamone, S.J. (1999) "Prevalence of Drugs Used in Cases of Alleged Sexual Assault", *J. Anal. Toxicol.*, 23 (3), pp. 141–146.

Engelhart, D.A., Lavins, E.S. and Sutheimer, C.A. (1998) "Drugs of Abuse in Nails", *J. Anal. Toxicol.*, 22, pp. 314–318.

Forney, R., Hulpieu, H. and Hughes, F. (1962) "The Comparative Enhancement of the Depressant Actions of Alcohol by Eight Representative Ataractic and Analgesic Drugs", *Experientia*, 18, pp. 468–470.

Fuller, D.C. and Anderson, W.H. (1992) "A Simplified Procedure for the Determination of Free Codeine, Free Morphine, and 6-acetylmorphine in Urine", *J. Anal. Toxicol.*, 16 (5), pp. 315–318.

Grinstead, G.F. (1991) "A Closer Look at Acetyl and Pentafluoropropionyl Derivatives for Quantitative Analysis of Morphine and Codeine by Gas Chromatography/Mass Spectrometry", *J. Anal. Toxicol.*, 15 (6), pp. 293–298.

Guillot, J.G., Lefebvre, M. and Weber, J.P. (1997) "Determination of Heroin, 6-acetylmorphine, and Morphine in Biological Fluids Using Their Propionyl Derivatives with Ion Trap GC-MS", *J. Anal. Toxicol.*, 21 (2), pp. 127–133.

Hammargren, W.R. and Henderson, G.L. (1988) "Analyzing Normetabolites of the Fentanyls by Gas Chromatography/Electron Capture Detection", *J. Anal. Toxicol.*, 12 (4), pp. 183–191.

Heishman, S.J. (ed.) (1998) "Pharmacodynamics". In *Drug Abuse Handbook*, pp. 203–306. Boca Raton, FL: CRC Press LLC.

Hoja, H., Marquet, P., Verneuil, B., Lotfi, H., Dupuy, J.L. and Lachatre, G. (1997) "Determination of Buprenorphine and Norbuprenorphine in Whole Blood by Liquid Chromatography-Mass Spectrometry", *J. Anal. Toxicol.*, 21 (2), pp. 160–165.

Jenkins, A.J. and Cone, E.J. (1998) "Pharmacokinetics: Drug Absorption Distribution and Elimination". In *Drug Abuse Handbook*, pp. 151–201. Boca Raton, FL: CRC Press LLC.

Jennison, T.A., Wozniak, E., Nelson, G. and Urry, F.M. (1993) "The Quantitative Conversion of Morphine 3-beta-D Glucuronide to Morphine Using Beta-glucuronidase Obtained from Patella Vulga-a as Compared to Acid Hydrolysis", *J. Anal. Toxicol.*, 17 (4), pp. 208–210.

Karch, S.B. (1996) *The Pathology of Drug Abuse*, pp. 281–408. Boca Raton, FL: CRC Press LLC.

Kerr, B., Hill, H., Coda, B., Calogero, M., Chapman, C.R., Hunt, E., Buffington, V. and Mackie, A. (1991) "Concentration-related Effects of Morphine on Cognition and Motor Control in Human Subjects", *Neuropsychopharmacol.*, 5 (3), pp. 157–166.

Kerrigan, S. and Goldberger, B.A. (1999) "Opioids". In Levine, B. (ed.) *Principles of Forensic Toxicology*, pp. 202–220. Washington, DC: AACC Press.

Kintz, P., Tracqui, A. and Mangin, P. (1996) "Sweat Testing in Opioid Users with a Sweat Patch", *J. Anal. Toxicol.*, 20, pp. 393–397.

Kiplinger, G.F., Sokol, G. and Rodda, B.E. (1974) "Effect of Combined Alcohol and Propoxyphene on Human Performance", *Arch. Int. Pharmacodyn.*, 212, pp. 175–180.

Kuhlman, J.J., Jr., Magluilo, J., Jr., Cone, E. and Levine, B. (1996) "Simultaneous Assay of Buprenorphine and Norbuprenorphine by Negative Chemical Ionization Tandem Mass Spectrometry", *J. Anal. Toxicol.*, 20 (4), pp. 229–235.

Lee, H.M. and Lee, C.W. (1991) " Determination of Morphine and Codeine in Blood and Bile by Gas Chromatography with a Derivatization Procedure", *J. Anal. Toxicol.*, 15, pp. 182–187.

Moffat, A. C. *et al.* (eds) (1986) *Clarke's Isolation and Identification of Drugs* (2nd edn) pp. 55–69. London: The Pharmaceutical Press.

Pacifici, R., Pichini, S., Altieri, I., Caronna, A., Passa, A.R. and Zuccaro, P. (1995) "High Performance Liquid Chromatographic-Electrospray Mass Spectrometric Determination of Morphine and its 3- and 6-glucuronides: Application to Pharmacokinetic Studies", *J. Chromatog. B*, 664, pp. 329–334.

Paul, B.D., Mell, L.D., Jr., Mitchell, J.M., Irving, J. and Novak, A.J. (1985) "Simultaneous Identification and Quantitation of Codeine and Morphine in Urine by Capillary Gas Chromatography and Mass Spectroscopy", *J. Anal. Toxicol.*, 9 (5), pp. 222–226.

Polettini, A., Groppi, A. and Montagna, M. (1993) "Rapid and Highly Selective GC/MS/MS Detection of Heroin and its Metabolites in Hair", *Forensic Sci. Int.*, 63, pp. 217–225.

Sawe, J., Dahlstrom, B., Paalzow, L. and Rane, A. (1981) "Morphine Kinetics in Cancer Patients", *Clin. Pharmacol. Ther.*, 30, pp. 629–635.

Schneider, U., Bevilacqua,C., Jacobs, R., Karst, M., Dietrich, D., Becker, H., Müller-Vahl, K., Seeland, I., Gielsdorf, D., Schedlowski, M. and Emrich, H. (1999) "Effects of Fentanyl and Low Doses of Alcohol on Neuropsychological Performance in Healthy Subjects", *Neuropsychbiol.*, 39, pp. 38–43.

Slawson, M.H., Crouch, D.J., Andrenyak, D.M., Rollins, D.E., Lu, J.K. and Bailey, P.L. (1999) "Determination of Morphine, Morphine-3-glucuronide, and Morphine-6-glucuronide in Plasma After Intravenous and Intrathecal Morphine Administration Using HPLC with Electrospray Ionization and Tandem Mass Spectrometry", *J. Anal. Toxicol.*, 23, pp. 468–473.

Tatsuno, M., Nishikawa, M., Katagi, M. and Tsuchihashi, H. (1996) "Simultaneous Detection of Illicit Drugs in Human Urine by Liquid Chromatography-Mass Spectrometry", *J. Anal. Toxicol.*, 20, pp. 281–286.

Tracqui, A., Kintz, P., Ludes, B., Jamey, C. and Mangin, P. (1995) "The Detection of Opiate Drugs in Nontraditional Specimens (Clothing): A Report of Ten Cases", *J. Forensic Sci.*, 40 (2), pp. 263–265.

Tyrefors, N., Hyllbrant, B., Ekman, L., Johansson, M. and Langstrom, B. (1996) "Determination of Morphine, Morphine-3-glucuronide and Morphine-6-glucuronide in Human Serum by Solid-phase Extraction and Liquid Chromatography-Mass Spectrometry with Electrospray Ionisation", *J. Chromatog. A*, 729, pp. 279–285.

Venho, I., Eerola, R., Venho, E. and Vartiainen, O. (1955) "Sensitization to Morphine by Experimentally Induced Alcoholism in White Mice", *Ann. Med. Exp. Biol. Fenn.,* 33, pp. 249–252.

Veselis, R.A., Reinsel, R.A., Feshchenko, V.A., Wronski, M., Dnistrian, A., Dutchers, S. and Wilson, R. (1994) "Impaired Memory and Behavioral Performance with Fentanyl at Low Plasma Concentrations", *Anesth. Analg.*, 79 (5), pp. 952–960.

Wang, W.L., Darwin, W.D. and Cone, E.J. (1994) "Simultaneous Assay of Cocaine, Heroin and Metabolites in Hair, Plasma, Saliva and Urine by Gas Chromatography-Mass Spectrometry", *J. Chromatog. B*, 660, pp. 279–290.

Watts, V. and Caplan, Y. (1988) "Determination of Fentanyl in Whole Blood at Subnanogram Concentrations by Dual Capillary Column Gas Chromatography with Nitrogen Sensitive Detectors and Gas Chromatography/Mass Spectrometry", *J. Anal. Toxicol.*, 12 (5), pp. 246–254.

White, R. (1955) "Intravenous Ethyl Alcohol Analgesia with Intravenous Pitocin Induction of Labor", *Amer. J. Obstet. Gynec.*, 70, pp. 983–986.

Wilkins, D.G., Rollins, D.E., Seaman, J., Haughey, H., Krueger, G. and Foltz, R. (1995) "Quantitative Determination of Codeine and its Major Metabolites in Human Hair by Gas Chromatography-positive ion Chemical Ionization Mass Spectrometry: A Clinical Application", *J. Anal. Toxicol.*, 19, pp. 269–274.

Wright, A.W. and Smith, M.T. (1998) "Improved One Step Solid Phase Extraction Method for Morphine, Morphine 3 Glucuronide and Morphine 6 Glucuronide From Plasma and Quantitation Using High Performance Liquid Chromatography with Electrochemical Detection", *Ther. Drug Monitoring,* 20, pp. 215–218.

Zacny, J.P. (1995) "A Review of the Effects of Opioids on Psychomotor and Cognitive Functioning in Humans", *Exp. Clin. Psychopharmacol.*, 3, p. 432.

Zuccaro, P., Ricciarello, R., Pichini, S., Pacifici, R., Altieri, I., Pellegrini, M. and D'Ascenzo, G. (1997) "Simultaneous Determination of Heroin 6-monoacetylmorphine, Morphine, and its Glucuronides by Liquid Chromatography – Atmospheric Pressure Ionspray-Mass Spectrometry", *J. Anal. Toxicol.*, 21 (4), pp. 268–277.

CHAPTER 8

MISCELLANEOUS PRESCRIPTION AND OVER-THE-COUNTER MEDICATIONS

Graham Jones
Peter Singer

This chapter will discuss the availability, pharmacodynamics, pharmacokinetics and analysis of a number of prescription and non-prescription drugs, including the antihistamines, antidepressants, antipsychotics, barbiturates, chloral hydrate and other sedatives. However, although each group of drugs has some unique properties, some comments can be made which are applicable to all of them.

PROPERTIES OF DRUGS USED TO COMMIT DFSA

Drugs used for drug-facilitated sexual assault, have one or more of the following properties: cause sedation, cause amnesia, are odorless and tasteless, dissolve readily in alcoholic or other beverages, and are rapidly absorbed after oral administration. Although the short-acting benzodiazepines probably come closest to the so-called "ideal" properties, the reality is that a wide range of other drugs could be, and have been, used to "drug" potential sexual assault victims. Alcohol is the most common substance because it is widely available and may already have been willingly consumed by the victim. However, almost any drug with even mildly sedative properties might be used by a perpetrator, especially if it is readily available to him or her. Some drugs are "over-the-counter" (OTC) and can be purchased by anyone. Others may be available through the perpetrator's employment (e.g. medical, paramedical, veterinary), via a legitimate prescription (self, friend or family member), or illegally bought on "the street."

DETECTABILITY BEFORE INGESTION

Most drug formulations will dissolve or at least disperse in beverages or food of various types. Tablets, and sometimes capsules, will often have some type of inert filler which will disperse, but not necessarily dissolve. Whether that insoluble residue is noticeable would depend on the type of beverage (e.g. light vs. dark, opacity), the physical and social circumstances (e.g. lighting, noise, distractions) and whether the victim is already intoxicated with alcohol. Whether or not the victim is able to "taste" the intoxicant will also depend on a number of factors. Most medications have some degree of bitterness. However, whether that bitterness would be noticed by the victim also depends on a number of circumstances: for example, how strongly tasting the beverage or food itself is and how familiar the victim is with it. A drug spiked into a club soda with vodka might be more easily detected than if the same drug was spiked into a "bitter" style beer or a "gin and tonic."

ONSET OF ACTION

The presence of large amounts of food may delay absorption and will often lower the peak blood concentrations of most medications. This is well documented for alcohol and is known to be the case for other medications. However, how quickly a person "feels" the effects of an illicitly administered drug will depend on how quickly it is ingested, how large the dose is, the amount of undigested food in the stomach, and the degree of pre-existing alcohol intoxication (if any). Therefore onset of action will be very variable, and even subjective. For some drugs, 30 min or more may elapse before any significant effect is noticed. Other drugs, notably short-acting sedatives, may exert a powerful effect within 10–15 min, especially in the absence of food and presence of alcohol.

DETECTION AND MEASUREMENT

SPECIMEN TYPE

[1] Whole blood is comprised of red and white blood cells, in a complex protein solution called "plasma." If whole blood is drawn and centrifuged before it is allowed to coagulate, the red and white blood cells form the red sediment in the bottom portion of the tube; the clear, straw-colored fluid on top is "plasma." If the blood is centrifuged after the blood has clotted, the straw-colored fluid on top is called "serum." Serum is the same as plasma, except that serum does not contain the clotting agent fibrinogen and platelets. For forensic toxicology purposes, serum and plasma are usually regarded as equivalent.

The preferred specimen for the detection of a drug in a DFSA case is usually, but not always, urine. The reason is that many drugs or their breakdown products (metabolites) are more easily detected in urine, than in blood or serum,[1] and are usually detectable for longer (days rather than hours). With the exception of barbiturates and other sedatives, most of the drugs discussed in this chapter (antihistamines, antidepressants and antipsychotics) have a chemically "basic" character, and even though many are extensively metabolized, they tend to occur at much higher concentrations in urine than in blood. Also, while most good forensic toxicology laboratories can readily analyze whole blood or serum, the preferred specimen for most clinical toxicology laboratories for "drug screening" is urine.

SCREENING TESTS

With the exception of barbiturates and tricyclic antidepressants, sensitive automated screening methods (e.g. immunoassay) are not generally available for the drugs discussed in this chapter. However, many are detectable in blood for several hours after ingestion, and for one or more days in urine, if other appropriate techniques are used. All of the drugs discussed in this chapter are "unique" chemicals and therefore their presence will invariably be proof of ingestion and cannot be confused with naturally occurring substances (unlike, for example, GHB, which is a naturally occurring biomolecule). However, the length of time a specific drug can be detected after ingestion will vary tremendously, depending on a number of factors – including the capabilities of the laboratory. Specific testing techniques are discussed below.

Immunoassay

Several drugs of abuse, including barbiturates, can be detected using various types of immunoassay. The advantage of immunoassay testing is that it is sensitive, can be automated, and has a relatively low cost per unit test. The disadvantages of immunoassays are that by their nature they are not specific enough to be relied on as the sole forensic test, and they may not detect all drugs in a particular class (either at all, or with sufficient sensitivity). Immunoassay tests can therefore indicate the presence of a drug or drug class, but cannot identify it specifically. Most immunoassays, although not all, are matrix-sensitive; that is, some cannot be used on whole or hemolyzed blood or may give unreliable results. For forensic purposes, all immunoassay presumptive positive results must be confirmed by another non-immunoassay technique such as GC/MS.

Thin layer chromatography (TLC)

TLC has been used for years as a screening test for drugs in urine. It has the advantage that it is relatively inexpensive, can detect a wide range of drugs, and potentially give more information about the identity of a drug than can immunoassay. The disadvantages of TLC are that it is difficult to effectively automate, it requires significant skill and training to interpret, it is generally less sensitive than immunoassay and other techniques, and it cannot readily be applied to blood or serum without extensive sample preparation. For these reasons, the use of TLC in forensic toxicology screening is diminishing in favor of other chromatographic[2] techniques. Ironically, in a few specific circumstances TLC may give results which are as or more diagnostic than mass spectrometry in detecting certain antidepressants and antipsychotics.

[2] Chromatography is the science of separation, and can take place in both the liquid (TLC, HPLC and capillary electrophoresis) and gas phases (e.g. GC).

Gas chromatography (GC)

GC has been used for decades as an analytical technique for screening and quantitating drugs and other toxins in biological fluids. Once sample preparation is completed, GC analysis can be automated, it is sensitive, and can be very specific if used in combination with mass spectrometry (MS). A disadvantage is that single samples can take 10–20 min to analyze (even after sample preparation), it is relatively expensive (especially in combination with mass spectrometry), and requires skilled and highly trained personnel to operate. GC-based screening methods and quantitative assays may use detectors other than mass spectrometry. These include flame ionization detection (FID), which is relatively non-specific; virtually all carbon-based substances will produce a response. One of the most common detectors for drug analysis is the nitrogen-phosphorus detector (NPD), also called a thermionic specific detector (TSD). It will detect most drugs and other compounds which contain at least one nitrogen or phosphorus atom (which most do). Less commonly used, but very valuable for certain types of drugs, is the electron capture detector (ECD), which gives a relatively selective response for compounds such as benzodiazepines which contain halogens (e.g. fluorine, chlorine, bromine).

Other techniques

Several other techniques may be used to detect drugs in blood or urine. These include high-performance liquid chromatography (HPLC, increasingly used in combination with mass spectrometry) and capillary electrophoresis (CE). Most or all of the chromatographic techniques (including CE) can be used to detect and identify the vast majority of drugs covered in this chapter. However, whether or not they actually do, or do so with sufficient sensitivity, depends on the individual laboratory and the specific methods used. HPLC and CE are most commonly used with ultraviolet (UV) or photodiode array (PDA) detectors, which measure the absorption of UV wavelength light by different substances.

A general discussion of the analytical techniques used to detect and identify drugs and their metabolites is given in various standard texts and papers (Karch, 1997; Maurer, 1992; Moffat, 1986).

The laboratory and the results

It cannot be emphasized enough, that whether or not a specific DFSA drug is detected depends not only on the properties of the specific drug, but also its dose, the time since ingestion that the blood or urine sample was collected, and, most importantly, on the specific analytical methods used. It is very important to understand the significance of a reported "negative" result. Obviously, a "negative" result may mean that no drugs were involved in the assault. It may mean that sufficient time had elapsed between the alleged administration and when the sample was collected, that the drugs had been cleared from the body, or that the concentration was below the detection limit of the test. However, a "negative" result may also mean that the methods used by the laboratory would not have detected the presence of a particular drug, no matter what the concentration, or that the sensitivity of the test used was not adequate for the purpose. It has to be borne in mind that the concentrations of drugs to be detected after a DFSA may be significantly less than someone taking the drug daily for medical treatment, especially if collection of a blood or urine sample was delayed several hours. Notwithstanding, no single analytical test will detect all potential drugs used to facilitate sexual assault. For example, some laboratories, particularly smaller clinical or forensic toxicology laboratories, may rely almost solely on a panel of immunoassay tests for drug detection, and may even lack the means to properly confirm presumptive positive results. Even supposedly comprehensive and sensitive GC/MS techniques used by large forensic laboratories will not readily detect all potential DFSA drugs, including some antihistamines, antidepressants, antipsychotics, and sedatives. It is important to know whether or not the testing laboratory has adequately sensitive methods, that they know the type of drugs which could be present, and that the concentrations may be very low. As with any forensic toxicology testing, it will assist the laboratory if specific drugs are suspected. And if the name of specific drugs is not suspected, knowing that the specimens are from a suspected sexual assault victim will help direct the analyses appropriately.

DIPHENHYDRAMINE AND RELATED ANTIHISTAMINES

AVAILABILITY

Antihistamines are used for the treatment of a variety of allergic reactions and, in some cases, nausea. Although most are available over the counter (OTC), some (e.g. hydroxyzine) are only available by prescription. Diphenhydramine and doxylamine are specifically approved as OTC "sleep-aids." Diphenhydramine and other antihistamines are marketed in tablet, capsule, and liquid formulations, either on their own, or combined with other drugs such as caffeine, dextromethorphan, decongestants (e.g. phenylephrine, phenylpropanolamine and pseudoephedrine) and sometimes analgesics (e.g. acetylsalicylic acid [Aspirin, ASA], acetaminophen, ibuprofen) in so-called cough and cold medications. Antihistamines are probably one of the most widely available OTC medications, second only to analgesics.

It is worth noting that diphenhydramine is also available as a component of dimenhydrinate (most commonly marketed as Gravol). Dimenhydrinate is the 8-chlorotheophylline salt of diphenhydramine. Therefore, when dimenhydrinate is taken, it readily dissociates into its component parts, although only diphenhydramine is usually detected and measured. Confusion can result because there is a common misconception that diphenhydramine and dimenhydrinate are unrelated substances; they are essentially the same.

PHARMACODYNAMICS

As the names suggests, antihistamines counter the undesirable effects of histamine. Histamine is a chemical which is released in response to allergic reactions or irritation of various types, including environmental allergens and drugs. The primary effects of histamine include peripheral vasodilation (dilation of the small blood vessels), which causes "flushing" or reddening of the skin, itching (H_1 receptor effects), and constriction or tightening of the airway and increased secretion of gastric juice (H_2 receptor effects). The main pharmacological effect of diphenhydramine and other antihistamines is to block H_1 receptors, inhibiting the action of histamine on the small blood vessels. However, while the older, "classical" antihistamines, such as diphenhydramine, are highly effective, they also have pronounced sedative action, due to their action on H_1 receptors in the CNS. They also produce side-effects such as dry nose and mouth due to an additional anticholinergic effect. The "classical" antihistamines include chlorpheniramine, brompheniramine, doxylamine, promethazine, hydroxyzine and triprolidine.

However, the newer generation antihistamines such as terfenadine, astemizole, and cetirizine cause far less sedation than the older drugs such as diphenhydramine. Many studies have looked at the sedative potential of antihistamines: while few, if any have been found to be totally without any sedative action, the effect is minimal for many. Any sedative effects are usually dose-related (Carruthers *et al.*, 1978; Hindmarch and Shamsi, 1999; Woodward, 1990).

As for almost any drug which causes sedation, antihistamines have at least an additive depressant effect in combination with alcohol and any other sedative or narcotic drugs the victim may have taken. The more sedating an antihistamine is when taken on its own, the more likely it is to cause even greater sedation in combination with alcohol. However, for ethical reasons, few studies have quantified this relationship, especially at higher blood alcohol concentrations.

The most important side-effects of diphenhydramine and related antihistamines include sedation, impairment of motor skills, dizziness, tinnitus, fatigue, blurred vision, and paradoxically, euphoria, nervousness, and insomnia. After overdosage, diphenhydramine can cause exaggerated side-effects, but more seriously reduced consciousness, cardiac arrhythmias, coma and death.

PHARMACOKINETICS

Diphenhydramine and related antihistamines are all readily absorbed after oral administration, either from tablet, capsule or liquid formulations. Peak blood

Antihistamine	Sedative activity[1]	Anticholinergic activity[2]	Half-life (hours)[3, 5]	Plasma levels ng/ml (dose mg)[4, 5]	Trade names[6]
Astemizole	NS	0	20–24	<1.0 (10)	Hismanal®
Brompheniramine	S		15–22	15 (8)	Dimetapp®, Dimetane®, Puretane®
Cetirizine	NS	+/++	6.5–10	400 (10)	Zyrtec®
Chlorpheniramine	S	0/++[7]	12–43	17 (12)	usually in combination e.g. Chlor-Tripolon®
Clemastine	S	+/++	21	0.6–1.6 (2)	Tavist®
Cyclizine	S		7–24	69 (50)	Marezine®
Diphenhydramine	S	++	3–14	83 (50)	Benadryl®, Nytol®, Gravol® (as dimen-hydrinate)
Doxylamine	S		10	99 (25)	Unisom®, Bendectin®
Fexofenadine	NS		9–20	0.2 (80)	Allegra®
Hydroxyzine	S		13–27	70 (50)	Atarax®, Vistaril®
Loratadine	NS	0	3–20	5 (10)	Claritin®
Promethazine	S	++	9–16	29 (50)	Phenergan®, Remsed®, Zipan®
Terfenadine	NS	0	15	1.5 (60)	Seldane®
Tripelennamine	S		2.9–5.3	60 (100)	Pyribenzamine®
Triprolidine	S	++	2–5	7–25 (2.7)	usually in combination e.g. Actifed®

1   Adapted from Hindmarch and Shamsi (1999).
2   Adapted from Woodward (1988).
3   The half-lives quoted are average from the literature; half-lives for some individuals are outside these ranges.
4   The plasma concentrations quoted are averages or ranges for a particular study, concentrations for some individuals may differ and will invariably be higher for multiple doses.
5   Ellenhorn, 1997; Baselt, 2000 and references therein.
6   Some of the common North American trade names are given; many "generic" medications may have trade names of their own; some of the "older" antihistamines may be available under multiple generic names or as one constituent in numerous multi-component cold/allergy preparations.
7   Dose-dependent.

concentrations for diphenhydramine are reported to occur at 1.5–3 hours, although the onset of action would begin considerably sooner. The half-life of the antihistamines in blood varies considerably, being about 9 hr (range 3–14 hr) for diphenhydramine and averaging 20 and 24 hr for hydroxyzine and chlorpheniramine, respectively (Simons *et al.*, 1984; Vallner *et al.*, 1982). It can

Table 8.1

Properties of some antihistamines.

be expected that in general terms, the longer the half-life of the antihistamine, the longer it can be detected in blood and urine.

ANALYSIS

Automated screening techniques (e.g. immunoassay) are not generally available for antihistamines. However, many of the common sedating antihistamines are detectable in urine by a variety of techniques, including TLC and GC/NPD or GC/MS. The detection limit for many of the antihistamines by TLC (e.g. Toxi-Lab™), including diphenhydramine, is about 0.5 to 1.0 mg/L in urine. However, TLC does not generally have sufficient sensitivity to detect antihistamines in blood or serum. For example, one study reported an average plasma concentration of 0.083 mg/L three hours after administration, falling to less than 0.01 mg/L after 24 hours (Bilzer and Gundert-Remy, 1973). For this reason, GC is preferred to TLC, if possible in combination with mass spectrometry. In fact some form of mass spectrometry analysis is virtually essential if the results are to have forensic value. Most antihistamines are extensively metabolized, although sufficient of the unchanged drug persists in the blood for detection several hours after administration, if sufficiently sensitive techniques are used. Detection times are typically much longer in urine, even extending to two or more days after a single dose (Maurer and Pfleger, 1988a; Maurer and Pfleger, 1988b). Use of the newer antihistamines as DFSA drugs is less likely due to their relative lack of sedative properties.

AMITRIPTYLINE AND RELATED ANTIDEPRESSANTS

AVAILABILITY

All antidepressant drugs are available only by prescription or via illicit means. They are most commonly available in tablet or capsule formulation. As with the antihistamines, the individual antidepressants vary significantly in their abuse potential as DFSA drugs, in terms of their ability to sedate, and their ability to cause amnesia.

Antidepressants, as the name implies, are used to treat several types of clinical depression, and for some (e.g. clomipramine), obsessive compulsive disorders. The antidepressants vary tremendously in their theoretical ability to act as DFSA drugs. In general terms, amitriptyline and other tricyclic antidepressants (TCAs) have the greatest potential for such abuse because of their anticholinergic action. In contrast, the newer SSRI (selective serotonin reuptake inhibitor) antidepressants would theoretically have relatively little effectiveness as DFSA drugs because they have little or no anticholinergic action and seldom cause much sedation. Examples of the TCAs include amitriptyline, nortriptyline, imipramine, desipramine, trimipramine, clomipramine, doxepin, and protriptyline. The SSRI antidepressants are regarded as causing less sedation and being less toxic than the TCAs, and include fluoxetine, paroxetine, sertraline, fluvoxamine, citalopram, and mirtazapine. Other, related, "cyclic" antidepressants include trazodone, maprotiline, and amoxapine, and

Table 8.2

Properties of some antidepressant drugs.

Drug	Sedative activity[1]	Anticholinergic activity[1]	Half-life (hours)[2, 4]	Peak level ng/ml (dose mg)[3, 4]	Trade names[5]
Amitriptyline	+++	+++	8–51	16–35 (50)	Elavil®
Nortriptyline	+	+	15–91	30–61 (70)	Aventyl®; Pamelor®
Imipramine	++	++	6–20	8–84 (75)	Tofranil®
Desipramine	+	+	12–54	8–15 (50)	Norpramine®; Pertofrane®
Doxepin	+++	++	8–25	24 (75)	Sinequan®
Dothiapin			24	25–95 (75)	Prothiaden®
Protriptyline	+	+	74	10–22 (30)	Vivactil®
Trimipramine	+++	+++	16–39	15–51 (50)	Surmonyil®; Stangyl®
Maprotiline	+	+	36–105	45–60 (50)	Ludiomil®
Trazodone	+++	0	4–7	1100 (100)	Desyrel®
Fluoxetine	0	0	24–72	15–55 (40)	Prozac®
Paroxetine	0	(+) slight	7–37	1–33 (20)	Paxil®
Citalopram	0	0	25–35	42–52 (50)	Celexa®
Mirtazapine	++	+	20–40	5–100 (15–80)	Remeron®
Moclobemide	0	0	1–4	100–600 (50)	Aurorix®; Manerix®
Venlafaxine	0	0	3–7	70 (50)	Effexor®

1 Adapted from Rudorfer *et al.* (1994), with additional information added, based on information in the manufacturer product monographs.
2 The half-lives quoted are average from the literature; half-lives for some individuals are outside these ranges.
3 The plasma concentrations quoted are averages or ranges for a particular study; concentrations for some individuals may differ and will invariably be higher for multiple doses.
4 Ellenhorn, 1997; Baselt, 2000 and references therein.
5 Some of the common North American trade names are given; many "generic" medications may have trade names of their own; some of the "older" antidepressants may be available under multiple generic names.

are reputed to be of intermediate toxicity between the TCAs and the SSRIs. Yet another, distinct class of antidepressants are the monoamine oxidase inhibitors (MAOIs), which include phenelzine, tranylcypromine, and moclobemide; their potential as DFSA candidates is difficult to assess.

PHARMACODYNAMICS

The pharmacological action of amitriptyline and the other TCAs is not completely understood, but is related to their effect of blocking reuptake of one or more neurotransmitters in the central nervous system, thereby prolonging and potentiating their action. The effect is known to be more complex than originally thought, since TCAs usually take 2–3 weeks to fully develop their antidepressant effect when given therapeutically. However, it is the undesirable side-effects of the TCAs which makes them candidates as DFSA drugs. Amitriptyline and most TCAs exhibit side-effects which including sleepiness, lightheadedness, a slight drop in blood pressure, and unsteadiness. Furthermore, the TCAs also exhibit anticholinergic (atropine-like) effects, which include a dry mouth, blurred vision, and urinary retention. It is the anticholinergic action that is thought to cause the amnesic effects of amitriptyline (Curran *et al.*, 1988; Sakulsripong *et al.*, 1991).

Toxic effects of amitriptyline overdose include exaggerated side-effects such as sedation, but also paradoxical nervousness and restlessness, in addition to more severe anticholinergic actions such as dry mouth, dilated pupils, urinary retention, tachycardia (rapid heart-beat) and intestinal stasis. In severe cases of poisoning, cardiac arrhythmias, seizures, and coma may result. The toxicity of TCAs is more likely to be increased in the presence of high blood alcohol concentrations and in persons with pre-existing heart disease.

PHARMACOKINETICS

Virtually all antidepressants are given orally. In fact for most, the onset of antidepressant action takes several days or weeks so there is seldom benefit in administering the drugs parenterally. The half-lives of the TCAs tend to be quite long. For example, the half-life of amitriptyline is around 24 hr (range 8–51 hr) (Rogers *et al.*, 1978). Therefore, with appropriate analytical techniques, it should be possible to detect the parent drug or their metabolites in blood for several hours after ingestion, and perhaps for several days, particularly in urine. It should be remembered by testing laboratories that blood or plasma concentrations may be much lower after DFSA than after chronic therapy for depression. For example, single 50 mg doses have been reported to produce peak serum concentrations in the range 0.016 to 0.035 mg/L after 2–4 hr (Garland,

1977). That is significantly lower than the 0.10–0.30 mg/L typically attained after chronic therapeutic dosing, and well below the concentrations which post-mortem toxicology laboratories typically screen for. Urine may be a better specimen. However, most of the antidepressants are extensively metabolized, and therefore ability to detect amitriptyline or other TCA after ingestion will depend on the ability of the laboratory to detect metabolites. If only the parent drug is targeted, results will be very variable.

There are two major metabolic pathways for the TCAs. The first major pathway is demethylation, in most cases forming a metabolite that has pharmacological activity. For example, amitriptyline is demethylated to nortriptyline (a drug in its own right), imipramine forms desipramine (also a marketed drug); doxepin, trimipramine and clomipramine also form the corresponding "desmethyl" metabolites. The second major pathway is hydroxylation and subsequent conjugation to the glucuronide metabolites. These metabolites represent most of what will be found in urine. Therefore, the ability of a laboratory to detect the hydroxylated metabolites is key to providing evidence that the parent drug was given, since the parent drug may not be present. Detection of the hydroxylated TCA metabolites will provide unique evidence that the parent drug was ingested. However, few toxicology laboratories target analysis of these metabolites, unless specifically asked to do so.

ANALYSIS

Commercial immunoassays are available for the detection of TCAs as a "class" in serum or plasma. However, such assays will not detect all drugs in the class with equal sensitivity, due to differing crossreactivity. Also, such assays may not be sufficiently sensitive for detection of a TCA which was ingested several hours before, especially if the dose was not large and the perpetrator was relying on the additional presence of a high concentration of alcohol in the victim. One other disadvantage of commercial immunoassay tests is that they often have reduced sensitivity in the presence of hemolyzed red cells and may not work at all with whole blood. Such assays may or may not work well with urine samples due to unknown or unpredictable crossreactivity with the TCA metabolites. In any event, confirmation by a non-immunoassay technique is required for forensic purposes.

Detection of amitriptyline and the other TCAs may therefore be best done with chromatographic tests such as GC or HPLC, and preferably in combination with MS. There are innumerable methods in the literature which describe the measurement of TCAs in serum, plasma or blood, although less for urine. However, as stated above, sensitive detection of TCA ingestion requires an assay which will identify the hydroxylated metabolites, if urine is used. A protocol for the sensitive detection of a wide range of antidepressant drugs in urine has been described (Maurer, 1992; Maurer and Bickeboeller-Friedrich, 2000).

CHLORPROMAZINE AND RELATED ANTIPSYCHOTICS

AVAILABILITY

Like the antidepressants, all antipsychotic medications are only available on prescription, or by illicit means. The use of chlorpromazine dates back to the 1950s, although it is still a valuable drug and remains in common use. It is a derivative of phenothiazine, and therefore chemically related antipsychotic drugs are commonly referred to as "phenothiazines." These include methotrimeprazine, thioridazine, trifluoperazine, prochlorperazine, triflupromazine, fluphenazine and perphenazine. Pharmacologically, they used to be referred to as "major tranquilizers," because they were the first therapeutic choice for calming or sedating psychotic patients. Over the past 20–30 years other types of antipsychotics have been developed, including haloperidol, loxapine, chlorprothixene, thiothixene, pimozide, clozapine, and more recently risperidone and olanzapine.

Antipsychotics are also sometimes referred to as neuroleptics. Most of the phenothiazines and many of the other drugs are available in both oral (tablet, capsule, solution) and injectable forms. In injectable form (usually intramuscular), sedative action of the antipsychotics takes effect almost immediately and certainly within a few minutes. Unlike antidepressants, antipsychotic medications are sometimes required to be given in emergency situations to sedate a disturbed patient. Some potent antipsychotic medications are also given as long-acting oily "depo" intramuscular injections.

PHARMACODYNAMICS

Chlorpromazine and the other antipsychotics primarily have a depressant action on the central nervous system (CNS). They are used clinically to control various types of abnormal behavior, including psychoses and schizophrenia. Their mechanism of action is thought to be related primarily to inhibition of the neurotransmitter, dopamine. When used for the treatment of psychiatric disorders, the range of dosage used can be enormous, sometimes ranging over 100-fold from one patient to another, depending on the specific drug. However, tolerance to very high doses is usually attained over an extended period of time. Many antipsychotics, including chlorpromazine, also have a powerful antiemetic (anti-nausea) action and are sometimes used for that purpose where the nausea is severe; prochlorperazine is a good example. Although less

Antipsychotic	Sedative activity[1]	Anticholinergic activity[1]	Half-life (hours)[2, 4]	Plasma levels ng/ml (dose mg)[3, 4]	Trade names[5]
Chlorpromazine	+++	Yes	18–30	18 (150)	Largactil®
Methotrimeprazine	+++	Yes	17–78	80 (300–400)	Nozinan®
Thioridazine	+++	Yes	26–36	240 (100)	Mellaril®
Trifluoperazine	+	Yes			Stelazine®
Haloperidol	+	0	14–41	3 (10)	Haldol®
Clozapine	+	Yes	6–17	140 (100)	Clozaril®; Leponex®
Olanzapine	0	0	21–54	20 (15)	Zyprexa®
Quetiapine	+	0	3–9	140–365 (75)	Seroquel®
Risperidone	0	0	3–20	8 (1)	Risperdal®

1 Adapted from Gilman (1990), Rudorfer et al. (1994), plus additional information based on information in the manufacturer product monographs.
2 The half-lives quoted are average from the literature, half-lives for some individuals are outside these ranges. The half-lives of many of the antipsychotic medications are pharmacogenetically determined.
3 The plasma concentrations quoted are averages or ranges for a particular study; concentrations for some individuals may differ and will invariably be higher for multiple doses.
4 Ellenhorn, 1997; Baselt, 2000 and references therein.
5 Some of the common North American trade names are given; many "generic" medications may have trade names of their own; some of the "older" antipsychotics may be available under multiple generic names.

commonly used as antihistamines, many of the phenothiazines also have that property. In fact promethazine was commonly used as an antihistamine until largely replaced by less sedating drugs. Promethazine was commonly used as a premedication cocktail, before receiving general anesthesia.

Table 8.3

Properties of some antipsychotic drugs.

In an individual not taking the drug chronically, the primary effect of the chlorpromazine and other antipsychotic drugs is sedation and lightheadedness. In addition, the phenothiazines, in particular, have anticholinergic effects which will cause similar effects as described for the TCAs (dry mouth, blurred vision, urinary retention). That anticholinergic action may also produce some degree of amnesia or memory loss. In common with narcotics and other sedative drugs, the antipsychotics will potentiate the effects of alcohol. Therefore, someone who might feel slightly intoxicated after a couple of drinks, is likely to feel much more intoxicated if they are given even a single dose of an antipsychotic medication. After chronic dosing, patients receiving antipsychotics may become tolerant to the sedative effects, although that may not be relevant to a DFSA situation. So-called extra-pyramidal side-effects (Parkinson-like tremors and other effects) will develop after long-term use, and may sometimes be evident after short-term use if the dosage is high. Phenothiazine antipsychotics can also lower the seizure threshold, which could pose a risk to victims with pre-existing epilepsy.

High, toxic doses of chlorpromazine and the other antipsychotics will potentiate the hypotensive and sedative effects. In the early stages of intoxication, paradoxical excitement, restlessness, and confusion may result, as well as miosis (dilated pupils). Severe toxicity can include seizures, cardiac arrhythmias, loss of thermo-regulation, and eventually loss of consciousness, coma and death.

PHARMACOKINETICS

The pharmacokinetics of chlorpromazine and the phenothiazines is complex. These drugs are extensively metabolized and blood levels vary tremendously from one drug to another, and even one patient to another. Chlorpromazine has an "average" half-life in blood of about 18–30 hr, although stated to range from seven hours to five days (Whitfield *et al.*, 1978). Doses of chlorpromazine low enough to produce significant sedation in a person not accustomed to taking the drug (e.g. 25 mg) will produce a peak plasma level of about 0.001 mg/L. Even a 150 mg dose of chlorpromazine may only produce a peak plasma level of 0.018 mg/L (0.010–0.026 mg/L) (Hollister *et al.*, 1970). Modest single therapeutic doses of many of the other phenothiazines will produce peak plasma levels which are even lower. The dosage of many phenothiazines is low enough that their detection is all but impossible except by specifically targeted analysis. This is partly because most phenothiazines are very extensively broken down by the liver, often forming dozens of different metabolites (Maurer and Pfleger, 1983; Maurer and Pfleger, 1984).

ANALYSIS

Commercial immunoassay tests for phenothiazines and other antipsychotic medications do not exist, or at least are not readily available. Detection of these drugs must therefore rely on chromatographic methods such as GC or HPLC, in combination with MS or other suitable detectors. As for other drug groups, confirmation of any findings by MS is highly desirable, if not essential. However, while some of the higher dose phenothiazines, including chlorpromazine, can be detected in blood or plasma if sufficient care is taken, some of the lower dose antipsychotics are extremely difficult to detect, even with a "targeted" analysis. Blood concentrations of some of the antipsychotics are very low due to their small dosage and extensive metabolism (e.g. fluphenazine, perphenazine), whereas for others the drug is simply not detected by routine screening tests, as well as having low dosage (e.g. pimozide, risperidone).

If there is any "good news," it is that the higher dose phenothiazine drugs (e.g. chlorpromazine, methotrimeprazine, thioridazine) are readily detected in urine by suitable techniques, and should be detectable for several days after an alleged assault. However, even with these drugs, little if any of the parent drug will be evident, especially after a few hours, and the laboratory must be prepared to search for hydroxylated and other metabolites. A reasonably comprehensive protocol for the detection of several antipsychotic drugs in urine has been reported (Maurer and Pfleger, 1983; Maurer and Pfleger, 1984).

BARBITURATES AND OTHER NON-BENZODIAZEPINE SEDATIVES

AVAILABILITY

All drugs in this section are available only by prescription or illicit sources. The barbiturates are one of the oldest categories of drugs in this group, dating back to their introduction in the very early 1900s. They were used as tranquilizers, general sedatives and hypnotics, and to treat a variety of psychiatric disorders prior to the introduction of the phenothiazines. As anxiolytic, sedative and hypnotic drugs, the barbiturates have largely been replaced by the benzodiazepines, and for other psychiatric disorders by phenothiazines and other antipsychotics. Some of the barbiturates are available in both oral and injectable form, including phenobarbital and pentobarbital; thiopental and thiamylal are only available in injectable form.

Other non-barbiturate sedatives include chloral hydrate, meprobamate, carisoprodol, zolpidem, and zopiclone. Meprobamate is an older-style carbamate sedative, which is still prescribed occasionally, but has largely been replaced by the benzodiazepines. Carisoprodol is a centrally acting muscle relaxant, which has pronounced sedative action and is extensively metabolized to meprobamate. Zolpidem and zopiclone are hypnotic/sedative drugs which have pharmacological actions similar to the benzodiazepines, but which are structurally unrelated. Zopiclone is not available in the USA, but is widely used in Europe and Canada. All of these drugs except chloral hydrate are available only in solid dosage form.

Choral hydrate deserves special mention. It is one of the oldest sedatives still used in modern medicine and has been used since before 1900. Chloral hydrate is still used occasionally as a night-time sedative, rarely as a general daytime tranquilizer, and as an acute sedative for pediatric dentistry, and for medical procedures requiring sedation such as CAT scans and MRI exams. Chloral hydrate used to be the original "Mickey Finn" – a drink (usually alcoholic) which had been spiked with a sedating drug.[3] Chloral hydrate is formulated as liquid-filled gel-caps, or as a syrup. It is worth noting that chloral hydrate has a vile taste, which is difficult to mask with conventional drinks. However, it is not inconceivable that a person already intoxicated might be persuaded to drink a chloral hydrate-laced drink if it was in the form of a strongly tasting liqueur.

PHARMACODYNAMICS

Phenobarbital is the only barbiturate which is still widely used in general practice medicine, as an anticonvulsant in the treatment of epilepsy. It is still widely used in emergency medicine for the treatment of acute seizure activity. Pentobarbital is still occasionally used to decrease brain pressure resulting from acute brain injury. Amobarbital and secobarbital are still occasionally prescribed as sedatives or hypnotics, although such use has been discouraged for a number of years, due to tolerance and addiction. Similarly, butalbital continues to be prescribed for dismenorrhoea and similar pain, in combination with caffeine, ASA (Aspirin) and sometimes codeine (e.g. Fiorinal-C). The ultra-short-acting barbiturates thiopental and thiamylal continue to be used as induction agents in general anesthesia, but reports of their use or abuse outside the medical field are rare. Pharmacologically, the barbiturates are general CNS depressants, their primary effect being to induce sedation and sleep. Their ability to suppress "excitable tissues" is the underlying reason why barbiturates have antiepileptic activity, although only phenobarbital is still widely used for that purpose.

The toxic effects of the barbiturates and other drugs in this category are an extension of their primary therapeutic effect, that is pronounced CNS depression, causing notably increasing drowsiness, sedation, and impairment of cognitive function. In fact, the reason why barbiturates fell out of favor as tranquilizers was their relatively narrow therapeutic index (i.e. the doses required to reduce anxiety were not much lower than doses which caused impairment of motor function and even speech). Severe intoxication can cause a decreased level of consciousness, respiratory depression, hypotension, nausea and aspiration, renal failure, cardiac arrhythmias, and death. As with all CNS depressants, the toxicity of barbiturates and related sedatives is potentiated by alcohol. Chloral hydrate is reportedly more cardio-toxic than the other CNS depressants after overdosage, although it has a wider therapeutic index after normal doses and is therefore regarded as safer than the barbiturates.

[3] "An alcoholic beverage that is surreptitiously altered to induce diarrhea or stupefy, render unconscious, or otherwise incapaitate the person who drinks it. Etymology: probably after a notorious Chicago bar shut down in 1903, allegedly because its cutomers were served spiked drinks and then robbed." (American Heritage, 2000)

Sedative/hypnotic	Half-life (hours)[1, 3]	Plasma levels mg/L (hypnotic dose mg)[2, 3]	Trade names[4]
Secobarbital	15–40	1 (100)	Seconal®
Pentobarbital	15–48	1–3 (100)	Nembutal®
Amobarbital	8–42	1.8 (120)	Amytal®
Phenobarbital	48–140	18 (600)	
Meprobamate	6–17	7.7 (400)	Equanil®; Miltown®
Carisoprodol	1–2.5	2.1 (350)	Soma®
Methyprylon	7–11	3.5–8.4 (300)	Noludar®
Chloral hydrate[5]	6–10	8.0 (1000)	Noctec®
Ethchlorvynol	19–32	1.2 (200), 6.5 (500)	Placidyl®
Zopiclone	3.5–6.5	0.08 (7.5)	Imovane®
Zolpidem	1.5–4.5	0.1 (10)	Ambien®

1 The half-lives quoted are average from the literature; half-lives for some individuals are outside these ranges.
2 The plasma concentrations quoted are averages or ranges for a particular study; concentrations for some individuals may differ and will invariably be higher for multiple doses.
3 Ellenhorn (1997); Baselt (2000) and references therein.
4 Some of the common North American trade names are given; many "generic" medications may have trade names of their own; some of the "older" antipsychotics may be available under multiple generic names.
5 Half-life and plasma levels are of the primary active metabolite, trichloroethanol.

PHARMACOKINETICS

The short to intermediate acting barbiturates (e.g. secobarbital, pentobarbital) are rapidly absorbed, with onset of action stated to be 10–15 min and half-lives in the range 15–40 hr. The intermediate acting barbiturates (e.g. amobarbital, butalbital) have a longer onset of action of 30–60 min and similar half-lives of about 15–40 hr. On the other hand, phenobarbital, a long-acting barbiturate, has an onset of action of about 60 min and a half-life of 80–120 hr (3–5 days). As a result of their relatively long half-lives, all except the ultra-short-acting anesthetic barbiturates (thiopental, thiamylal) tend to produce a "hangover" effect, due to their slow excretion.

Peak plasma concentrations of zolpidem are in the range 60–270 ng/ml following a 10 mg dose, with a half-life of about 2.5 hr (range 1.4–3.8 hr)

Table 8.4

Properties of some barbiturates and other non-benzodiazepine sedatives/anxiolytics.

(Searle, 1999). While the parent drug is fairly rapidly cleared from blood, zolpidem metabolites are excreted in urine for up to four days following a single dose. (Fraisse *et al.*, 1996). Zopiclone has a slightly longer half-life (4–6 hr) than zolpidem (Viron *et al.*, 1990). Single 7.5 and 15 mg doses of zopiclone have produced average peak serum concentrations of 76 and 131 ng/mL respectively (Fernandez *et al.*, 1993; Marc-Aurele *et al.*, 1987).

Peak plasma levels of carisoprodol have been reported to average 3.5 mg/l 0.8 hr after a 700 mg dose, with a half-life of about 1–2.5 hr; peak concentrations of the metabolite, meprobamate average 4.0 mg/l after 3.7 hr (Olsen *et al.*, 1994). In a separate study, plasma concentrations of meprobamate averaged 7.7 mg/12 hr after a single 400 mg dose (Meyer *et al.*, 1978). The plasma half-life of meprobamate is 6–17 hr (Hollister and Levy, 1964).

Chloral hydrate is rapidly absorbed following oral ingestion, with an onset of action of about 10–15 min. The half-life of chloral hydrate is only a few minutes, but the active metabolite, trichloroethanol, has a half-life of about 8 hr (range 4–12 hr). The half-life of the terminal metabolite, trichloroacetic acid, can range up to about 100 hr (Breimer *et al.*, 1974). Blood concentrations of trichloroethanol are reported to average 8.0 mg/l (range 2.0–12) 1 hr after a single oral dose of 1000 mg (Kaplan *et al.*, 1967).

ANALYSIS

Several commercial immunoassays are available for plasma and urine, which crossreact with all of the barbiturates. The barbiturates are usually quantitated by either GC/NPD or GC/FID, or by HPLC/UV; confirmation is usually by GC/MS. The barbiturates are detectable in blood or serum for several hours after ingestion. Their detection in urine may depend on excretion of sufficient unchanged drug. Detection of the hydroxylated barbiturate metabolites in urine may extend the detection time for several hours, and probably days. However, few laboratories target their testing towards the metabolites and typically only test for the parent barbiturates. A comprehensive protocol for the detection and identification of a wide range of barbiturates and other sedatives in urine, including their metabolites, in urine by GC/MS, has been described (Maurer, 1990; Maurer, 1999).

Carisoprodol, and meprobamate, are extensively metabolized by hydroxylation and subsequent conjugation. Less than 1% of a carisoprodol dose is excreted unchanged in a 24-hour period, and only about 5% as meprobamate (Baselt, 2000). Despite their extensive metabolism, both substances can be detected in urine by TLC, and in blood or plasma by GC, although carisoprodol undergoes thermal breakdown when analyzed by GC. The metabolite, meprobamate, is considerably more stable and may be detected for several hours in blood or even days in urine. However, many clinical and forensic laboratories rely on nitrogen-phosphorus detection for drug screening by GC, which is almost completely insensitive to meprobamate.

Zolpidem has been analyzed in blood by GC/NPD, GC/MS and HPLC (Durol and Greenblatt, 1997; Lichtenwalner and Tully, 1997; Meeker *et al.*, 1995; Stanke *et al.*, 1996). The analysis of zolpidem is difficult due to extensive metabolism to acid metabolites, which are not detected by commonly used drug screening methods. However, due to the long terminal half-life of these metabolites, they may be detected for at least two days if an appropriately targeted assay is used.

Zopiclone is best analyzed by GC/ECD or GC/MS (Gaillard *et al.*, 1993; Van Bocxlaer *et al.*, 1996). Detection of zopiclone may be difficult by routine screening techniques because concentrations are low, it is unstable in the acidic conditions often used for routine drug screening extractions, and it is frequently masked by cholesterol. Urine is the specimen of choice for the detection of zopiclone, since concentrations are at least an order of magnitude higher than in blood.

Chloral hydrate is rapidly broken down to trichloroethanol, therefore analytical methods must focus on this metabolite. Unfortunately, trichloroethanol is not detected by most routine drug-screening protocols, and requires a targeted test. The Fujiwara spot test can be readily applied to urine and can be adapted for blood or plasma. (Moffat, 1986). The test detects "halogenated hydrocarbons," including chloroform, and, in the case of chloral hydrate, probably detects the terminal metabolite, trichloroacetic acid. However, in order to specifically detect trichloroethanol in blood, plasma or urine, the analyst has to use GC/FID or GC/ECD, and lower the column temperature sufficiently to separate the metabolite from the solvent.

TELAZOL®

Telazol® is a proprietary veterinary medication, developed in the late 1960s by Parke Davis for use as anesthetic agent for animals. It contains tiletamine (a dissociative anesthetic similar to ketamine) and zolazepam (a benzodiazepine similar to diazepam) in a 1:1 ratio. It is only available to veterinary practices. There is very little data available regarding the pharmacodynamics and pharmacokinetics of tiletamine and zolazepam in humans. However, tiletamine is reported to have similar pharmacological properties to ketamine and phencyclidine, and is reported to produce taming and immobilizing effects, as well as general anesthesia (see Chapter 6). Zolazepam has similar properties to the other benzodiazepines (see Chapter 4), including anterograde amnesia at higher doses, sedation, and muscle relaxation. An extensive review has been published on the use of Telazol® in veterinary medicine (Lin *et al.*, 1993). Three human fatalities have been attributed to the abuse of Telazol® or use as a suicidal agent. Both tiletamine and zolazepam are stable drugs which may readily be analyzed by GC/NPD or GC/MS. In common with the other benzo-diazepines, zolazepam may also be analyzed by GC/ECD (Chung *et al.*, 2000; Wade *et al.*, 2000).

CONCLUSION

A large number of diverse drugs may be used for DFSA. Not all are classic "sedatives," but may include a number of other drugs where sedation or amnesia is only a side-effect. While the analysis of most of these drugs is well documented in the scientific literature, their detection and identification poses special problems in the context of DFSA. Analytical methods for the vast majority of clinical and forensic toxicology laboratories are designed to detect toxic concentrations of drugs, and may not detect the very small or trace amounts present several hours or days after a single dose. Detection of many drugs in these circumstances demands that the analyst search not just for the parent, but for one or more metabolites which might not ordinarily be looked for during routine testing. The DFSA investigator and the analyst should be aware of this. At the very least, the analyst should be made specifically aware of the general circumstance of the investigation, and wherever possible, any suspicions about the involvement of specific drugs which might not ordinarily form part of the routine analytical search.

REFERENCES

American Heritage (2000) "Mickey Finn". In *The American Heritage® Dictionary of the English Language* (4th edn). Boston: Houghton Mifflin.

Baselt, R.C. (2000) *Disposition of Toxic Drugs and Chemicals in Man* (5th edn). Foster City, CA: Chemical Toxicology Institute.

Bilzer, W. and Gundert-Remy, U. (1973) "Determination of Nanogram Quantities of Diphen-hydramine and Orphenadrine in Human Plasma Using Gas–Liquid Chromatography", *Eur. J. Clin. Pharmacol.*, 6 (4), pp. 268–270.

Breimer, D.D., Ketelaars, H.C.J. and Van Rossum, J.M. (1974) "Gas Chromatographic Deter-mination of Chloral Hydrate, Trichloroethanol and Trichloroacetic Acid in Blood and in Urine Employing Head-space Analysis", *J. Chromatogr.*, 88, pp. 55–63.

Carruthers, S.G., Shoeman, D.W., Hignite, C.E. and Azarnoff, D.L. (1978) "Correlation Between Plasma Diphenhydramine Level and Sedative and Antihistamine Effects", *Clin. Pharmacol. Ther.*, 23 (4), pp. 375–382.

Chung, H., Choi, H., Kim, E., Jin, W., Lee, H. and Yoo, Y. (2000) "A Fatality Due to Injection of Tiletamine and Zolazepam [In Process Citation]", *J. Anal. Toxicol.*, 24 (4), pp. 305–308.

Curran, H.V., Sakulsriprong, M. and Lader, M. (1988) "Antidepressants and Human Memory: An Investigation of Four Drugs with Different Sedative and Anticholinergic Profiles" (published erratum appears in Berl (1989) *Psychopharmacol.*, 97 (1), p. 139). In Berl *Psychopharmacol.*, 95 (4), pp. 520–527.

Durol, A.L. and Greenblatt, D.J. (1997) "Analysis of Zolpidem in Human Plasma by High-Performance Liquid Chromatography with Fluorescence Detection: Application to Single-Dose Pharmacokinetic Studies", *J. Anal. Toxicol.*, 21 (5), pp. 388–392.

Ellenhorn, M.J. (1997) *Ellenhorn's Medical Toxicology: Diagnosis and Treatment of Poisoning* (2nd edn). Baltimore: Williams and Wilkins.

Fernandez, C., Maradeix, V., Gimenez, F., Thuillier, A. and Farinotti, R. (1993) "Pharmacokinetics of Zopiclone and its Enantiomers in Caucasian Young Healthy Volunteers", *Drug Metab. Dispos.*, 21 (6), pp. 1125–1128.

Fraisse, J., Garrigou-Gadenne, D. and Thenot, J. P. (1996) "Pharmacokinetic and Metabolic Profiles of Zolpidem". In Freeman, H., Puech, A.J. and Roth, T. (eds) *Zolpidem: An Update of its Pharmacological Properties and Therapeutic Place in the Managment of Insomnia*. Paris: Elsevier.

Gaillard, Y., Gay-Montchamp, J.P. and Ollagnier, M. (1993) "Gas Chromatographic Determination of Zopiclone in Plasma After Solid-Phase Extraction", *J. Chromatogr.*, 619 (2), pp. 310–314.

Garland, W.A. (1977) "Quantitative Determination of Amitriptyline and Its Principal Metabolite, Nortriptyline, by GLC-Chemical Ionization Mass Spectrometry", *J. Pharm. Sci.*, 66 (1), pp. 77–81.

Gilman, A. (1990) *Goodman and Gilman's The Pharmacological Basis of Therapeutics* (8th edn). New York: Pergamon Press.

Hindmarch, I. and Shamsi, Z. (1999) "Antihistamines: Models to Assess Sedative Properties, Assessment of Sedation, Safety and Other Side-effects", *Clin. Exp. Allergy*, 29 (Suppl. 3), pp. 133–142.

Hollister, L.E. and Levy,G. (1964) "Kinetics of Meprobamate Elimination in Humans", *Chemotherapia*, 9, pp. 20–24.

Hollister, L.E., Curry, S.H., Derr, J.E. and Kanter, S.L. (1970) "Studies of Delayed-Action Medication. V. Plasma Levels and Urinary Excretion of Four Different Dosage Forms of Chlorpromazine", *Clin. Pharmacol. Ther.*, 11 (1), pp. 49–59.

Kaplan, H.L., Forney, R.B., Hughes, F.W. and Jain, N.C. (1967) "Chloral Hydrate and Alcohol Metabolism in Human Subjects", *J. Forensic Sci.*, 12 (3), pp. 295–304.

Karch, S. (1997) *Drug Abuse Handbook*. Boca Raton: CRC Press.

Lichtenwalner, M. and Tully, R. (1997) "A Fatality Involving Zolpidem", *J. Anal. Toxicol.*, 21 (7), pp. 567–569.

Lin, H.C., Thurmon, J.C., Benson, G.J. and Tranquilli, W.J. (1993) "Telazol – A Review of its Pharmacology and Use in Veterinary Medicine", *J. Vet. Pharmacol. Ther.*, 16 (4), pp. 383–418.

Marc-Aurele, J., Caille, G. and Bourgoin, J. (1987) "Comparison of Zopiclone Pharmacokinetics in Patients with Impaired Renal Function and Normal Subjects. Effect of Hemodialysis", *Sleep*, 10 (Suppl. 1), pp. 22–26.

Maurer, H.H. (1990) "Identification and Differentiation of Barbiturates, Other Sedative-Hypnotics and their Metabolites in Urine Integrated in a General Screening Procedure Using Computerized Gas Chromatography-Mass Spectrometry", *J. Chromatogr.*, 530 (2), pp. 307–326.

Maurer, H.H. (1992) "Systematic Toxicological Analysis of Drugs and their Metabolites by Gas Chromatography-Mass Spectrometry", *J. Chromatogr.*, 580 (1–2), pp. 3–41.

Maurer, H.H. (1999) "Systematic Toxicological Analysis Procedures for Acidic Drugs and/or Metabolites Relevant to Clinical and Forensic Toxicology and/or Doping Control", *J. Chromatog. B Biomed. Sci. Appl.*, 733 (1–2), pp. 3–25.

Maurer, H.H. and Bickeboeller-Friedrich, J. (2000) "Screening Procedure for Detection of Antidepressants of the Selective Serotonin Reuptake Inhibitor Type and their Metabolites in Urine as Part of a Modified Systematic Toxicological Analysis Procedure Using Gas Chromatography-Mass Spectrometry [In Process Citation]", *J. Anal. Toxicol.*, 24 (5), pp. 340–347.

Maurer, H. and Pfleger, K. (1983) "Screening Procedure for Detecting Butyrophenone and Bisfluorophenyl Neuroleptics in Urine Using a Computerized Gas Chromatographic-Mass Spectrometric Technique", *J. Chromatogr.*, 272 (1), pp. 75–85.

Maurer, H. and Pfleger, K. (1984) "Screening Procedure for Detection of Phenothiazine and Analogous Neuroleptics and Their Metabolites in Urine Using a Computerized Gas Chromatographic-Mass Spectrometric Technique", *J. Chromatogr.*, 306, pp. 125–145.

Maurer, H. and Pfleger, K. (1988a) "Identification and Differentiation of Alkylamine Antihistamines and their Metabolites in Urine by Computerized Gas Chromatography-Mass Spectrometry", *J. Chromatogr.*, 430 (1), pp. 31–41.

Maurer, H. and Pfleger, K. (1988b) "Screening Procedure for the Detection of Alkanolamine Antihistamines and their Metabolites in Urine Using Computerized Gas Chromatography-Mass Spectrometry", *J. Chromatogr.*, 428 (1), pp. 43–60.

Meeker, J.E., Som, C.W., Macapagal, E.C. and Benson, P.A. (1995) "Zolpidem Tissue Concentrations in a Multiple Drug Related Death Involving Ambien", *J. Anal. Toxicol.*, 19 (6), pp. 531–534.

Meyer, M.C., Melikian, A.P. and Straughn, A.B. (1978) "Relative Bioavailability of Meprobamate Tablets in Humans", *J. Pharm. Sci.*, 67 (9), pp. 1290–1293.

Moffat, A.C. (1986) *Clarke's Isolation and Identification of Drugs* (2nd edn). London: The Pharmaceutical Press.

Olsen, H., Koppang, E., Alvan, G. and Morland, J. (1994) "Carisoprodol Elimination in Humans", *Therap. Drug Monitor*, 16 (4), pp. 337–340.

Rogers, H.J., Morrison, P.J. and Bradbrook, I.D. (1978) "The Half-life of Amitriptyline", *Brit. J. Clin. Pharmacol.*, 6 (2), pp. 181–183.

Rudorfer, M.V., Manji, H.K. and Potter, W.Z. (1994) "Comparative Tolerability Profiles of the Newer Versus Older Antidepressants", *Drug Safety*, 10 (1), pp. 18–46.

Sakulsripong, M., Curran, H.V. and Lader, M. (1991) "Does Tolerance Develop to the Sedative and Amnesic Effects of Antidepressants? A Comparison of Amitriptyline, Trazodone and Placebo", *Eur. J. Clin. Pharmacol.*, 40 (1), pp. 43–48.

Searle, G.D. (1999) *Ambien (Zolipdem Tartrate) Prescribing Information*. G.D. Searle and Co.

Simons, F.E., Simons, K.J. and Frith, E.M. (1984) "The Pharmacokinetics and Antihistaminic of the H1 Receptor Antagonist Hydroxyzine", *J. Allergy Clin. Immunol.*, 73 (1 Pt 1), pp. 69–75.

Stanke, F., Jourdil, N., Bessard, J. and Bessard, G. (1996) "Simultaneous Determination of Zolpidem and Zopiclone in Human Plasma by Gas Chromatography-Nitrogen-Phosphorus Detection", *J. Chromatog. B Biomed. Appl.*, 675 (1), pp. 43–51.

Vallner, J.J., Kotzan, J.A., Stewart, J.T., Brown, W.J., Honigberg, I.L., Needham, T.E. and Dighe, S.V. (1982) "Blood Levels Following Multiple Oral Dosing of Chlorpheniramine Conventional and Controlled Release Preparations", *Biopharm. Drug Dispos.*, 3 (2), pp. 95–104.

Van Bocxlaer, J., Meyer, E., Clauwaert, K., Lambert, W., Piette, M. and De Leenheer, A. (1996) "Analysis of Zopiclone (Imovane) in Postmortem Specimens by GC-MS and HPLC with Diode-Array Detection [See Comments]", *J. Anal. Toxicol.*, 20 (1), pp. 52–54.

Viron, B., De Meyer, M., Le Liboux, A., Frydman, A., Maillard, F., Mignon, F. and Gaillot, J. (1990) "Steady State Pharmacokinetics of Zopiclone During Multiple Oral Dosing (7.5 mg Nocte) in Patients with Severe Chronic Renal Failure", *Int. Clin. Psychopharmacol.*, 5 (Suppl 2), pp. 95–104.

Wade, N.A., Spies, C.E. and Cooley, S.M. (2000) "Telazol: A Dissociative Animal Anesthetic Agent Found in Two Fatalities", Society of Forensic Toxicology 30th Annual Meeting, p. 39.

Whitfield, L.R., Kaul, P.N. and Clark, M.L. (1978) "Chlorpromazine Metabolism. IX. Pharmacokinetics of Chlorpromazine Following Oral Administration in Man", *J. Pharmacokin.
Biopharm.*, 6 (3), pp. 187–196.

Woodward, J.K. (1988) "Pharmacology and Toxicology of Nonclassical Antihistamines",
Cutis, 42 (4A), pp. 5–9.

Woodward, J.K. (1990) "Pharmacology of Antihistamines", *J. Allergy Clin. Immunol.*, 86 (4
Pt 2), pp. 606–612.

CHAPTER 9

COLLECTION OF EVIDENCE FROM DFSA

Marc LeBeau
Ashraf Mozayani

Proper collection, preservation, and analysis of physical evidence is essential to the successful investigation and prosecution of sexual assault cases. When drugs are used to facilitate an assault, the victim's recollection of the events may be unclear, inconsistent, or completely absent, making the physical evidence even more critical to these cases. The greatest challenge surrounding the physical evidence from DFSA cases is the collection of proper biological specimens. These samples must be collected in adequate volumes and in a timely manner. In addition, the typical evidence from non-DFSAs should also be collected in DFSAs. This includes items that will be analyzed for DNA, trace evidence (i.e. hairs and fibers), and possible lubricants.

TOXICOLOGY EVIDENCE

As the previous chapters have explained, there are numerous drugs which can be used to facilitate an assault. These drugs have a wide variety of pharmacological properties, but many are very potent, low-dose medications that cause central nervous system depression (LeBeau, 1999). These low-dose drugs and their metabolites are increasingly difficult to detect in biological fluids, especially after there has been a delay in reporting the incident and collecting the appropriate specimens. Understanding the pharmacokinetic parameters of a drug – that is, understanding the body's effect on ingested drugs – allows one to appreciate the preferred specimen(s) for toxicology testing in cases of DFSA.

After drugs are orally ingested, they must be absorbed into the bloodstream to be effective. This requires the drug to cross cellular membranes in the stomach and small intestine. Once absorbed, the drug is carried throughout the body by means of the blood vasculature. As it moves through the body, the drug will leave the bloodstream (distribution) and interact with cellular receptors in tissues. In DFSA cases, the drug's primary site of action is the central nervous system. It is here, in the brain, that most of these drugs will interact with receptors to disrupt the brain's normal function, resulting in the drug's effect on the body (pharmacodynamics).

The bloodstream is also responsible for carrying drugs to the liver. The liver is a very important organ as it contains enzymes that metabolize most drugs. The biotransformation of drugs usually results in alternate forms (metabolites) that are more hydrophilic, or water soluble, than the original drugs. This leads to the final stages of pharmacokinetics – excretion and elimination of drugs.

Once a drug becomes hydrophilic, it is readily passed from the blood into urine via the kidneys. A function of the kidneys is to concentrate urine by returning most of the aqueous portion back to the blood. Thus, the drugs and any polar metabolites become highly concentrated in the urine.

COLLECTION OF URINE SPECIMENS FOR TOXICOLOGICAL ANALYSES

In cases of DFSA, urine specimens should always be considered the specimen of choice for toxicological testing (LeBeau *et al.*, 1999). Since most drugs and metabolites are present at higher concentrations in the urine, toxicologists can detect their presence for longer periods of time. As it is impossible to reliably predict *exactly* how long a drug or its metabolite will remain at detectable levels in urine, it is essential that efforts be made to collect the first available urine specimen from the victim.

When there has been a substantial delay in the collection of a urine specimen, the likelihood of detecting the presence of a commonly encountered DFSA drug or metabolite decreases dramatically. It has been suggested that a "96-hour" rule be used to collect urine in these cases (LeBeau *et al.*, 1999); that is, a urine specimen should be collected within 96 hours of the alleged drugging. It is important to emphasize that this is 96 hours post-ingestion, not after the victim wakes up. The logic behind this suggestion is that while *most* of the common DFSA drugs will no longer be detectable at 96 hours, some with longer half-lives may still be. The 96-hour rule minimizes the likelihood of failure to collect a urine specimen when it may still contain evidence of the drugging.

Every time the victim urinates, evidence of drug consumption is essentially lost. It is important that the victim be instructed not to urinate until the specimen can be collected. In circumstances where the victim cannot wait until the sexual assault examination, then he/she should collect the urine themselves in a clean container and take it with him/her to the examination (Ledray, 1996). Then, during the examination, a second urine specimen can be obtained and the results of the two specimens compared.

It is recommended that at least 100 mL of urine be collected in a standard urine collection cup (LeBeau *et al.*, 1999). This volume of urine allows for a very comprehensive, sensitive toxicological analysis to be performed. If the victim cannot produce 100 mL of urine, then collect what he/she can produce or take a second collection when they can produce more urine. It is not advisable to have the victim drink a large quantity of water to generate this urine as this may render a more diluted sample than would normally be produced. Instead, allowing the body to naturally produce the urine will likely yield the most useful result.

Once collected, there is no need to add a preservative to the urine specimen. No research studies exist that suggest a significant loss of drugs in urine samples due to lack of preservatives. However, as with all biological specimens, it is important that the urine be maintained in a refrigerated or frozen condition. This will prevent putrefaction of the specimen which may interfere with certain toxicological assays or prevent the detection of certain drugs.

COLLECTION OF BLOOD SPECIMENS FOR TOXICOLOGICAL ANALYSES

Blood specimens are also useful to forensic toxicologists, especially when the victim of a DFSA is able to report the crime shortly after the drugging. In general, blood should only be collected during the first 24 hours after the drugs were suspected to have been ingested (LeBeau *et al.*, 1999). After 24 hours, most DFSA drugs and metabolites are no longer at detectable levels in the blood.

Blood for toxicological testing should be collected by a qualified medical professional into gray-stoppered tubes. These tubes contain sodium fluoride (preservative) and potassium oxalate (anticoagulant) and are not the same tubes used for forensic serology and DNA testing. Failure to collect the blood in a proper specimen tube can prevent the laboratory from deriving a meaningful toxicological analysis (Fieler *et al.*, 1998; LeBeau *et al.*, 2000; Stevens and Coleman, 1999). The blood samples should always be collected *in addition* to the urine. It is desirable to collect 10–30 mL of blood from the victim. Unfortunately, the blood collection tubes contained in most sexual assault kits do not contain the desired preservative and anticoagulant for toxicological specimens (LeBeau *et al.*, 2000).

COLLECTION OF HAIR FOR TOXICOLOGICAL ANALYSES

Hair would appear to be a logical specimen choice following a suspected DFSA, particularly when there has been a delay in reporting the incident. There are numerous instances where hair has shown a history of drug use. However, when dealing with DFSA cases, there are many limitations as to the usefulness of hair specimens.

Currently, there are very few forensic laboratories that analyze hair specimens for drugs. Furthermore, the majority of published methods for drug testing of hair samples are designed to detect chronic drug use in an individual (Cirimele *et al.*, 1997; Ropero-Miller *et al.*, 2000; Tsatsakis *et al.*, 2000). Until recently, drugs that have been identified in hair are those that are generally consumed in relatively high doses. Many of the commonly encountered DFSA drugs are low-dose formulations. Thus, there is very little drug available to incorporate into the hair. Additionally, most DFSA cases involve a one-time exposure to the drug, unless the victim was chronically abusing the substance.

It should be noted that hair specimens are not conducive to comprehensive drug screens. Testing for a few drugs or classes of drugs may consume all of the available hair sample. In addition, hair cannot be used to screen for the most commonly encountered DFSA drug – alcohol. Thus, it is essential to have a good idea as to what the likely drugging agent(s) is/are prior to the hair analysis.

Of course, hair length should also be considered. Human hair grows at a rate of approximately $1/2$ inch (~1 centimeter) per month. If the victim has short hair or there is a delay of months in collection of the hair sample, evidence of the drugging may have been removed with his/her last hair cut. It takes one to two weeks for drugs to begin to appear in the hair above the scalp. Hair should be cut by isolating a $1/4 - 1/2$ inch section of head hair from the victim using rubber bands, ensuring that the end closest to the scalp is clearly marked. The hair should be cut close to the scalp and placed into a paper envelope.

While hair specimens may not yet yield widely useful information in most DFSA cases today, new technological advancements and increasingly sensitive instrumentation may become available to allow for successful analysis of hair in these types of cases in the future (Muller *et al.*, 2000; Negrusz *et al.*, 1999; Negrusz *et al.*, 2000). Thus, consideration should be made to routinely collect hair in these cases, especially when there has been a substantial delay in reporting the crime.

ADDITIONAL SPECIMENS THAT MAY BE USEFUL FOR TOXICOLOGICAL ANALYSES

As previous chapters have discussed, nausea and vomiting are common symptoms of many of the drugs related to DFSA. These drugs take time to completely absorb into the bloodstream after ingestion. When a victim vomits shortly after ingestion of a drug, the substance may not have had an opportunity to completely absorb into the bloodstream. Thus, the vomitus may contain a significant amount of the drugging agent, so collection and analysis of this specimen should be assessed in these cases.

If the vomitus has dried prior to collection, the article that contains the vomitus should be submitted to the laboratory for testing. If it has not dried, it should be carefully transferred into a clean container, such as a urine collection cup.

There are other stains that may be discovered in these cases that should be collected for toxicological testing. Occasionally, the victim may release her bladder and a urine stain may be present on bedding materials or clothing. Also, there may be stains on items as a result of vaginal or rectal bleeding. If these stains are large enough, these items may also be analyzed for many of the same drugs and metabolites that would be found in a traditional urine or blood specimen.

EVIDENCE FOR CHEMICAL EXAMINATIONS

Crime scene investigations and execution of search warrants in cases of DFSA often lead to the discovery of items that require chemical identification and/or comparison. Such items may include: suspected recreational drugs or prescription medications; bottles, cups, or cans; used condoms; or sexual stimulation devices. The importance of each of these will vary from case to case, but it is best to initially collect, preserve, and store these items for later testing, if necessary.

COLLECTION OF PILLS, TABLETS, OR SUSPECTED DRUGS

There are more than a handful of drugs that can be used in DFSA cases (Schwartz *et al.*, 2000). During the execution of a search warrant, it is important to search for pills and tablets that may be used in this manner.

Typically the perpetrator will choose to use a drug or drugs readily available to him. If he belongs to a gym or frequents "rave" parties, then one should take extra care to look for GHB or GBL containers. If the perpetrator suffers from depression, then one should look for sedative antidepressants such as amitriptyline or desipramine. If he/she has a family member that takes sleeping pills, then one should search for benzodiazepines or related drugs.

Although a perpetrator may have a "stash" of pills secretly hidden, the investigator should not overlook the obvious, such as the medicine cabinet. Any and all sedative medications should be recorded and collected for possible future analysis. It may be useful to have contact with a pharmacologist or toxicologist during the search to assist in determining possible drugs used in the assault (APRI, 1999). When submitting pills and tablets to the laboratory, they should remain in their original containers, if present. Alternatively, medications may be sealed in a plastic bag prior to submission to the laboratory.

One of the most overlooked drugs at a crime scene is GHB. Since it is typically dissolved in water and is colorless, it may be stored in water bottles or may be colored and stored in sports drink bottles. It may also appear as a cleaning product, health drink, eyedrop solution, or even hair spray. GBL and 1,4-butanediol may also appear in such containers. All liquids should be tightly capped and double-sealed in plastic bags. Excessive heat should be avoided when storing these samples.

COLLECTION OF CUPS, CANS, CONTAINERS, DISHES, ETC.

Drugs used to commit DFSA have been administered to a victim in almost every conceivable manner. While delivery through a beverage in a cup, glass, can, or bottle is the classic example, these drugs have also been administered in food or through voluntary ingestion by the victim.

Occasionally, a search of the crime scene may reveal evidentiary items such as a cup, can, or bottle that the victim believes the drug was delivered in. Analysis of remaining liquid or residue in these containers may reveal the drugging agent used. The evidence should be collected in such a manner as to preserve its original condition. If some liquid remains in the container, it should be documented and then transferred to a sterile container that can be tightly sealed. Both the container and the liquid should be chemically analyzed for the presence of common DFSA drugs. Dried residues that remain in a cup or bottle should also be documented before packaging, and submitted. Suspect food should be frozen to prevent spoilage.

It is good practice to obtain a control sample of any food or beverage that is believed to have been spiked. This facilitates the chemical examination by allowing the analyst to look for abnormalities in the questioned specimen in comparison to the control sample. Whenever possible, controls from the same batch or lot should be obtained.

COLLECTION OF CONDOMS AND SEXUAL DEVICES FOR CHEMICAL EXAMINATIONS

While analyses for DNA and hairs are usually the most important examinations done on condoms or sexual devices, chemical examination of this evidence may occasionally provide useful information as well.

Condoms discovered at a crime scene may contain spermicide and lubricants that can be compared to condoms found in the possession of a suspect (Blackledge, 1995; Blackledge *et al.*, 1994). Additionally, latex additives may allow for a more unique comparison to be made.

Lubricants are often used to sodomize victims in sexual assaults. These lubricants may consist of petroleum jelly, lotion, or oils. When traces of lubricant are discovered on a sexual device or swabs from the sexual assault examination, chemical comparison to a suspect lubricant can exclude or include it as a source.

Condoms and sexual devices should be placed in paper bags and appropriately sealed. Visible lubricant on these devices may be swabbed and placed into small, paper envelopes. If such swabs are taken, be certain to include control swabs in a separate envelope.

Occasionally, the investigation may be enhanced through determination of the use of a spermicide. For example, the suspect may use a condom coated with nonoxynol-9. Highly sensitive techniques may allow the identification of such a spermicide on swabs from the sexual assault examination (Hollenbeck *et al.*, 1999).

EVIDENCE FOR DNA ANALYSIS

Recent advancements in DNA technology are enabling law enforcement officers to solve cases previously thought to be unsolvable. DNA, or deoxyribonucleic acid, is the fundamental building block for an individual's entire genetic make-up. It is a component of every cell in the human body (except red blood cells); therefore making the DNA in a person's blood (white blood cells) the same as the DNA in their saliva, hair, skin cells, semen, perspiration, liver, and every other cell in the body.

DNA is a powerful forensic tool because each person's DNA is unique (except for identical twins). DNA collected from a crime scene may link a suspect to the evidence or exonerate them. Furthermore, when biological evidence from one crime scene is compared to evidence from another, those scenes may be linked to a perpetrator using DNA analysis.

Investigators and forensic laboratory staff should work together to exploit every possible piece of evidence. They must also be aware of important issues concerning the identification, collection, preservation, transportation, and storage of DNA evidence. Their understanding of each of these aspects is the first step to a successful case investigation.

IDENTIFYING DNA EVIDENCE

DNA evidence can be collected from practically anywhere. Sexual assault investigators should be able to identify evidence from traditional and nontraditional sources. They must remember the process of evidence exchange that occurs at every crime scene. For example, during a sexual assault, an exchange of DNA may occur between the victim and perpetrator. Semen may be recovered from the smears and swabs that were collected as part of the sexual assault examination. Additionally, the victim's epithelial cells or blood may be found in the suspect's underwear. When a condom is used, it may also contain useful semen evidence, in addition to cellular material and/or blood.

Investigators should consider identifying and collecting blood, seminal fluid, and hair on the victim. Additionally, they should also consider collecting common items of evidence such as blankets, pillows, sheets, swabs, clothing, dirty laundry, used condoms, and facial tissue.

COLLECTION AND PRESERVATION OF DNA EVIDENCE

It should be noted that valuable DNA can be found on evidence that is decades old, although several factors can affect the DNA left at a crime scene. Contamination and environmental factors such as heat, sunlight, moisture, bacteria, and mold are all factors that may prevent DNA evidence from being viable.

Polymerase Chain Reaction (PCR) technology allows for extremely small samples of DNA to be used as evidence. This increased sensitivity requires that greater caution be taken to eliminate the chances of contamination. This is particularly important for the evidence collector responsible for the identification, collection, and preserving of DNA evidence. To eliminate the chances of contamination, evidence should be collected while wearing clean gloves, a mask, and hairnet. Additionally, the gloves should be changed frequently and the use of disposable instruments will help minimize the chances of contamination.

BLOOD FOR DNA EXAMINATIONS

Blood samples from the victim and perpetrator should be collected by qualified medical personnel and preserved for DNA testing. These samples are best collected in purple-top (EDTA) tubes. Red-top (no preservative or anticoagulant), gray-top (sodium fluoride/potassium oxalate), or green-top (heparin) tubes are not recommended. It should be standard procedure to label the known blood specimens with the name of the individual, date, time, offense number, and the collector's initials. In addition, blood specimens for DNA examinations should be refrigerated if used within a few days. For prolonged storage, a bloodstain card should be made.

It may also be necessary to collect and analyze blood samples from spouses, boyfriends, or recent sexual partners of the victim. This will allow the DNA analyst to differentiate DNA from a consensual partner and that of the suspected rapist.

SALIVA FOR DNA EXAMINATIONS

Another common specimen collected in sexual assault kits is buccal swabs. Cheek swabs collected from an individual may, in fact, contain a high concentration of cells with DNA. However, it should be noted that blood is always the better "known" sample of choice to be collected from the victim for DNA analysis. In fact, the need to resample "knowns" from the victim is much higher with cheek swabs than with liquid blood. This is especially true when the epithelial cheek cells are contaminated with the perpetrator's DNA following an oral assault or if the victim's mouth is bleeding.

It is recommended that food and drink be withheld at least 20 minutes prior to collection of a saliva sample. These samples are best taken with a clean, cotton-tipped swab like those provided in sexual assault kits. The inside of the mouth (cheeks and gums) should be swabbed and the swab should be smeared onto a microscope slide. The swab should then be air dried before packaging in a paper (not plastic) envelope for submission to the laboratory. The sample should be identified with the subject's name, date, time, collector's name or initials, and appropriate case numbers. These specimens do not require refrigeration.

PENILE, VAGINAL, AND RECTAL SWABS FOR DNA EXAMINATIONS

In all sexual assault investigations, swabs of the penis, vagina, and rectum are especially important. These swabs may reveal the presence of semen or other body fluids. The collection should be completed using multiple clean, cotton swabs to efficiently collect as much material as possible.

MISCELLANEOUS EVIDENCE FOR DNA EXAMINATIONS

The sexual assault investigator should recognize that useful DNA evidence does not stop at the body of the victim. Evidence also includes sheets and blankets, "sex toys," or other devices used to sodomize the victim. These items should be submitted in their original condition without the investigator attempting to take samples from them. For example, it is desirable to collect and submit undergarments worn after an assault rather than attempting to cut or swab stains in the crotch of the undergarment. Occasionally, the submission of the original item is impractical. In this case, a cutting may be taken to remove the possible evidentiary stain from the substrate. Prior to cutting, it is wise to draw a sketch, photograph, or diagram the item and the cut section for future reference. One may also choose to swab the material from the substrate. If the material is wet, then a clean, cotton swab can be used to collect the material. If dry, a drop of deionized water can be placed onto a cotton swab prior to the swabbing process. All swabs should be air dried completely prior to their packaging.

At times, the naked eye may fail to reveal useful biological fluids at a sexual assault crime scene. There are a number of useful tools that will allow the investigator to find this valuable evidence. Acid phosphatase (AP) "mapping" is one method for collection of such evidence. This method involves swabbing or blotting the suspect area and determining the presence of AP. Luminol, another essential tool, will reveal traces of blood that can be missed by the naked eye. Finally, one can use alternative light sources (i.e. ultraviolet light) to detect semen on bedding or clothing. With a trained eye, body fluids can be differentiated from other fluids just by the color of the luminescence that is emitted.

TRANSPORTATION AND STORAGE OF DNA EVIDENCE

When transporting and storing potential DNA evidence, it is important to keep the evidence dry and refrigerated. The evidence should be secured in paper bags or envelopes and sealed, labeled, and transported in such a way that ensures proper identification and chain of custody. Never place DNA evidence in plastic bags, as this will retain potentially damaging moisture. Also, avoid direct sunlight, warm temperatures, or repetitive freeze–thaw cycles as this may cause degradation of DNA.

EVIDENCE FOR TRACE ANALYSIS

Trace evidence in DFSA can be very valuable. For example, a suspect's pubic hair recovered from an assault scene may support the victim's recollection of being raped at that location. Furthermore, debris such as human tissue or clothing fibers recovered under the fingernails of a victim may also support her claim of resisting the attack.

HAIR FOR TRACE ANALYSIS

There are two types of evidential hair samples – loose and pulled. The two can be differentiated by whether or not a bulb or root is present on the end of the hair. Pulled hairs will contain this bulb, while loose hairs will not contain this material. When collecting hairs from the victim of a DFSA, pull 5–10 hairs from the front, back, center, left, and right of the victim's head. Five to ten pulled pubic hairs should also be collected. The head and pubic hairs should be packaged separately and labeled accordingly.

Loose hairs should also be collected from the victim. This is accomplished by placing a sheet of paper under the victim's head and, using a sterile comb (provided in some sexual assault kits) or gloved hand, combing the loose hairs down onto the paper. A similar collection of loose hairs from the pubic area should be made with another sheet of paper. The paper sheets should be folded so that none of the hairs fall out. These paper bindles need to be properly packaged, sealed, and labeled.

FINGERNAIL SCRAPINGS FOR TRACE ANALYSIS

Scraping from under the fingernails of the victim are easy to obtain with the wooden nail scrapers provided in many sexual assault kits. Scrape the material from under the fingernails onto a clean sheet of paper. The paper should be folded in such a manner as to prevent the loss of the collected material. The specimens should also be appropriated packaged, labeled, and initialed.

MISCELLANEOUS DEBRIS FOR TRACE ANALYSIS

General debris, outer clothing, and materials on the body should be collected onto a separate clean sheet of paper. This is to prevent loss of important evidentiary material as the victim disrobes.

If the clothing is wet, the collector should allow it to air dry before packaging. Clothing may be packaged into paper bags and properly sealed.

Finally, once nude, the victim should stand over another clean sheet of paper to collect any remaining debris from the attack. All paper should be folded so that no debris will fall out. Additionally, it is important to remember to label and package the specimen appropriately.

OTHER EVIDENCE IMPORTANT TO DFSA CASES

While every DFSA case is different with its own peculiarities, a commonality among many of these cases is the suspect's desire to photograph or videotape the victim during the assault. The photographs and video can prove to be very important evidence documenting the scene and the victim's condition during the assault.

Other important evidence that may be uncovered during the execution of a search warrant include pornographic magazines, newspaper articles, books on pharmacology, sexually explicit literature, or other items that provide information about DFSA or the pharmacodynamics of drugs.

The Internet has provided the free exchange of information like we have never before seen. Unfortunately, this exchange of information has included tips on committing criminal actions. DFSA owes its popularity in part to the Internet. There are numerous sites that provide information about the drugs that can be used to commit this crime, how to administer them without being detected, where to buy the drugs, and even how to make them at home. When faced with a DFSA case, it may prove beneficial to seize the suspect's computer to determine if he/she has taken an interest in DFSA by looking at their Internet browser's "favorites" or "bookmarks" as well as the historical account of websites visited prior to the assault.

CONCLUSION

Much of the evidence collected from victims and scenes of DFSA is the same as that collected from non-DFSA cases. The introduction of drugs as a weapon to commit sexual assault requires the investigator to collect a urine specimen from the victim as soon as possible. Also, it is important that an investigation of the suspect begin immediately. One goal of this type of investigation should be to determine likely drug candidates that may have been used to cause the symptoms described by the victim. This allows the toxicologist to initially focus on these drugs instead of looking for a "needle in a haystack."

Investigators involved in the collection of DNA evidence should use common sense and not allow such collections to intimidate them. By following the proper procedures, valuable evidence can be obtained in a safe manner. It is important that crime scene investigators are aware of the field tests that can be done to assure the proper collection and submission of DNA evidence. The accuracy by which these tasks are performed may determine whether or not justice will be served.

REFERENCES

American Prosecutors Research Institute (1999) *The Prosecution of Rohypnol and GHB Related Sexual Assault.* Alexandria, VA.

Blackledge, R.D. (1995) *J. Forensic Sci.*, 40, pp. 467–469.

Blackledge, R.D. and Vincentri, M. (1994) *J. Forensic Sci. Soc.*, 34, pp. 245–256.

Cirimele, V., Kintz, P., Staub, C. and Mangin, P. (1997) *Forensic Sci. Int.*, 84, pp. 189–200.

Fieler, E.L., Coleman, D.E. and Baselt, R.C. (1998) *Clin. Chem.*, 44, p. 692.

Hollenbeck, T.P., Siuzdak, G. and Blackledge, R.D. (1999) *J. Forensic Sci.*, 44, pp. 783–788.

LeBeau, M.A. (1999) *Forensic Sci. Comm.*, 1, p. 1.

LeBeau, M.A., Andollo, W., Hearn, W.L., Baselt, R., Cone, E., Finkle, B., Fraser, D., Jenkins, A., Mayer, J., Negrusz, A., Poklis, A., Walls, H.C., Raymon, L., Robertson, M. and Saady, J. (1999) *J. Forensic Sci.*, 44, pp. 227–230.

LeBeau, M.A., Montgomery, M.A., Jufer, R.A. and Miller, M.L. (2000) *J. Anal. Toxicol.*, 24, pp. 383–384.

Ledray, L. (1996) *Am. J. Clin. Health Aff.*, 79, p. 3.

Muller, C., Vogt, S., Goerke, R., Kordon, A. and Weinmann, W. (2000) *Forensic Sci. Int.*, 113, pp. 415–421.

Negrusz, A., Moore, C., Deitermann, D., Lewis, D., Kaleciak, K., Kronstrand, R., Feely, B. and Niedbala, R.S. (1999) *J. Anal. Toxicol.*, 23, pp. 429–435.

Negrusz, A., Moore, C.M., Kern, J.L., Janicak, P.G., Strong, M.J. and Levy, N.A. (2000) *J. Anal. Toxicol.*, 24 (7), 614–620.

Ropero-Miller, J.D., Goldberger, B.A., Cone, E.J. and Joseph, R.E. (2000) *J. Anal. Toxicol.*, 24 (7), pp. 496–508.

Schwartz, R., Milteer, R. and LeBeau, M. (2000) *South. Med. J.*, 93, pp. 558–561.

Stevens, B. and Coleman, D.E. (1999) *J. Forensic Sci.*, 44, p. 231.

Tsatsakis, A.M., Psillakis, T. and Paritsis, N. (2000) *J. Clin. Psychopharmacol.*, 20 (5), pp. 560–573.

CHAPTER 10

ANALYSIS OF BIOLOGICAL EVIDENCE FROM DFSA CASES

Marc LeBeau
Carla M. Noziglia

TOXICOLOGICAL ANALYSIS

Whereas the vast majority of collected evidence in cases of sexual assaults is subjected to routine examinations, some evidence in DFSA cases must be handled differently. This is particularly true with specimens requiring a toxicological analysis. While previous chapters have discussed a number of challenges surrounding the toxicological analysis of evidence from DFSA, this chapter will address the analytical issues and provide recommendations to overcome them.

MAKING THE NON-ROUTINE TOXICOLOGICAL ANALYSIS ROUTINE

As an investigator or a forensic toxicologist dealing with a DFSA case, one of the most important concepts to understand is that the analyses in these cases usually do not follow a set routine. There are many factors that determine which analyses should be performed on the submitted specimens. Many of these factors are dependent upon the investigation of the case. In fact, the investigation actually drives the testing that will be performed on the specimens (LeBeau, 1999). Therefore, it is always important that a thorough investigation begin immediately and that it does not wait for toxicological results from the victim's samples before starting.

Other chapters deal with the investigator's role in DFSA cases, yet it is important that the investigator and toxicologist have a thorough discussion of the case in order to make smart decisions as to the analytical scheme to follow (LeBeau, 1999). Table 10.1 lists some of the topics that may be important to a toxicologist's analytical scheme.

Many laboratories do not have a means of addressing DFSA cases. Therefore these samples may get batched in with the more routine cases (i.e. driving under the influence, overdoses, determination of chronic drug use). Following this protocol, many DFSA cases fall through the cracks, missing the extra attention they require.

A toxicology laboratory that is serious about investigating DFSA cases should recognize the difficulties of these cases and develop a procedure for the non-routine nature of these cases. This procedure may address things such as:

Information about the crime	Information about the victim	Information about the suspect

Dates and times of:
  Drugging
  Assault
  Awakening
  Specimen collection
Location of crime
Evidence collected from crime scene
	Age
	Sex
	Alcohol, drugs,
	  or medications used
	Victim's description of symptoms
	Witnesses' descriptions of symptoms
	Types of specimens collected
	  from victim
		Age
		Sex
		Alcohol, drugs,
		  or medications used
		Drugs or medications
		readily available to suspect
		Occupation and hobbies

1. which cases to accept as DFSA candidates;
2. specimens to require for their investigation and the length of time that specimens can be collected after ingestion of these drugs;
3. what information they will require for their examinations;
4. how the specimens will be treated to improve detection limits;
5. which drugs will be routinely tested for;
6. which drugs will occasionally be tested for;
7. when to "call it quits," and
8. how to report the findings.

"PERFECT" DFSA CASES

In the eyes of the forensic toxicologist, a "perfect" DFSA case will involve a victim that reports immediately after the assault and provides urine and blood specimens for the toxicological analysis. It will include a thorough investigation of the suspect(s) and will uncover the drug(s) likely to have been used to incapacitate the victim. Then the analysis can target that drug and its metabolites and will not require a search for the "needle in the haystack" as so often occurs in DFSA cases. But these cases are few and far between. The more likely scenario will involve a victim who does not report the crime for 24, 48, or even 96 hours after the crime occurs. It may involve the collection of only blood from the victim without any thought to the value of urine to the case. Or perhaps an unmotivated officer or the lack of a suspect to the crime may delay the investigation. The laboratory should establish criteria to determine which cases it will accept for analysis, and which it will refuse when their analyses will not provide probative information.

SPECIMEN SELECTION

Chapter 9 proposes specific volumes of blood and urine that are recommended for the toxicological investigation of DFSA: refer to that chapter for a complete discussion of this topic.

INFORMATION TO REQUEST AS PART OF THE TOXICOLOGICAL INVESTIGATION

A serious concern of most toxicologists is the breakdown in communication between investigators and the scientists trying to assist them in finding the truth. This, of course, also holds true in DFSA cases. Communication can be the difference between solving a case or allowing a perpetrator to remain free and capable of continuing the committed crime. Therefore, it is wise for toxicologists to develop a list of questions which they will expect the investigators to answer prior to agreeing to work on their DFSA case (LeBeau, 1999). These questions should serve as the first "screen" for toxicologists to attempt to focus their analysis to the likely drug candidate(s). This protocol prevents useless analyses and the wasting of valuable biological evidence. A list of such questions can be found in Table 10.2.

What symptoms did the victim describe?	How much ethanol did the victim consume?
How long was the victim unconscious?	Did the victim take any drugs (recreational, pre-scription, or over-the-counter)?
What specimens were collected?	Did the victim urinate prior to the collection of a urine specimen? If so, approximately how many times?
How much time passed between the alleged drugging and the collection of specimens?	What drugs does the suspect have easy access to?

Table 10.2
"Screening" questions for toxicological investigation of DFSA.

IMPROVING SENSITIVITY OF THE TOXICOLOGICAL ANALYSIS

It seems that every few years technological advances allow toxicologists to detect increasingly lower levels of drugs or metabolites in biological samples. For example, in the 1970s toxicologists were generally capable of measuring only microgram levels of drugs; today picogram levels (a million times less than a microgram) can be detected. With newer technology, toxicologists will only get better at detecting low levels of drugs that are used to commit DFSA. But today many laboratories are constrained by small budgets that do not allow them to purchase the "latest and greatest" instrumentation that technology has to offer. Laboratories are forced to rely on technology that is five, ten, or even twenty years old. While these laboratories cannot be expected to reach the low detection levels of laboratories with larger budgets, they can take some com-monsense approaches to improve their detection limits for DFSA cases and other cases that may require it.

One obvious technique to lower the detection limit of an analytical procedure is to increase the amount of analyte that the instrument is "seeing." This may be accomplished by increasing the volume of the specimen that is extracted and analyzed. For example, if a laboratory's standard procedure for analysis for hallucinogens uses 2 mL of urine, increasing that volume to 10 mL will result in an approximately five-fold increase in sensitivity.

Another way to increase what the instrument "sees" is to hydrolyze specimens to detect polar metabolites that would otherwise go undetected. This is particularly true with benzodiazepines like Rohypnol®, Xanax®, and Halcion®. Enzymes in the liver often convert benzodiazepines into water-soluble products by forming a conjugate with an endogenous substance. These hydrophilic compounds are not detected by many standard benzodiazepine procedures. This can be overcome through the use of a simple acid or enzymatic hydrolysis to free the benzodiazepine metabolite allowing for its detection.

Polar drugs and metabolites that may not be readily detected by standard techniques can be derivatized or chemically modified to improve their detection. There are numerous derivatizing agents and it is beyond the scope of this chapter to detail each. The individual chapters on the drugs used to commit DFSA provide more detail on analysis for these polar analytes.

Another common technique used by many toxicology laboratories to improve sensitivity is a process known as selective ion monitoring (SIM) mass spectrometry (MS). This is an instrumental experiment that lowers background noise, thus increasing sensitivity. While it is a popular technique within the field, it should be used with caution. The technique does not provide the same level of discriminating power as full scan MS. Therefore, the analyst must carefully measure ion ratios and show they are similar ratios to reference standards or controls at similar concentrations. But with the proper validation and precautions, SIM MS is a reasonable means of improving an assay's sensitivity.

An increasingly popular form of MS involves the use of chemical ionization (CI). This is a form of MS that provides a "softer" fragmentation pattern than seen with traditional electron impact (EI) MS. The result for most analytes is a CI mass spectrum composed primarily of a protonated molecular ion ($[M+H]^+$) with little additional fragmentation. Additionally, it is common to see adduct ions from the chemical reagent used to ionize the analyte. This has a number of advantages over EI MS. First, this technique allows the analyst to determine the molecular weight of an unknown analyte. Further, since there is less fragmentation and the signal is mainly focused in $[M+H]^+$, it results in higher mass-to-charge ratios of these fragments. This in turn means there will be less chemical noise and a higher signal-to-noise level, ultimately allowing for lower detection levels.

While not all laboratories can afford the newest technology that is available, those that can have witnessed how the technology has improved capabilities in drug analysis. One such improvement, liquid chromatography/mass spectrometry (LC/MS), has proven to be useful in DFSA analyses, particularly when looking for benzodiazepines (LeBeau *et al.*, 2000). LC/MS has a number of advantages over traditional GC/MS techniques including the capability of analyzing polar, non-volatile, and thermally labile analytes that do not fare well by GC/MS techniques. Further, it can do so without derivatization and often with greater sensitivity. As technological advances continue, the capabilities of toxicology laboratories will only improve.

TESTING FOR THE "ROUTINE" DFSA DRUGS

As previously mentioned, the investigation of the crime drives the toxicological analysis required for each individual case. For example, if a suspect has access to GHB, the analysis should include this drug if the specimen was collected within a logical time period. Unfortunately, many DFSA investigations do not turn up the "likely" drug. Thus, the laboratory is forced to screen specimens for "routine" DFSA drugs. This list should include drugs that are generally recognized as DFSA drugs, as well as other commonly encountered recreational drugs. Of course, each laboratory's list of routine drugs may vary based on their capabilities. Additionally, the levels for which the laboratory is capable of testing must be low enough to address the question the investigators are asking – was the victim under the influence of some drug or drugs? Table 10.3 is an example of what may be considered routine DFSA drugs by some laboratories (LeBeau *et al.*, 1999). It is not meant to be a comprehensive list of every drug that may be used to commit DFSA. Instead, it serves as a logical starting point for addressing these cases.

TESTING FOR THE "NON-ROUTINE" DFSA DRUGS

At times the investigation may warrant a more comprehensive toxicological analysis than looking for routine DFSA drugs. Perhaps the investigation has revealed that the suspect had prescription sleeping pills that are not considered routine. Or perhaps chemical analysis of a cup that the victim drank from revealed the presence of another "non-routine" DFSA drug. On other occasions, the history of the case combined with the victim's symptoms may warrant a more comprehensive screen. Then it becomes essential that the forensic toxicologist perform targeted analyses for these non-routine drugs in biological specimens from the victim. Table 10.4 lists what may be considered non-routine DFSA drugs that have been suspected or proven to have been used in DFSA cases.

Table 10.3

Example list of "routine DFSA drugs".

Ethanol	Cocaine*
Gamma Hydroxybutyrate (GHB)	Marijuana*
Gamma Butyrolactone (GBL)*	
1,4-Butanediol*	Opiates:*
	Heroin
Benzodiazepines:*	Morphine (Roxanol®)
Alprazolam (Xanax®)	Codeine
Chlordiazepoxide (Librium®)	Hydrocodone (Vicodin®)
Clonazepam (Rivotril®)	Hydromorphone (Dilaudid®)
Diazepam (Valium®)	Oxycodone (Oxycontin®)
Flunitrazepam (Rohypnol®)	
Lorazepam (Ativan®)	Barbiturates:
Temazepam (Restoril®)	Amobarbital (Amytal®)
Triazolam (Halcion®)	Phenobarbital (Phenob®)
	Pentobarbital (Nembutal®)
Amphetamines:	Secobarbital (Seconal®)
Amphetamine (Adderall®)	
Methamphetamine (Desoxyn®)	Sedative Antidepressants:*
Methylenedioxyamphetamine	Amitriptyline (Elavil®)
(MDA)	Desipramine (Norpramine®)
Methylenedioxymethamphetamine	
(MDMA)	Sedative Antihistamines:*
	Diphenhydramine (Benadryl®)
	Brompheniramine (Dimetapp®)
	Doxylamine (Unisom®)

* Screens should include major metabolites in addition to the parent drug.

Table 10.4

Example list of "non-routine DFSA drugs".

Anticonvulsants:*	Muscle Relaxants:*
Chloral hydrate (Noctec®)	Carisoprodol (Soma®)
Ethchlorvynol (Placidyl®)	Cyclobenzaprine (Flexeril®)
Valproic acid (Depakene®)	Meprobamate (Equanil®)
Hallucinogens:*	Sedatives:*
Dextromethorphan (Robitussin®)**	Clonidine (Catapres®)
p-Methoxyamphetamine	Zolazepam (Telazol®)
Scopolamine	Zolpidem (Ambien®)
Tiletamine (Telazol®)***	

*   Screens should include major metabolites in addition to the parent drug.
**   Dextromethorphan is a sedative hallucinogen when taken in large doses.
*** Telazol is a veterinarian medication composed of a dissociative anesthetic agent and a strong sedative.

CALLING IT QUITS

Knowing when to "throw in the towel" on DFSA cases is an additional challenge to the forensic toxicologist. Often, the specimen itself makes the decision as its volume becomes increasingly depleted. On other occasions, the cost of the analytical testing may draw the analyses to a close.

But often, it is up to the toxicologist to determine when they are through with the case. This decision may not come easily, particularly when the investigators are insistent that *some* drug must have been used. Nonetheless, once the routine DFSA drugs are ruled out, the decision to address nonroutine drugs must be investigation-driven. The investigators should not expect the laboratory to rule out every nonroutine DFSA drug unless they are prepared to prove that their suspect had access to these drugs. For example, if investigators insist that zolazepam should be targeted in a DFSA case, they should be prepared to provide reasonable proof that the suspect had such a drug at his disposal (i.e. prescription, word of mouth, etc.). Without such, toxicologists must use their professional judgment to determine when the case is "finished."

REPORTING RESULTS

The significance of the results of the toxicological analysis of DFSA specimens is often quite confusing to both the toxicologist and investigators. Therefore, it is important to establish some consistency in reporting the results.

One common area of confusion is through the use of concentration units. Some laboratories report concentrations as nanograms per milliliter (ng/mL); others use micrograms per milliliter (μg/mL). Given the 1,000-time difference between nanograms and micrograms, it is imperative that the readers of a toxicology report understand their meaning. A case in point involves GHB. While most laboratories report their GHB findings in μg/mL or milligrams per liter (mg/L), some laboratories have reported their GHB findings in micrograms per deciliter (μg/dL). This results in confusion in interpretation as the numbers appear 100 times higher to the untrained eye. Thus a measured amount of GHB of 2 μg/mL in a urine sample, considered an endogenous level, may be misinterpreted when reported as 200 μg/dL. While there are attempts to encourage laboratories to become more consistent in the units that are used to report their quantitative results, tradition sometimes overrules common sense. Therefore, Table 10.5 provides conversions between the most commonly used concentration units.

When reviewing the report of a toxicological analysis it is important that the reader understand what a "positive" result and a "negative" result really mean. The positive result indicates that the individual was exposed to that drug at some time prior to the collection of the specimen. If the specimen is urine, then the possible time frame may be limited to only 12 hours (e.g. GHB) or it may be as long as days to weeks (e.g., Rohypnol®) (Hoes *et al.*, 1980; Negrusz *et al.*, 1999). If a blood specimen is analyzed, then the possible exposure time is shortened. It may be as low as a few hours (e.g. ethanol, GHB) to as long as a day or so (e.g. phenobarbital). Based on the levels that are measured, a trained

1 mg/L = 1 µg/mL
1 mg/mL = 1000 µg/mL
1 µg/mL = 1000 ng/mL
1 mg/dL = 10 µg/mL
100 µg/dL = 1 µg/mL

toxicologist or pharmacologist may be able to give a *rough* estimate of how recent the ingestion took place, but will never be able to say that the ingestion occurred at a specific time.

A negative result means one of two things. It may indicate the specimen was collected after the drug had been cleared from the body to a level that was no longer detectable by that laboratory. But it may also indicate that the victim was not exposed to any drug. Since most specimens are collected with some delay after the drugging, it can be difficult to distinguish between the two, and it is best emphasized that both are reasonable scenarios.

IMMUNOASSAYS

A common tool in the analytical toxicologist's or chemist's "toolbox" is a technique known as an immunoassay. This assay is based on the concept of an antibody against a particular drug competitively binding to the drug itself (the antigen). Smith (1999) provides an excellent overview of immunoassays.

While immunoassays are generally reliable tools when determining if someone died of a drug overdose or if someone was under the influence of a drug at the time of specimen collection, these same tests may not possess the ability to adequately determine if an individual was drugged hours to days before the specimen was collected. Of the commonly available immunoassays, the benzodiazepine class of drugs tends to be the most troublesome in this area. A number of commercially available immunoassays do not detect low levels of today's more common benzodiazepines. Therefore, toxicologists and investigators must be wary of "negative" results produced by this technique. If the assays are available, they should nearly always be utilized (if specimen volume permits); however, negative results should not be regarded as "no drug or metabolite is present."

A common practice when working with immunoassays is to look for a positive deviation from the negative controls that are run as part of the assay. Such a rise may be an indication that low levels of the drug or metabolite are present, but not at high enough levels for the instrument to call it "positive." This practice helps improve the effectiveness of immunoassays in DFSA investigations.

As mentioned earlier, another means of improving the sensitivity of benzodi-azepine immunoassays is to incorporate a hydrolysis step into the assay. This will free the conjugated polar metabolites, allowing for better cross-reactivity and improved performance of the immunoassay (Beck *et al.*, 1992; Meatherall and Fraser, 1998; Simonsson *et al.*, 1995; Weijers-Everhard and Végh, 2000).

DETECTION LIMITS OF OTHER TECHNIQUES

While immunoassays have been much criticized for their inability to detect low levels of common DFSA drugs, a number of other commonly used analytical techniques also suffer the same ineffectiveness. It has been suggested that in order to be effective at DFSA investigations, the toxicology laboratory needs to fine-tune its procedures to detect all of these drugs (with the exceptions of GHB and ethanol) at levels of 10 ng/mL or lower (LeBeau *et al.*, 1999). It should be recognized that this is just a "line in the sand" and that the true determining factors of how low a laboratory should go will depend on the drug used, the specimen(s) collected, and the amount of time between ingestion and collection of the specimens. The 10 ng/mL level is meant as a starting point to get laboratories thinking of how they can increase the sensitivities of their procedures to better address the question that hangs over these cases – "Was the victim drugged?"

SEROLOGY AND DNA ANALYSIS

DNA analysis has made dramatic improvements in recent years. New methods of testing are usually quicker, use less sample and give better results. The old method of DNA analysis, RFLP (Restriction Fragment Length Polymorphism), took weeks to complete and needed a large sample to test. The new PCR (Polymerase Chain Reaction) method needs only a small sample and an entire sexual assault case can be completed in less than five days. The results depend upon which method is used. One hair can yield a comparable DNA type using PCR, but that same hair is useless using RFLP. This is why old cases and laboratory results must be looked at keeping this concept in mind.

QUALITY CONTROL

A quality assurance/quality control (QA/QC) scheme is vital to the reconstruction and evaluation of analyses performed in a forensic laboratory. It is for this reason that forensic laboratories performing DNA testing are required to have a Quality Assurance Manual that defines policy, documentation, and methodology.

It is the goal of the forensic laboratory to maintain a high standard of quality in analysis and reporting that meets or exceeds national standards. The QA/QC system is a compilation and consolidation of the many recommendations approved by the DNA Advisory Board (DAB), the Scientific Working Group on DNA Analysis Methods (SWGDAM), the National Research Council (NRC), and the American Society of Crime Laboratory Directors/Laboratory Accreditation Board (ASCLD/LAB). The DNA Advisory Board's guidelines outlined in their *Quality Assurance Standards for Forensic DNA Testing Laboratories* became the standard for all DNA testing laboratories on October 1, 1998. The guidelines are also the standard by which all DNA testing laboratories are currently audited. These guidelines are the basis for the Forensic Laboratory Quality Assurance Manual.

MULTIPLE SUSPECTS

The presence of multiple male (or female) DNA types in one sample will cause the interpretation of results to be quite different from a sample containing only one male and one female type. Probabilities are difficult to determine and may not be performed by the analyst. Rely on the good judgment of the forensic scientist to know the limitations of the evidence and the testing protocol.

AVAILABILITY OF KNOWN SAMPLES

It is essential that known samples be submitted from all victim(s), suspect(s), consensual partner(s), and any other potential contributors to the sample. If these are not available, testing may be suspended pending their submission. Collection of these samples is much easier now that buccal swabs are collected and not blood. Blood can certainly be submitted, but is not the specimen of choice. If a known sample absolutely cannot be collected because of death or the condition of the body, samples can be collected from the parents and/or siblings of the unknown person. In old cases, blood samples may be unavailable. Hairs may be used as good known reference standards.

MISCELLANEOUS FACTORS

As anyone knows who has collected evidence from a crime scene, analyzed it in the laboratory, or admitted evidence into court, no two cases are alike: anything can happen, and usually does. Murphy had to have been a law-enforcement officer, a forensic scientist, or a lawyer. Temperature, humidity, animal and human activity, wind, and artificial interference are some of the variables at the crime scene. Fatigue, skill, interest level, and personal matters may interfere with the ability of the crime scene and/or laboratory analyst on a given day.

Mechanisms are in place in the forensic laboratory to make sure that these circumstances do not infringe on the correct analysis procedures.

LIMITATION OF TESTS

There are a number of limitations to the DNA and serological testing on evidence from sexual assault victims. For example, tests for semen, seminal fluid, and spermatozoa will be negative if ejaculation did not occur or if a condom was used. Further, no spermatozoa will be found in men with aspermia or a successful vasectomy.

Penetration with no ejaculation will probably yield all negative results, but tests for amylase may be "positive" if licking or kissing occurred. Washing, douching, urinating, and defecating decrease the chance of "positive" tests. It is important to realize that these tests sometimes read "positive" over 72 hours after sexual contact, but they cannot determine how the stain got where it is, why it is there, or how long it has been there.

SEROLOGY

The word "serology" means the study of serous fluids, fluids in the body. It has come to mean the "old" technology used prior to DNA analysis that identified genetic proteins and enzymes such as PGM (phosphoglucomutase), Pep A (peptidase A) and PGM sub (phosphoglucomutase sub-type).

With the advent of DNA testing, previously used tests such as acid phosphatase are no longer used, and the importance of others such as prostatic acid phosphatase have decreased and are now used only as screening tests. Methods such as electrophoresis and ELISA have been replaced with quicker, more sensitive methods such as the Abacus method (results in ten minutes).

DNA is robust and has been found in evidence kept at room temperature for many years. If kept in a dry atmosphere, out of bright sunlight, DNA can be detected for more than 30 years.

DNA testing is extremely sensitive and as many as 40 DNA runs can be performed on a sample the size of the period at the end of this sentence. The current limit of 72 hours for evidence collection is still the norm, but with advances in technology this will be extended in the future.

GENERAL FORENSIC LABORATORY PROTOCOL

There are two separate kinds of tests performed: preliminary (or screening) tests, and confirmatory tests. Preliminary tests "indicate" the presence of the tested substance; confirmatory tests "identify" the tested substance.

Table 10.6

Definitions relevant to DNA analysis.

Acid phosphatase	Enzyme found in both seminal fluid and vaginal fluid. Test is limited in usefulness in sexual assault cases and not currently used as a presumptive test.
Amylase	Enzyme found in saliva.
Buccal swab	Swab collected from the inside area of the cheek. Now used in lieu of blood as a "known" sample from victim and suspect.
Confirmatory test	Final, definitive test.
Contamination	Introduction of a foreign material.
DNA	Deoxyribonucleic acid present in all cells of the body except red blood cells and platelets. Of particular importance to sexual assault cases, DNA is found in sperm as well as the epithelial cells in seminal fluid and saliva.
Exclusion	Any condition other than a complete match between a reference sample and a non-mixture evidentiary sample for every allele in every locus.
Inclusion	A complete match between a reference sample and a non-mixture evidentiary sample for every allele in every locus.
Locus/Loci	A locus is a point on the chromosome. Loci is plural and means places on a chromosome.
Mixture	More than one body fluid or donors. A DNA profile providing three or more alleles for any two loci.
Non-mixture	One body fluid or one donor. DNA profiles containing no more than two alleles per each locus analyzed.
Non-probative alleles	Alleles expected to be present (or whose presence is not unexpected) on the evidentiary evidence.
p30	Protein weighing 30,000 Daltons. Antigen from the prostate found in seminal fluid. Confirmatory test for the presence of seminal fluid. "Positive" even in samples from vasectomized males or other males with no spermatozoa.
PCR	Polymerase Chain Reaction. Method of DNA analysis.
Presumptive test	Screening test. Preliminary test.
Prostatic acid phosphatase	Enzyme from the prostate found in high levels in human seminal fluid. Presumptive test for seminal fluid.
RFLP	Restriction Fragment Length Polymorphism. Method of DNA analysis.
Secretor	One of 80% of the population to secrete his ABO type into body fluids. Tests for secretor status are no longer routinely performed.
Semen	Ejaculate from the male that contains spermatozoa (sperm) in seminal fluid. 60% of semen comes from the seminal vesicles, 20% from the prostate, 5% from sperm, and 15% from other sources.
Seminal fluid	Liquid portion of semen that contains prostatic acid phosphatase and p30.
Spermatozoa	Plural for two or more spermatozoon (sperm) – the reproductive cell of the male. Has characteristic shape. Formed in the testes. Comprises less than 5% of the semen volume. Degrade rapidly in the vagina.
STR	Short Tandem Repeats.

The sexual assault kit, samples taken from the victim, clothing, bedding, and other evidence are examined. Stains, hairs, fibers and anything of interest are noted. Preliminary tests are conducted on stains to determine if blood, semen, or saliva is indicated. If positive, a portion of the stain is tested further. Extraneous material such as leaves, hairs and fibers are removed and packaged for further testing.

In the past, many laboratories kept positive samples in the laboratory after testing. Since so little of the stain is used in DNA testing, this is no longer necessary and evidence may be returned to evidence storage or the submitting agency after testing.

Suspected semen stains are tested for the presence of spermatozoa and seminal fluid. A slide is made from the evidence and examined microscopically for the presence of spermatozoa. A portion of the evidence is subjected to prostatic acid phosphatase screening. If positive, confirmatory p30 testing using a monoclonal anti-human p30 antibody is performed. Seminal fluid diluted up to one in a million should be detectable. Table 10.7 provides examples of how the test results should be interpreted.

Findings	Interpretation
Positive p30 with presence of spermatozoa	Semen identified
Positive p 30 with no spermatozoa present	Seminal fluid identified
Spermatozoa	Spermatozoa identified
Positive amylase	Amylase identified – saliva indicated

Table 10.7
Interpretation guidelines for serological tests.

DNA

A good forensic analyst makes the final report as objective, simple, and direct as possible. If a distinct conclusion cannot be reached from the DNA profiles in a case, it is completely acceptable to report inconclusive results. Analysts should never be made to feel pressured to report conclusive results from less than conclusive data. All efforts should be made to err conservatively when data may be ambiguous.

There are three main types of DNA profile data: reference sample profiles, non-mixture profiles, and mixture profiles.

REPORTING RESULTS

Many forensic laboratories do not include a table of DNA profiling results in the final report because these tables are difficult to understand and confusing for the non-scientist. However, a results section is included in the report that will summarize the pertinent DNA information obtained from the samples, notably:

- A statement describing whether DNA profiling results for reference samples were complete or incomplete. If incomplete, a listing of the locus/loci for which allelic information was not obtained will be provided.[1]

  "A complete DNA profile was obtained from this individual."
  or
  "A DNA profile was obtained from this individual. Information from the STR locus/loci _____ was not obtained."

- A statement describing whether evidentiary samples appear to be mixtures or not.

  "DNA information obtained from this item appears to have come from a single source."
  or
  "DNA information obtained from this item appears to be a mixture."

[1] The reasons why a profile is incomplete are many, and a profile that was incomplete may still be used with confidence as discussed later.

REPORTING CONCLUSIONS

In the conclusion section of the final report the DNA information found in the evidentiary samples is compared to the DNA profile information of the reference samples. Based upon the comparison, DNA profiles will either be included in or excluded from a group of possible donors of the DNA information found in the evidentiary samples. Inclusions need to be qualified by a statistical value determined from the DNA information. The method for comparing and calculating will vary, depending upon whether the evidentiary DNA information appears to be a mixture of DNA profiles from two or more individuals or not.

NON-MIXTURES

Match criteria and calculations are defined by the NRC in *The Evaluation of Forensic DNA Evidence* (National Research Council, 1996), are applicable only for non-mixtures and are applied in the following order. First, reference samples are compared to each evidentiary sample to determine if the donor of the reference sample can be included in or excluded from the possible donor of the evidentiary sample. Inclusion is a complete match between a reference sample and a non-mixture evidentiary sample for every allele in every locus. Exclusion is any condition other than a complete match between a reference sample and a non-mixture evidentiary sample for every allele in every locus. If the reference or evidentiary sample is missing allelic information from one or more loci, exclusion/inclusion can still be determined.

- Inclusions/complete DNA match:

  "The suspect/victim/individual cannot be excluded as a potential donor of the DNA information observed."

- Exclusions/incomplete DNA match or DNA non-match:

  "The suspect/victim/individual is excluded as the potential donor of the DNA information observed."

An exclusion between a complete reference sample and a non-mixture evidentiary sample requires no further report statements. An inclusion between a complete reference sample and a non-mixture evidentiary sample must be further qualified by providing a statistical value. The statistical value given in this situation should not be thought of as the statistic for inclusion, because this thinking leads to the faulty assumption that some sort of relatedness exists between the individual's profile and the evidence. Instead, the statistical value is merely the probability of drawing that particular DNA profile (which has been found on both the reference sample and the evidentiary sample) at random from a population.

The NRC in Recommendation 4.1 provides calculation methods and formulae. Most laboratories use the "Product Rule" for all inclusion calculations involving nonmixtures. The conservative Theta value of 0.03 is used in these calculations.

The statistical value must be defined within a particular population. The population must be defined in the statistical statement and is determined by which population database is used to calculate the statistical value. For example, if a Norwegian database were used, the statement would indicate this by stating, "1 in XX Norwegians." It is common for forensic laboratories to use three population databases in calculations. A statistical value for each of the three population databases is usually included in the statement, regardless of suspect/victim background. The frequencies usually used in the calculations are the United States Caucasian, African–American, and Hispanic values as reported in the database compiled by the US Federal Bureau of Investigation (FBI). The database has been statistically validated and published.

A statistical statement should follow the inclusion statement above as follows:

> "The probability of selecting an individual at random who could have contributed this information is 1 in (XX) U.S Caucasians, 1 in (XX) African Americans, and 1 in (XX) Hispanics.

In the event that an incompletely profiled reference sample is compared to a non-mixture evidentiary sample, the above guidelines and formulae apply, but the locus/loci not observed in the reference sample cannot be used in any of the calculations.

MIXTURES

Mixtures can be compared to reference samples in much the same way that non-mixtures can with some exceptions.

Non-probative alleles are defined as alleles expected to be present (or whose presence is not unexpected) on the evidentiary evidence. For example, you would expect to find an individual's profile on an item of that individual's clothing or on a swab taken from that individual's body. If a sample of a victim's clothing gave a mixture of DNA information (e.g. a mixture of a suspect's DNA profile and that victim's DNA profile) it is reasonable to subtract the DNA information that could have been contributed by the victim. This leaves only the DNA information that could have been contributed from another individual or individuals. The remaining DNA information can then be compared to the suspect's reference DNA profile. Inclusions or exclusions can be made based on the remaining information.

> "After subtracting the DNA information attributable to the victim, no DNA information that is suitable for comparison remains."

> *or*

> "After subtracting the DNA information attributable to the victim, DNA information that is suitable for comparison remains."

> *or*

> "After subtracting the DNA information attributable to the victim and the victim's boyfriend/husband, no DNA information that is suitable for comparison remains."

> *or*

> "After subtracting the DNA information attributable to the victim and the victim's boyfriend/husband, DNA information that is suitable for comparison remains."

then

"The suspect/victim/individual can/cannot be excluded as a potential donor of the DNA information observed."

plus

"The probability of selecting an individual at random who could have contributed this information is 1 in (XX) US Caucasians, 1 in (XX) African–Americans, and 1 in (XX) Hispanics."

The following report indicates that there must be at least one more person's DNA present. The investigator must get a sample from another suspect, boyfriend, the husband, etc. before a good interpretation can be made.

■ *(apparent mixture)*: The suspect cannot account for all of the remaining DNA information, but he/she cannot be excluded as a potential contributor of at least a portion. In other words, portions of the DNA information obtained appear to be from an individual for whom a reference sample was not submitted.

This means the suspect is included but the DNA from someone else is also present.

■ *(apparent mixture of three)*: Neither suspect A nor suspect B can be excluded as potential contributors of portions of the DNA information obtained from this item. However, suspect A and B cannot account for all of the information obtained. Remaining DNA information appears to have come from an individual for whom a reference sample was not submitted.

This means the two suspects are included but the DNA from someone else is also present.

MISCELLANEOUS STATEMENTS

The following statements may be applicable in some instances:

■ Reporting unaccounted for DNA information obtained from a non-mixture evidentiary sample/stain:

"All suspects/victims/individuals can be excluded as potential donors of the described evidentiary stain. The DNA profile on described evidentiary stain/sample is from an individual/male/female for whom a reference sample was not submitted."

All the knowns are excluded and there is DNA from someone present.

REPORTING FORMAT

Once case results have been completely analyzed, the analyst prepares a report. The written report is a summation of the results obtained during the examination of the evidence and any conclusions the analyst has drawn from these results. All reports prepared by one forensic laboratory should conform to the same reporting format. Table 10.8 lists the information usually included in a forensic report.

Table 10.8

Information included in a forensic report.

Incident/case number
Property number
Crime
Full names of victim(s) and suspect(s)
Name of requesting agency/person
Description of evidence
Relevant test results

COURT PRESENTATION

How the jury perceives DNA evidence depends largely upon the way the evidence is presented. It is difficult to educate a jury about DNA, so the expert must be depended upon. For the most part, the use of charts and graphs has been discontinued by scientists because of the difficulty nonscientists (jury, judge, and attorney) have in understanding and interpreting them.

A study at the University of Texas at Austin found that juries reached different conclusions depending upon the presentation of the data regarding DNA (Koehler, 1999). In the study, mock jurors were presented with the same testimony from DNA experts presented in two mathematically equivalent but different ways. The testimony differed in only one respect – the description of the likelihood that the DNA came from the suspect.

One group heard the odds expressed as a percentage: "The suspect has a 0.1 per cent probability of matching the DNA found purely by coincidence." The second group heard the odds as a frequency: "One in 1,000 other people also match the DNA."

Eighty-two per cent of jurors in the first group thought that the DNA came from the suspect. Most of the jurors were very confident of their judgement. Forty-three per cent of the jurors in the second group thought that the DNA came from the suspect. Only ten per cent of the jurors were very confident of their judgement.

The key to the understanding of the forensic laboratory report is communication. The work done by the law enforcement officer, the attorney, and the forensic scientist is important, and it is necessary for each to understand the work of the other. If you don't understand, ask. There is no such thing as a stupid question.

CONCLUSIONS

Most evidence collected in sexual assault cases will be subjected to the same routine examinations as other sexual assaults; however, DFSA cases require that additional precautions surrounding the toxicological examination be undertaken. This chapter has described some of these precautions and has provided suggestions to improve the analysis of biological fluids collected from alleged victims of DFSA and the understanding of the forensic laboratory reports.

REFERENCES

Beck, O., Lafolie, P., Hjemdahl, P., Borg, S., Odelius, G. and Wirbing, P. (1992) *Clin. Chem.*, 38, pp. 271–275.

DNA Advisory Board (1998) *Quality Assurance Standards for Forensic DNA Testing Laboratories.*

Hoes, M.J.A.J.M., Vree, T.B. and Guelen, P.J.M. (1980) *L'Encephale*, VI, pp. 93–99.

Koehler, J.J. (1996) "On Conveying the Probative Value of DNA Evidence: Frequencies, Likelihood Ratios and Error Rates", *Univ. Col. Law Rev.*, 82, pp. 43–78.

LeBeau, M.A. (1999) *Forensic Sci. Comm.*, 1, p. 1.

LeBeau, M.A., Andollo, W., Hearn, W.L., Baselt, R., Cone, E., Finkle, B., Fraser, D., Jenkins, A., Mayer, J., Negrusz, A., Poklis, A., Walls, H.C., Raymon, L., Robertson, M. and Saady, J. (1999) *J. Forensic Sci.*, 44, pp. 227–230.

LeBeau, M., Montgomery, M., Wagner, J. and Miller, M. (2000) *J. Forensic Sci.*, 45 (5), pp. 1133–1141.

Mattimore, V. and Noziglia, C. M. (1999) *Tulsa Police Department Biology Section: Case Management.* Quality Assurance and Standard Operating Procedure Manuals.

Meatherall, R.C. and Fraser, A.D. (1998) *J. Anal. Toxicol.*, 22, pp. 270–273.

National Research Council (1996) *Evaluation of Forensic DNA Evidence*, National Academy Press.

Negrusz, A., Moore, C., Deitermann, D., Lewis, D., Kaleciak, K., Kronstrand, R., Feely, B. and Niedbala, R.S. (1999) *J. Anal. Toxicol.*, 23, pp. 429–435.

Simonsson, P., Liden, A. and Lindberg, S. (1995) *Clin. Chem.*, 41, pp. 920–923.

Smith, M.L. (1999) "Immunoassay". In Levine, B. (ed.) *Principles of Forensic Toxicology.* American Association for Clinical Chemistry.

Weijers-Everhard, J.P. and Végh, C. (2000) *Bull. Intern. Assoc. Forensic Tox.*, 30 (4), pp. 8–10.

CHAPTER 11

SEXUAL ASSAULT NURSE EXAMINERS

Linda Ledray

HISTORY AND NEED FOR SANE-SART PROGRAMS

The impetus to develop SANE programs began in the United States with nurses, other medical professionals, counselors, and advocates working with rape victims who came for medical care in traditional settings such as hospital emergency rooms. It was obvious to these individuals that the services to sexual assault victims were inadequate. They were not receiving the same standard of care as other medical patients (Holloway and Swan, 1993; O"Brien, 1996). Rape victims often had to wait as long as four to twelve hours in a busy, public area, competing unsuccessfully for medical staff time with the critically ill (Holloway and Swan, 1993; Sandrick, 1996; Speck and Aiken, 1995). They were often not allowed to eat, drink, or urinate while they waited, for fear of destroying evidence (Thomas and Zachritz, 1993).

Emergency department (ED) services were inconsistent and problematic, with the typical rape survivor facing a time-consuming, cumbersome succession of examiners, some with only a few hours of orientation and little experience. Not only were the doctors and nurses treating them often not sufficiently trained to do the medical-legal exam required, but many were also unwilling or lacking in their ability to provide expert witness testimony if the case went to court (Lynch, 1993). When they had been trained to complete the evidentiary exam, staff often did not complete a sufficient number of exams to maintain their level of proficiency (Lenehan, 1991; Tobias, 1990; Yorker, 1996). Even when the victim's medical needs were met, their emotional needs all too often were overlooked (Speck and Aiken, 1995), or even worse, the survivor was blamed for the rape by the emergency department (ED) staff (Kiffe, 1996).

Often the only physician available to do the vaginal exam after the rape was male (Lenehan, 1991). While approximately half of the rape victims in one study were unconcerned with the gender of the examiner, for the other half this was extremely problematic. In this same study, even the male victims indicated they preferred to be examined by a woman, as they too were most often raped by a man and experienced the same generalized fear and anger toward men that female victims experience (Ledray, 1996a).

There are many anecdotal and published reports of physicians being reluctant to do the exam. This is reported to result from many factors including the physicians lack of experience and training in forensic evidence collection (Bell, 1995; Lynch, 1993; Speck and Aiken, 1995), the time-consuming nature of the evidentiary exam in a busy ED with many other medically urgent patients waiting to be seen (DiNitto et al, 1986; Frank, 1996), and the potential that if they completed the exam they may then be subpoenaed and taken away from their work in the ED to testify in court and be questioned by a sometimes hostile defense attorney (Frank, 1996; Speck and Aiken, 1995; Thomas and Zachritz, 1993). This often resulted in documentation of evidence that was rushed, inadequate, or incomplete (Frank, 1996). Staff physicians assigned residents to do the forensic examinations when they were available, or physicians even refused to do the exam (DiNitto *et al.*, 1986). In one case it was reported that a rape victim was sent home from a hospital without having an evidentiary exam completed because no physician could be found to do the exam (Kettelson, 1995).

As information became more readily available on the complex medical–forensic needs of rape victims, nurses and other professionals realized the importance of providing the best ED care possible (Lenehan, 1991). For 75% of these victims the initial ED visit was the only known contact they had with medical or professional support staff (Ledray, 1992a). Nurses were also very aware that while they were credited with only "assisting the physician with the exam," in reality they were already doing all of the medical–forensic examination except the pelvic speculum exam (DiNitto *et al.*, 1986; Ledray, 1992a). It was clear to these nurses that it was time to re-evaluate the system and consider a new approach.

To better meet the needs of this population, Sexual Assault Nurse Examiner (SANE) programs were established in Memphis, Tennessee, in 1976 (Speck and Aiken, 1995), Minneapolis, Minnesota, in 1977 (Ledray, 1993b; Ledray and Chaignot, 1980), and Amarillo, Texas, in 1979 (Antognoli-Toland, 1985). Unfortunately, these nurses worked in isolation, unaware of the other very similar programs' existence until the late 1980s. In 1992, 72 individuals from 31 SANE programs across the United States and Canada came together for the first time at a meeting hosted by the Sexual Assault Resource Service and the University of Minnesota School of Nursing in Minneapolis. It was at this meeting that the International Association of Forensic Nurses (IAFN) was formed (Ledray, 1996b).

While the initial SANE development was slow, with only three programs operating by the end of the 1970s, development today is progressing much more rapidly, especially with the high program visibility that resulted with the publication by the US Department of Justice, Office for Victims of Crime (OVC) document *The SANE Development and Operation Guide* (Ledray, 1999). Only 86 SANE programs were identified and included in the October 1996 listing of SANE programs published in *Journal of Emergency Nursing* (Ledray, 1996b). There are currently 182 SANE programs registered on the OVC grant-funded web site *www.sane-sart.com* and the number of SANE programs is expected to grow much more rapidly in the years to come. The American Nurses' Association (ANA) officially recognized Forensic Nursing as a new specialty of nursing in 1995 (Lynch, 1996). SANE is the largest sub-specialty of forensic nursing. At the 1996 IAFN meeting in Kansas City, Geri Marullo, Executive Director of ANA, predicted that the Joint Commission on Accreditation of Health Care Organizations would eventually require every hospital to have a forensic nurse available (Marullo, 1996).

THE ROLE OF THE SANE

Since forensic nurse examiner programs began independently and functioned independently until the founding of IAFN in Minneapolis in 1992, different terminology has been used across the country to define the new role in which they function. At the October 1996 IAFN annual meeting held in Kansas City, the SANE Council voted on the terminology it wanted to use. The overwhelming decision was to use the title – "Sexual Assault Nurse Examiner". A Sexual Assault Nurse Examiner (SANE) is a registered nurse, RN, who has advanced education in forensic examination of sexual assault victims. In programs where physicians are also used they are primarily referred to as Sexual Assault Forensic Examiners (SAFE). They too must have advanced education in sexual assault forensic evidence collection.

The primary mission of a SANE program is to meet the needs of all male and female victims of sexual assault or abuse by providing immediate, compassionate, culturally sensitive, and comprehensive forensic evaluation and treatment by trained, professional nurse experts within the parameters of the individual's state Nurse Practice Act, the SANE standards of the IAFN, and the individual agency policies. SANE programs may provide services to children, adolescents, and adult victims.

In addition to documentation and collection of forensic evidence, prophylactic treatment of sexually transmitted infections (STI) and prevention of pregnancy are provided by the SANE. The SANE conducts a limited medical examination to identify trauma, not a routine physical examination.

While the SANE is not a legal advocate, she does provide the rape survivor with information to assist her in anticipating what may happen next, in making choices about reporting and deciding who to tell, and to ensure that she gets the support she will need after she leaves the SANE facility. This usually includes a discussion between the victim and the SANE about reporting to law enforcement.

If she has made a choice not to report, they will need to discuss why she may be hesitant to report. While the decision to report is always ultimately the victim's, in most cases the SANE will encourage the survivor to report the crime and make referrals to legal advocacy agencies which can provide the support necessary to help her through the criminal justice process. The SANE will also provide emotional support and crisis intervention, working with advocacy support when available.

HOW TYPICAL SANE-SART PROGRAMS OPERATE

To be optimally effective and provide the best service possible to victims of sexual assault, the SANE must function as part of a team of individuals from community organizations, usually referred to as a Sexual Assault Response Team (SART). At a minimum, the SART will include the SANE, advocate, law enforcement, and prosecutor. The SANE is usually available on-call, off premises, 24 hours a day, seven days a week. The on-call SANE is paged immediately whenever a sexual assault or abuse survivor enters the community's response system. If a rape advocate is available, the staff or SANE will also page the advocate on call.

During the time it takes for the SANE to respond (usually no more than an hour), the ED or clinic staff will evaluate and treat any urgent or life-threatening injuries. If treatment is medically necessary, the ED staff will treat the client, always considering and documenting the forensic consequences of the life-saving and stabilizing medical procedures.

THE SANE EVIDENTIARY EXAM

After obtaining a signed consent, the SANE will conduct a complete medical forensic exam, including:

- the collection of evidence in a rape kit;
- further assessment and documentation for drug-facilitated sexual assault;
- assessment and documentation of injuries;
- risk evaluation and prophylactic care for sexually transmitted diseases (STDs);
- evaluation of pregnancy risk and preventive care;
- crisis intervention;
- referrals for medical and psychological follow-ups (Table 11.1). In most agencies a complete evidentiary exam is conducted for up to 72 hours from the time of the sexual assault as recommended by the American College of Emergency Physicians (1999) and the SANE Development and Operation Guide.

Forensic evidence collection

STD evaluation and preventive care

Pregnancy risk evaluation and prevention

Crisis intervention

Care of injuries (completed by the medical staff)

Table 11.1
Essential components of the complete medical forensic examination.

THE SANE ROLE WITH DFSA

The role of the SANE in dealing with the issue of DFSA begins by ensuring that all SART members are familiar with the clinical symptom picture that would indicate a possible DFSA. These are addressed throughout this book and include:

- a history of being out drinking, having just one or two drinks (too few to account for the extreme level of intoxication), quickly becoming extremely "intoxicated";
- a moment where she recognized suddenly feeling "very drunk" or "disoriented";
- reports from witnesses or from the victim that she acted "intoxicated" within about 15 minutes after drinking a beverage that she accepted from someone, or drinking a beverage that she left unattended;
- the victim remembers very little of the incident after accepting the beverage until awakening, other than flashes of memory, sometimes referred to as "cameo appearances";
- a reported history of "cameo appearances" in which she remembers "waking up" or "coming-to," but being unable to move, and passing out once again;
- these cameo appearances may be associated with a loud noise or pain;
- a history of feeling or being told she suddenly appeared drunk, drowsy, with impaired motor skills, judgment, or amnesia;
- the victim awakened, hours later, and found herself undressed, or partially dressed, and possibly in bed with a male she may or may not know;
- possible nausea and vomiting upon awaking (not always – this is drug dependent, as discussed in other chapters);
- the victim awakes with vaginal or rectal soreness making her believe she has been raped;
- history of being told she was given "Roofies," "Mexican Valium," "R-2," "Special K," "Ecstasy," etc.

INSTRUCTIONS FOR ED STAFF

The SANE protocol should include ED staff instructions and responsibilities for collecting and handling urine for a drug screen. These may include the following:

- If possible, ask the victim not to void until the SANE arrives so that evidence is not lost or destroyed.
- If the victim must void, ask her to save the urine in a forensic urine collection container, if available, or in a clean catch urine specimen container.
- The victim should be instructed to not wipe when she voids to avoid loss of sperm evidence.
- If the victim must void, the ED nurse should take possession of the urine from the victim and begin a chain-of-custody record (the SANE should have a chain-of-custody available in the ED for the ED staff).
- If the victim brings a urine specimen with her to the ED, this should not be discarded, but should be kept in the victim's possession until the SANE arrives.
- The staff should also know to record the victim's behavior, medical presentation, such as nausea and vomiting, disorientation, and assault history when volunteered to the ED staff.

DFSA BIOLOGICAL EVIDENCE COLLECTION AND HANDLING

When the SANE determines that the assault history is suspicious of DFSA she will collect a blood and a urine specimen in the ED, maintaining proper chain-of-custody. If the victim has brought a urine specimen with her, the SANE will take possession of the urine and begin chain-of-custody from that point. It is also important to document when the urine was collected by the victim, where it was between collection and the SANE taking possession, and who else had access to the urine. The first voided urine specimen should also be collected and proper chain-of-custody maintained on that specimen. Both should be sent for toxicological analysis by an appropriate laboratory.

BLOOD EVIDENCE

As a part of the forensic evidentiary examination of the sexual assault victim the SANE will always draw the victim's blood for DNA analysis (Frank, 1996). In addition, it is recommended that an additional tube of blood routinely be drawn that can be held for blood and alcohol analysis should this become an issue later when the case is charged (Ledray, 1992a). Since many of the drugs used to facilitate a sexual assault, including alcohol, are metabolized quickly, the blood specimen should be collected within 24 hours or it will be unlikely to test positive. (It is still, however, recommended that a blood specimen be routinely collected as a part of the SANE examination recognizing the limitations.)

URINE EVIDENCE

As noted in this book, urine is a better specimen for detection of metabolites of many of the drugs used to facilitate a sexual assault. Scientists are in the process of developing more sensitive testing procedures than are currently available. While these processes are currently only in research stages, once developed they may allow for the identification of substances as long as 28 days post-ingestion of a single 2 mg dose of flunitrazepam (Negrusz *et al.*, 2000).

Victims may report a history of having only a couple of alcoholic beverages but quickly becoming extremely intoxicated. When the victim awakens, sometimes more than 12 hours later, she may find herself undressed, or partially dressed, with vaginal or rectal soreness making her believe she has been raped. The victim can often remember very little of the incident prior to awakening, other than flashes. Even though there is little memory and perhaps no certainty of a sexual assault, the SANE should adhere to the standard sexual assault protocol and collect the first voided urine for a drug screen. If the victim calls prior to coming to the hospital or clinic, she should be told to not void unless necessary, and if she must void to collect her first voided urine in a clean container and bring it with her (Ledray, 1996b). Whenever the victim's story is consistent with a DFSA, or suspicious, the SANE will collect a urine specimen for DFSA analysis as a part of the sexual assault evidentiary examination.

HAIR EVIDENCE

Head hair is also a source for identification of some drugs, such as benzodiazepines and amphetamines; however, a large number of false negatives are usually found (Cooper *et al.*, 1999). Most laboratories today do not have the ability to analyze hair specimens for drugs used in a DFSA; however, when they do, it is a very expensive process. While with special equipment and procedures drugs may be detected as early as 24 hours after ingestion, toxicologists prefer hair specimens collected 14 days later to allow for absorption of the drug into the hair as it grows. When hair is to be used for drug screening, it should not be collected as a part of the routine SANE evidentiary exam. Arrangements should be made for the victim to return at a later date for collection of hair specimens, which can be cut close to the skin. The hair does not need to be pulled.

The collection of head hair and pubic hair from all sexual assault victims at the time of the initial examination is controversial. State crime laboratories have requested up to 50 pulled head hairs and 50 pulled pubic hairs from every victim. This is a very painful experience for a victim who has recently been raped, and most of these hair specimens have historically never been used for comparison purposes. Most SANE programs have, as a result, discontinued the routine pulling of head and pubic hair. In the few cases where hair is needed it can be obtained at a later point in time. It is not evidence that will be lost (Ledray, 1999b). In the case of a possible DFSA, it will even be more useful evidence when collected later.

ADDITIONAL SOURCES OF EVIDENCE

HISTORY OF ASSAULT

Unfortunately, in most cases of suspected DFSA a positive blood, urine, or hair specimen is not obtained. As analytical techniques become more sophisticated in the future, this will likely change. Today, however, police and prosecutors must rely primarily on verbal history from the victim, or witnesses, and other physical evidence collected by the SANE. It is thus essential that other potential sources of evidence be carefully evaluated.

Because the SANE is conducting a medical examination, she can testify in court as to what the victim reported during the exam, and this testimony is admissible as an exception to the hearsay rule. Normally the court will not allow one person to testify as to what another person told them because it is considered "hearsay." The other time this type of testimony is admissible into court as an exception to the hearsay rule is "an excited utterance," when a victim reports immediately after the sexual assault.

This testimony can be important corroborating evidence and very useful in court. Knowing this, it is extremely important that the SANE accurately document what the victim tells her, using quotes of the victim's words whenever possible. In addition, the SANE should document the victim's behavior and emotional response during this process. She should also always note if the victim is or is not oriented to "person" (who she is), "place" (where she is), and "time" (date and time). Her ability to recall past events should also be documented. In addition, it is helpful for the SANE to note if the victim's speech is clear, if her gait is steady, and if there are any other visible physical signs of intoxication at the time of the examination. This is important not only to document possible drug intoxication, but also because the credibility of the victim will often be challenged should the case go to trial. For instance, if the victim reports "coming to" and trying to move her arms or legs, and states, "I couldn't move my arms or legs. It was like they were not attached to my body," this is valuable evidence for the SANE to document in quotes.

PHYSICAL EXAMINATION AND EVIDENCE COLLECTION

In many DFSA cases it is unclear if a sexual assault took place. Once the SANE has as complete and detailed history of the assault as the victim can provide, she will know where to look further for potential evidence of physical trauma or recent sexual contact that can corroborate the victim's assault history. If, as often occurs in DFSA, the victim cannot give an account of the assault other than a few vague memories, the SANE will need to do a complete head-to-toe visual examination looking for areas of redness, swelling, abrasions, bruising, scratches, or cuts. It is important to palpate for areas of soreness as well.

In addition the oral, rectal, and vaginal orifices should be examined for trauma and specimens taken for sperm and acid phosphatase to show if recent sexual contact occurred. It is important to note that while positive specimens will prove that recent sexual contact did occur, negative results without trauma and without sperm or acid phosphatase do not prove that recent sexual contact did not occur (Ledray, 1999b).

NONGENITAL INJURY EVIDENCE

Physical injuries are the best proof of force and should always be photographed, described on drawings, and documented in writing on the SANE Exam Report as evidence of force (Ledray, 1992b). Photographs are, however, not meant to take the place of good charting (Pasqualone, 1996). It is also important to note that the absence of injuries does not mean force or coercion was not used. Lack of injury does not prove consent (Tucker *et al.*, 1990). Especially in a DFSA where the victim may be unconscious or immobilized by the drugs and unable to resist, it is unlikely that physical injury will result.

Specific consent to photograph is necessary but may be included as a standard part of the exam consent. In a facility which maintains medical records, two sets of pictures should always be taken. One set always remains with the medical record. The second set should be given to law enforcement (although some programs give it to the victim) and will usually be the pictures used in court. Whenever pictures are taken, the first picture should always be of the victim's face, and others should follow in a systematic order, such as head to toe, or front to back. They should be taken first without a scale to show nothing is being hidden, then with a standard gray photographic scale to document size and color. While a coin such as a quarter is sufficient, a gray photographic scale will also assist with color determination. Each picture should include a label with the victim's name in the picture. When possible, a camera with a macro lens should be used that allows for close-up photography. If a Polaroid camera is used, the SANE should print her name and title, the date, the time, and the client's name and record number on the back of every Polaroid. It is possible to use the medical record number instead of the victim's name.

Photographic documentation of injuries using a 35 mm camera should be completed with a standard 50 mm lens, or a 35–110 zoom lens, and 100–200 speed (ASA) color film. A disadvantage of 35 mm pictures is that they must be sent out for developing and are often not available to law enforcement when they investigate or to prosecutors when they are deciding if they will charge the case. Because of this limitation, some SANE programs will take 35 mm and Polaroid pictures. Polaroid photography has the advantage of allowing the SANE to give the victim one set of pictures to take with her when the exam is completed, and of being available to the police during their initial investigation. The older, less expensive Polaroid cameras have the disadvantage of poorer quality, especially for close-ups. Polaroid film is also very expensive (Sheridan, 1993).

The nurse must be knowledgeable about patterns of injuries resulting from violence so she knows the appropriate questions to ask and where to look for injuries on the basis of the history (Sheridan, 1993). The most common injuries in non-DFSA are broken eardrums from severe slapping, neck bruising from choking, punch bruising to the upper arm, and "defensive posturing" injuries to the outer mid-ulnar areas of the arms. Also common are whip- or cord-like injuries to the back; punch or bite injuries to the breasts and nipples; punch injuries to the abdomen, especially in pregnant women; punch and kick injuries to the lateral thighs; and facial bruising, abrasions, and lacerations (Sheridan, 1993). There are no data available on DFSA injury patterns.

"Patterned injury" is different from the similar term, "pattern of injury" discussed above. Both are, however, important forensic terms. "Patterned injuries" are injuries where one can easily identify the object used to inflict the injury by the pattern left on the victim, such as a coat hanger, iron, extension cord, belt, or the imprint of a ring worn by the assailant. Bite marks are important patterned injuries that can be linked to a suspect's dental pattern. Since most assailants choke using their dominant hand, the fingertip pattern can identify the assailant's handedness. A right-handed assailant will usually grab the victim's anterior neck so as to leave a single thumb bruise at the right lateral neck and several fingertip bruises to the left lateral neck (Sheridan, 1993).

It is not advisable to try to date the age of a bruise by its color. Individuals vary greatly in their rates of healing, and medications may affect bleeding and healing response as well. Sheridan suggests that deep blue-purple bruising is best documented as a "relatively recent bruise" or as "consistent with Mary Jane's report of being punched by Jim Smith 24 hours prior" (Sheridan, 1993).

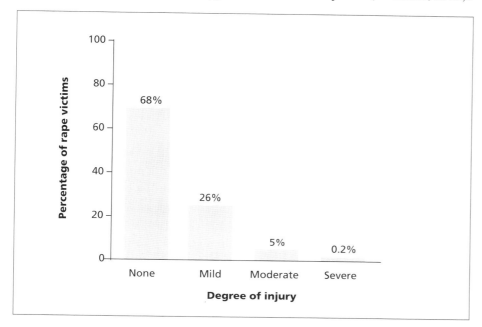

Figure 11.1

Non-genital injuries suffered during rape. Percentage of sexual assault victims with mild, moderate, severe, and no injuries (Tintinalli and Hoelzer, 1985). ED rape cases (N = 372).

As Figure 11.1 indicates, physical injuries resulting from sexual assault are relatively rare. In a review of 372 ED rape cases, 68% of the victims seen had no injury, 26% had mild injuries, 5% moderate injuries, and less than 1% (0.2%), were severely injured. Victims 50 years old and over were twice as likely to be injured, 63%, compared with 32% of the victims under 50 years old (Tintinalli and Hoelzer, 1985).

Another study found only 5% of victims had major nongenital injuries. However, women over 35 years of age were nearly twice as likely to be injured (Marchbanks *et al.*, 1990). In another study of 440 rape victims, 46% had some nongenital trauma; however, only 1% required hospitalization (Cartwright *et al.*, 1986). In a study of 98 rape victims, only 27% had even minor nongenital injuries not requiring treatment, 3% had injuries requiring treatment, and less than 1% required hospitalization (Tucker *et al.* 1990).

GENITAL TRAUMA EVIDENCE

Genital trauma is useful to show both recent sexual contact and force. Just as with nongenital trauma, the absence of genital trauma does not indicate consent (Cartwright *et al.*, 1986). While the examiner will usually not find genital injuries, this should not influence testimony regarding the validity of the rape, since most rape victims do not experience genital injury as a result of a rape (Bowyer and Dalton, 1997). In one study, vaginal injuries represented only 19% of the total injuries and were always accompanied by complaints of vaginal pain, discomfort, or bleeding (Tintinalli and Hoelzer, 1985). Another study found that 22 of 83 (27%) victims had genital injuries following a rape (Bowyer and Dalton, 1997). Still another study found only 1% of rape victims had genital injuries so severe that they required surgical repair, 75% of which were upper vaginal lacerations (Geist, 1988). They also found that upper vaginal lacerations usually presented with profuse bleeding and pain, and lower vaginal lacerations were more common in virgins.

The pattern of genital injury in female sexual assault victims has been a more recent area of study. Since the posterior fourchette is the point of greatest stress when forceful stretching occurs, and it is the point of first contact of the penis with the vagina, the resulting injury is characterized as an "acute mounting injury" (Slaughter and Brown, 1992; Slaughter and Brown, 1997). Because no posterior fourchette injuries were found in a control group of sexually active adolescents, and injuries were found in 33% of the abused population, the researchers concluded that posterior fourchette injuries are indicative of sexual assault (McCauley et al., 1986).

In a study that compared the physical vaginal examination findings of 311 rape victims to a group of 75 women after consenting sexual intercourse, researchers found that 213 (68%) of the rape victims had genital trauma and only eight (11%) of the consenting women had genital trauma. Furthermore, none of the women who were examined after consenting sex had injury in more than one site (Slaughter and Brown, 1997). Of the 213 victims with trauma, however, they found that 200 (94%) had trauma at one or more of four sites including posterior fourchette, Labia minora, hymen, or fossa navicularis; 162 (76%) had 3.1 sites of injury, making injury at more than one site indicative of rape. Trauma varied by site, tears appeared most often on the posterior fourchette and fossa navicularis; abrasions appeared on the labia; and ecchymosis was seen on the hymen. They also found that all women with tears reported vaginal bleeding. Five victims mistakenly reported that their menstrual period had begun. Researchers also concluded that timing of the exam was crucial because beyond 24 hours, the likelihood of identifying injury was significantly reduced. At follow-up examination, which occurred beyond four days (average of 25 days), all injury was resolved and there was no scarring and no evidence of the previous trauma. They also found that with the exception of hymenal tears, which were nearly four times more common in adolescent victims, injury was not related to age.

The literature also suggests that colposcopic examination to magnify genital tissue is an important asset to the identification of genital trauma (Frank, 1996;

Peele and Matranga, 1997; Slaughter and Brown, 1992; Slaughter and Brown, 1997). With the use of a colposcope, the number of cases increased by 8% because three or more genital injuries were identified as compared to identification with the naked eye (O"Brien, 1997). Photographic equipment, both still and video, can be easily attached for forensic documentation. In one study, 28% of 440 rape victims had genital trauma; however, only 16% were identifiable without staining or colposcopic exam (Cartwright *et al.*, 1986). In the legal arena, the use of the colposcope is well documented as an accepted practice in the examination of adults and children. The fact that it is noninvasive makes it particularly valuable for examination of young or elderly clients. The colposcopic exam is especially important as a part of the pediatric protocol (Soderstrom, 1994).

With visualization alone, positive genital findings occur in only 10% to 30% of the cases (Cartwright *et al.*, 1986; Tintinalli and Hoelzer, 1985). With colposcopic examination, genital trauma has been identified in 87% (N = 114) of sexual assault cases (Slaughter and Brown, 1992). When a colposcope is used, the magnification must always be documented, the pictures or video must be well focused and clear, standard positions for examination should be used and documented, and a method of measurement should be used (Soderstrom, 1994).

In a study of genital trauma in a consenting population using the colposcope, 11 (61%) of 18 volunteers, who had consenting sex within six hours, had positive findings of micro trauma. This trauma was not visualized with gross visualization but required the use of the colposcope (Norvell *et al.*, 1984).

While there are no data available today, in a DFSA, since the victim is relaxed and not resisting the sexual penetration, it may be even less likely that genital trauma will result.

SEMINAL FLUID EVIDENCE

Seminal fluid evidence is used for two purposes: to show that recent sexual intercourse occurred, and to identify the assailant. It is important to remember that the absence of sperm or seminal fluid findings does not disprove recent sexual intercourse. This is especially likely since 34% or more of rapists are sexually dysfunctional (Groth and Burgess, 1977) and others wear condoms (Norvell *et al.*, 1984). Even when sexual intercourse has occurred, sperm may also not be found if the assailant has had a vasectomy, is sexually dysfunctional, or the sperm deteriorated due to the time between the exam and the forced penetration (Tucker *et al.*, 1990).

Vaginal secretions can be screened for the presence of sperm with a wet mount during evidence collection. While any microscope can be used, a light staining microscope developed specifically for use by the SANE aids significantly in simplifying this procedure. The light staining microscope enhances and makes the color of the sperm more distinct without staining the slide or altering it in any way. The image viewed through the light staining microscope is optically enhanced to make the sperm appear bright yellow against a blue background. It also eliminates the need for the user to find the optimal magnification. This enhanced image can also be photographed through an attachable camera for evidence (O'Brien, 1996; Peele and Matranga, 1997). It can also be attached to the same monitor as the colposcope (Peele and Matranga, 1997).

Seminal fluid evidence is analyzed for sperm presence, often also for motile or nonmotile sperm, and for acid phosphatase (ACP). ACP is actually an array of related isoenzymes which is found in much greater concentration in semen than in any other body fluid (Davies, 1978). Vaginal secretions have been found to contain very low levels of endogenous ACP. The exact tissue source of the vaginal ACP is uncertain, but is believed to be endometrium. The two specific ACPs most often analyzed in the evaluation of sexual assault are prostatic acid phosphatase (PAP) and prostatic specific antigen (PSA). Since vaginal ACP and prostatic ACP cannot be distinguished biochemically, the only reliable differentiation is the quantitative level. Since prostatic ACP found in semen is in much higher concentration than vaginal ACP, a high level would indicate that there has been recent sexual contact with seminal fluid being left in the vagina (Green, 1988). This may be especially useful information in the DFSA case in which the victim is unsure if a sexual assault occurred. The interpretation of actual numeric results of analysis will be different depending on the specific substrate used by the laboratory as there is no standard. The laboratory must indicate how the analysis was done in order to determine how to interpret the findings as positive or negative for prostatic ACP.

Cases that are "negative" for sperm and "positive" for acid phosphatase typically involve an assailant who has had a vasectomy, but this result is also possible in cases involving an assailant who is a chronic alcoholic (Enos and Beyer, 1980).

In a sexually functional, nonrape population, sperm has been found on examination within 24 hours after consenting sexual intercourse with known ejaculation, as often as 100% of the time (N = 15) in one study (Soules *et al.*, 1978), 65% (N = 980) in another study (Silverman *et al.*, 1978), and in as little as 25% (N = 542) in yet another study (Randall, 1986).

In a study of 1,007 rape victims examined, sperm was found in only 1% (N = 4) of the 369 cases involving oral rape (Figure 11.2). All of the positive oral specimens were collected within three hours of the rape. Of the 210 cases with rectal involvement, only 2% (N = 4) were positive for sperm. These exams were

Figure 11.2 (opposite, above)

Specimens positive for sperm: results of a study by Tucker et al. (1990) indicating the prevalence of spermatozoa findings following oral and anal rape.

Figure 11.3 (opposite, below)

Vaginal specimens positive for sperm: results of a study by Tucker et al. (1990) indicating the prevalence of spermatozoa findings following vaginal rape.

all completed within four hours of the rape. In the 111 skin specimens collected, 19% (N = 12) were positive. All but two of the positive specimens were collected within four hours of the rape (Tucker *et al.*, 1990).

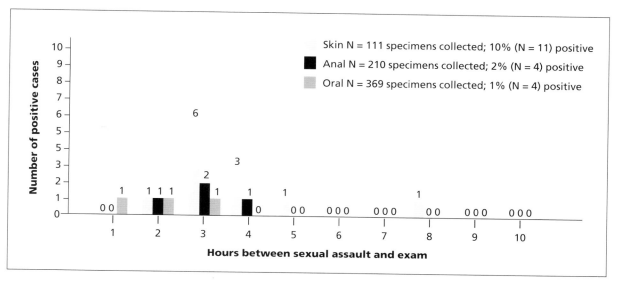

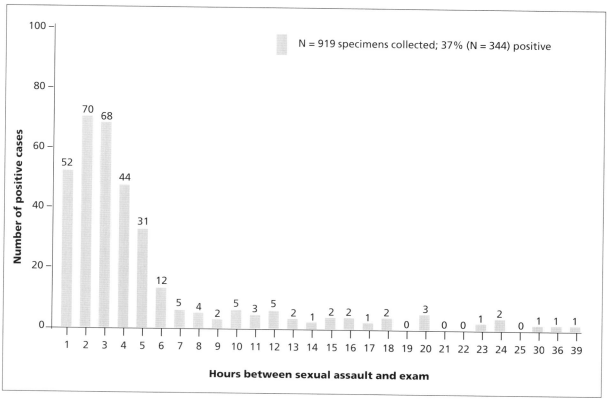

Of the 919 vaginal specimens (Figure 11.3), 37% (N = 317) were positive. Of these, the majority, 83% (N = 263) were examined within five hours, and 307 were examined within 12 hours of the rape. Only six of the positive specimens were collected more than 20 hours after the rape (Tucker *et al.*, 1990). These data clearly indicate that the vaginal site is the most likely site to obtain specimens positive for sperm. It also indicates that by far the majority of positive results will be collected within the first five hours after the assault, and that even then, it is rare that specimens positive for sperm will be obtained in any site other than the vaginal site. It is imperative that the SANE is aware that this does not, however, mean sexual contact did not occur (Tucker *et al.*, 1990).

Figure 11.4

Results from a study by Tucker et al. *(1990) using a prostatic acid phosphatase (PAP) test as an indication of semen.*

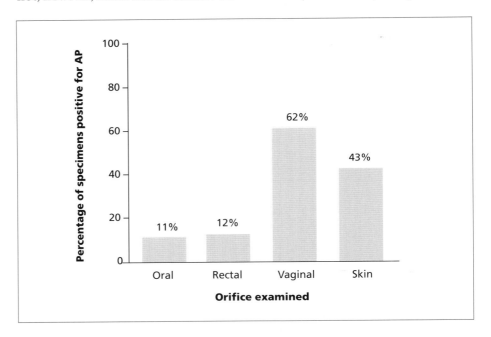

Because of the small percentage of positive sperm specimens, the literature indicates that it can be very helpful to also analyze the specimens collected for prostatic acid phosphatase (PAP). While it is still more likely that specimens will be negative than positive, the results are more likely to be positive for PAP than for sperm. Figure 11.4 indicates that of the oral specimens, 11% (N = 40) were positive for PAP; of the rectal specimens, 12% (N = 32) were positive for PAP; of the skin specimens, 43% (N = 72) were positive for PAP; and of the cases involving vaginal assault, 62% (N = 566), were positive for PAP (Tucker et al, 1990).

In another study of 212 women who had consenting sex within four days, comparing PAP to PSA, researchers obtained better results with PAP than PSA analysis (Figure 11.5). While both were positive in 59% of the cases, PAP was positive 84% of the time and PSA was positive 60% of the time. PAP was negative only 2% of the time when PSA was positive, and PSA was negative 25% of the time when PAP was positive (Roach and Vladutiu, 1993). Most programs collect vaginal sperm and acid phosphatase specimens using cotton tip swabs. A few programs use a vaginal normal saline aspirate, or vaginal washes for this purpose (Osborn and Neff, 1989).

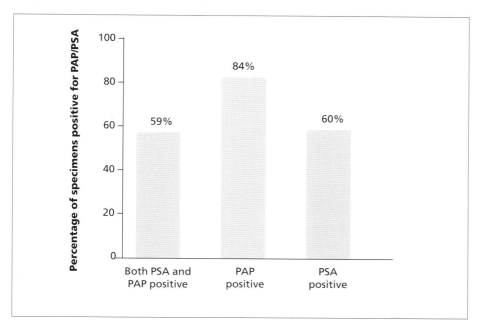

Figure 11.5

Comparison of prostatic acid phosphatase (PAP) and prostatic specific antigen (PSA) test results following consensual sexual intercourse (N = 212).

DFSA BIOLOGICAL SPECIMEN ANALYSIS: WHERE CAN IT BE COMPLETED?

It is essential that SANE-SART programs identify laboratories that can do a sensitive drug toxicology screen when a blood, urine, or hair specimen is obtained for DFSA testing. Many laboratories can identify benzodiazepines, but not flunitrazepam (Rohypnol®), for instance. Not all laboratories, not even all crime laboratories, can do a sufficiently specific analysis to detect these substances. Private laboratories will often charge more than $800 for a complete drug toxicology screen. Many state crime laboratories can analyze for GHB or flunitrazepam, but only do the specific test when it is requested by law enforcement. They do not routinely do a broad drug screen. Many agencies mistakenly equate DFSA with only GHB or flunitrazepam when these substances are just a small part of the DFSA problem today.

Unfortunately, there is often little specific information on what drug was likely given to the victim, so a specific test for only one or two drugs, GHB or flunitrazepam (Rohypnol®) is less helpful. While a broad drug screen is usually preferable, it is also controversial what drugs should be screened for, and the victims should always give informed consent prior to testing. For instance, should illegal drugs that are often used recreationally such as marijuana, cocaine, or amphetamines be included in testing? Should alcohol be routinely included in testing? Should there be different time guidelines when specific substances are suspected?

If a complete drug screen is going to be conducted, it is essential that the SANE explain to the victim what drugs will be included in the screen. It is also important that the SANE explain to her that if she has been using drugs recreationally or by prescription they may be detected in the screen. If so, it is important for the SANE to know this ahead of time in order to have the least negative impact on the victim's credibility. In most communities, if voluntary use of illegal drugs is not disclosed until after a positive drug screen, it will likely do irreparable damage to the victim's credibility. An otherwise good case may not be charged as a result. However, if the drug use is disclosed, it is more likely the prosecutor will decide they can either exclude the information from court, or deal with it in court. It is essential for the SANE to discuss the impact of illegal drug use with the victim. The client needs to know if they will be charged criminally if they admit to illegal drug use. In most communities the answer will be a definitive "NO." They also need to know how law enforcement and the prosecutor will view a positive screen for an illegal substance they took willingly. How will this potentially impact the investigation and charging of their case?

WHO SHOULD PAY FOR DRUG TESTING?

Hoffman La Roche paid for complete urine drug screens at ElSohly Laboratories from June 1996 through December 1999 in an attempt to determine the role their drug Rohypnol® played in DFSA. They abruptly terminated payment in January 2000. Testing for a single substance such as GHB or flunitrazepam can cost $80 each. A complete drug toxicity screen can cost more than $800. This is more than the total amount available to most SANE programs and medical facilities as reimbursement for the complete sexual assault evidentiary examination, including personnel costs, other laboratory testing, and medications. It is unreasonable to expect the SANE program or the medical facility to assume this cost without adequate reimbursement.

When a sexual assault report has been made and there is other evidence such as the clinical symptom pattern described above to suggest that this was a DFSA, it is clear that law enforcement or the prosecutor's office should pay for the drug screen if one is requested. Since this is costly, it will be important to have specific guidelines for testing and reimbursement.

Who should pay for testing in the cases that are not clear? What if the clinical picture and history provided by the victim clearly do not fit the expected DFSA scenario, but the victim or her parents are "certain" that she was drugged and raped and they are insisting that a complete urine screen be completed? Should a screen be done and, if so, who is responsible for paying for it? If the victim makes a report and wants the test, should one be conducted for her satisfaction? What if she does not want to decide about reporting until the test results return? Can her insurance be billed? If she does not have insurance and no report is made, who should be expected to pay? Should government funding be available to pay for these tests? Even if insurance or government funding is available for drug testing, unnecessary testing without guidelines could only further burden limited resources.

The responsible SANE-SART clearly needs to have protocols in place to address when testing should be completed and who will be expected to pay, so that the victim will be able to make an informed decision about her options.

WHAT ABOUT INFORMED CONSENT FOR DRUG TESTING?

What informed consent options should be considered? Should the victim have the right to refuse testing for a specific drug or group of drugs, and if she refuses, how will this information be used? Who will have access to it? How can it affect her legal case? Should her decision impact payment? Since national guidelines are not currently available, local SANE-SART programs must develop policies to guide their decisions and practices to insure consistency.

While a urine, blood, or hair specimen obtained from the victim after a suspected DFSA is clearly the best evidence to lead to an arrest and conviction, with today's techniques these positive specimens are often not obtained. However, there is still valuable evidence that the SANE can obtain to facilitate the law enforcement investigation and help answer the victim's question, "Was I drugged and raped?"

REFERENCES

American College of Emergency Physicians (1999) *Psych. Clin. N. Am.*, 18, pp. 139–153.

Antognoli-Toland, P. (1985) *J. Em. Nursing*, 11 (3), 132–136.

Bell, K. (1995) "Tulsa Sexual Assault Nurse Examiners Program", *Oklahoma Nurse*, p. 16.

Bowyer, L. and Dalton, M. (1997) *Brit. J. Ob. Gyn.*, 104, pp. 617–620.

Cartwright, P.S., Moore, R.A., Anderson, J.R. and Douglad, H. (1986) *J. Reprod. Med.,* 31 (11), pp. 1043–1044.

Cooper, G.A., Allen D.L., Scott, K., Oliver, J.S., Ditton, J. and Smith, I.D. (1999) *J. Forensic Sci.*, 45, pp. 400–406.

Davies, A. (1978) *Med. Sci. Law,* 18 (3), pp. 174–178.

DiNitto, D., Martin, P.Y., Norton, D.B. and Maxwell, S.M. (1986) *Am. J. Nursing*, 86 (5), pp. 538–540.

Enos, W.F. and Beyer, J.C. (1980) *J. Forensic Sci.*, 25, pp. 353–356.

Frank, C. (1996) *Redbook*, 12, pp. 104–120.

Geist, R.F. (1988) "Sexually Related Trauma", *Em. Med. Clin. N. Am.*, p. 299.

Green, W. (1988) *Rape: The Evidential Examination and Management of the Adult Female Victim*, pp. 97–127. MA University of California-Davis, School of Medicine: Lexington Books.

Groth, A. Nicholas and Burgess, A.W. (1977) *New Eng. J. Med.*, pp. 764–766.

Holloway, M. and Swan, A. (1993) *Nursing Standard*, 7 (45), pp. 31–35.

Kettleson, D. (1995) Unit News/District News District East Hawaii. June, 1.

Kiffe, B. (1996) Thesis, Augsburg College MSW, Minneapolis, MN.

Ledray, L.E. (1992a) *J. Em. Nursing*, 18 (3), pp. 217–220

Ledray, L.E. (1992b) *J. Em. Nursing*, 18 (3), pp. 223–232.

Ledray, L.E. (1993a) *Clin. Iss. Perinat. Wom. Health Nursing*, 4 (2), pp. 180–190.

Ledray, L.E. (1993b) "Sexual Assault Nurse Clinician: An Emerging Area of Nursing Expertise". In *Perinatal and Women's Health Nursing*, L.C. Andrist (ed.), J.B. Lippincott, Co.: Philadelphia, pp. 1–18.

Ledray, L.E. (1996a) *J. Em. Nursing*, 22 (5), pp. 460–464.

Ledray, L.E. (1996b) *J. Em. Nursing*, 22 (1), p. 80.

Ledray, L.E. (1999a) *J. Em. Nursing*, 25 (1), pp. 63–64.

Ledray, L.E. (1999b) *SANE Development and Operation Guide.* US Dept. of Justice, Office of Victims of Crime.

Ledray, L.E. and Chaignot, M.J. (1980) "Services of Sexual Assault Victims in Hennepin County", *Eval. Change,* Special Issue. Garland Publisher, Inc. pp. 181–193.

Lenehan, G.P. (1991) *J. Em. Nursing*, 17 (1), pp. 1–2.

Lynch, V.A. (1993) *J. Psychosoc. Nursing*, 132 (3), pp. 7–14.

Lynch, V.A. (1996) Presented at the Fourth Annual Scientific Assembly of Forensic Nurses, Kansas City.

Marchbanks, P., Lui, K.J. and Mercy, J. (1990) *Am. J. Epidemiology*, 132 (3), pp. 540–549.

Marullo, G. (1996) Presented at the Fourth Annual Scientific Assembly of Forensic Nurses. Kansas City.

McCauley, J., Gorman, R.L. and Guzinski, G. (1986) *Pediatrics,* 78 (6), pp. 1039–1043.

Negrusz, A., Moore, C., Stockham, T., Poiser, K., Kern, J., Palaparthy, R., Pharm, B., Le, N.L., Janicak, P. and Levy, N. (2000) *J. Forensic Sci.*, pp. 1013–1022.

Norvell, M.K. (1984) *J. Reprod. Med.*, 29 (4), pp. 269–271.

O'Brien, C. (1996) *J. Em. Nursing*, 23 (5), pp. 532–533.

O'Brien, C. (1997) *J. Em. Nursing*, 23 (5), pp. 460–462.

Osborn, M. and Neff, J. (1989) *J. Em. Nursing*, 15 (3), pp. 284–290.

Pasqualone, G.A. (1996) *J. Psychosoc. Nursing*, 34 (10), pp. 47–51.

Peele, K. and Matranga, M. (1997) *Nurse Practitioner*, 22 (4), pp. 250–252.

Randall, B. (1986) *J. Forensic Sci.*, 32 (3), pp. 678–683.

Roach, B.A. and Vladutiu, A.O. (1993) *Clinica Chimica Acta*, 216, pp. 199–201.

Sandrick, K.J. (1996) *Hosp. Health Networks*, pp. 64–66.

Sheridan, D.J. (1993) *J. Pychosoc. Nursing*, 31 (11), pp. 31–37.

Silverman, E.M. and Silverman, A.G. (1978) *JAMA*, 240 (17), pp. 1875–1877.

Slaughter, L. and Brown, C. (1992) *Am. J. Obstet. Gynecol.*, 166, p. 1.

Slaughter, L. and Brown, C. (1997) *Am. J. Obstet. Gynecol.*, 176, p. 3.

Soderstrom, R.M. (1994) *J. Reprod. Med.*, 39, p. 1.

Soules, M.R., Pollard, A.A. and Brown, K. *et al.* (1978) *Am. J. Obstet. Gynecol.*, 130, pp. 142–147.

Speck, P. and Aiken, M. (1995) *Tennessee Nurse*, pp. 15–18.

Thomas, M. and Zachritz, H. (1993) *J. Oklahoma St. Med. Assoc.*, 86, pp. 284–286.

Tintinalli, J. and Hoelzer, M. (1985) *Ann. Emerg. Med.*, 14 (5), pp. 447–453.

Tobias, G. (1990) *Practitioner*, 234, pp. 874–877.

Tucker, S., Ledray, L.E. and Werner, J.S. (1990) *Wisc. Med. J.*, July, pp. 407–411.

Yorker, B. (1996) *Georgia Nursing*, 5.

CHAPTER 12

INVESTIGATING DFSA CASES

Joanne Archambault
Trinka Porrata
Peter Sturman

CLUB DRUGS, THE RAVE CULTURE, AND DFSA

As the saying goes, the times are changing. Each generation has its own special music, dance trends, sports heroes, and recreational drugs. Understanding these differences is important in the investigation of DFSA cases. For now, the "rave" culture is the newest and, thus, the least understood trend. In the 1960s and 1970s, it was the "Free Love" era in which Woodstock-type concerts were the trademark. LSD ("Acid"), MDMA ("Ecstasy," the "Love Drug," the "Hug Drug"), phencyclidine ("PCP"), marijuana, mushrooms ("Shrooms") and other psychedelic drugs were the rage. Sex at these events was often open and notorious. Today, it's the rave and club drug cultures you may have to investigate.

Though society at large may have little awareness and understanding of its existence, the rave phenomenon is becoming dramatically widespread. Rave parties have often been announced in cyberspace, beyond the vision of most parents, teachers, and law enforcement. Today, raves (now also being called "dance parties" to escape the stigma of "raves") are common at neighborhood clubs and bars. A juror from the "Free Love" era may not understand the rave climate without some help.

People may wonder why this generation is attracted to such parties. It is not about sex: it's about closeness and instant, drug-induced friendship and openness. It is not about alcohol either: this body-conscious group views alcohol with disdain and prefers "non-calorie" drugs such as MDMA, ketamine, GHB, and others. MDMA, commonly referred to as "Ecstasy," is the single most widespread drug of abuse at raves. Use of any disinhibiting or impairing drug, especially when used with other drugs, may render the victim either more susceptible to becoming involved in sex, or render her powerless to avoid it. These drugs are also abused outside of the rave scene, such as in the club crowd where alcohol use is often an added element. These drugs are also on campuses, both college and high school. The gay community also presents an additional group of sexual assault cases (including numerous drug-facilitated assaults) with new challenges to investigation and prosecution. It is important to remember that sexual predators exist in all elements of society.

Finally, in a society that still looks with suspicion at a rape victim who drank even just one alcoholic beverage, we need to emphasize the concept that voluntary ingestion of alcohol, marijuana, or any other drug does not constitute an open invitation to have sex.

RAVES

Raves are traditionally underground parties held in remote places that typically last all night. They are out of reach of society's rules and regulations. The phenomenon started in England in the 1980s and worked its way to North America. In the United States and Canada, not all raves are underground. They may be held at fairgrounds, skating rinks, and in many popular nightclubs. Electronically generated "Techno music" (also called Trance or Jungle or House, etc.) is popular. The beat is set between 100 and 300 beats per minute and puts listeners into a trance-like state. Attendees blend with the beat of the music and become one with it. The drugs add to their trance, keeping them up dancing all night, fixated on their intensified sensations.

POPULAR CLUB DRUGS

MDMA (3,4-METHYLENEDIOXYMETHAMPHETAMINE)

MDMA is an hallucinogenic stimulant. It has a number of popular street names as listed in Table 12.1. Presently it is the single most widely abused drug in the rave and club drug scenes in the United States. It is also often seen on college and high school campuses. There are also designer variations of MDMA (i.e. MDA, MDMB, etc.) but MDMA is the desired product. MDMA comes primarily from European countries such as Denmark and Germany, but is sometimes manufactured in the United States. When demand exceeds supply, products sold as MDMA may really be stimulants (e.g. methamphetamine ephedrine, caffeine) alone or with hallucinogens (e.g. ketamine, LSD, dextromethorphan), or they may be some related drugs (i.e. PMA (paramethoxyamphetamine) – an old drug that resurfaced in Illinois and Florida in 2000, quickly killing 12 people because it is more powerful than MDMA). While MDMA may be found as a powder, it is most commonly abused as little pills with a wide variety of colors, shapes, and logos. They are designed to look "innocent" and attract no more attention than a handful of candies or children's vitamins.

MDMA may cause muscle spasms and teeth-grinding. Abusers often suck on baby pacifiers or lollipops in an effort to reduce the grinding. "Ravers" may dress in infantile or other exotic dress to distract from the pacifier. MDMA is not a potent stimulant but enables users to dance for hours. Additionally, it is not a powerful hallucinogen, yet users do have altered or enhanced perception. The most common symptoms are dilated pupils, raised pulse, blood pressure, and body temperature. Dangers include the risk of hyperthermia, intense depression, long-term brain damage, dental and jaw damage, and even death. It is primarily used and known for its "mind expansion" qualities. It reportedly opens the mind and intensifies perceptions and assures instant friendship with those around the user. It makes the user feel they belong in any group. Colors and lights are intensified (thus the use of light wands and flashing lights), smell is more pronounced (thus the use of a vapor rub on face masks to get the tingling feeling from eucalyptus), and sense of feel is heightened (thus the baggy clothing made of soft fabrics, the fuzzy necklaces and other items). MDMA users tend to be passive and obsessed with "sensations." This condition makes a young female highly susceptible to being touched and caressed by a virtual stranger, leaving her at the mercy of a sexual predator. A rave documentary in early 2000 showed a 15-year-old female talking openly about how she had taken Ecstasy. She claimed that every touch felt good. During this conversation, a young man was intensely caressing her all over. She referred to him as her "boyfriend" yet she had just met him two hours before. A more detailed description of MDMA and related hallucinogens can be found in Chapter 7.

Common name	Chemical name	Street name
MDMA	3,4-methylenedioxy-methamphetamine	Ecstasy, X, XTC, E, Hug Drug
GHB	Gamma hydroxybutyrate	G, Scoop, Easy Lay, Liquid X, Grevious Bodily Harm, Liquid E, Salty Water
LSD	Lysergic acid diethylamide	Acid, Pyramids, Microdots, Blotter Paper, Stamps, Sunshine, Window Panes
Ketamine	Ketamine	K, Special K, Vitamin K
Psilocybin	Psilocybin	Shrooms, Magic Mushrooms
Nitrous oxide	Nitrous oxide	Laughing gas, Whippets

Table 12.1
Club drugs.

GHB (GAMMA HYDROXYBUTYRATE)

GHB is the drug creating the most immediate concern and risk of danger in the area of DFSA. While a more detailed description of GHB (and related analog products) can be found in Chapter 6, a brief overview is warranted here.

The effects are somewhat comparable to an alcohol high, but with some added elements, such as out-of-body experiences. GHB puts its users at high risk, especially when other drugs are ingested. Respiration can be severely depressed, sometimes as low as six breaths per minute. When GHB puts an individual into a comatose state, the person is without a protective gag reflex and can thus aspirate on their vomit or simply stop breathing. Unfortunately, party hosts and guests often fail to get medical assistance for these individuals, believing that the user can just sleep the GHB off. There is no antidote for a GHB overdose. Treatment typically entails advanced life support to keep the patient breathing until the effects of GHB pass. Sexual predators at raves, bars, or parties may slip this drug into an unsuspecting victim's drink. Alternatively, they may talk the victim into ingesting it for a wild high. Once the drug takes effect, it affords the opportunity for the predator to sexually assault the victim.

GHB has no distinctive odor but may have a salty taste. Poor quality GHB may have an excessively high pH level which will cause a "burning" sensation when ingested. Taking GHB with other drugs can prevent the user from "feeling" the effects of the drugs. This puts the user at risk of overdosing by taking more and more drugs to reach or maintain a desired sensation.

GHB is particularly troublesome in sexual assault cases because it distinctively lowers inhibitions. This is why many exotic dancers voluntarily take GHB. Once ingested, memory may be fragmented or completely absent. First responders and investigating officers of a DFSA need to understand this aspect of GHB and consider it another challenge to work through. Sexual assault reports should be documented even when witnesses describe sexual behavior on the part of the victim or when her memory is extremely blank or fragmented.

While under the influence of GHB, a sexual assault victim may not be in control of her body and reactions. A classic, tragic case of GHB's impact occurred in Utah. The incident involved a young woman who drank a tonic containing GHB with her boyfriend. A male friend of the boyfriend arrived and asked to try the drink. The boyfriend lapsed into a semi-comatose stage, seeing what was going on around him but being unable to react. Meanwhile, his friend began inappropriately touching the woman. She resisted and made it to her boyfriend's side for help but the GHB rendered him physically helpless to assist. The suspect dragged the victim into another room where he sexually assaulted her. The victim's boyfriend was very distraught over his inability to rescue her from the attack and committed suicide before the trial began. His statements to police, backing up her claim of resistance to the suspect's advances, were not provided to the jury. During the trial, the suspect testified that it was the greatest sex of his life and claimed she was responsive and involved. There was no expert testimony on the effects of GHB and the jury acquitted the man.

LSD (LYSERGIC ACID DIETHYLAMIDE)

LSD is extremely common at rave parties. It often is seen in liquid or gel form, perhaps even more so than in the traditional blotter paper format. Little bottles of breath mints are a common transportation method and may not be recognized by law enforcement, parents, and teachers.

KETAMINE

Ketamine (aka Special K) is a veterinarian tranquilizer, but also has legitimate use in human medicine. Ketamine is legitimately manufactured but smuggled from foreign countries or stolen from local veterinary clinics or medical supply sources. It normally is supplied as a liquid injectable; cigarettes may be dipped in it and then smoked analogous to PCP. More commonly, ketamine is dried into a powder and then snorted. A bad trip puts one into the " K Hole." Users have described this experience as "seeing God in the disco ball" or "your body disappears and you are just a head rolling along." Ketamine can cause flashbacks and may depress respiration to dangerously low levels. Chapter 7 provides more detail on ketamine and other hallucinogens.

PSILOCYBIN

Psilocybin is an active hallucinogenic found in some mushrooms. It is common at raves, though not necessarily in large quantities. The dried, hallucinogenic mushrooms may be chewed or appear as brown powder in gelatin capsules.

NITROUS OXIDE

Nitrous oxide is widely abused in the rave and youth cultures and seems to be growing in popularity. It gives an intense rush and is very short-lived. It is not controlled federally or in any state, though five states have established some minor criminal offenses for abuse or sales of it for human consumption. It causes a depletion of oxygen to the brain, which can cause death or serious brain damage in an uncontrolled environment. NO_2 may be obtained from tanks diverted from dental offices, medical supply houses, high-performance vehicle shops (it is "adrenaline" for high-performance vehicles), store-purchased cans of whipped cream or from the "whippet" canisters sold to power home-made whipped cream makers. The later are common in major coffee houses where hundreds of canisters may be in a store's stockroom. The whippets can also be purchased by the hundreds over the Internet. Devices called "crackers" are used to crack the whippets and fill balloons with the gas.

These crackers may be plastic, brass, or aluminum and sold in sex shops, head shops or via the Internet. They serve no other purpose than to open the canisters of NO_2.

Of course, other drugs may also be found at rave parties. These drugs include marijuana, methamphetamine, and other stimulants, asthma inhalers, other depressants, including benzodiazepines (which includes the other infamous "rape drug," flunitrazepam, also known as "roofies" or the trade name Rohypnol®), peyote, mescaline, and various other hallucinogenic drugs. It is important to stress that use of these drugs in this crowd is akin to general use of alcohol in other crowds.

INVESTIGATING THE DFSA

Unfortunately DFSAs are not new. An old saying went "Candy is dandy, but liquor is quicker!" Club drugs bring an entirely new element to this saying. Most sexual assaults occur by someone the victim thought they knew and could trust. The Bureau of Justice Statistics (BJS) 1998 National Crime Victimization Survey (NCVS) revealed that 74% of rape/sexual assault victims knew their assailant. Between 1994 and 1996, 1,228 sexual assaults reported to the San Diego Police Department Sex Crimes Unit were analyzed. In 13% of all the cases, the victim had met the suspect for the first time within 24 hours of the assault. These cases are referred to as "brief encounter" assaults. Among the non-stranger sexual assaults, 20% of the cases involving adolescents were brief encounters while 17% of the adult non-stranger cases involved this type of assailant (Lindsay, 1998). 53% of the adolescent victims in the brief encounter group self-reported using drugs or alcohol prior to the sexual assault. In contrast, 34% of the adult victims in the brief encounter category self-reported using drugs and alcohol prior to the assault. The investigating officer must understand that the dynamics of these circumstances will direct the entire course of the investigation.

Most suspects in DFSA cases will claim a "consent" defense rather than deny a sexual encounter. In a consent defense, it is not a question of whether the defendant had sex with the victim, but the circumstances of the act (i.e. whether the victim consented or if she was unable to consent due to her level of intoxication or lack of consciousness). The skills and ability of the investigator will be thoroughly challenged while working DFSAs. Corroboration of the sexual assault is critical and every strategy should be considered and explored with an open mind.

COMMUNITY PROTOCOLS

When a person suspects they have been the victim of DFSA, they must always be treated professionally and appropriately. The victim should not be ignored even if the scenario sounds implausible to the officer. Allow the investigation to determine whether or not a crime took place. Do not allow inaction due to first impressions to risk the loss of a case. If the victim was given or voluntarily took a mind-altering drug, she may be in a state of confusion. Dependent on the drug dose and the time elapsed since its ingestion, the victim may have the ability to recollect what has happened to her, or she may have little to no recollection at all. Often, a victim may suspect she was sexually assaulted because she feels sore, smells like sex, or has a vaginal discharge. It should be remembered that if the drug is still in the victim's system when the report is made to the police, it might affect her behavior and the way she presents.

Sexual assault victims often reflect upon what has happened, questioning whether they were at fault or if they may have given the "impression" of consent. It is critical that these victims are treated as other rape victims, irrespective of how confused their recollection may be. The allegation must be taken seriously and the victim must feel that she is believed.

When a victim calls the police to report the assault, the communications personnel must be properly trained to ask a number of questions. They need to determine if the victim has showered or bathed, if she has urinated (the number of times) and if she has laundered the clothes she wore prior to or after the assault. It is important to ask these questions in such a manner that the victim will not feel "ashamed" and try to hide the fact that she might have done some of these things. The victim's initial report is one of the most important times during the investigation, and her interaction with law enforcement at this point may be crucial in her decision to proceed with the investigation and subsequent criminal charges.

Victims reporting soon after the attack must be encouraged not to urinate. However, since it may be many hours before the police can respond to a delayed sexual assault report, it is ridiculous to tell someone who has to go to the bathroom, not to urinate. Some drugs can leave the body in as little as 12 hours or less as they pass from the blood into the urine and are thus removed from the body when one urinates. For this reason, the best chance of detecting a drug will be in the first or second urination after the offense. In cases where the victim needs to relieve herself, she should be encouraged to collect the sample in a clean container with a lid. The sample should then be refrigerated until it can be given to the proper law enforcement authorities or a forensic examiner. Although this may create a question regarding possible contamination and proper chain of custody, the sample may be the only chance of detecting the presence of some of the drugs used to commit DFSA. A urine sample should be obtained from the victim as soon as possible, but the presence of most DFSA drugs will no longer be detectable 96 hours after the assault. At the time a urine sample is taken at the hospital, the forensic examiner should note the approximate number of times the victim urinated since ingesting the drug and the assault. Whether it is a forensic examiner, counselor, or patrol officer, the person taking the initial report must ensure all information is passed on to the investigating officer. It is important that detailed and accurate information is obtained and acted upon immediately. Building a "time line" of events is particularly critical in a DFSA case. This allows the drug to "do the talking," providing important clues as to which drug or family of drugs might have been used.

SEXUAL ASSAULT EVIDENCE KITS

Forensic evidence kits must include the appropriate means of collecting biological samples. In a DFSA, urine is needed to ensure longer detection times of drugs. Therefore, evidence kits must include containers for urine collection or the collection site should have a supply on hand. Forensic examiners and officers should document the amount of urine collected. Law enforcement agencies must also establish proper storage guidelines for blood and urine samples. The San Diego County Sexual Assault Response Team Systems Review Medical Sub-committee developed a form to ensure the forensic examiner asks the appropriate questions and documents all the necessary information (Appendix A). The Examiner completes the form at the time of the interview based on the patient's history and/or signs/symptoms observed by the examiner. The sample collection procedures may need to be standardized, as is done in the United Kingdom (Sturman, 2000).

INTERVIEWING DFSA VICTIMS

First responding officers and detectives must interview a victim of DFSA without judging her or leading her to believe that she will be arrested for drug use or possession. The officer also needs to determine the victim's prior experience with prescription and recreational drugs, including alcohol. In San Diego, California, nearly 60% of all felony sexual assaults involve victims between the ages of 14 and 25 (San Diego Police Department Sexual Assault statistics). Their life experience and frame of reference may be very different from that of the investigating officer. The officer should not make assumptions. For example, in a high-profile case in San Diego, four suspects sexually assaulted an 18-year-old female. The victim was asked if she had been drinking and she said that she had. It was assumed that the victim had become drunk. Later, upon further questioning by a detective, it was discovered that the victim had taken a couple of sips of wine. More important, she had also taken two hits from a "blunt" (a cigar laced with an unidentified drug). The victim was actually very inexperienced with alcohol and drugs. At the conclusion of the investigation, the detective felt that a drug was used to facilitate the sexual assault. A search warrant was executed at one of the suspect's homes, which revealed literature taken from the Internet on DFSA and drugs. The information about the victim's experiences with drugs and alcohol would have been extremely helpful if it had been obtained earlier in the investigation. Conversely, investigators, forensic examiners and rape crisis advocates must be careful not to lead victims to believe that a DFSA will not be taken seriously unless the drug was given to them surreptitiously. As professionals working in the field of sexual assault, we need to be responsible for the image we continue to help perpetuate about DFSA. This includes contributing to this stereotype through media campaigns, news reports, training manuals, and publications that focus solely on surreptitious DFSA. Although many states can add or enhance charges for this type of offense, in most states it is no longer necessary for the suspect to give the intoxicating substance to the victim to meet the elements of DFSA. Most states only require that the suspect had knowledge that the victim was incapacitated and could not give informed consent. A DFSA should be investigated regardless of whether the victim voluntarily engaged in drug and alcohol abuse, and a victim's history of drug or alcohol abuse should not be held against her. Often, it may be evidence to support the DFSA. However, if a sexual assault victim lies about her own substance abuse, these lies will be used to discredit her and the case will likely fail to move through the criminal justice system. "A Study of the Effect of Evidence Factors and Victim Characteristics on Prosecutors' Charging Decisions in Sexual Assault Cases" conducted by Spears and Spohn (1997) at the University of Nebraska at Omaha validated that the prosecution is affected by the victim's moral character and behavior at the time of the incident regardless of the strength of the evidence in the case. Therefore, sex crimes detectives must complete a thorough, unbiased investigation to shift the burden from the victim to the evidence. There are a number of questions that need to be asked of the victim. Table 12.2 lists such questions.

Establishing force is not necessary in DFSA. In fact, a forcible sexual assault may contradict DFSA since most DFSAs are based on the premise that the victim was rendered too intoxicated to consent or resist. In these cases, the victim's intoxication level is a critical element of the DFSA. Documenting that witnesses observed the victim as "drunk" or "loaded" is not enough. The investigator needs to determine the victim's condition as she left the bar or the party (i.e. whether she was carried, assisted, passed out or vomited). Investigators also need to interview the victim's friends to help establish the victim's normal

How much alcohol was consumed?

- What type(s) of alcohol or drink(s)?
- Size of glasses or bottles?
- How long was she drinking?

What prescription or over-the-counter medications was the victim taking?

- What dose?
- When was the last pill taken?

What recreational drugs did the victim voluntarily ingest?

- How much was ingested?
- When was it ingested?
- How was it taken (orally, smoked, injected)?

How experienced is the victim with alcohol and drugs?

- Get detailed descriptions of symptoms the victim experienced, including information about vomiting, hang-over, how long she was "out," what she remembers of the assault, and when she feels the opportunity to drug her occurred.
- Have the victim describe her level of experience with alcohol and drugs.
- Have the victim describe how this experience was different from other times when she voluntarily ingested alcohol and/or drugs.

behavior compared to the behavior observed leading up to the assault. An effective technique is to ask witnesses to estimate both the victim's and suspect's level of intoxication based on a scale of one to ten (one being completely sober and ten being unconscious). Often, the suspect and witness will testify that the suspect was also under the influence. In many cases, a thorough investigation will establish that while the suspect had one or two drinks and may have engaged in some other substance abuse, he was cognizant and functioning capably when last seen by witnesses. DFSA victims will have little or no memory. The investigating officer must be very careful not to lead the victim or fill in blank spaces with assumptions and conclusions. An interviewer may feel inclined to jump ahead and ask questions such as "and then did you feel . . ." and "Did this happen?", anxious to identify the DFSA drug they recently learned about. Because of the trauma caused by the unknown element of a DFSA, victims will often work very hard to fill in the blank spots in their memory. They may recall some information from the evening, but they may also add information relayed to them by well-meaning friends, family, police, and medical personnel. For example, a woman was sexually assaulted and found comatose in a run-down hotel. The victim was transported to a trauma hospital where she underwent surgery to repair the vaginal trauma she suffered as a result of the sexual assault. Although there were no eyewitnesses to the assault, the evidence suggested to patrol officers and medical personnel that the suspect used his fist to penetrate the victim's vagina. The victim overheard conversations between the professionals and was later told by a friend that according to police, she had been raped with the suspect's fist. Initially, the victim told the first responding officer that she had no memory of the assault due to her state of unconsciousness. Witnesses supported this and the fact that the victim was comatose when police and paramedics arrived. Because of the victim's own need to understand what happened or because of law enforcement's need to establish the corpus of the crime, in a follow-up interview, the victim "remembered" that the suspect put his fist inside her vagina. Further questioning revealed the victim was filling in blank spaces in her memory with what she had heard. Let the drug do the talking through the victim's own words and then, if possible, identify which drug or drug class fits the pattern described.

A sexual assault victim should be fully informed if the forensic examination includes toxicology testing. A complete toxicological screen is necessary in the investigation of a DFSA. A victim's failure to agree to any aspect of a toxicology screen will most likely result in the termination of the investigation. The specialized panels of the tests required to detect these drugs can be expensive, and most law enforcement agencies will not pursue these avenues if common substances have not already been excluded.

TESTING THE SAMPLES

Law enforcement agencies must identify laboratories capable of conducting appropriate sensitive tests for drugs like GHB, ketamine, flunitrazepam and other benzodiazepines. If their local laboratory doesn't have the capability of reaching the desired level of service, it may be necessary to contract with other laboratories that are capable. The contracts must include provisions for laboratory personnel to make themselves available to testify in court. Experts must be knowledgeable about current DFSA literature and be prepared to explain the reasons for a negative toxicology result and current challenges with the toxicological testing of DFSA cases. This can be difficult since many labs may have difficulty admitting or acknowledging they cannot test to the levels required.

Many forensic toxicology laboratories are capable of testing blood alcohol levels and some general drug screens. Specialized screens are more complicated, especially in those cases where the victim has no idea what she may have ingested. In these cases, the toxicologist will need to test for specific drugs or groups of drugs. It follows that they will need some guidance as to what to test for. The San Diego Police Department has developed a form to help guide the investigating officer and the toxicologist communicate better (Appendix B).

It is important to remember that "alcohol" is ethanol and ethanol is a drug that is often ingested with other drugs. When mixed with most DFSA drugs, ethanol will enhance the effects of DFSA drugs. Of course, alcohol can also be used alone. In fact, alcohol is the most common substance used to facilitate sexual assault. Therefore a high blood alcohol concentration may support the allegation, not discredit it. If a person is not capable of consenting due to alcohol intoxication, they are as much a victim of a DFSA as someone who might have been given a tablet surreptitiously. It should also be noted that ingestion of a DFSA-type drug may result in disinhibition that causes the victim to ingest additional alcohol (without recall of doing so) that puts her blood alcohol level higher than she felt was possible. Keep in mind she may not be lying about what she drank, but was already under the grip of the drug and truly would not have ingested that much and does not remember doing so. In cases where there are limited quantities of urine, investigating officers should consult with a toxicologist capable of performing specialized drug screens before commencing with any toxicological analysis.

INTERPRETING TOXICOLOGY RESULTS

It is important to realize that a positive toxicological result is not likely in many DFSA cases. This should change as our testing capabilities are upgraded and training efforts of victims and first responders take effect. In many American states, it is not necessary to establish with certainty the exact drug used, but only to establish that the victim was drugged, impaired and unable to give consent. With or without positive results, your best bet is to immediately focus on developing a detailed time line. Your expert witness will need this in order to evaluate and present the case via symptomology. Details that normally appear unimportant may now play a crucial role in determining the sequence of events, the victim's state of mind, and her physical condition. Each detail may help back up her memory or fill in the gaps. It may establish her level and time of impairment or may substantiate any efforts to resist. For example, in one DFSA case in Los Angeles, CA, a victim awoke suddenly while being sodomized in a shower. She immediately called the police. She last remembered "throwing a fit" in a parking lot to avoid leaving with the suspect. She was unable to communicate her wishes to anyone around her or to escape due to her physical state. A parking lot attendant recalled the altercation. He didn't understand that the victim was attempting to get away from the suspect and, thus, did not intervene. His recall of this detail supported her statements and state of mind. The toxicology report on her blood (taken at least seven hours after ingesting the drink) was negative, as expected; urine was not collected. The prosecutor of the case felt it was strong without the DFSA issues, but the victim testified to being drugged and raped. The defense attorney introduced the negative toxicology report to discredit the victim. The judge refused to allow the prosecutor to reopen his case in chief and present the proper perspective on what the negative toxicological results meant. The judge ruled that expert witness testimony would be prejudicial. The defense claimed it was consensual sex and she became "hysterical" after it had progressed to anal intercourse. The trial resulted in a hung jury. When faced with a refiling and a promise that the DFSA issue would be prominent, the suspect pleaded guilty. Had a retrial been necessary, supporting evidence such as the parking lot episode would have been significant.

In assessing a toxicology report, it should be understood that our testing capabilities are inconsistent throughout the world, particularly as we react to new drug issues. For example, benzodiazepine immunoassay "screening" tests are probably the weakest screens and may not adequately detect these drugs at levels that will reveal if the victim was drugged by a benzodiazepine. Until this improves, investigators cannot readily rely on drug screens to rule out fluni-trazepam or to determine that this is not a DFSA without having some intimate knowledge of the laboratory's capabilities. A confirmation test is needed for benzodiazepines. Testing for GHB is also a problem. There are no rapid screens for GHB, thus hospitals are generally not capable of stating that GHB was or was not present. Many toxicology labs do not yet test samples for GHB. The lack of field test kits for GHB products has made identification of this usually liquid drug particularly difficult. GHB and its analogs may be concealed in literally any container capable of holding a liquid. The GHB analog products, commonly sold in supplement stores and over the Internet, are disguised as tonics, sleep aids, weight belt cleaners, etc., and are easily overlooked. The supplement bottles may or may not list the actual analog ingredients (under a variety of chemical name variations), or lie and claim other ingredients. The liquid may be thick or thin and may be dyed any color. Now that GHB is a federally con-trolled substance, companies making drug test kits are anxious to get in on this new market. Hopefully, this will ensure GHB field test kits are available in the near future.

Additionally, some private toxicology laboratories have been reluctant to produce their specifications and publish their cut-off levels. Results can be meaningless to prosecutors without knowledge of this information. This is espe-cially true with GHB because of the issue of low levels of endogenous GHB in urine. To aid in the investigation of DFSA, the San Diego Police Department Sex Crimes Unit and their laboratory have designed a laboratory request form to help detectives and toxicologists identify the type of substance that might have been used to facilitate a sexual assault (Appendix B). Teamwork and communication between the detective, prosecutor, toxicologist, and other experts are the keys. The goal should be to proceed as far as possible with the investigation and prosecution (regardless of the toxicological findings) using the victim's statements, eyewitness accounts, and a thorough investigation. An expert witness may then be needed to provide a framework for understanding the victim's symptomology and behavior. While prosecutors are accustomed to using street narcotics officers as "drug experts," this now can be a complicated arena. Unfortunately, many law enforcement agencies do not yet have many experts in-house to address DFSA. Agencies are struggling to develop expertise to explain drug packaging, the environment in which these drugs are used, the groups using them, trafficking issues, and recognition of those under the influence. Time and proper training can help fill that void. At a preliminary hearing, a detective probably will not be able to adequately address toxicology and pharmacology issues concerning these drugs. Also, many crime lab toxicologists or chemists are not adequately trained to address these issues. Do not rely on Internet searches for information on these drugs, and use caution in selecting an expert, especially regarding GHB or any other uncommon drug.

INVESTIGATIVE STRATEGIES

The holes in a DFSA investigation need to be filled as much as possible. Many DFSA cases involve multiple crime scenes (i.e. the location of the seduction, the location of the actual sexual assault, the location of the victim's clothing worn at the time of the assault or put on after the assault, etc.). Serving a search warrant for a crime scene should come to mind immediately, but first the "When," "Where" and "What" must be addressed. Appendix C contains a sample search warrant for DFSA investigations.

WHEN

In one high-profile case, detectives felt it was critical to hit the location of the assault with a search warrant as soon as possible. Symptomology from the victim and witnesses was indicative of GHB, and a pretext phone call gave solid hints as to what drugs were used. Probable cause was well in order. The upcoming Friday seemed perfect. It was the suspect's birthday, and he would likely be "stocked up" on his drugs of choice. Based on witness statements, the timing would also allow for the search to occur before he would be in the club again. However, investigative supervisors wanted to take a conservative approach and wait until the toxicology results came back. The toxicology reports were "negative" for GHB although the samples were collected "late", but "positive" for a stimulant (as predicted from the pretext call). The search warrant was eventually served but the expected drugs were not recovered. Meanwhile, the suspect had heard in the club that the victim had reported the assault to the police and he stated that he expected the police to show up. Timing is of the essence! On the other hand, one should not rush into a search warrant without adequate training for the identification of all drugs used in these crimes. For example, if GHB is suspected, the search warrant must be written to adequately cover the locations and containers in which it might be found, and the officers conducting the search need to be adequately trained to recognize these containers. Without adequate training, follow-up search warrants may be necessary and/or evidence may be lost.

WHERE

The appropriate places to search may include the scene where the sexual assault took place, the site where the victim may have been drugged, a vehicle (suspect's vehicle, victim's vehicle, or another vehicle used to transport the victim), a residence, college dorms, office area, work, or gym locker. Depending on the scene, a warrant may not be needed in all situations.

WHAT

If a specific drug is not suspected, make certain to consider drugs that will give the range of symptoms the victim experienced. Wording in each search warrant often needs to include multiple drugs or drug classes. A general DFSA search warrant is included in the resource material of this book, but the drug descriptions may not be exhaustive; adapt as needed for each case. Table 12.3 lists potential evidence that should be listed in the search warrant. Prior to conducting any search, make sure that those conducting the search are alerted as to what they are looking for to avoid missing crucial evidence. In an initial investigation, this may mean at least a quick phone call to a narcotics detective who is adequately familiar with the possible drugs involved. Suspects will "use what they have" to commit DFSA. This requires a thorough investigation of a potential suspect. His geographical location, for example, should be considered. If he lives near a foreign border, he will have more ready access to foreign drugs, such as flunitrazepam (Rohypnol®). His personal prescriptions should also be considered. If he has a prescription for sleeping pills or other benzodiazepines, he may be more likely to use those than to seek out Rohypnol®. Consider his profession and his associations. If he's a veterinary assistant, he may have ketamine or another tranquilizer readily available. He may be a drug user. A heroin addict may use heroin to incapacitate a victim, and is likely to also

Table 12.3

Common evidence for search warrants.

Drugs

Chemicals

Glasses, containers, bottles

Photographs (of current or prior victims and additional accomplices)

Videos (of current and/or prior victims and additional accomplices)

Computer records

Phone records

Articles about these drugs and/or their uses

Vomit

abuse benzodiazepines. Likewise, a methamphetamine or cocaine user is also apt to use depressants to ease the negative effects of the stimulants. Working with narcotics officers to make an undercover buy from the suspect or his associates may be in order to establish his involvement with, or access to, drugs. Suspects may also include opportunistic security guards, bouncers or patrons at clubs who encounter a comatose victim and take advantage of her condition to sexually assault her.

INNOVATIVE INVESTIGATIVE TECHNIQUES

In addition to search warrants, investigators may use a variety of strategies to investigate DFSA. As with all communities, many of the special populations you work with have their own communication system (i.e. gay/lesbian, transgender communities, active military personnel, university students). Friends and co-workers may suspect other unreported victims or may be aware of the suspect's use of or access to the drugs in question. In some cases, suspects have made incriminating statements as they brag to their friends about their sexual conquests. Many DFSAs involve more than one suspect. On college campuses, it may be helpful to contact the students to ask for assistance. In at least one case, an active student group took it upon themselves to contact their student body by e-mail to inquire about prior incidents of DFSA on campus. Computers allow some anonymity for students who are afraid to come forward. Once accessed, students may decide to come forward to reveal these prior acts (even if never prosecuted) so they can be used to corroborate a current victim's allegation. If the suspect is new to the community, be sure to check his previous locales for prior allegations of sexual assault.

Those working intensely with the drug GHB have found that the single largest category of GHB users still involve bodybuilders. This may include anyone working out at a gym regularly, competitive bodybuilders, or professional athletes. It is also widely abused by exotic dancers and their bodyguards. Abuse of GHB is also common within the group of employees and owners of health or sports supplement shops. Thus, any suspect with an athletic build who fits into any of these categories may employ GHB for sexual assault. In fact, in one incident, a female was introduced to an athletic man through mutual friends. During the evening, as her friends were gradually leaving, she observed him spike his own drink with a clear liquid. She inquired what it was and he told her that it was GHB. She questioned the danger of his actions and told him she would never take anything like that. In retaliation, he later dosed her drink and she became extremely intoxicated. He was later observed putting her into his car. Passers-by, who knew the victim, intervened, and he bragged that he had drugged her drink with GHB, saying he would take care of her. Fortunately, her friends rescued her and rushed her to the hospital where she nearly died. In the case of an athletic victim, or someone interested in getting into the workout scene, they may be talked into taking GHB or a related product as an energy tonic or sleep aid.

Perhaps one of the most valuable tools available to the sex crimes detective is the pretext phone call or confrontation call. Child abuse detectives have used this tool for decades. A pretext phone call refers to a scripted conversation that takes place between the victim and suspect at the suggestion of law enforcement or the prosecutor. If the victim is unable to manage a pretext phone call, a detective can pose as a friend, parent, counselor, or public health nurse. The conversation is usually tape-recorded. Keep in mind that these phone calls are illegal in some American states like Illinois, while other states require the consent of at least one party. Make sure you know the law for each state the investigation involves. For example, California has an evidence code that allows police officers to use this tool during the course of a criminal investigation. Nevada allows an officer to orchestrate the phone call but does not allow it to be recorded. So in Nevada, a detective can listen to the conversation and testify to the content in court. Unless these calls are strictly prohibited in your state, sex crimes detectives should be encouraged to use pretext phone calls, whenever possible. Detectives need to clearly understand the elements of a DFSA before scripting the call. Since the suspect will most likely claim that the sex act was consensual, the burden is not establishing sexual contact but getting the suspect to admit to the victim's level of incapacitation or lack of consent.

Pretext phone calls are most effective if they are made before the suspect is aware of the investigation. However, since so few sexual assault cases are prosecuted (a 1993 Senate Judiciary report indicates that 98% of sex offenders are never caught, tried, or imprisoned) a delay in the call may be advantageous since the suspect may believe that he got away with it. E-mail and voice mail messages are also useful and effective. This is especially true if your state does not allow the use of pretext phone calls.

Law enforcement officers often fear working with the media. However, working with news resources on DFSA cases can be crucial both in preventing and responding to these crimes. Ongoing efforts should be made to inform the public of developing trends regarding drugs and sexual assaults. This can serve as a public service to inform the general public about sexual predators and can educate future jurors about these crimes. For DFSA investigators, working with the media to get a suspect's face on television or in the newspaper, may bring out other victims. Prior victims of sexual assaults that occurred beyond the statue of limitations may corroborate your case and provide additional investigative leads.

INTERVIEWING THE SUSPECT

Most law enforcement officers are taught to hope for a confession, but confessions are actually rare. More often, sexual assault cases are built on statements of admission, inconsistencies, and absurdities. To get the most from a suspect's statement, officers must remember to be quiet and listen. This is not the time to confront the suspect with the implausibility of his statements. If the victim had a forensic sexual assault examination, or there is other physical evidence, absent a full confession, you want the suspect to deny all sexual contact. With denial, the suspect's defense is that someone else is responsible. Then it becomes a question of identification. In cases of identification, law enforcement has been well trained. To some degree, investigators understand footprints, latent fingerprints, tool marks, DNA, and trace evidence. Unfortunately, based on the expertise of the San Diego Police Department Sex Crimes Unit, in approximately nine out of ten sexual assaults, this is not the type of evidence that will be needed to corroborate the victim's allegations. In DFSA cases, the suspect will often admit that he had sex with the victim, but that it was a consensual act. The suspect may use the victim's history of substance abuse or promiscuous behavior to direct blame to her and hold her responsible for the sexual contact. In the case of a consent defense involving a DFSA, investigators should get the suspect to acknowledge the victim's extreme level of intoxication. For example, he may admit that she was throwing up and lying in her own vomit. He will often try to convince the investigator that the sex act was still consensual, but it becomes more difficult for a jury to believe. There have been a number of cases in which the sexual assault of an unconscious woman caused her tampon to be jammed into her cervix so far that it could not be removed without assistance. The prosecutor could easily argue that a coherent woman would have removed the tampon, if, in fact, she was going to consent to sexual intercourse. Other admissions include statements about sexual acts that go beyond the victim's normal sexual experience (i.e. anal intercourse, lack of contraception, or lack of protection from sexually transmitted diseases).

When the suspect claims consent was given, the investigator needs to question how he knew she consented. It should be determined what he thinks she said or did that led him to believe that she wanted to have sex with him. Witness statements may contradict his statement. For example, a DFSA that went to trial in San Diego involved a young woman who became very intoxicated at a party. Her friends allowed her to sleep it off in one of the bedrooms at the party house. Witnesses went to check on the victim several times because they were aware that she was extremely intoxicated, and when interviewed, they reported that the victim was totally unconscious. During one of these checks, her friends saw the suspect jump up from the bed and quickly pull up his pants while stating that he didn't do anything. The victim was still unconscious and could not be awakened. Paramedics and police were called. Both spent some time trying to wake the victim, including applying pain at pressure points and using smelling salts. After almost 45 minutes, the victim woke with no memory or knowledge of the sexual assault. When interviewed, the suspect claimed he went into the room to check on her even though she was a complete stranger to him. He said the victim "came on" to him, pulled him into her bed, took off his shirt, and suggested they have sex. The statements concerning the victim's level of intoxication and the time it took to revive her were critical for the jury's ultimate rape conviction.

Interviews should also include bartenders and bouncers to verify the suspect or victim's statement. They may have information about prior complaints involving the suspect. Remember that these suspects are often serial rapists. They may frequent the same locations, but because of severe under-reporting and failures by the criminal justice system, they are very active and confident they will never be caught or prosecuted.

Many businesses and residential complexes have security cameras that may have video evidence of elements of the crime. This video may depict the victim being escorted from the bar and, in at least one case, the suspect's license plate as he left the club with the victim. These videos must be discovered quickly as many businesses recycle their videotape every 24 hours.

REFERENCES

Lindsay, S.P. (1998) Doctoral dissertation, University of California at San Diego.

San Diego Police Department Sexual Assault statistics (1992–1999) *Non-Stranger Versus Stranger Sexual Assault.*

Spears, J.W. and Spohn, C.C. (1997) *Just Quart*, 14, p. 3.

State Judiciary Committee (1993) *The Response to Rape: Detours on the Road to Equal Justice*, Senator Joseph R. Biden, Jr.

Sturman, P.A. (2000) *Drug Assisted Sexual Assault – A Study for the Home Office*, Police Research Scheme.

CHAPTER 13

PROSECUTION OF DFSA

Karla Kerlin
Diana M. Riveira
Stephen J. Paterson

Drug-facilitated sexual assault (DFSA) poses many challenges for prosecutors. More common difficulties include delayed reporting, memory loss from the drugs used, lack of positive toxicological findings, and consensual use of drugs and alcohol by the victim. While these cases may seem difficult on their face, in reality they are no more challenging than traditional acquaintance rape cases lacking witnesses and physical injuries. Prosecutors must not shy away from prosecuting these cases only because of their complexity. Through training, experience, and working as a team with other criminal justice professionals, prosecutors can successfully prosecute even the most challenging DFSA cases.

ASSISTING IN THE INVESTIGATION

The key to overcoming the challenges of DFSA cases and successfully prosecuting them is teamwork. The prosecutor must work closely with all the members of the team, which includes law enforcement, forensic scientists, the victim advocate, and most important, the victim herself.

Early involvement of the prosecutor in a case of DFSA increases the chances of a successful outcome. By providing advice and guidance during the early stages of the investigation, the prosecutor can assist in analyzing the weaknesses of the case and suggest leads for further investigation. In addition, aggressive investigative and prosecutorial strategies can be identified and implemented.

PRE-FILING INTERVIEW

In DFSA cases, the prosecutor should ideally be someone who already has specialized training and experience in the prosecution of sexual assault crimes and, more specifically, acquaintance rape cases. Prior to interviewing the victim, the prosecutor should familiarize himself/herself with some of the classic signs of DFSA. This helps the prosecutor ask more appropriate questions and better understand and appreciate valuable facts in the victim's answers.

Although the victim may not remember the assault itself, she will have information that will be crucial to the case. The prosecutor must conduct a detailed interview with her and explain the necessity for the questions that are asked. At this stage, the prosecutor starts to piece together circumstantial evidence that will be vital to the success of the DFSA case (APRI, 1999). The victim has just experienced a life-altering trauma. It is important that the prosecutor encourage her to speak with a victim advocate for additional support. If the victim decides that she would like this support, make sure that the advocate is present during the interview.

As in all sexual assault cases, the prosecutor should interview the victim before making any filing decision. This interview gives the prosecutor the opportunity to assess the victim's rendition of events and to evaluate the victim's ability to testify as a witness in the courtroom. It also gives the prosecutor the opportunity to develop a rapport with the victim early on in the proceedings. This may enhance the victim's comfort level in proceeding with the prosecution. Additionally, it gives the prosecutor a chance to explain to the victim how the case will likely proceed to trial. Finally, the interview allows the prosecutor to discuss issues of victim confidentiality, to explain in basic terms the various stages of the criminal proceedings, and what may be expected from the defense during discovery and cross-examination.

So that the victim will know what to expect, the prosecutor needs to explain each step in as much detail as possible. The prosecutor should discuss trial procedure, presentation to the jury, defense depositions, potential discovery of related records (the sexual assault exam, including the presence of recreational drugs uncovered by a "comprehensive or full drug screen"; medical records; school transcripts and records; mental health counseling records), direct testimony, cross-examination, and what to realistically expect from plea agreements or sentencing of the defendant after trial. How the team interacts with the victim will affect her recovery from the assault, her view of the criminal justice system, and the outcome of the case. The victim must be kept informed and involved during every stage of the prosecution.

To every extent possible, the prosecutor should be prepared, and indeed should be invited by law enforcement, to participate in all law enforcement interviews with potential victims. A multidisciplinary approach wherein the prosecutor and law enforcement interview victims together has many advantages. First, it reduces the overall number of victim interviews. This usually makes the process easier for the victim. Second, a well-planned, thorough interview by the prosecutor and law enforcement should result in a single comprehensive follow-up investigation report and reduce the number of inconsistencies in the victim's statement from repetitive interviewing. Third, interviewing as a team provides an excellent opportunity to develop a rapport with the victim. As the victim gains familiarity with the people who will handle the prosecution of the case, her comfort level in proceeding with prosecution is enhanced.

During the interview, law enforcement and the prosecutor must stress the need for full disclosure and complete honesty by the victim, especially if there is an issue of voluntary ingestion of recreational drugs. Only with such absolute candor can the prosecutor be prepared to protect the victim in court against defense attack, by bringing the appropriate motions *in limine* to limit or exclude irrelevant, negative information (when appropriate and possible) or to present the negative evidence up front in the prosecution's case-in-chief.

This is another area where it is crucial for the prosecution to work closely with victim advocates. A victim has to understand the potential legal ramifications of waiving her rights to self-incrimination and disclosing actions that could be classified as criminal acts (e.g. ingesting illegal drugs). The best case scenario is where the police department and the prosecutor's office have policies in place where victims of sexual assault are not charged with ingesting illegal substances, and thus the focus is kept on building the strongest possible case against the true malefactor, the rapist. However, it cannot be overemphasized that in DFSA cases, where the victim may have consumed a great deal of alcohol or voluntarily ingested recreational drugs, it is imperative that the prosecutor knows this in advance. The prosecutor should be sensitive to the fact that the victim may be reluctant to disclose any alcohol consumption or recreational drug use, if for example she is under age and is accompanied by her parents. For this reason, victim interviews are best done outside the presence of anyone who could have a chilling effect on the victim's honesty.

Ideally, victim interviews should be scheduled at a time and place that are convenient for the victim. Prosecutors should also be aware of the effects of Post-traumatic Stress Disorder (PTSD), from which some rape victims suffer. This may cause the victim to "present" (or portray herself) differently at different times when she sees the prosecutor. For example, the victim may appear depressed yet willing to talk one day, but completely withdrawn and uncommunicative the next.

Accounting for the victim's state of mind and circumstances will require some flexibility in the prosecutor's schedule as he may need to accompany law enforcement to interview a victim in the evening or at a victim's home, workplace, or other neutral setting of the victim's choosing. When interviewing victims who live in remote areas, it may be beneficial to suggest that the victim meet the interviewing team halfway, or at a local police station. Even if the police station is a different agency than the one handling the case, law enforcement will usually cooperate in making an interview room available as a courtesy to other law enforcement officers. This strategy should also be considered if a victim does not want her friends or family to know that she is a victim of a sexual assault. Alternatively, victims can be interviewed at a convenient neutral setting such as a restaurant or a park close to their home.

In addition, when dealing with victims from different cultures, the prosecutor should educate herself as to any potential cultural differences, screen for language difficulties, and be aware of potential immigration concerns. Cultural sensitivity is especially important in cases of rape because of the added psychological strain of the victim if cultural prejudices exist against women who have been sexually assaulted.

When interviewing a DFSA victim, the prosecutor should exercise particular caution in not suggesting information to the victim. A DFSA victim may have gaps in her memory that she is eager to fill with information. As with any other type of crime, questions should be open-ended (to the extent possible) to generate information that is solely the independent recollection of the victim at the time of the interview. For example, if the prosecutor suspects that a particular drug was used in the assault, she should not ask leading questions about the victim's symptoms, but should instead ask the victim to completely describe her symptoms. Additionally, if the prosecutor is familiar with the perpetrator's *modus operandi*, he should avoid asking leading questions. Instead, the prosecutor should ask open-ended questions designed to elicit narrative-type answers from the victim. The prosecutor can then assess whether or not the assault on this victim fits the pattern of a suspected perpetrator's *modus operandi*. For example, rather than asking if the perpetrator injected a spermicide into the victim's vagina, the prosecutor could ask if the victim is aware of any form of birth control used by the perpetrator.

In most cases, the drug or substance used to commit DFSA is not known. It is essential that the prosecutor get all possible information from the victim. This may enable an expert to later give an opinion as to what drug may have caused the effects the victim describes. For example, the prosecutor should get detailed information regarding what the victim had to eat and drink, and the approximate times and amounts. Then, the interview should address the approximate time the victim thinks she may have been drugged, the length of time before the onset of symptoms, as well as the actual symptoms. Furthermore, the victim should be asked about how long the symptoms were experienced and any changes in the symptoms she may have experienced as time progressed. The victim should also provide information about how she felt in the ensuing day (or two) after the drugging. All of this information may later prove useful for an expert witness to proffer an opinion as to what drug or substance may have been used, without requiring the victim to be subjected to additional interviews. It may also help law enforcement in their investigation by targeting a suspected drug and in the drafting of an appropriate search warrant.

In DFSA cases, the perpetrator prearranges and deliberately takes advantage of the victim's impaired state to engage in a wide variety of sexual activity, and sometimes in unusual or deviant sexual behavior. A victim may come into the police station and report that strange and unorthodox things have been done to her. For example, a victim may remember waking up in the middle of the sexual assault and seeing a bright light. The victim may then fear that she was videotaped or photographed for pornographic personal use or commercial sale, or Internet website postings.

Law enforcement and prosecutors need to be sensitive to the fact that in a DFSA case, a victim's recollection of events may initially seem contrary to common sense, and consequently makes her seem less credible. For example, a victim calls 911 and states that she "may" have been raped, she doesn't remember, but she is sure "something" happened to her. Untrained law enforcement's initial response may be that the victim was drunk (or is still drunk or "high") and doesn't remember consenting to sex or now feels embarrassed. Trained law enforcement would instantly identify this as a classic case of DFSA and would commence a sexual assault investigation. The key to interviewing under these circumstances is to document everything the victim reports in a sensitive and nonjudgmental manner.

Some criminal justice professionals may mistakenly believe that victims of DFSA do not suffer the same trauma as other sexual assault victims since they do not remember the specifics of the crime that was perpetrated on them. However, many DFSA victims report agonizing trauma precisely because they do not remember exactly what happened to them. Thus, they are only left with their imagination, which may be more horrifying than the actual crime.

PRE-FILING REVIEW AND FOLLOW-UP INVESTIGATION

As with all types of crimes, the prosecutor needs to review the entire case packet from the assigned law enforcement officers before filing a DFSA case. The prosecutor may need to defer a filing decision and request that the detectives do further investigation. This additional investigation might consist of a pretext phone call, a search warrant or additional follow-up investigation based upon evidence recovered during the execution of a search warrant.

The prosecutor may need to strategize with law enforcement in targeting items to be searched during the execution of a search warrant. Evidence may include videotapes or photographs of victims; the drugs suspected to have been used; compounds used to synthesize a particular drug; recipes, books or articles on DFSA or drugs; "souvenirs" from the victims (e.g. panties, evidence of additional victims). It is important not to overlook the obvious. Perpetrators commit crimes with what is readily accessible to them. A search warrant must cover medicine cabinets (or other locations where medicines are kept) and prescription drugs found therein (or elsewhere) such as muscle relaxants and sleep aids.

If a search warrant yields information that leads law enforcement to suspect that there are additional victims, further investigation will need to be done to see if these potential victims can be located and interviewed. If any person is suspected to be a victim of a DFSA or to have additional information to offer, then a follow-up, in-person interview should be scheduled.

All evidence that supports the victim's version of events must be fully developed and investigated. Other corroborating evidence may include: prescriptions from the US and foreign countries, especially sleeping aids, muscle relaxants, and sedatives; eye-drop bottles or sports bottles (containers for GHB); Internet information or pamphlets on Rohypnol® and GHB, and on using these and other drugs in the commission of sexual assaults or for other purposes; (if robbery is suspected) the victim's possessions or pawn shop slips for a sale of the victim's possessions; multiple victims who experience similar symptoms or experiences after being with the same perpetrator; or admissions made by the perpetrator. The prosecutor should also determine if there are any "fresh complaint" witnesses, or persons to whom the victim first reported the crime. These individuals may be able to testify as corroborating witnesses.

Other avenues of corroborating evidence should be pursued as well. If a victim was with her girlfriends in a nightclub, the friends may be able to testify as to what they observed the victim drink, or to the fact that they were not aware of the victim or anyone else ingesting drugs on that evening. Friends might also be able to testify that it was unusual for the victim to have left the club without telling them, because they had a long-standing agreement never to do so. They may also be able to testify to the "out of character" behavior of the victim (e.g. dancing on tables or flirting with an individual they had just met). Information of this type can corroborate the victim's story and strengthen an otherwise weak case.

In some situations, it may be necessary to complete all scientific testing before a case filing decision is made. In cases with little or no corroborating evidence, the prosecutor may need to know the results of chemical, DNA, toxicological, or other testing. Once those results are available, the prosecutor can then evaluate whether there is enough evidence to ethically file the case. This in no way means that a prosecutor should only file cases where there is a positive toxicological report. It is anticipated that in the majority of DFSA cases there will not be a biological sample. However, prosecutors need to be aggressive and work with the multidisciplinary term to amass a strong circumstantial case against the suspect.

REQUESTS FOR FORENSIC TESTING

Several types of scientific testing may be needed in cases of DFSA. If substances were seized that are believed to be legal or illegal drugs, testing will be needed to verify the type of drug and the amount possessed by the perpetrator. If fluids (such as beverages) were seized as part of the investigation, they will need to be analyzed to see what drugs, if any, are contained therein. If biological samples, such as blood or urine, were taken from the victim, these samples need to be tested for the presence or absence of drugs and alcohol.

The prosecutor, in conjunction with law enforcement, should request that a forensic laboratory perform the appropriate narcotic, toxicological, and other necessary or special tests required for the case. If the jurisdiction's forensic laboratory does not have the capacity to adequately test samples for the suspected drugs, it may be necessary to send toxicological or other samples to a reputable outside laboratory. It is imperative, therefore, that the prosecutor understands enough of the science of DFSA to be able to discuss testing issues with the appropriate criminal forensic laboratory, and that she is familiar with the testing capabilities of the other available forensic laboratories. The local crime lab may be able to perform some of the testing, with the remainder performed by an outside agency.

A laboratory experienced in DFSA cases will conduct a "comprehensive drug screen." Experienced forensic scientists know that it is very difficult to narrow down the potential drug utilized in a DFSA based solely on the facts of a particular case. A laboratory with less experience in DFSA cases will need guidance. The prosecutor must understand the science of DFSA to discuss with crime laboratory personnel the substances for which testing will be done.

Not every crime laboratory will have the capability of testing the sample at adequate levels to detect the drugs ingested. For example, screening tests for benzodiazepines currently used in most toxicology laboratories may not detect benzodiazepines such as Rohypnol® or their metabolites, particularly if present in residual amounts. Therefore, it is important to determine whether the laboratory used by law enforcement in your jurisdiction is capable of carrying out these tests or whether the samples will have to be sent to another laboratory.

For experienced laboratories, the scientists and the prosecutor's office may wish to work together to develop a "DFSA Testing Request Form." This form should detail the dates and times of the assault, the medical examination, and collection of any biological samples; the symptoms experienced by the victim; and the drug panel(s) for which testing should be done. A sample form that can be adapted for your jurisdiction can be found in Appendix B. A "comprehensive drug screen" should be conducted with *informed victim consent* and include testing for the following drugs: benzodiazepines, amphetamines, muscle relaxants, sleep aids, antihistamines, cocaine, marijuana, barbiturates, opiates, ethanol, GHB, ketamine, and others as indicated in other chapters (; LeBeau, 1999; LeBeau *et al.*, 1999). Before ordering a "comprehensive drug screen," the investigating officer should explain to the victim what is entailed and obtain her informed consent. In fact, some American states require the investigating officer to obtain the victim's consent before ordering a "comprehensive drug screen."

Some sexual assault coalitions that operate on the local level to prevent such crimes and to assist victims have expressed serious concerns over conducting a "comprehensive drug screen" which may reveal that a victim ingested other recreational drugs. Depending upon the results of such a drug screen, the information may be used by the defense to discredit the victim, thereby hurting her chances of a successful prosecution. It is essential that victims have an advocate available to thoroughly explain the ramifications of any type of drug testing, be it a full or partial drug screen. Without all of the accurate information, victims will not be able to truly give *informed consent* to such a test. Neither law enforcement nor prosecutors should use the results of a "comprehensive drug screen" to automatically prevent a sexual assault case from going forward in the criminal justice system. The presence of recreational drugs is not evidence of the victim's consent to the sexual act.

INCLUSION OF BLOOD ALCOHOL TESTING IN FULL DRUG SCREEN

It is important to get a blood alcohol level on the victim as a formal part of the drug screen. If the victim had very little to drink before being drugged, it is important to show that her blood alcohol level was inconsistent with the symptoms she displayed. Second, if the victim had consumed a large amount of alcohol, it is important to know how much and exactly what her blood alcohol level was as evidence of her impairment level. Finally, certain drugs will have enhanced effects when combined with alcohol. Thus, the expert witness will need to know the amount of alcohol the victim consumed to better testify as to the results of the combined ingestion of alcohol and drugs. When submitting a request for toxicological testing, the prosecutor must remember to ask for blood alcohol (ethanol) testing in addition to testing for drugs.

CHARGING DECISIONS

In the majority of DFSA cases, the prosecutor may not have the benefit of a positive urine test result if the drug was metabolized before the sample was taken, the laboratory methodologies were not capable of detecting low levels of the drug(s) used, or if no sample was even taken. For these reasons, it is important to build relationships with law enforcement and the local crime laboratory to ensure that the lab is equipped to handle DFSA cases; that a comprehensive drug screen is conducted on each sample; that the most sensitive assays are used to detect residual levels of the drugs; and that the toxicologist or pharmacologist is available to testify at trial.

If a urine sample is not available, or there are no positive toxicological results, the prosecutor and the detective need to be aggressive and work together with the rest of the team to gather enough supporting evidence to be able to file a case. The prosecutor should consider consulting with a forensic scientist or pharmacologist at this point to evaluate the case and work with the prosecutor on the substance of forensic testimony. In addition, the expert's testimony will explain the drug's effects and, if there is no positive toxicology result, the reason why there is not a positive toxicology result in every case. Together the prosecutor, the investigator, and the forensic scientist will be able to accurately evaluate the case and determine whether there is sufficient corroborative evidence (where there is no positive toxicology result) to be able to charge the case.

If there is no urine sample, but the case is proceeding on an alternate theory such as rape of a disabled person, the prosecutor may need to present evidence that the victim was "drugged" which, in turn, rendered her incapacitated or helpless, and incapable of giving consent. Evidence of the victim's state can be presented through victim and witness testimony. However, such facts must first be established in order to make any subsequent expert testimony relevant to the case.

Prosecutors should encourage law enforcement to always make a report, even in the rare case when it is doubtful that the incident will lead to a fileable case. Even in non-filed DFSA cases, if several reports from victims regarding strange or suspicious conduct of an individual are compiled, then a pattern emerges that suggests this perpetrator is committing DFSA. Since there is some evidence that DFSA perpetrators tend to be serial offenders, having a report ensures an accurate historical record of incidents involving a particular individual, and can lead to valuable corroborating witnesses or additional victims. If reports are not made by law enforcement, valuable prosecution evidence may be lost.

If a prosecutor determines that there is insufficient information to file a case, a victim should nevertheless be thanked for coming forward and making the disclosure. With the increased admissibility of "other acts" evidence, it may be possible in a future case to use a previous victim (for whom a case could not be filed due to insufficient evidence) as a corroborating witness. Or, it may be possible to revive a previous report when a more current incident is reported against the same offender.

The prosecutor should be knowledgeable about "sex crimes" laws and enhancements in his jurisdiction, as these will be the primary charges filed. The most common charge in these cases is "Rape by Drugs," which may also be titled "Rape by an Intoxicating or Anesthetic Substance." An additional or alternate charge (depending on the facts of the case) may be "Rape of an Unconscious Person" or "Sexual Assault with a Physically Helpless or Physically Incapacitated Victim." Should the victim attempt to resist the assault or become conscious during the sexual assault and attempt to halt the attack, "Forcible Sexual Assault" charges should be considered.

Once the primary decision is made on charging the DFSA, secondary charges also need to be considered. A prosecutor should be creative in charging options because there may be several other crimes that accompany the sexual assault charge. And, even in the event that a sexual assault count cannot be charged, there may still be other charges that are legally supported by the existing evidence.

In some states, the courts have held that the use of drugs is tantamount to a use of force (*People v. Dreas* (1984)). Using such an argument creatively can allow for charging of crimes such as "Kidnaping" where there were no other indicia of force used to move the victim. In courts that have accepted the use of drugs as the equivalent of the use of force, enhanced sentencing penalties for forcible sex crimes were also held to be applicable. This has yielded sentences higher than those for which the defendant otherwise would have been eligible. In addition to the statutes, the prosecutor must know the applicable caselaw in his jurisdiction. The prosecutor may wish to pursue a creative argument based upon another state's law if nothing similar exists in the prosecutor's state.

The prosecutor should also consider other non-traditional charges. The facts may warrant charges of "Kidnaping to Commit a Forcible Sexual Assault," "Kidnaping," "Poisoning," or "Administering a Controlled Substance to Commit a Crime." If the drugs are found on the suspect or in the suspect's home or car, you may charge possession and/or distribution of the drug. If the victim is a minor, you may be able to file charges for contributing to the delinquency of a minor, or for felony distribution of a controlled substance to a minor. Depending on the particular facts of a DFSA case, other charges such as "Sexual Battery with a Deadly Weapon," "Aggravated Battery," "Kidnaping/ False Imprisonment," "Drug Possession/Distribution," "Contributing to the Delinquency of a Minor," "Burglary/Robbery/Grand Theft Auto," or "Adulteration of Food or Drink" should be considered. In addition to these substantive charges, there may be additional enhancements for the "Administration of a Controlled Substance During the Commission of a Felony" which would attach to the sexual assault or other charges.

Thus, the prosecutor must know what charges are in his arsenal and should creatively file the case in such a way as to give options to the jury. For example, a particular jury may be uncomfortable with charges of "Rape by Drugs" in cases that lack positive toxicological findings, yet may be comfortable with charges of "Forcible Rape" or "Rape of an Unconscious Person" as an alternative. Although dependent upon the prosecutor's jurisdiction, the key is to file in the alternative, when permissible, to give the jury a number of options.

In jurisdictions that have no statutes to criminalize the conduct encompassed by DFSA, or no enhancements or increased penalties for such crimes, the prosecutor may need to submit legislation through her office. Prior to drafting proposed legislation, the prosecutor may wish to consult with experts in surrounding or similar jurisdictions to see what laws other states have enacted and to evaluate any problems experienced with those statutes. Reviewing the laws of other states can help determine which statutes and penalties will improve the chance of the successful enactment of the legislation.

Finally, the prosecutor should be aware that, in addition to state statutes, there are currently two federal available statutes available to charge DFSA offenses: The Drug-Induced Rape Prevention and Punishment Act of 1996 (21 U.S.C. §§801 & 841), and The Hillary J. Farias and Samantha Reid Date-Rape Drug Prohibition Act of 1999 (21 USC §§801 note. & 812 note.). Both of these statutes have resulted in successful prosecutions.

CONSULTATION WITH EXPERTS

DFSAs involve drugs that may produce amnesia in the victim. As a result, the prosecutor's usual key witness, the victim, may not be able to relay the details of the sexual assault. In these circumstances, the testimony of a credible expert witness often makes the difference between a conviction and an acquittal. As part of a thorough preparation, the prosecutor may wish to speak to other professionals who have been involved in the prosecution of such cases. The prosecutor may wish to consult with law enforcement experts, other prosecutors, toxicologists, pharmacologists, and others.

These experts can share their experiences and provide valuable information on what was successful and what was not. In particular, prosecutors can share information about how a case was filed; the case theme that was used; the expert witnesses called or consulted; what defense was presented; how that defense met and challenged; and the arguments that were made. Prosecutors may also share transcripts of expert testimony. This enables a prosecutor to evaluate how an expert witness has previously testified and the types of questions that were presented to the expert. Consultation with others serves to strengthen the prosecutor's knowledge base to better prepare her to proceed with the case.

SELECTING AN EXPERT WITNESS

Often, in cases of DFSA, having the right expert witness can be key to the ultimate outcome. Many experts specialize in a particular drug or drug class (e.g. gamma hydroxybutyrate (GHB) or benzodiazepines), and it is therefore important to get a witness with expertise in the drug that the prosecutor and law enforcement suspect was used. Additionally, the prosecutor may need to call several expert witnesses in one case. For example, the prosecutor may need to call a chemist to testify to the actual testing of drugs recovered during the investigation, a toxicologist to testify to the testing of biological samples, and a pharmacologist or psychopharmacologist to testify to the effects of the drugs.

To determine the expert witness's limitations, the prosecutor needs to meet with the individual in advance to discuss the witness's level of expertise and comfort in testifying to each of the desired areas of inquiry. The prosecutor should carefully peruse the curriculum vitae of the expert witness and should review it with that individual. The expert should be asked about his specific area of expertise and where that expertise is best reflected in the witness's curriculum vitae (i.e. research, publications).

If there are no "positive" toxicological findings in a case of suspected DFSA, early involvement with an expert witness can help narrow the likely drug or drugs used based upon the symptoms displayed by the victim. Consultation with an expert early in the investigation may assist in the preparation of a search warrant and in the determination of what items to look for during the execution of that warrant.

PRE-TRIAL AND TRIAL

CIVIL LAWSUITS

A victim of a DFSA, as with any sexual assault case, may file a concurrent civil lawsuit. The prosecutor must be prepared to confront this issue during the case-in-chief. The simplest way is to ask the victim, during her direct testimony, about the civil lawsuit and why the victim caused such a suit to be filed. Since civil lawsuits have a short statute of limitations, the victim may not be able to wait until the completion of the criminal case to decide whether or not to proceed civilly. Usually in these cases, a lawyer has suggested filing a suit to preserve the victim's rights. This information should be relayed to the jury so they have an understanding of why the civil lawsuit was filed so quickly. Of course, this matter should be discussed with the victim in advance to determine the victim's reasons for bringing a civil suit.

Obviously, the defense perspective on civil lawsuits is that the victim brought the lawsuit with the hopes of financial gain. The defense will try to portray the defendant as the true victim. Despite the negative impact that civil lawsuits can have on the criminal case, the prosecutor needs to deal with this issue up front to protect against a defense attack.

When a civil lawsuit is brought, the defense may use the civil suit as a means of gathering discovery to use in the criminal case. The defense may rush to schedule a victim's deposition to get testimony under oath in advance of the criminal case. The prosecutor should explain to the victim's civil lawyer the negative impact a civil case can have on a criminal case. The prosecutor should also encourage the civil lawyer to attempt to postpone the victim's deposition until the criminal trial is concluded. If a deposition of the victim is taken, the prosecutor should ask the victim's civil lawyer for transcripts of the victim's testimony. This transcript is important, as it will be in the possession of the defense at the time of the criminal trial.

PREPARING THE VICTIM FOR DEFENSE ATTACK

The prosecutor should prepare the victim for defense attack by discussing all areas of anticipated cross-examination or problem areas for the case. Of course, the victim should be reminded that absolute candor will work to her benefit and she should not tailor her testimony in any way in an attempt to make the facts look better.

In a DFSA case, common areas of defense attack include consensual use of drugs and alcohol, delays in reporting, memory loss, and civil lawsuits brought by the victim. Typically, the defense will attempt to portray the victim of a DFSA as a sexually promiscuous party-girl who is out drinking, using drugs and looking for a good time. The defendant may even portray himself as the Good Samaritan who tried to help the inebriated victim. The prosecutor should discuss any anticipated problem issues with the victim in advance so she is prepared to testify as comfortably and effectively as possible.

PRE-TRIAL MOTIONS

To protect the victim from attack by the defense, the prosecutor should aggressively make motions *in limine*. The prosecutor should avail himself of the rape shield laws in his jurisdiction. This prohibits the defense from inquiring into the victim's sexual history without showing relevance. This type of hearing should be made either in advance of the trial or before the victim's testimony, and outside the presence of the jury. The prosecutor should also ask for offers of proof regarding evidence the defense intends to use to cross-examine or impeach the victim. Through appropriate motions *in limine*, the prosecutor may be able to severely limit or even exclude the defense presentation of irrelevant and prejudicial information. For example, the prosecutor may be able to exclude the fact that the victim previously worked as an exotic dancer, attended a drug rehabilitation program, or appeared in pornographic magazines.

For the prosecutor to prepare the victim for defense attack, the prosecutor must be familiar with the skeletons in the victim's closet. The prosecutor should explain to the victim that the defense investigator will likely have done exhaustive investigation to find out this information. In order to protect the victim from attack, the prosecutor must level the playing field and know what potential issues exist. The prosecutor should ask the victim outright to share any such issues. The prosecutor can then address these areas in pre-trial motions so that the trial court makes the appropriate exclusionary or limiting rulings.

In addition to motions *in limine*, the prosecutor should avail herself of the use of "other acts" evidence whenever applicable in a particular case. Basically, this means that the prosecutor needs to be familiar with the prior conduct of the defendant to know if there might be admissible prior sexual assaults or attempted assaults. In order to bring the appropriate motion, the prosecutor needs to be familiar with the laws of her jurisdiction governing the admission of such "other acts" evidence. The trend in the law generally is to liberally allow for the admission of such evidence subject to the appropriate balancing test by the trial court. If the prosecutor's jurisdiction does not allow for the use of "other acts" evidence, this is an additional area where legislation might need to be proposed to enact appropriate statutes.

A motion *in limine* may need to be brought, or a trial brief filed, to address the issue of consent. In jurisdictions with a rape by drugs (or similar) statute, consent may not be a defense to the charge since it is not usually an element which the prosecutor needs to prove. Consent, however, is probably the most frequently presented defense in DFSA cases. The prosecutor may need to educate the judge as to the law and this esoteric point to preclude or limit the defense from presenting a consent defense. In cases without positive toxicological findings, this may be more difficult since the defense will likely argue that there were no drugs, thus there was no rape by drugs, and the sexual conduct was consensual. Nevertheless, the prosecutor should be aware whether or not consent is a defense, be mindful of this fact as the evidence unfolds, and make objections as appropriate.

JURY SELECTION

Jury selection is the first exposure the prosecutor and the jury have to one another and the only chance the prosecutor has to speak with prospective jurors. Therefore, jury selection and *voir dire* should be viewed as not only an opportunity to identify specific jurors who should be challenged, but also as the first chance the prosecution has to introduce the ultimate jury to the overall case themes.

ATTITUDES AND EXPERIENCES

Research has shown that attitudes and experiences are the most important determinants of juror behavior. Therefore, the first step in preparing for jury selection is to identify what attitudes and experiences will be most important to how a juror makes decision in a DFSA case. In particular, because the process of jury selection is really a process of "jury de-selection" (i.e. elimination of those jurors who could not be fair and impartial), the prosecutor should focus his or her attention on developing a profile of the type of person who would likely hold a defense bias in such a case. For example, attitudes relating to the police and police investigations could be critical to how a juror views the evidence in a particular DFSA case, especially if there is a question as to police conduct. Those prospective jurors who have negative attitudes toward the police may be significantly more defense-oriented. Another example is attitudes about individual responsibility. The prosecutor may conclude that those prospective jurors who hold strong beliefs about self-reliance and personal responsibility will also be more defense-oriented in these types of cases. The important thing for the prosecutor to do in preparing for jury selection is to identify the types of attitudes and experiences that he or she believes defense-oriented jurors will possess. This preparation can be done with the assistance of jury research (in the form of polling), in consultation with other prosecutors who have similar case experiences, and/or, most important, using the prosecutor's own judgment and case experience. This profile will provide the prosecutor with a framework to which she can compare each prospective juror.

QUESTIONING

Once profiling is complete, the next step is to develop *voir dire* questions. These questions can be administered either during oral *voir dire* and/or through the use of a juror questionnaire. The prosecutor should devote substantial resources to the development of *voir dire* questions. These questions should be designed to:

1. elicit information from jurors for purposes of evaluating whether they should serve;
2. inoculate jurors against defense attempts to elicit responses that will be used to support a challenge for cause; and
3. introduce case themes.

When trying to elicit information from a prospective juror, the best mechanism to use is an "open-ended" question. Questions such as "Tell me about what you know about the so-called date rape drugs," or "What do you think about the use of these drugs to commit rapes?" allow the juror to expand beyond a simple "Yes" or "No" answer and provide the prosecutor with a great deal more information by which to assess a person. They also serve to make the prospective juror more comfortable in an otherwise uncomfortable and unfamiliar environment.

Often the prosecutor may want to "protect" a prospective juror from defense questions designed to justify a defense challenge for cause. With these types of jurors, it is best to anticipate what these question areas will be and inoculate against them. For example, a prospective juror may indicate in a written questionnaire that he or she would tend to believe that a police officer would be more likely to tell the truth than other witnesses would. In this situation, the prosecutor would want to explain the law relating to witness testimony and then obtain a commitment from the juror that they would do their best to follow the law and the judge's instructions.

Finally, the prosecutor may want to introduce case themes through the use of *voir dire* questions. Questions designed to identify juror experiences and attitudes can be used to implant case themes directly into the minds of jurors. For example, suppose one of the themes in a DFSA case relates to "betrayal" and "violation of trust." The following questions can serve to address this theme in front of the prospective jurors. "How many of you here have ever been betrayed? Please raise your hands." "For those of you who raised your hands, how many of you feel that your trust was violated by that betrayal? Please raise your hands."

POTENTIAL AREAS OF INQUIRY

While *voir dire* questions must be tailored to the facts of the particular DFSA case, there are several general areas of inquiry that will likely apply in most cases.

DFSA cases are likely to garner a lot of pre-trial publicity. The prosecutor should ask questions about exposure to media reports on the case, or ones similar to it, to ensure that potential jurors have not prejudged the case based on media reports.

Because expert witnesses will likely testify, potential jurors should be asked attitudinal questions about their feelings toward expert witnesses who may testify frequently, and whether the jurors believe this affects a witness's credibility. As some of the expert witnesses may work for government laboratories, potential jurors should be questioned as to whether they believe this affects the objectivity of such a witness's testimony.

Depending on the facts of the particular case, jurors should be asked about their background in science, medicine, DNA, or pharmaceuticals. Specific questions can be tailored to the properties of the drug used in the case. For example, potential jurors could be asked whether they would have difficulty believing that a drug could cause memory loss, yet still allow a victim to walk around and interact with other people.

Other areas of inquiry might cover juror attitudes about whether it is less traumatic for a woman to be raped while unconscious rather than while awake. Potential jurors can be questioned about their attitudes toward a defendant who was also drunk or high from voluntary intoxication of alcohol and/or drugs. Finally, jurors can be asked standard sexual assault *voir dire* questions such as whether they would be uncomfortable listening to graphic sexual details, and whether they, or someone close to them, has been the victim, or the accused, of a sexual assault.

JUROR QUESTIONNAIRES

Sometimes the trial judge will allow the use of juror questionnaires. In addition to demographics (e.g. age, gender, occupation, etc.), these questionnaires are very helpful in obtaining attitudinal information about prospective jurors. The most straightforward way to address this in a questionnaire is to construct scaled-response questions. Scaled-response questions not only tell the prosecutor what attitude a particular juror has on an issue, but the intensity with which that attitude is held. For example, suppose toxicology records evidence will be central to the prosecution's case and the prosecution team is concerned about prospective jurors who do not trust toxicological test results. One way to address this in a questionnaire is to ask the following question:

> *Please tell us how much you disagree or agree with the following statement on a scale from 1 to 7, where 1 is disagree strongly and 7 is agree strongly, and you can use any number in between 1 and 7 as well.*

Toxicological evidence in a trial is an effective means of identifying drugs used.

1	2	3	4	5	6	7
Disagree strongly					**Agree strongly**	

The prosecutor may conclude that the most favorable jurors on this issue would answer a 6 or 7. Any prospective juror answering 5 or less would therefore be viewed as less favorable.

Where scaled-questions are not feasible, the prosecutor may want to consider open-ended questions. Care must be taken, however, with the use of too many open-ended questions in a juror questionnaire. Jurors may get tired and resentful if they are required to write too much, and the questionnaires become unwieldy to analyze and evaluate because of the large amount of information contained in the answers.

Advance notice of the intent to use a juror questionnaire should be given to the court so that both sides can submit proposed questionnaires to the judge. Often it is easier to obtain court approval if the prosecution and defense can submit a joint questionnaire. Questionnaires are also very helpful if a prosecutor is accused of exercising his challenges for improper reasons. They can support the prosecutor's race- and gender-neutral reasons for exercising a peremptory challenge on a particular juror.

OPENING STATEMENT

The prosecutor should use an opening statement to introduce the case theme, or reinforce the theme that was introduced during jury selection. This theme should be one that will be underscored by the presentation of evidence in the case and will be reiterated in argument. The use of a theme gives the jury a context or an idea of what the case is about and prepares them for the evidence they will see and hear. For example, in a case of DFSA, a theme may be that the defendant was a hunter or predator and the victim the prey. Of course, the facts of a particular case will determine the appropriate case theme.

In the opening statement, the prosecutor should prepare the jury for any negative facts the jury will hear about the victim or the evidence. For example, the prosecutor should let the jury know if there are no positive toxicological findings, if the victim used alcohol or drugs consensually, or if there was a delay in reporting. The prosecutor's presentation will prepare the jury to deal with these facts, and will preclude the defense from surprising the jury. Additionally, it weakens the defense case. An honest presentation deals with the negative and positive facts up-front and allows the jury to make a determination as to whether or not the charges have been proven beyond a reasonable doubt.

USE OF AN EXPERT WITNESS

The importance of expert testimony in DFSA trials cannot be overemphasized. An expert witness will be able to educate the judge and jury on the effects of the drug and the reasons for the victim's inability to remember all or any of the details about the incident. In addition, in cases where the victim did not sustain any physical injury as a result of the assault, a doctor or sexual assault nurse examiner (SANE Nurse) may testify about the reasons for the lack of injury, as in any other sexual assault case. It is important to remember, in these cases where the drugged victims are frequently unconscious or in an incapacitated state when sexually assaulted, there may not be evidence of injury or physical evidence of a struggle, such as torn clothing or broken fingernails.

The types of experts that are needed in sexual assault cases include:

- forensic drug chemists (who analyze seized drug samples);
- toxicologists (who analyze the body fluids of victims for drugs and may testify about the effects of the drugs);
- pharmacologists or medical doctors (who can discuss the overall pharmacology of the drugs involved in the case);
- forensic specialists in the areas of DNA analysis;
- medical doctors;
- other health-care professionals involved in the physical and psychological examination of the victim.

Before a prosecutor attempts to put an expert on the stand, the expert's testimony must be made relevant to the case. If there is no urine sample and the case is proceeding, for example, on a "Sexual Assault with a Physically Helpless or Physically Incapacitated Victim" charge, the prosecutor must put on evidence that the victim was "drugged," which rendered her incapacitated or helpless. This can be done through victim and witness testimony. However, these facts must be established in order to make the subsequent pharmacologist's testimony relevant to your case.

QUALIFYING THE EXPERT

The prosecutor should think carefully about how to use the expert witness. The goal is not only to elicit scientific information for the record, but also to have the jury actually understand the scientific evidence. It is also important not only to qualify the forensic scientist as an expert in a specific discipline (i.e. toxicology, pharmacology, etc.) but also to have them qualified based on their expertise with DFSA. One way to do this is to humanize the expert so that the jury begins to see him or her as a multifaceted person and not as just a "dull scientist." If the case comes down to the scientific evidence, the testimony may become a "battle of the experts," and the jury will decide based on the expert they find the most credible. Part of this jury assessment of credibility will depend on the "extras" they know about the expert's background.

Since there will be a limited number of experts that may be utilized in the area of DFSA cases, the prosecutor's office should invest the time in setting up "prosecution and defense experts case files" with trial transcripts. If funds are lacking, the prosecutor's office should contact local or national prosecutor organizations, such as the American Prosecutors Research Institute, which routinely set up such databases.

PROFFERING THE EXPERT

Depending on state law, the prosecutor may have to proffer the witness as an expert at this point. Be specific as to what type of experience the expert has. For example, if the expert has experience with GHB, she should be qualified as an expert experienced in analyzing that specific drug. This will set up a possible objection on relevance grounds to a defense expert with no specific experience in DFSA drugs. The prosecutor needs to be familiar with the rules of evidence in his jurisdiction that govern the determination of expert witness qualifications.

THE EXPERT TESTIMONY ITSELF

It is important to understand that not every victim will respond in the same way to drugs. The victim's reaction will depend on a number of factors such as the amount of a drug ingested, the size of the victim, whether the drug was ingested with alcohol, or if the victim has a tolerance to the drug. The expert needs to explain to the jury that there is no such thing as a classic case, and every case has to be analyzed individually by the forensic expert.

There are a number of other areas the expert witness can testify to that may help explain the facts or difficulties of the case. For example, the expert witness can discuss why the drugs cause memory loss. The expert can also testify to the effects of any drugs or alcohol the victim may have voluntarily consumed. Further, the expert may be called upon to explain such phenomena as the seeming willingness of the victim to accompany the defendant from one location to another, sexual arousal of the victim, or the loss of motor control. Additionally, the expert witness can testify to other effects of the drugs (e.g. nausea and vomiting). Once the expert witness has explained about the effects of the drug, the prosecutor can more easily explain why the victim would delay in reporting the incident or account for the so-called problems with the case.

To detail every area of the prosecution's direct examination of the forensic scientist would be impracticable (APRI, 1999). The one area that must be briefly covered is one of the greatest challenges in a DFSA case. This is expert testimony where there is no positive toxicological result, and the drug used has not been identified by other means. In states like New York and California, a DFSA case can still be successfully prosecuted because the specific drug used does not need to be identified. New York requires (New York Penal Law §130.00 (6)) that there be "incapacitation using a narcotic or an intoxicating substance." California requires that the victim be prevented from resisting by "an intoxicating or anesthetic substance."

If the statute in your jurisdiction reads like that of New York or California, present the pharmacologist with the symptomology experienced by the victim, and ask whether these symptoms are consistent with the language of the particular statute (e.g. "incapacitation using a narcotic or an intoxicating substance"). Provide your pharmacologist with the victim's alcohol and recreational drug consumption (if any) on the date of the incident (through the victim's testimony or witnesses's testimony) and also with the victim's past history of alcohol and recreational drug consumption (to determine tolerance, etc.).

Since the defense may attempt to argue that the victim's symptoms were produced by her voluntary alcohol consumption, ask the pharmacologist to discuss the amount of alcohol necessary to produce similar symptoms. Because of the occurrence of vomiting as a symptom, the ingestion of GHB will be more of a target for the defense in its attempts to analogize it to alcohol consumption. Closely follow the language used in the applicable state's statute when describing the drug (e.g, "narcotic," "intoxicating substance," or "anesthetic substance").

It is very important that the expert witness and the prosecutor meet to discuss the expert's testimony and to organize the direct examination questions to bring out all the necessary information. Experts may need to address the biological analysis of the urine samples and account for all the drugs present in the sample, the analysis of any seized drugs, and whether or not the victim's symptoms are consistent with the drugs involved. The expert may also need to explain the process of metabolism and how this process affects the testing procedure.

CROSS-EXAMINATION OF THE PROSECUTION'S FORENSIC SCIENTIST

Forensic scientists are crucial in a DFSA case. These experts may be able to assist the prosecutor in identifying and anticipating the information on which the defense will cross-examine them. The expert can make an educated guess as to the substance of a defense expert's testimony (e.g. would alcohol produce the same effects). The expert may also suggest issues on which to cross-examine the defense's expert witnesses.

Probably, the most prevalent area of cross-examination in DFSA cases focuses on whether large quantities of alcohol consumption would produce the same effect as being drugged with the drug in question. For example, the defense may attempt to establish on cross-examination that a victim consumed alcohol the night of the sexual assault. Then, the defense will cross-examine the prosecution's expert on the fact that there are general studies that indicate that people routinely underestimate the amount of alcohol they consume. Most of these studies will be drawn from the "driving under the influence" arena. The defense will conclude by arguing that even the victim herself admitted that she consumed alcohol that evening, and even the prosecution's own expert had to admit that people routinely underestimate how much alcohol they consume. The defense will further argue that it is impossible for the jury to conclude "beyond a reasonable doubt" that the victim was drugged with whichever drug by the defendant, and that she was probably just suffering from the effects of a large quantity of alcohol consumption.

The prosecution needs to counter this argument with the fact that it would take an extremely large volume of alcohol for the same symptoms to occur as would occur when ingesting a drug. The prosecutor can illustrate the time frame necessary for the body to process that much alcohol and result in a loss of consciousness.

Another defense tactic when a victim has ingested a DFSA drug like a benzo-diazepine and also a stimulant like cocaine, is to insinuate that the drugs cancel out each other and the victim is not impaired. If necessary and applicable, have the victim testify as a rebuttal witness. Go through the victim's history of alcohol use. Have the victim state how much alcohol she actually consumed. Corroborate the amount of alcohol she consumed through witness testimony, if available. Obtain the specific opinion of the expert on whether or not the specific amount of alcohol mentioned by the victim could account in total for the symptoms mentioned in her testimony. Prior to testifying, the expert witness must be informed, as accurately as possible, of the amount of alcohol that the victim claims to have consumed prior to the assault. In addition, the expert should also be familiar with the history of alcohol and other drug use by the victim.

Corroboration is key. Corroborate the expert's redirect testimony with the testimony of bystander witnesses that can testify as to how much alcohol the victim consumed the night of the sexual assault. Contact and speak with as many witnesses as possible. Interview the people who may have seen the victim that night. Think chronologically. Did room-mates, family, friends, or neighbors see the victim before she left for the party or bar? What do they remember about her condition? Who saw her as the evening progressed? Who saw her after the sexual assault? What was her appearance and behavior before she left and when she got home? How many and what type of drinks did she have? Did she exhibit unusual behavior? Who saw her when she got home? Ask the witnesses if the victim left on her own or if she was carried or assisted.

Talk to the suspect's friends and room-mates. Establish if they remember seeing the victim, and what they saw. Get the details that will determine the per-petrator of the drugging itself (e.g. they saw the suspect handing the victim drinks). Ask them if the suspect made any statements to them about the victim before or after the sexual assault. Identify any possible co-defendants or co-conspirators and the location of any potentially corroborating evidence. Conclude with the bystander witnesses' commonsense statement/conclusion that it seemed "odd" to them that the victim appeared so intoxicated for having drunk so little.

CROSS-EXAMINING THE DEFENSE EXPERT

The two basic areas on which to focus during cross-examination of the defense expert, are relevance and financial interest. With respect to relevance, if the prosecutor establishes that the defense expert has no prior experience with DFSAs, then he can make the argument that the defense witness lacks the requisite background to give an expert opinion in this DFSA case. This is especially true if the prosecution's expert was very specifically qualified as an expert in DFSA cases. The prosecutor needs to be familiar with the rules of evidence in her jurisdiction to know what is required to qualify an expert witness. The federal courts (Fed. R. Evid., 702), as well as many state courts, will allow for the qualification of an expert if it "will assist the trier of fact to understand the evidence or to determine a fact in issue . . ." As to financial bias, the prosecutor may properly inquire if the defense expert has any financial interest that would color his objectivity. Additionally, the prosecution's expert may be able to provide appropriate questions to ask of the defense expert.

ARGUMENT OR CLOSING

During argument, the prosecutor should repeat the case theme. By now, this theme should be familiar to the jury and give them a general review of the case. The standard rules of argument apply in this arena as in any other trial; namely, juries like visual aids, and the prosecutor should prepare whatever charts and visuals are necessary to illustrate the focal points of the argument.

The prosecutor will need to put a spin on any bad facts and turn them in his favor. For example, perpetrators frequently make calculated choices when selecting victims for DFSAs. These perpetrators often pick victims who are unlikely to report or may not be believed if they do report. A perpetrator may select someone who has been out drinking or has voluntarily consumed some drugs. The perpetrator himself may offer the drugs to reduce the likelihood that the victim will report. The prosecutor can argue under all of these facts and cast them in a positive light by asking the rhetorical question: Who makes the better target from the perpetrator's perspective – a straight-A, hard-working, church-going student or someone who can be characterized as a party girl, an exotic dancer, or someone with a drug problem?

SPECIAL ISSUES IN MULTIPLE-VICTIM CASES

Drug-facilitated sexual offenders are often serial offenders. The prosecution of these multiple-victim cases presents a unique set of issues.

VICTIM INTERVIEWS

In multiple-victim cases of DFSA, a common theme, pattern, or *modus operandi* will usually develop as additional victims are interviewed. As a pattern emerges, the prosecutor and law enforcement should refine the interview questions to elicit information from the victim that will reveal whether her incident is within this common pattern or differs in any way. The prosecutor may wish to re-interview victims in an attempt to uncover information not previously given which would fit this pattern.

CATEGORIZATION OF VICTIMS

In cases with numerous victims, the prosecutor may elect to not bring charges for all of the potential victims. Furthermore, some of the victims may decline to prosecute or may prefer to be corroborating witnesses rather than charged victims. Other victims may be outside the statute of limitations, but they are beneficial as "other acts" evidence victims. Some victims may weaken the prosecution's case as they have entirely too many personal issues. Therefore, the prosecution must categorize the pool of victims into a formation that will allow for the strongest presentation. An example of such categorization of victims is demonstrated in Table 13.1.

Table 13.1

Example categorization of victims as witnesses against a serial drug-facilitated sexual offender.

"Charged victims" – Victims for whom charges have been brought
"Other Acts" witnesses
Rebuttal witnesses
Remaining victims not directly used

PRETRIAL AND TRIAL

To maximize the impact of the expert witness's testimony at trial, the prosecutor may wish to call the expert witness out of order and before all of the victims have testified. Calling the expert earlier than expected may require the advance approval of the court. If the expert testifies before all of the victims have testified, the jury is educated about the type of drug believed to have been used and the symptoms the victims would likely have displayed. Then, when the remaining victims testify, the jury can easily process the victims' experiences and decide if their symptoms are consistent with the expert's testimony.

A very useful tool for trial preparation and the trial itself is a chart or charts of the common themes or pattern of the incidents. One chart might just list the common themes. Another might list all of the victims in one column, with succeeding columns representing the common themes. The blocks could then be filled with the specific facts for each victim. For example, if each victim was given a different type of cocktail, the column for the general theme would be that the victim was given a beverage. The victim-specific block would indicate which cocktail the victim was given.

The use of these types of charts is invaluable in case preparation and presentation. A chart of the common themes can be shown to the jury and discussed during the opening statement. The jury is then prepared and can identify the themes as each victim testifies to her incident. The charts can then be utilized again during closing arguments. A large chart that includes both the common themes and the victim-specific facts can enable the prosecutor to easily and thoroughly argue the case and illustrate the *modus operandi* without the use of notes. This will greatly enhance the effectiveness of the prosecutor's presentation.

CONCLUSION

While DFSA cases pose many challenges for the prosecution, these cases can be extremely interesting and rewarding. With increased education of the public, law enforcement, prosecutors, and the judiciary, improvements can be made to the system that will lead to an increase in the successful prosecution of DFSA cases.

Law enforcement education should stress how to identify this type of crime. It should also emphasize the importance of taking a report, even if the case does not appear capable of being filed at that time. Additionally, law enforcement should understand the importance of a urine sample. These specimens should be collected as soon as possible to avoid the potential loss of critical evidence.

The community needs a better understanding of DFSA and the types of drugs that are used. Then, when members of the public sit as jurors, they have some knowledge about DFSA crimes, and such crimes will not seem so alien or unbelievable. The community also needs education about this crime so they can decrease the likelihood of being a victim themselves.

Prosecutors need to develop training for themselves and for the law enforcement agencies with which they work. This will improve the recognition and investigation of DFSA crimes. Prosecutors need education on the science of

DFSA. They also need to keep abreast of which substances are commonly being used in their jurisdictions. Prosecutors need to learn to make the proper requests for toxicological analyses and other testing. They should also be able to interface with the appropriate expert witnesses to maximize the effectiveness of their prosecutions. Finally, prosecutors must speak with others who have experience with these cases. They should learn from the successes and failures of other prosecutors. Through education, a cooperative team effort with law enforcement and the victim(s), and thorough preparation, DFSA cases can be successfully prosecuted.

Victims have described DFSA as the "perfect crime in a pill." Victims of DFSA are helpless against the opportunist perpetrators because of the incapacitating effects of the drugs specifically sought out and used by their rapists. Prosecutors need to be prepared to go the extra mile in these cases. They should be prepared to work with the victim and investigators to discover every piece of evidence to corroborate the victim's complaint and to build a strong case. The victim's involvement will help in the development of investigative leads and will help her become empowered as she experiences the process of recovery from the assault.

Finally, always remember that the investigation and prosecution of a DFSA is a team effort. These are challenging cases because the prosecutor's main witness, the victim, cannot provide a complete account of the crime perpetrated on her. The prosecutor cannot win this case alone.

A successful trial depends upon the cooperation of the victim, law enforcement, victim advocate, and expert witnesses. Foster those relationships as soon as possible. Early prosecution involvement in these cases is key. While abiding by ethical guidelines, do not be afraid to be creative or aggressive in prosecuting these sexual assaults.

REFERENCES

American Prosecutors Research Institute (APRI) (1999) "The Prosecution of Rohypnol and GHB Related Sexual Assaults" videotape and accompanying manual. Sections of this chapter drafted by Diana Riveira were mostly excerpted from APRI's Manual, which she co-authored. This manual was prepared under Grant Number 96-WT-NK-K001 for the U.S. Department of Justice, Office of Justice Programs, Violence Against Women Office.

Cal. Penal Code Section 261(a)(3).

Emerging Problems Under the Federal Rules of Evidence: A Study of the Federal Rules of Evidence by the Section of Litigation, American Bar Association, A.B.A. Sec. Lit. 214 (1998).

Fed. R. Evid. 702.

LeBeau, M., Andollo, W., Hearn, W.L., Baselt, R., Cone, E., Finkle, B., Fraser, D., Jenkins, A., Mayer, J., Negrusz, A., Poklis, A., Walls, H.C., Raymon, L., Robertson, M. and Saady, J. (1999) *J. Forensic Sci.*, 44, pp. 227–230.

LeBeau, M. (1999) *Forensic Sci. Comm.*, 1.

N.Y. Penal Law Section 130.00(6).

People v. Dreas 153 Cal. App. 3d 623 (1984).

People v. Lusk 170 Cal. App. 3d 764 (1985).

APPENDIX A

SAMPLE QUESTIONNAIRE FOR DFSA INVESTIGATORS

SAN DIEGO SEXUAL ASSAULT RESPONSE TEAM
SART/SANE PROGRAM

ADDENDUM
DRUG-FACILITATED SEXUAL ASSAULT
96-HOUR DRUG HISTORY

The SART nurse will complete this form at the time of the interview based on the patient's history and/or signs/symptoms observed by the examiner.

Please circle: A: Patient History B: Observed A&B: Both

Disturbance of Consciousness	Memory Impairment	Neurological	Psychophysiological	GI/GU
● Drowsiness A B	● Confusion A B	● Muscle relaxation A B	● Excitability A B	● Nausea A B
● Sedated← A B	● Memory Loss A B	● Dizziness A B	● Aggressive behavior A B	● Vomiting A B
● Stupor A B	●	● Weakness A B	● Sexual stimulation A B	● Diarrhea A B
● Loss of Consciousness A B	●	● Slurred Speech A B	● Loss of inhibitions A B	● Incontinence Urine/Feces A B
●	●	● Paralysis A B	● Hallucinations A B	●
●	●	● Seizures A B	● Dissociation A B	●
●	●	● Pupil Size Reaction: _____	●	●

How long was the patient unconscious: _____

Date and time of suspected ingestion: _____

Specimen collected: Urine _____ _____ _____ cc's collected _____
                                        Date   Time   1st Void
                            Urine _____ _____ _____ cc's collected _____
                                        Date   Time   2nd Void (If needed)
                            Blood _____ _____ (Grey Top Tube)
                                        Date   Time
How many times has the patient voided prior to this collection? _____

How much alcohol did the patient consume? _____

Type of alcohol: _____

← Name of drugs taken (recreational, prescription or over the counter)	Last dose:
	Date: Time:
	Date: Time:

Has patient vomited? ● Yes   ● No   Where is specimen? _____

Nurse: _____ Date: _____ Time: _____

APPENDIX B

SAMPLE TOXICOLOGICAL
REQUEST FORM FOR DFSA CASES

SAN DIEGO POLICE DEPARTMENT
FORENSIC SCIENCE SECTION

SEX CRIMES TOXICOLOGY REQUEST		

Unit/M.S.	Case No.	Today's Date
Subject's LAST Name	Subject's First Name	Subject's DOB
Detective's Name	Phone	Sergeant's Name	Phone
Property Tag No.	Blood Alcohol No.	Urine Alcohol No.
Date/Time of Assault	Date/Time of Forensic Examination	Number of Hours Between Incident and Sample Collection
? BLOOD BA result, if known: _____	? FIRST VOID URINE TIME:_____	? SECOND VOID URINE TIME:_____

SUBJECT SYMPTOMS

Please circle: A: Patient History   B: Observed   A&B: Both

Disturbance of Consciousness	Memory Impairment	Neurological	Psychophysiological	GI/GU
? Drowsiness A B	? Confusion A B	? Muscle relaxation A B	? Excitability A B	? Nausea A B
? Sedated* A B	? Memory Loss A B	? Dizziness A B	? Aggressive behavior A B	? Vomiting A B
? Stupor A B	?	? Weakness A B	? Sexual stimulation A B	? Diarrhea A B
?Loss of Consciousness A B	?	? Slurred Speech A B	? Loss of inhibitions A B	? Incontinence Urine/Feces A B
?	?	? Paralysis A B	? Hallucinations A B	?
?	?	? Seizures A B	? Dissociation A B	?
?	?	? Pupil Size Reaction:_____	?	?

How long was the subject unconscious:_____
Date and time of suspected ingestion:_____
How many times did the subject void prior to the urine collection?_____
How much alcohol did the subject consume?_____
_____
Type of alcohol:_____

*Name of drugs taken (recreational, prescription or over the counter)	Last dose:
	Date: Time:
	Date: Time:

BASED ON HISTORY AND SYMPTOMS, SELECT DRUG PANEL(S):

? General Drugs (Urine)	Amphetamines Cocaine Opiates Phencyclidine Benzodiazepine Marijuana
? Prescription Drugs (Urine)	Chlorpheniramine Orphenadrine Carisoprodol Diphenhydramine Amitriptyline Desipramine Brompheniramine Meprobamate Imipramine Dextromethorphan Methaqualone Lidocaine Meperidine Barbiturates Thioridazine Verapamil
? Specialized Sex Crimes (Urine) _____ Sergeant's Approval Required	Barbiturates Soma Ketamine Rohypnol GHB Scopolamine

Nurse: _____   Date: _____   Time: _____

Patient Name: _____   Patient ID: _____
G:Sexcrimes/Archambault/Drug-Facilitate form.doc   July 00

APPENDIX C

SAMPLE SEARCH WARRANT FOR DFSA CASES

? Other (Urine)	Specify:
? Alcohol (Blood)	

SW No._____

STATE OF CALIFORNIA-- COUNTY OF _____

SEARCH WARRANT AND AFFIDAVIT

(AFFIDAVIT)

_____, being sworn, says that on the basis of the information within this Search Warrant and Affidavit and the attached and incorporated **Statement of Probable Cause**, he/she has probable cause to believe and does believe that the property described below is lawfully seizable pursuant to Penal Code Section _____, as indicated below, and is now located at the locations set forth below. Wherefore, affiant requests that this Search Warrant be issued.

_____, NIGHT SEARCH REQUESTED: YES [ ] NO [ ]

(Signature of Affiant)

(SEARCH WARRANT)

THE PEOPLE OF THE STATE OF _____ **TO ANY SHERIFF, POLICEMAN OR PEACE OFFICER IN THE COUNTY OF** _____: proof by affidavit having been made before me by _____, that there is probable cause to believe that the property described herein may be found at the locations set forth herein and that it is lawfully seizable pursuant to Penal Code Section _____ as indicated below by "x" (s) in that it:

___   was stolen or embezzled

___   was used as the means of committing a felony

___   is possessed by a person with the intent to use it as means of committing a public offense or is possessed by another to whom he or she may have delivered it for the purpose of concealing it or preventing its discovery.

___   tends to show that a felony has been committed or that a particular person has committed a felony.

___   tends to show that sexual exploitation of a child, in violation of PC Section 311.3 has occurred or is occurring.

YOU ARE THEREFORE COMMANDED TO SEARCH:

See attachment " A "

FOR THE FOLLOWING PROPERTY:

See attachment " B "

AND TO SEIZE IT IF FOUND and bring it forthwith before me, or this court, at the courthouse of this court. This Search Warrant and incorporated Affidavit was sworn to and subscribed before me this _____day of _____, 20__ at _____ A.M./P.M. Wherefore, I find probable cause for the issuance of this Search Warrant and do issue it.

_____, NIGHT SEARCH APPROVED: YES [ ] NO [ ]

(Signature of Magistrate)

Judge of the Superior/Municipal Court, Los Angeles Judicial District.

ATTACHMENT "A"

LOCATION TO BE SEARCHED

(——Insert address and description of location (detailed as to color and type of building and how numbers are marked, etc. so that a reasonable person could find the right location based on your description————)

PERSONS TO BE SEARCHED

(——If appropriate, include specific suspects to be searched, including true name if available or nickname and/or physical description————)

VEHICLES TO BE SEARCHED

(———If appropriate, include vehicles to be searched, including license number if available or description . . . or any vehicle registered to persons located at premises or . . . as appropriate————)

ATTACHMENT "B"

FOR THE FOLLOWING PROPERTY

FLUNITRAZEPAM (Rohypnol®, aka roofies, poor man's quaaludes, the forget me pill, pingas, roches, ruffies, ropies, R-2's or R-1's, Mexican Valium) **or other benzodiazepines,** including but not limited to diazepam (Valium® or other foreign trade name), clonazepam (Klonopin® or Rivotril®), alprazolam (Xanax®), triazolam (Halcion®), lorazepam (Ativan®), temazepam (Restoril®) chlordiazepoxide (Librium®) or other benzopiazepines not approved for use in the United States and thus not controlled substances at this time, such as bromazepam (Lexotan®) **or other depressants** such as chloral hydrate. These medications may most commonly be found in pill or capsule form but may also be encountered in powder form or dissolved into liquid form. Flunitrazepam may be encountered as a small white pill bearing the inscription "ROCHE" with a "1" within a circle, though there are other brands as well. The "new" formulation of flunitrazepam manufactured by Roche may be in a blister pack and may appear as a small, oval shaped dark blue or dark greenish pill. Any paraphernalia relating to use and/or possession, purchase or sales of CNS depressants such as storage containers, vitamin bottles, pill bottles, blister packs (opened or unopened), ziplock baggies. Any printed material or literature regarding the use, abuse, dosage units and pharmacological effects of the above or indications of prescriptions, purchases or other sources of the above drugs.

KETAMINE (Ketamine Hydrochloride (hcl), aka Special K, K, Vitamin K, Chemical Virtual Reality, Psychedelic Heroin) an animal tranquilizer (behavioral analog of PCP) also used in human surgical procedures, any medical bottle marked Ketamine, Ketalar, Vetalar, Ketaset or with label removed containing a clear liquid (slightly thicker than water in appearance), box or label or product information sheet regarding Ketamine, any syringe containing a clear liquid or empty which may have been used and may contain residue or any white powdered substance on plate or other surface or in ziplock baggie or other container commonly associated with transporting powdered drugs, any plate, oven pan, microwave dish or interior of microwave or oven which may contain residue of Ketamine being dried upon or in that item. Any computer or other articles re Ketamine use and abuse; any packaging material with evidence of shipment from veterinary or other medical supply location. Small amber bottles or tiny "coke" spoons, straws, rolled papers or monetary bills used for snorting powdered substances.

GAMMA HYDROXY BUTYRATE (GHB aka Scoop, G, Liquid X, Liquid Ecstasy, Easy Lay, Great Hormones at Bedtime, Salt Water, Water, Sodium Oxbate or Oxybutyrate, Grievous Bodily Harm, Female Viagra, Georgia Home Boy, Everclear, Aminos); any active analog of GHB, including but not limited to 1,4 Butanediol (aka, tetramethylene glycol or Sucol B), Gamma Butyl Lactone (an analog and precursor, with an aka of 2(3H) furanone di-hydroxy); Sodium 4-hydroxyvalerate (aka, GHV or 4-Methyl GHB) and narcotics paraphernalia consisting in part of, including but not limited to: Any container capable of holding a liquid, such as water bottles, sports drink bottles (Gatorade or other brands), mouthwash bottles (large or sample size), vitamin and other pills bottles, spice bottles (clear or brown glass, such as vanilla or almond extract or food coloring), eyedroppers, medicinal style bottles with eyedropper in lid; child's bubble container, hair spray bottle (large or purse size), gallon jugs of auto window wash solution or any cleaning agent bottle, liquid eyewash or breath mint containers, any container marked GHB, whether liquid or powder, or marked Biosul or Borametz (or other name with ingredients listed as Russian pine needle oil extract) or marked Renewtrient, Blue Nitro, Revivarant, Regenergize, Firewater, Invigorate, Eclipse, G3, Gamma G, GHG or GHGold, Reactive, Rest-eze or Remforce (which may list the ingredient 2(3H)furanone di-hydroxy or di-hydro). The analog 1,4 butanediol may be listed as tetramethylene glycol or Sucol B on products with names such as Enliven, Serenity, Revitalize Plus, Thunder Nectar, Weight Belt Cleanser, Amino Flex, Jolt, Verve, Rejoov, Dream On, BVM, GHRE, NRG3, Promusol, etc.

   While GHB is most commonly encountered in liquid form (in original form will be clear and only slightly thicker than water, but may be diluted or mixed with other drinks or colored for concealment), it may also be found in powdered form (it is hydroscopic and thus, if not well sealed, may turn into a mushy or putty form) and may be found as a powder in capsule form. Therefore, search to also include container which would be capable of holding a powder or pills, such as glass or plastic containers with screw on or snap on lids (such as butter containers, cosmetic cream containers, etc.), ziplock baggies; medical type containers for storage and dispensing of liquids (vials or injectable fluid types, possibly labeled "For research only"); or other containers associated with the storage and use of GHB. Also to be searched, refrigerators and freezers for containers of liquid, ice cube trays, blocks or other frozen containers of GHB or its analogs.

Any container of GHB precursor Gamma Butyl Lactone (size may vary from a few ounces to 55 gallon drum), sodium hydroxide or lye, baking soda (may be used in lieu of sodium hydroxy or lye), vinegar, muriatic acid, acetone (re powdered GHB or attempt to convert to powder), heating element (optional), multiple empty containers such as listed above for use in distribution. Also U.S. currency and any papers and documents tending to show possession for sale, such as lists of names or addresses or pay and owe records, buyers, sellers, manufacturers, chemical supply houses, order forms or receipts for purchase from chemical supply houses of above ingredients, shipping records, bills of lading, recipes, any bodybuilding magazine articles re GHB use, other magazine or computer articles re GHB use and manufacturing.

Any and all computer equipment or other electronic storage devices capable of storing electronic data regarding above items, including magnetic tapes, floppy disks, hard drive, viewing screens, disk or tape drives, central processing units, printers, and all software necessary to retrieve electronic data, including operating systems, database, spreadsheet, word processing and graphics programs, all manuals for operation of computer and software together with all handwritten notes or printed confidential password lists to enter secured files. Also any print outs throughout location or trash re above items. Check for indication of Internet usage and "favorite" or "bookmark" Internet locations.

Any and all camera equipment, including cameras, lights, tripods, lens, staged scenery items; any negatives, photographs and undeveloped film, which might contain photographs of current or past victims and/or evidence of drug use.

SAMPLE STATEMENT OF PROBABLE CAUSE FOR SEARCH WARRANT

I, Karen Keyser, do on oath make complaint, say and depose the following on this 24th day of March, 2000: that I have substantial probable cause to believe and I do believe that I have cause to search the premises, including all rooms, safes, storage areas, containers, surrounding grounds, trash areas, garages and outbuildings assigned to or part of the residence located at 12345 Calle Hermosa Avenue, Poway, California, County of San Diego, 92064; the residence is contained in a single story single family dwelling having a primarily light green stucco exterior with avocado color wood trim, having the numbers "12345" located on the upper right corner of the attached garage; all rooms, desks, safes, storage areas, containers, and lockers assigned to the employee known as John Smith at the business known as "Help-U Movers" located at 12345 Hawley Street, Poway, California; the building is a white in color multi-story commercial building with the "12345" written in red on the north side of the building; and the vehicle, including the passenger compartment, trunk, engine compartment, living areas and all parts and containers therein or part of the vehicle described as an approximately 1995 Saturn automobile; the vehicle is primarily tan in color and bears California license plate number 123XYZ, and is believed to be parked at or near the above described residence; for the following property, to wit: controlled substances, tranquilizers and other drugs including flunitrazepam (also known as roofies or the trade name Rohypnol), and gamma hydroxy butyrate (also known as GHB); any containers or packaging for the described drugs; to seize and analyze any glassware for the presence of such substances; clothing, including undergarments; jewelry including a gold bracelet; handwritings, fingerprints, papers, documents and effects which tend to show possession, dominion and control over said premises including keys, photographs, taped voice and/or video images, computer tapes or disks, pagers, anything bearing a persons' name, social security number, drivers' license number or other form of identification, including the interception of incoming calls during execution of the warrant.

I am a peace officer employed by the San Diego Police Department (hereafter SDPD) and have been so employed for about 12 years. I am currently assigned to the Sex Crimes Division and have been so assigned for about 9 months. During my career, I have investigated at least 70 cases involving sexual assault.

During the course of my duties, I have learned the following information based upon my discussions with the named witnesses or by having read the reports of or talked with other SDPD officers who have spoken directly with the named witness. All references to dates refer to the current calendar year unless otherwise stated.

I have read and considered the attached six-page report prepared by SDPD Officer D.R. Bishop, ID# 4424. I hereby request incorporation by reference herein of said report as if fully set forth and identified as ATTACHMENT A.

In synopsis, Robin XXXXX, told police she became unconscious after having consumed one and one half alcoholic beverages with John Smith. When she awoke later, she noticed bruises on her body, and experienced vaginal pain. A Sexual Assault Response Team (hereafter, SART) nurse with Villa View Hospital saw injuries on XXXXX consistent with vaginal intercourse and forcible sodomy.

I know based on my training and experience that persons involved in sexual assaults will attempt to render their victims compliant through the surreptitious use of drugs classified as depressants. These drugs include Rohypnol® (also known as Flunitrazepam), and Gamma Hydroxy Butyrate (also known as GHB), and have been referred to as "rape" drugs. I know these drugs are illegal in the United States. Your affiant is aware that since September 28, 1997, gamma hydroxy butyrate (GHB) is a Schedule II controlled substance in California. Possession is charged under 11377 of the Health and Safety Code (H&S); possession for sales, 11378 H&S; and sales, 11379 H&S. Furthermore, the analogs of Schedule I and II substances are covered under 11400/11401 H&S. Flunitrazepam became illegal in California on January 1, 1997. However, they are legal in Mexico and other countries, and are easily obtained. GHB is also readily available illegally over the internet. I have received training through my department at seminars on sexual assault investigations, educational newsletters, and law enforcement training bulletins. I have learned how the drugs affect the victim. I have also learned how the drugs are administered. I know that flunitrazepam is commonly seen in pill form. I also know that GHB typically appears in liquid form, but may also be seen in capsules, powder or even a "putty" form. Pills may be crushed into powder and either the pill or powder can quickly be deposited into a beverage. I know that the liquid form of GHB is also commonly mixed with a beverage as a way of deceiving the victim and may be transported in non-distinct containers such as common eye solution bottles to avoid detection. I know flunitrazepam and GHB or related drugs are commonly used in sexual assaults because these drugs remain in the victim's system for a relatively short period of time. Since urinalysis rarely detects the presence of the drugs, it is difficult to establish that the suspect administered them to the victim.

I know that flunitrazepam is known for its disinhibiting and nearly paralyzing effect, and its propensity to cause amnesia in the victim. It is used in some countries as a pre-surgical tranquilizer. It is used by abusers of the drug to render compliant a victim of a sexual assault. Often the victim is unaware he or she was sexually assaulted during the resulting state of memory loss, semi-consciousness or unconsciousness. GHB is a central nervous system depressant originally abused by body builders who believed it would stimulate the body's production of growth hormone. It is legitimately available in the United States solely on a restricted basis as an "orphan" drug for experimental treatment of narcolepsy. It is known by abusers of the drug for its intense intoxicating capabilities, amnesia effects and enhancement of sexual interest.

When I spoke with Ms. XXXXX, I did so in person and had the opportunity to observe her demeanor. She appeared to be telling me the truth regarding the amount of alcohol she consumed. I could detect no inconsistencies in her statements to law enforcement. Based on the amount of alcohol XXXXX consumed I believe the suspect may have rendered her unconscious by adding a drug to her beverage. I also believe this based on XXXXX's own statement regarding her complaints of dizziness while dancing, and her awareness of the dangers of becoming too intoxicated with a man she did not know well. Also, XXXXX became dizzy after consuming a beverage which the suspect had brought to her. It is significant to me that XXXXX did not see this beverage poured by the bartender. I know that for the suspect to administer a drug to the beverage it is common that the victim leave the beverage unattended for some period of time or be distracted even briefly.

I know that XXXXX was examined by SART personnel at VillaView Hospital, where blood and urine were obtained. Laboratory analysis was performed on the blood and urine to determine whether any drugs could be detected in her system. These tests did not show positive for the presence of any drugs. However, XXXXX was examined approximately 18 hours after the assault. As stated earlier, research has shown that GHB in particular remains in the system for only a very short period of time. It is common for GHB to be undetectable, unless conducted within 12 hours of ingestion. Even drugs remaining in the urine longer, such as flunitrazepam, may be difficult to detect under current laboratory practices. Also, if the recipient of the drug urinates after ingestion of this drug this often produces a negative result in later voids obtained by hospital personnel. It should be noted in this case XXXXX told me she did urinate prior to going to the hospital after the assault.

I acquired a photograph of John Smith through official police records. I prepared a photographic lineup with the photograph of Smith along with the photographs of four other similar-looking individuals. I showed the lineup to the victim and she positively identified Smith as the person who was present with her at the described bar. I conducted an additional records check to learn where Smith lived. I found through Smith's previous place of employment (Gooseline Tours, Inc.) that Smith lived at 12345 Calle Hermosa Avenue, more fully described above. A Department of Motor Vehicles check also confirmed this. XXXXX told me at one time she worked with Smith at Gooseline Tours, Inc. When I spoke with employees of Gooseline Tours, Inc., they also told me

Smith currently worked at "Help-U Movers" in Poway, more fully described above.

On January 21, 2000, I conducted a pretext telephone call with the permission of XXXXX. She telephoned Smith at his place of business (Help-U Movers). XXXXX spoke with Smith on the telephone while I listened with XXXXX's permission. Smith admitted that he had both vaginal and anal intercourse with victim. He said it was consensual and she was extremely intoxicated when these acts occurred in his personal vehicle, while parked across the street from the bar parking lot. XXXXX asked Smith if he put something in one of her beverages. He denied doing that.

It is my training and experience that the above described property, or a portion thereof, is currently at the described premises, business, and vehicle and is necessary in providing corroborating evidence that a sexual assault occurred, that a drug was used to facilitate the sexual assault, and the identity of the perpetrator. My experience indicates that the objects searched for can be found at any of the above locations. Although the assault on XXXXX occurred on January 17, I believe that the property to be searched for will still be present at the places to be searched. I believe this because I know that perpetrators of this type of crime will keep more of the described drugs available so they can cause the involuntary intoxication of future victims. I also know that even if the perpetrator has the presence of mind to dispose of the drugs he often fails to dispose of the packaging materials for those drugs. The perpetrator does not ordinarily recognize the significance such materials have in demonstrating that the sexual encounter was against the will of the victim.

Furthermore, my training and experience indicates that persons in control of premises leave evidence of their identification such as fingerprints and handwritings, which are subject to expert identification, routinely in the normal course of living within their premises. Also, clothing, photographs, cancelled mail and the like are routinely maintained in a person's premises as necessary and incident to maintaining such premises. In addition, by intercepting phone calls at the premises while the search warrant is being executed, I expect to talk with persons who are familiar with the persons in control of the premises and will so testify. Such callers and described dominion and control evidence is vital to proving control over the described property to be seized. Therefore, based on my training, experience, and the above facts, I believe that I have substantial cause to believe the above described property or a portion thereof will be at the described premises when the warrant is served.

Based on the aforementioned information and investigation, I believe that grounds for the issuance of a search warrant exist as set forth in Penal Code section 1524.

I request that this declaration, the affidavit, search warrant and supporting attachments be sealed pending further order of the court. I make the request for the following reasons. Without sealing, the affidavit and supporting documentation and warrant become a matter of public record within ten days. Penal Code section 1534(a). Sealing is justified even against discovery by the defendant based on the governmental privilege that allows for the protection of the identity of informants pursuant to Evidence Code section 1041. *Swanson v. Superior Court* (1989) 211 Cal.App. 3d 332. Also, Penal Code section 293 provides that a victim of a sex offense be advised that his or her name will become a matter of public record unless he or she requests that it not become a matter of public record. The victim in this case has not yet stated whether or not she will allow her name to become a part of the public record. For this reason, I believe all information identifying the victim should remain sealed pending further order of the court.

I, the affiant, hereby pray that a search warrant be issued for the seizure of said property, or any part thereof, from said premises at any time of the day, good cause being shown therefore, and that the same be brought before this magistrate or retained subject to the order of this Court.

This affidavit has been reviewed for legal sufficiency by *(name)* under my hand and dated this 24th day of March, 2000.

AUTHOR INDEX

SUBJECT INDEX